A Player's Place

DAVID GARFIELD

A Player's Place

The Story of
The Actors Studio

MACMILLAN PUBLISHING CO., INC.

NEW YORK

Macmillan Publishing Co., Inc.
866 Third Avenue, New York, N.Y. 10022
Collier Macmillan Canada, Ltd.

Library of Congress Cataloging in Publication Data

Garfield, David.
    A player's place.

    Bibliography: p.
    Includes index.
    1. New York (City).   Actors Studio.   I.   Title.
PN2078.U62N38   792'.028'097471   80–10585
ISBN 0–02–542650–8

---

10   9   8   7   6   5   4   3   2   1

Printed in the United States of America

*This book is for my
mother and father*

Contents

Introduction

THE ASSERTION that The Actors Studio has been one of the greatest single influences on American acting in this century would, in all probability, provoke little objection. In company with "The Method," its famous approach to performance, and by dint of its association with such stars as Marlon Brando and James Dean, whose iconographic portrayals have become part of the national consciousness, the Studio can properly claim to have made an unmistakable contribution not only to the art of acting, but to American culture at large. From its very beginnings, through the more than three decades of its controversial existence, there has been little question of its effect, at first subtle, but ultimately marked, on the character and quality of the player's craft in this country. Indeed, with a membership that includes a score of America's leading performers and a history that boasts the participation of many outstanding theater artists, the Studio cannot be denied its preeminent place as a significant force in the evolution of American acting.

The fact of the Studio's importance, of its influence, has seldom been questioned. The nature and consequence of that influence *have* been—continually and often heatedly. The Studio has always had its admirers. One of them, Thornton Wilder, said of it, "It is my deep-rooted conviction that The Actors Studio is the most important thing and the finest influence in our theatre. Its repudiation of all recourse to stereotype and mere effect has enhanced the actor's art in our time. Part of its greatness is its power to capture the gifted young." [1] Others, while not wholehearted supporters of the workshop, have at least given it the benefit of the doubt, as in Tony Richardson's estimation that "the Studio's most significant contribution . . . is the creation of a committed state of mind about acting—committed about its relevance to contemporary life and its seriousness as a craft." [2]

A good number of critics, however, pointing to the "limitations" of the American actor, have been less sympathetic to the Studio. It has not been unusual for them to arraign the workshop and Lee Strasberg, its artistic director, for malfeasances against American acting (at times ascribing to the Studio all the ills of the American theater), while refusing to acknowledge that the Studio has contributed anything to the development of those special qualities that give the American actor his particular distinction.

A number of years ago, for instance, in an article entitled "Are Britain's Actors Better Than Ours?," Robert Brustein accused The Actors Studio of encouraging what he called the American actor's "subjective, autobiographical approach to performance." He cited the Studio for promoting, "through a mistaken reading of Stanislavski," acting techniques that were "responsible for developing not character actors, willing to submerge themselves in the life of another, but rather personalities (many of them movie and TV stars) who often exploited their own personal quirks."

At the same time, he noted and underscored in his conclusion that "for all its erraticism, clumsiness and sheer waste of talent, American acting, at its best, somehow manages to penetrate more deeply than anything found on the English stage," [3] and yet, characteristically, did not give the Studio any particular credit for helping to make possible that phenomenon.

To what extent has criticism of the Studio and Strasberg been justified, and how much has been the result of misunderstanding? *Has* the Studio encouraged subjective, "personality" acting? *Is* its famous Method "a mistaken reading of Stanislavski"? Precisely what is taught there, and exactly what *does* Lee Strasberg advocate? How has this body of technique contributed to making the American actor's art "penetrate more deeply" than acting in other national traditions? Where and how has it come up short?

These are some of the questions this book, by presenting for the first time a comprehensive account of The Actors Studio, attempts to answer. Such an account is long overdue; for despite the fame of the workshop and the years of controversy over it, there is a surprising lack of information about The Actors Studio.

The Studio has been the victim of press-agentry ballyhoo, the misguided advocacy of true believers, the distorted and exaggerated antagonism of those too ready to extrapolate and to generalize from individual failings and shortcomings, and of its own privatism and laxity in explaining itself adequately. All of this has helped create the aura of mystery and misunderstanding that has surrounded the workshop for more than thirty years.

Some demystification is in order. Norman Mailer, who was once a member of the Studio's Playwrights Unit, hyperbolically described the workshop as "a cavern where mysteries of acting are invoked in soul-shifting states of ceremony." [4] The truth is far more prosaic. The Studio is not the home of esoteric rites; it is, quite simply, a place for working actors to develop their craft and to find practical solutions to professional problems.

The Method is not some arcane set of rituals or mystic invocations. It is a pragmatic way of working to create both the interior life and the logical behavior of a character—a way that can be taught, practiced, monitored, and corrected.

What it is specifically and concretely, how it evolved, how it is used by Strasberg in his work at the Studio, and why, paradoxically, it has both unleashed the dramatic creativity of generations of actors and, at the same time, produced enormous confusion and frustration is examined in detail in what follows.

The Studio and its famous Method are part of a tradition, an approach to acting and theatrical presentation that has its roots in the explorations of Stanislavski in prerevolutionary Russia and its earliest American manifestation in the work of the Group Theatre during the 1930s. Lee Strasberg, Harold Clurman, Cheryl Crawford, Elia Kazan, Robert Lewis, and the many others who founded and worked in that organization were motivated by a missionary zeal to create something vitally new in the American theater.

Their fervency was passed on to The Actors Studio, where the idealism of a visionary art of the theater, based on a concept of the essential and profound creativity of the actor, has continuously drawn enthusiastic professionals eager for a nourishment often lacking in the commercial American theater.

The Studio has always been a hotbed of strong feelings. Dealing as it does in the most personal realities of the actor's mind, character, and sensibility, the work at the Studio has often elicited both passionate defenses and fierce condemnations—sometimes from the same people. Ambivalence toward the Studio is not uncommon among its members and others who have participated in the activities there. Why this is so is, again, the subject of this book.

What follows is an attempt to make the reality, as opposed to the image, of The Actors Studio more apparent. As a pioneering effort at presenting the uncharted history of that organization, it strives for an overview of the entire record of the workshop's ideas, influences, accomplishments, and failures, while at the same time it aims to distill the very specific flavors of particular events and personalities. Certainly it is to be hoped that someday other books will be written that will explore individual aspects of the subject in even greater detail.

As a member of the Studio since 1970, I might be open to the charge of presenting a prejudiced view of the subject. There may indeed be discernible predispositions in the handling of this material but, as best as I have been able, I have made every effort to be scrupulously objective in my evaluation of the particulars. Having encountered and examined the full range of sentiment on the Studio, from the most devoted *parti pris* enthusiasms to expressions of extreme and unforgiving vitriol, I have tried to take the measure of this multitude of opinions and interpretations of events and to filter them through my own experiences of the Studio and my awareness of the objective facts in order to render as honest a picture of the workshop as I am capable. The results, I hope, will speak for themselves.

DAVID GARFIELD
New York, 1980

CHAPTER **1**

The Group Theatre Heritage

Tℍᴇ ʀᴏᴏᴛs of The Actors Studio reach through two decades of American theatrical experience to the nurturing subsoil of the formative twenties and thirties, the period Harold Clurman has celebrated as "The Fervent Years." During those twenty years the future founders and leaders of the Studio learned their craft, defined their theatrical ideals and ideology, and set out to revolutionize the American theater and American acting. The theorics and techniques they first championed then, innovations that have had such an enormous impact on the development of American actors, were the seeds that blossomed a generation later into their most influential and enduring offspring: The Actors Studio.

The central figure in the chronicles of the Studio, the individual whose ideas and decisions defined its nature and molded its course, is Lee Strasberg. Any examination of the life of that organization has to take into account the aesthetic and spiritual guidance he provided. His experience, therefore, is the ground upon which the whole of the Studio's history must be drawn.

Born to Baruch Meyer and Ida (Diner) Strasberg on November 17, 1901, in the Galician village of Budzanow (at that time in Austria-Hungary, now part of the USSR), Lee Strasberg was brought to America at the age of seven and a half. When he arrived in New York he spoke only Yiddish and was at first enrolled at the

[*1*]

Poale Zion School, where instruction was in Yiddish and Hebrew. Eventually he entered the New York public school system, although to this day he cannot remember how he learned English. His earliest awareness and experience of acting and theater, it therefore should not be surprising to note, was not of the American stage with its English-speaking actors, but of something quite different: the drama and performance of his own, vibrant, East European Jewish heritage.

In the midst of a rich immigrant Jewish culture, Strasberg was inevitably exposed to the emotional vitality of the Yiddish theater in its heyday on Manhattan's Lower East Side. The very first plays he saw in his impressionable youth were Yiddish ones, featuring such Jewish stars as Ludwig Satz, Boris Thomashevsky, Jacob Adler, and David Kessler. The last of these was the young Strasberg's favorite—the first actor in his experience whom he could single out as being special.

David Kessler was noted in the Yiddish theater for the high standard of his acting. Though he was not above the common and sometimes outrageously delicious Yiddish-theater practice of breaking the theatrical illusion—when some inconsiderate latecomers made a noisy entrance during one of his scenes, he exclaimed loudly, "Aha, they're here again, the slummers!"—his performances had integrity. They were intense, vital, and impressive. To some observers his "full acting" style seemed, in retrospect, comparable to Method acting. One Yiddish-theater scholar went so far as to say, "Kessler *was* the Method!" [1]

Several years before he saw Kessler, before he had seen any actors perform, for that matter, Strasberg made his own debut as a performer. At the age of ten he was asked to appear in a Yiddish play for the Progressive Dramatic Club, an amateur theater group that seriously aspired to improve the literary and artistic quality of Yiddish theater,[2] taking its inspiration from the Independent Theater Movement represented by André Antoine's Théâtre Libre in France and Otto Brahm's Freie Bühne in Germany. Sporadically, over the next few years, he acted there in a variety of Yiddish amateur productions. When he was almost fourteen, he played the hero Mordechai in an annual *Purimspiel*, the uniquely Jewish theatrical genre celebrating the victory of the biblical Esther over Haman, the enemy of the Jews. One of his teachers complimented him on how good his performance was, only to have another teacher say to the first, "You shouldn't tell him that!" (God forbid a Jewish boy should be encouraged to pursue a career in acting!)

Strasberg's career in the theater did temporarily come to an end as the result of a traumatic experience he had in the Progressive Dramatic Club's production of Sudermann's *Glick Im Winkle* (*Luck in the Corner*), which was presented at the Liptzin Theater when he was sixteen. In one scene he had to light a lamp to set the mood, and then exit. Having rehearsed without props, he was surprised to find a chimney lamp on stage the night of the performance. Unused to handling such a device, he tried putting a lighted match down the glass tube. It flashed up at him and he blacked out. How he got off stage, he does not remember, but the accident so upset the shy and impressionable young boy that it discouraged him from participating in theatrical activities for many years.

It was not until the early twenties that he became reinvolved with theater on a regular basis. Forced to drop out of Townsend Harris Hall High School at the end of his second year when a younger brother died in the influenza epidemic of 1918, Strasberg became an office clerk in a shop that manufactured ladies' wigs, eventually buying himself a partnership in the firm.

With his scholarly temperament and his sensitivity, however, he did not seem cut out for a career in the wig business. (His family considered him their "black sheep"; he was always off in his own world with his nose buried in a book or magazine.) He felt a need to be involved with something creative, something artistic, something that would provide an outlet for his cultural interests.

He joined the Students of Art and Drama (SAD), a group of amateurs who gathered socially at the Chrystie Street Settlement House to work on theatrical projects. It was there that he met his first wife, Nora Z. Krecaun, a vivacious amateur actress whom he married in 1926.

Though he did not entertain any serious thoughts about a career in the theater at the outset, he was soon using his involvement with the "SADs" to test his abilities, first as an actor and, eventually, as a director. His experiences at the settlement house stimulated his interest in the theater, which he began to study intensively. The first play in English he had seen was *Hamlet* with Walter Hampden; now he attended plays with some regularity.

Having dropped formal schooling, he undertook a personal schooling in his chosen field that would last a lifetime. Books on the theater and on acting became his passion, his obsession. From the time he bought his very first one, Hiram Moderwell's *Theatre of Today*, he was constantly reading, constantly pressing volumes on people for their own edification. He devoured histories of performance, actors' biographies, tracts on aesthetics, and carefully studied their end-page bibliographies, seeking out further volumes that had somehow slipped his attention earlier. He eventually developed the invariable habit of visiting old bookstores every week of his life. (To this day, he can be found perusing the dusty stacks of the used bookshops of Fourth Avenue every Saturday morning, constantly looking for something new.) People sent him tomes, pamphlets, artifacts, from all over the world, especially on a subject they knew interested him. Many of the volumes he collected he could not read —they were in Chinese, Japanese, Polish, Swedish, and practically every other European language. But whatever he could read, in English, German, French, and Yiddish, he did read—sometimes in depth, making notes; sometimes skimming, when key words let him know that the matter at hand covered familiar territory. Strasberg eventually had so many volumes, he would sometimes forget what he already owned and unwittingly purchase second, third, and even fourth copies of certain texts.

By the time he came to settle in the Central Park West apartment he still lives in, his collection was incredible. Books lined every room of his home. Once, when his tax return was challenged because he had deducted a large proportion of his apartment as an office/study, an incredulous tax auditor was led from room to room to inspect the thousands of volumes lining the walls of living rooms, bedrooms, kitchen, closets, hallways, bathrooms, and piled in heaps on the floor, on chairs, stools, and other furniture (people were always moving books or records when they sat down). His deductions were allowed.

Second only to his preoccupation with books was his passion for collecting records by the hundreds—old 78s as well as new releases. He would have dozens of discs sent to him from abroad, purchasing from foreign catalogues titles unavailable in America. He would not think twice about spending eighty dollars on a rare recording if he wanted it. (That is what he paid for a transcription of Toscanini rehearsing with and yelling at the NBC orchestra.) At one time

Strasberg reportedly spent two or three hundred dollars a week on recordings.

During the seventies, when he came to live half the year in New York and half the year on the West Coast, parts of his record and book collections were duplicated so that he could have them readily at hand in both locations. The weekend hunting trips to rare-book shops were to continue in California, as Strasberg discovered un-tapped treasure troves along the byways of Los Angeles County.

From early on what Strasberg absorbed from his voracious reading became the common coin of his conversation on theater. People were impressed and intimidated by his knowledge of the field, although sometimes the sheer extravagance with which he larded it on seemed suspiciously like a parading of knowledge for its own sake, or like the show of learning of an autodidact overeager to establish his intellectual credentials.

Strasberg, with several notable exceptions, would always retain a certain resentment toward established theater scholars. He would speak with disdain and undisguised contempt of various cloistered theoreticians who wrote about the theater without any firsthand knowledge of the subject. If there was a hint of defensiveness in the face of these academic authorities, there was also the justifiable arrogance of an original practitioner who thought freshly and who worked creatively in his field.

Of the many writers whom he read on the subject during the twenties, the one above all who set him to thinking seriously about the theater and his own involvement with it was Gordon Craig.[3]

"The generation of which I am a part," Strasberg was to later write, "came into the theatre on the wings of a dream."[4] That "dream," shared by many, was the vision of a new Art of the Theater, as set forth in the writings of Adolphe Appia and Edward Gordon Craig. Craig, the revolutionary scenic-designer son of Ellen Terry, especially helped to ignite Strasberg's interest in the theater by projecting an aesthetic that sought to make of the theater a unified and coherent art form worthy of the highest respect and admiration. The visionary theatrical idealism of his *On the Art of the Theatre*, dedicated "TO THE SINGLE COURAGEOUS INDIVIDUALITY IN THE WORLD OF THE THEATRE WHO WILL SOME DAY MASTER AND REMOULD IT. . . . You are a young man; you have already been a few years in a theatre, or you have been born of theatrical parents; . . . or you have been a manufacturer," [5] had enormous appeal for Strasberg, the young "manufacturer" of women's hairpieces who was already deeply involved in amateur theatrics and susceptible to the idea of devoting his life to becoming a true "artist of the theatre of the future."

"It was the reading of Gordon Craig that first gave me the idea of what theater was and excited my imagination, my interest, and my enthusiasm for it. I doubt that I ever would have actually embarked in the theater professionally if not for this eye-opening sense of what theater was, could be, should be, might be," Strasberg has said.

"What the theater should be" very much revolved around the art of the actor, and Strasberg's study of acting was thorough indeed. He familiarized himself with all the historical discussions of the subject, finding of particular value Luigi Riccoboni's "Pensées sur la déclamation," which he once called "the sanest essay on acting ever written" (Stanislavski was so delighted with the "Pensées" when he read them in 1914, he exclaimed, "Oh, the darling, the darling! I could embrace him! I could kiss him!" [6]); Talma's "Réflexions . . . sur l'art théâtral"; William Gillette's "The Illusion of the First Time in Acting"; critic George Henry Lewes's *On Actors and the Art of Acting;* and, as a vital source of raw information on the actor's problems, William Macready's diaries and reminiscences.

He was especially taken with the historical accounts of the great, early-nineteenth-century English actor, Edmund Kean, of whom Coleridge remarked, that to see him act "was to read Shakespeare by flashes of lightning." William Hazlitt's famous discussions of this genius of the English stage, classic pieces in the history of dramatic criticism which drew vividly insightful portraits of the actor's artistry, contributed preeminently to Strasberg's enthusiasm for the man. The unique qualities of this wildly emotional romantic actor—when he played Sir Giles Overreach in Massinger's *A New Way to Pay Old Debts,* the prodigious emotional power of his performance is said to have caused people in the audience and even some of his fellow cast members to faint—made him, for Strasberg, the greatest actor of all time.

Strasberg rather enjoyed identifying himself with his favorite performer. They were apparently the same height and had similar bantam physiques, and Strasberg even imagined they looked somewhat alike. Over the years he would half-jokingly extend the comparison to ostensible similarities in temperament and talent whenever he discussed Kean at The Actors Studio.

Certain outstanding actors of the nineteen twenties played a part in shaping Strasberg's evolving theatrical tastes as well. Their general characteristics as performers and their special qualities in specific roles helped him define for himself what he valued most in the art of acting. Among those he particularly admired were Eva Le Gallienne, for her "fragility and beauty"; the young Joseph Schildkraut, whose performances he would later characterize as a "somewhat exaggerated forerunner of what would today be labeled the Actors' Studio style"; Jeanne Eagels for "the strange vibrancy" in her performance in *Rain;* Pauline Lord for "the driving quality" she brought to *Anna Christie* and *They Knew What They Wanted;* Jacob Ben-Ami for his "flair and emotional depth" in *Samson and Delilah;* Alfred Lunt, for his "creation of levels of perception and characterization"; and the Barrymores for their "glamour and excitement." [7]

Strasberg also admired Charlie Chaplin, whom he was to meet years later through their mutual friend, Clifford Odets. The famous comedian was important to him, Strasberg says, because he "could not do anything that was purely verbal or mental" in his performing. Chaplin's use of his whole body and his ingenious physical expressivity were the subjects of frequent commentary by Strasberg over the years.

Most influential of all, however, were the mighty Chaliapin, the great Russian basso from whom Stanislavski had drawn so much inspiration and whose Boris Godounov and Mephistopheles were among the great theatrical experiences of Strasberg's life, and two very special Italian actors: Giovanni Grasso and Eleonora Duse.

Grasso's performances, which the eminent American theater critic Stark Young singled out for their "wild animality, speed, passion and impetus," had a visceral impact on Strasberg. Watching him play a death scene once, he had to grip the arms of his theater seat and repress the urge to yell "Save him, do something!" because for him the actor *was* dying. And later, on the subway home to Queens, Strasberg and his wife did not speak; they had just seen a man perish.

Gabriele D'Annunzio, the poet-playwright and quondam lover of the incomparable Duse, described her running with her wolfhounds:

she was a wolfhound; if standing near a tree: she was a tree. Her sensibility was of such an order as to let her become one with the object of her involvement. Strasberg never tired of speaking of her ineffable qualities. For him she was, above all, "the actress who exemplified the poetry of reality."

In 1923, the same year that he saw Duse in her farewell appearances in Ibsen's *Ghosts* and *Lady From the Sea*, and D'Annunzio's *The Dead City*, Strasberg attended the Moscow Art Theater's (MAT) premiere season of productions at Al Jolson's Fifty-ninth Street Theatre in New York. This first American visit of Constantin Stanislavski and his troupe was a watershed experience for the young American amateur. By his own account, it demonstrated concretely to Strasberg that the ideas about the theater and acting he was assimilating from his reading and thinking could become a tangible reality.

Strasberg had, of course, already examined all the available literature on Stanislavski and his theater. Craig had written about his 1908 visit to the MAT in *On the Art of the Theatre*, praising its "admirable actors . . . the best set of actors upon the European stage" for their seriousness and devotion, and the organization itself for its aliveness and its "character and intelligence." [8] Articles about Stanislavski had appeared in American periodicals as early as 1906. *Theatre Arts* had featured a piece on the MAT in August 1917, the year of the Russian revolution. Huntly Carter and Oliver Sayler wrote extensively of the MAT in their volumes on the Russian theater. In addition, Sayler and others wrote a number of articles on the Russians during the early twenties and just prior to their arrival, whetting America's appetite for the impending visit.

In two seasons in New York, the Russians presented over a dozen plays from their repertory. The first year featured the original productions of a number of the Moscow Art Theater's earliest successes (with most of the original casts), including the company's very first presentation, *Tsar Fyodor Ivanovich*, dating from 1898, Gorky's *The Lower Depths*, and two Chekhov plays, *The Three Sisters* and *The Cherry Orchard*. The second year opened with *The Brothers Karamazov* and featured two additional Chekhov plays, *Uncle Vanya* and *Ivanov*. Strasberg saw every one of these productions, most of the others, and a number of them more than once.[9]

He was not especially taken by the quality of the individual productions; like many others, he felt they were somewhat "tatty" and not so definitely successful from an aesthetic point of view. Neither was he overawed by the quality of any particular performance; individually speaking, there had been equally fine acting from many American actors. What really made an impression on him was the overall effect of the ensemble work and the sense of a theater as a long-lived enterprise in which the totality of what has been produced over many years has significance above and beyond any individual plays presented along the way. American production had created the ensemble effect to a certain extent—Strasberg was impressed with the Jewish Art Theatre for this reason—but compared to the kind of "three dimensional totality of living on the stage by every one of the actors" of the Moscow Art Theater, these native attempts at a unified approach to production had been relatively external. The Russians underscored, for Strasberg, Craig's advocacy of the unification of all theatrical elements, especially in the way each actor was "alive and vivid in a coherent relationship to the concept of the play."

In essence, the MAT actors summed up what Strasberg had concluded from his reading, thinking, and observing of actors and acting, "the conviction that acting is living on the stage." Riccoboni had stated "the actor must feel what he acts," Talma had argued the central importance of the actor's "sensibility," and numerous actors had discussed the questions of emotion, belief, and "living" the role. Strasberg had come to the conclusion that great acting demanded of the performer belief of such an order as to enable him to really live and to really experience on the stage.[10] But the question of how this was to be accomplished remained open. In 1923 Strasberg had yet to become acquainted with the special techniques Constantin Stanislavski had developed precisely to achieve these aims.

By 1924 he was sufficiently inspired by the example of the Moscow Art Theater and his experience of Craig finally to attempt to make his way in the professional theater. At first he enrolled at the Clare Tree Major School of the Theatre, where he studied for about three months, appearing in *The Rivals* and as Cassius in *Julius Caesar*. Then he heard about a new school associated with the American Laboratory Theatre, the group founded by the Russian émigré actors Richard Boleslavsky and Maria Ouspenskaya. Dissatisfied with the acting training he had been receiving, he auditioned for the Laboratory Theatre school and began a course of study that was to influence crucially his entire subsequent career in the theater.

Richard Boleslavsky had been a pupil and disciple of Stanislavski's for over fifteen years when he decided to leave Russia and make a life for himself in the United States. He was eighteen when he first auditioned for the MAT's school in 1906 and was accepted with two other pupils to study under Stanislavski. His three-year course of training, largely a period of apprenticeship under the leading MAT actor, Ivan Moskvin, coincided with Stanislavski's earliest work on his famous System. Boleslavsky was first exposed to elements of the System in the first MAT presentation which drew upon Stanislavski's evolving theories, the 1909 production of Turgenev's *A Month in the Country*, in which the young actor played Beliaev.[11]

Boleslavsky also played a major role in the famous First Studio of the Moscow Art Theater, where, as a founding member, he participated in experimentation with Stanislavski's System under the supervision of Leopold Sulerjitsky, Stanislavski's intimate friend and closest associate. He put the System to use in the production of Heyerman's *The Wreck of the Hope*, which he directed for the First Studio. Stanislavski said of the production that it "showed clearly that the young actors could perform with a simplicity and depth of which we had not even suspected them. I credited that, with some justification, to our joint 'system' effort." [12] He also appeared with Eugene Vakhtangov and Michael Chekhov in Sulerjitsky's stage version of Dickens's *Cricket on the Hearth*, the production that once and for all "legitimized" the System for the older members of the MAT, who up to then had resisted Stanislavski's ideas. After Sulerjitsky's death in 1916, he worked closely with Vakhtangov, who was appointed the new head of the First Studio. According to Strasberg, Boleslavsky's thinking about the System was heavily influenced by his contact with Vakhtangov, who was the definitive teacher of the System, even in Stanislavski's eyes, till his death in 1922.

When the MAT arrived in New York in January of 1923, Boleslavsky, who had immigrated to America a year earlier, was here to greet them. Stanislavski invited him to act with the company in America, and he did briefly, appearing in such roles as Prince Shakhovsky in *Tsar Fyodor Ivanovich* and (alternating with Stanislavski) as Satin in *The Lower Depths*. More important, however, were his efforts to capitalize on the developing American interest in the Moscow Art Theater. Ten days after *Tsar Fyodor* opened, he began a series of lectures on the MAT and the Stanislavski System at the Princess Theater at Broadway and Twenty-ninth Street, the same building in which The Actors Studio would hold its first meeting a quarter of a century later. These lectures, which Boleslavsky gave twice a week for about two months, stimulated considerable interest in Stanislavski's theory and practice among New York theater people.[13] He also published an article in the April 1923 issue of *Theatre* magazine, entitled "Stanislavsky—The Man and His Methods" and, in the July 1923 issue of *Theatre Arts* magazine, "The Laboratory Theatre," in which he explained his hopes for an American theater modeled along the lines of the MAT and its First Studio.

As a result of the growing interest in his advocacy of the Stanislavski approach to acting training, Boleslavsky was invited to teach at the Neighborhood Playhouse, where he began holding classes in the summer and fall of 1923. He thus became the first teacher of the Stanislavski System in America.[14] Later in the fall of 1923 Boleslavsky started his own school, which he hoped to turn into a producing organization modeled on Russian prototypes. This was the American Lab Theatre, where Strasberg studied. Maria Ouspenskaya, who came to America with the MAT and who remained in this country when Stanislavski and his actors returned to Russia, joined Boleslavsky at the Lab as his principal teaching colleague.

Originally a student at the Adasheff Studio, a private school run by some actors of the Moscow Art Theater (Sulerjitsky taught the earliest form of the System there before the founding of the First Studio, and Vakhtangov, who joined the classes in 1909, was his prize pupil), Ouspenskaya was accepted as a member of the MAT in 1909. She was also one of the original members of the First Studio, where, like Boleslavsky, she studied Stanislavski's System with Sulerjitsky and Stanislavski himself. Over the years she came to be esteemed as one of the outstanding actresses in the ranks of the Moscow Art Theater. And Stanislavski evidently valued her highly as a pedagogue as well; he is said to have called her one of the very best teachers of his System.

Madame Ouspenskaya, or "Madame," as she was addressed, was an awesome little figure. Sitting in her chair, her feet on a footstool, her head covered by a shawl, she would light a small black cigar and with a piercing look command her students to begin an exercise. If their work displeased her, she let them know it in no uncertain terms. Once, in her later teaching career in Hollywood, she assigned her students a group exercise involving shipwrecked travelers drowning in the sea. After diligently attempting to create this underwater drama for her, Ouspenskaya's young actors were startled to see her lying stretched out supine on the classroom floor. Her assistant, carefully placing a flower in her folded hands, said dolefully to the wide-eyed performers, "Look what you've done! You've bored Madame to death with your acting!"

Ouspenskaya's powers of observation were astonishing. Her students were constantly amazed at her uncanny analyses of their work; her intense and vehement criticism often brought them to tears, and apparently this was an intentional element in her pedagogy. She believed it was necessary to break through her students' habitual defensive armor to reach, release, and cultivate the emotional life within them. She frequently provoked a student to emotional outburst because she believed it was the only way to overcome his fearfulness or self-consciousness about being open and truthful on stage. Interestingly enough, Strasberg was to develop a similar reputation for extraordinary insight into the individual actor's problems as well as a tendency on occasion toward harsh criticism.

Strasberg was mightily impressed by Ouspenskaya, whom he remembers as both a marvelous actress and trainer of actors, "better in both capacities, probably, than any of the other Russian actors of the time who immigrated to this country." He was deeply influenced by her approach to acting training and by the emphasis she put on various elements of the Stanislavski System.

In her course "Technique of Acting," students did improvisations, one-minute plays, and explored ways of creating character, situation, and "mood." The procedures were designed to provide the actor with a working technique for stimulating and controlling feelings and emotions necessary in performance through the cultivation of sensorial memory. Evidently, she did not follow a prescribed routine of predetermined exercises. She selected them according to the needs of the particular students she was dealing with, a basic procedure Strasberg was to use in dealing with members of The Actors Studio decades later. Her emphasis on physical relaxation, concentration, and sense and emotion memory was to be reflected in Strasberg's own pedagogy throughout his career.

Some fifty years after having been her student, Strasberg would recall one of Ouspenskaya's concentration exercises at a session of The Actors Studio. He described how she directed her young actors to take a matchbox and to examine it carefully for five minutes. After studying every detail, they were to put it down, let a minute pass, and then write down what they could remember about it. Picking it up again, and reexamining it, they would realize how much they had not observed or remembered. Then she would tell them to look at the object closely. "What is the box made of? It's made of wood. Wood comes from trees. It took men and technology to cut down the trees and manufacture that little box. On the surface of the object are printed letters and designs, which presupposes a history of written communication and graphic arts. In short, the little matchbox should lead you to a consideration of all of human civilization, for all technology, culture, and civilization is represented in that little object." From then on, whenever the students would look at a matchbox, it would no longer be a prop, but a reality with a significance the actor could respond to.

Strasberg also retains vivid memories of Boleslavsky's course "Art of the Theatre." He still has the notes he took at the first lecture at the school's headquarters at 139 MacDougal Street (once the home of the Provincetown Playhouse). On that introductory occasion, the topic was not the System, but the two forms of acting: the kind that Stanislavski calls "the art of representation," which demands a highly skillful imitation or indication of preconceived forms of behavior, and the other kind, "the art of living the part," which requires the actor to really experience on stage. Years later he would recall how he sat there listening and jotting down his notes, experiencing the sensation that "this is it." Here were the means to create the kind of acting and the kind of theater he wanted to be involved with.

At subsequent class sessions Strasberg was introduced to what he has since characterized as the "classic form" of the Stanislavski System. Boleslavsky had published his "First Lesson" in the art of acting in *Theatre Arts* magazine at the very time he had started his school. That piece (on "Concentration") and his subsequent *Theatre Arts* articles on "Memory of Emotion," "Dramatic Action," "Characterization," "Observation," and "Rhythm"—all of which were later published as *Acting: The First Six Lessons* [15]—together with his unpublished Princess Theater lectures, develop many of the ideas he taught in his course.

Among the topics receiving special attention that made a lasting impression on Strasberg were relaxation and concentration. An actor, before beginning any exercise or scene, must achieve muscular relaxation; he must deal with the body's tensions and a lifetime of physical conditioning. This was achieved, first of all, by concentrating on muscle groups throughout the body with a conscientious effort made to allow them to slacken one by one, and, second, by a series of simple exercises, such as walking, sitting down, lighting a cigarette, and lacing a shoe, using only the amount of strength absolutely necessary for each activity.

Also fundamental to the actor's work was what Boleslavsky called "spiritual relaxation," the task of overcoming the inner pressures and distractions of modern life. For this he asked the actor to concentrate on past sensory experiences, such as handling a personal object (e.g., a childhood toy) or wearing a familiar piece of clothing, to the point where the remembered sensations elicited an emotional response from the actor to the exclusion of actual stimulation coming from the outside. This arousing of feelings through imaginary stimuli—what would generally come to be called sense-memory exercises —was to play a very important role in Strasberg's work. "The realism that Stanislavsky preaches is internal, not external," observed Boleslavsky. "An Actor who can stand in an imaginary snow-drift and actually make an audience shiver has mastered the reality of his art." [16]

Concentration is essentially the obverse complement of relaxation. Muscular relaxation depends on a concentration of attention to focus the effort to release tension; to be able to concentrate, one must relax. "Spiritual concentration" stands in a similar relation to "spiritual relaxation" as a means of honing or refining one's sensory apparatus to bring one's "inner" life under the control of the will. In addition to such procedures as Madame Ouspenskaya's dealing with the matchbox, Boleslavsky prescribed a long list of exercises in concentration to give the actor control of his emotions. " 'Spiritual Concentration' is the ability to say to any of your feelings: 'Stop, and fill my entire being!' This faculty can be developed and trained as much as one can train a human body,—and this training is the main problem of a creative school of acting." [17]

The central purpose of "spiritual concentration" and, indeed, the key objective of the creative actor's work is the cultivation of the "life of our inner feelings." Specifically, according to Boleslavsky, this involves the development and use of the actor's "affective memory." This phenomenon of recalling and reexperiencing previously felt emotions was described by the French psychologist Théodule Ribot in *La psychologie des sentiments* (1896) and *Problèmes de psychologie affective* (1910). Stanislavski, who read Ribot's discussions of the process, developed exercises with which the actor, by recalling the sensory details that accompanied an emotional experience, could entice the emotion from his subconscious and reexperience it. Madame Ouspenskaya, says Strasberg, used to call the actor's affective memories "golden keys," which unlocked some of the greatest moments in acting.

Marcel Proust, in the last four pages of the "Overture" section of *Swann's Way*, describes a perfect example of the affective-memory phenomenon and how it is linked to particular sensory keys that can unlock long-forgotten feelings.[18] The novel's narrator recalls how his mother served him some tea with "those short, plump little cakes called 'petites madeleines.'" He takes a sip of the tea into which he has dipped a piece of madeleine and suddenly experiences an exquisite sense of joy. He tries another sip of the tea and cake and then another, but the sensation seems to diminish. After considering for a moment, he concentrates on the gustatory *memory* of "the crumb of madeleine soaked in [a] decoction of lime-flowers," and immediately a flood of reminiscence is released: the Sunday mornings at Combray, when, as a child, his aunt Léonie used to give him a piece of the madeleine she had dipped in her own cup of lime-flower tea, the reexperiencing of which unfolds into the complex of recollection that becomes *Remembrance of Things Past*.

There are myriad examples in theater history of performers making unconscious use of their affective memories. Edmund Kean, for instance, was always terribly moved in the gravediggers' scene in *Hamlet* when he picked up the skull of Yorick. He would inevitably be reminded of a beloved uncle who had given him his first lessons in acting and who had introduced him to Shakespeare. Stanislavski provided an objective and systematic means for tapping these memories —for making connections to past experience—at will.

In the creative work of the actor, the affective memory is used as follows, according to Boleslavsky. After the performer analyzes his part to see what feeling or emotion is necessary at a particular point in a scene, he searches his own life for a remembered feeling or emotion that parallels the former. He then uses appropriate sensory exercises to retrieve the parallel emotion from his affective memory. He is not to be concerned with *how* the emotion will manifest itself, but only with finding it, creating the sensory realities that will unlock it, and trusting to his "instrument's" natural and unique response to what is released.

Strasberg's attention to "affective memory" and his insistence on its primary importance in the actor's creative work was to become the hallmark of his pedagogy and a source of enormous controversy over the years. Affective memory was, for him, essential to the basic idea of the actor's bringing a role to life and "living the part."

To Stanislavski and Vakhtangov, he would argue, affective memory was *the* central concept because it was what made possible the actor's ability to really experience on stage. Most acting involves the kind of thinking that leads to indicated performing, that is, the actor has an idea of how he should look or what he should be doing and executes that image as best he can. He thinks the character is afraid and tries to act "fearful." He thinks it is three in the morning and he is supposed to be drunk and tries to act "three o'clock A.M. and hung over." But his thoughts do not organically affect his behavior. His mental processes are closed circuits that do not directly impel behavior through the nervous system. The actor, in actuality, reverts to preconceived or cliché behavior, more or less skillful, depending on his talent and experience. Such acting, in short, tends to be *about* behavior and states of being rather than behavior and states of being in and of themselves. When the affective memory is tapped, the mental processes set in motion do cause psychophysical responses. They stimulate the player's physical and mental being with remembered sensations and emotions that color his or her behavior and vocal expression in ways that both the actor and the audience experience as viscerally real and exciting. And it is this, Strasberg would insist, that gives fine acting its "aliveness" and verisimilitude—that makes acting, in fact, a *creative* art.

Vakhtangov said, "Everything that the actor does on the stage is, whether he knows it or not, affective memory." By this he meant, according to Strasberg, that if the actor is properly repeating from night to night the sensory and emotional aspects of a role, a memory —not muscular and not mental—is functioning: memory of affect. The fact that the human organism has this capacity to remember sensations and emotions makes it possible for the actor's feelings to be there every time he needs them. The emotions, in fact, must be *remembered* emotions and not "real" ones. Real emotion, that is emotion actually provoked on the spot, has no place on the stage, according to Vakhtangov. If one actor has to beat up another actor in order to provoke tears, where is the art? Anyone will cry if he is actually hurt. The *art* of acting is that the actor has full control of his sensory and emotional apparatus and can bring it into operation at his will, creating the experience over and over solely through the creative manipulation of his imagination.

The reference to Vakhtangov is significant. The fact that Boleslavsky studied and worked with Vakhtangov at the First Studio and taught Stanislavski's ideas as filtered through the thinking of his great disciple made Boleslavsky's teaching all the more important to Strasberg. Stanislavski stated on more than one occasion that Vakhtangov taught the System better than he himself did. He even asked the younger man to coach him when he was working on the role of Salieri in Pushkin's *Mozart and Salieri*. Strasberg came to believe that Vakhtangov understood the theoretical implications of the Stanislavskian ideas better than Stanislavski did. Moreover, because of his Vakhtangov background, Boleslavsky was not limited by Stanislavski's directorial concepts. For this reason, according to Strasberg, Boleslavsky's explication of the System made its applicability to all styles of theatrical production much more understandable.*

Strasberg spent only one semester as a regular full-time student at the American Lab Theatre. By the winter of 1924, concluding that Boleslavsky's plans for a theater company were not really viable, he decided to strike out for Broadway as an actor. Two years later he returned to the Lab for five months to attend Boleslavsky's special course for "*régisseurs*." But the influence of his studies at the Lab

---

*For a dissenting view on the relationship between Vakhtangov and Boleslavsky, see Jerry Wayne Roberts, "The Theatre Theory and Practice of Richard Boleslavsky," Ph.D. dissertation, Kent State University, 1977, pp. 373–379.

was definitive and lasting. The exposure to Ouspenskaya, with her practical approach to work from an actor's point of view on the one hand, and to Boleslavsky, with his director's point of view and overall theoretical perspective on the other, provided a learning experience of enduring impact. In evaluating the effect of the Lab on his activities with the Group Theatre during the following decade, Strasberg later said, "There is no question that the technical work in the Group Theatre came definitely from the work that I had acquired, the knowledge that I had acquired in the Lab." [19]

In the period between his first enrollment at the Lab and the founding of the Group Theatre, 1924–1931, Strasberg experimented with the techniques he had studied there. He explored the possibilities of improvisation and affective memory in a variety of plays he directed for the SADs at Chrystie Street. Each play was chosen to investigate how the same approach to acting would have to be adjusted in order to solve particular stylistic problems. Heyerman's *Good Hope*, for instance, picked by Strasberg for his first directing effort at the settlement house because it had also been the initial project of the MAT First Studio, lent itself to completely realistic performances and production. Hofmannsthal's *Death and the Fool*, on the other hand, showed Max Reinhardt's influence. Anatole France's *The Man Who Married a Dumb Wife* used a Constructivist production format à la Meyerhold, while Synge's *Riders to the Sea* featured experiments with poetic language and Irish intonation.

Strasberg's 1926 production of the John Masefield translation of Racine's *Esther* is worth noting on several counts. It was the first play in which he directed Sanford Meisner, a young, onetime pianist turned performer who had gotten involved with the production in order to take advantage of Strasberg's work with his actors, and who would later become a founding member of the Group Theatre and an outstanding teacher of acting in his own right. It also offers us an interesting example of Strasberg's use of Vakhtangov-inspired procedures to solve the problem of making the Racinian world of kings and queens real to his Lower East Side amateurs. Casting about for an approach that would allow his performers to behave with belief in such a foreign and formal dramatic world, he struck on the idea of having his players imagine they were priests and nuns, figures from their everyday life to whom they could truthfully respond with a genuine awe and dignity that would, at the same time, create the appropriate "heightened" behavior from the audience point of view. This was an early use of the technique of "substitution," where a personal reality was substituted for a stage reality to help the actor believe in what he was doing and, therefore, create "truthful" and "organic" behavior.

An especially satisfying production for Strasberg, and his last at the Chrystie Street Settlement House, was the presentation of Jacques Copeau's *The House into Which We Are Born* (*La Maison Natale*), staged in honor of Copeau's visit to America in 1927, with the playwright himself attending the dress rehearsal. Strasberg had the gratification of seeing his use of affective memory and other techniques work to great effect: Copeau was so moved he wept. The amateur actors "were able to convey to this man who is himself a theatre person of distinct and definite ideas, and who had himself done the play, something alive enough and real enough so that it moved and touched him," Strasberg would recall.[20]

Strasberg had met Copeau and invited him to the Chrystie Street Settlement House when the Theatre Guild was preparing a production of the playwright's dramatization of *The Brothers Karamazov* (1927). Strasberg had been working for the Guild since December 1924, around the time he left the American Lab Theatre. Philip Loeb, casting director for the Guild, had seen him perform the role of a blind boy in a Maeterlinck play at the Chrystie Street Settlement House sometime earlier, and had told him to "look him up" if he ever wanted to start acting professionally. When Strasberg decided to try his luck on Broadway, he wrote to Loeb and within a few weeks was cast in John Howard Lawson's *Processional*, which opened on January 12, 1925. For the next two years, while working on various Guild projects, he continued his activities with the SADs as well.

Strasberg had no aspirations to become a famous actor nor any illusions that he might have a successful career as one. He was actually more interested in directing plays than in appearing in them. But he was a talented performer who could be quite funny in comic parts. He created the role of the peddler in *Green Grow the Lilacs* (1931), and "stopped the show" in the Theatre Guild's studio production of *Red Rust* (1929), in which he played a character called Pimples. "I was proud because I played him without makeup, though people swore they saw pimples on my face," he would recall. "At the time, of course, I considered that a triumph of acting."

It was Strasberg's performance of the leading role in a special Guild "trial performance" of Pirandello's *Right You Are If You Think You Are* (1927) that first brought him to the attention of Harold Clurman, who had been invited to see the production by Sanford Meisner, who was also in it. Clurman had just returned from Paris, where he had studied at the Sorbonne, and had made a start in the theater as an extra in the Provincetown Players production of Stark Young's *The Saint* (1924). When he first saw Strasberg, he had come to work at the Guild as an extra in *Caesar and Cleopatra* (1925). He had been promoted to stage manager when he finally met Strasberg at an audition for the *Garrick Gaieties of 1925*, a show the Guild was preparing to do at special Sunday matinees.[21] Philip Loeb introduced them, saying, "I think you two should know one another."

Loeb perhaps sensed that two such passionate young theater men would have much to offer one another, and apparently he was right, for they soon became fast friends. Both were upset by what they saw as the selfishness, the pettiness, the gross commercialism and triviality, of much of the American theater. Clurman, who had been tremendously impressed with Copeau's Théâtre du Vieux Colombier, which he had seen in operation firsthand during his stay in France, spoke of the possibility of emulating that organization in this country. Strasberg, for his part, introduced Clurman to the ideas of Craig and Stanislavski. Clurman observed Strasberg's work with his Chrystie Street amateurs and together they enrolled in Boleslavsky's course for directors (*régisseurs*) at the American Lab. It was at the Lab that they first met Stella Adler, whom Clurman later married. Before long they were considering forming a theater of their own based on the principles of Stanislavski, Craig, and Copeau.

Early in 1928, while they both continued to work for the Guild, they began rehearsing Waldo Frank's *New Year's Eve* in a "roof-garden hall" on the top of an apartment house owned by Sidney Ross, a real-estate man who was interested in the theater. To the group of young performers whom they had gathered together, they explained that they had no formal production plans for the play, but hoped that their work on it might lead to the birth of a new theater. In any case, the experience "would be instructive to the actors."

From the beginning, Clurman and Strasberg expressed special concern for the situation of the young actor, whose "individual problems as a growing craftsman" were usually swept aside by the exigencies of commercial production. Strasberg, who was reading a great deal of Marx, Lenin, and Trotsky at the time, defined the actor's problems in Marxist terms.

The actor in the American theater was a "commodity." He was a victim of the "type system," which in the craft of acting paralleled the capitalist system of production at its zenith. Typing an actor was industrializing him and turning him into a mechanism for manufacturing a specific product; typing or commodifying was the inevitable result of the capitalist development of the theater as a business. In such a theater the actor felt there was no opportunity to develop artistically or technically. He felt insecure and alienated from the system that provided his livelihood haphazardly. He felt exploited and, in fact, was exploited.

The new organization was to answer these felt wrongs. As part of a collective, the actor would have a sense of belonging. His economic and psychological well-being and the development of his talent would be a central concern of the organization. They would have to be, since they were crucial to the health of the group. The type system, for one thing, would be abolished as much as possible through the training in the Method, which would allow the performer's unique individual creativity, with all its possibilities of greater scope as well as greater depth in acting, to flower. When they spoke to prospective actors of their plans, Strasberg and Clurman emphasized that they would be paying careful attention to the actor's development. "Rehearsals themselves would constitute a schooling," Clurman stated. This was to remain a fundamental aspect of their work during the formative years of the Group Theatre.

But the Group was still a way off. The production of the Frank play had no immediate repercussions. Neither did their second project, the staging of Padraic Colum's *Balloon* later the same year, nor their presentation of the Soviet play *Red Rust* (1929) for the short-lived Theatre Guild Studio. This last production included a number of performers who were eventually to become permanent members of the Group: Strasberg, Luther Adler, William Challee, Ruth Nelson, Franchot Tone, and Eunice Stoddard.

They also joined forces with Cheryl Crawford, a graduate of Smith College who had attended the Theatre Guild School in 1926–1927. Miss Crawford, who earlier had been involved with the Provincetown Theatre on Cape Cod, had worked her way up from part-time casting secretary and third assistant stage manager to casting director for all the Guild plays and assistant director on the Guild's board.

She befriended Clurman when they worked together on the 1926 Guild production of *Juarez and Maxmillian*, she stage managing and executing a couple of tiny roles and Clurman playing a Mexican peon (his only line was "Ugh!"). Clurman explained his artistic ambitions to her, and, as he got to know her better, kept prodding her to join him and Strasberg. "This isn't what you really want, is it?" he would ask. Though she had been happy at her job, she was forced to admit that the Theatre Guild did not fulfill her dream of an ideal repertory company. She therefore gave up an opportunity to become a member of the Guild's board of directors and chose to join Strasberg and Clurman in their new venture.

Born in Akron, Ohio, on September 24, 1902, of quintessentially midwestern American Protestant stock, the soft-spoken Miss Crawford, with her short-cropped hair and squarely handsome, clean-cut features tending toward the severe, seemed an anomalous companion to the very vocal, very Jewish Strasberg and Clurman. They needed her organizational and managerial talents very badly, however, and she needed their idealism and fervency just as much. Though worlds apart from them in temperament and personality, she was to prove a very valuable ally in the formation, financing, and day-to-day running of the new theater.

It was in her apartment that Harold Clurman began his series of twenty-five Friday evening lectures to prospective participants in the new project. Then, as interest and the crowds grew, Steinway Hall was rented, and as many as one hundred or two hundred actors came to these meetings, which started close to midnight and went on into the early hours. Clurman was a spellbinding speaker; his impassioned oratory was as dramatic as it was powerful. He would grab the back of a chair and would hammer home his points while twisting it, brandishing it about, and beating it against the floor. Boris Aronson, the gifted scenic artist who was to create a number of the Group's sets, commented wryly once, "Well, I finally understand him; if he wouldn't have been the director of the Group Theatre, he would have been Father Divine!"

Clurman's talks were humorous, graceful, and full of his very real culture and intellect (years later, when he began writing for *The*

Nation, he would earn a reputation as one of America's outstanding theater critics). They attempted to crystallize every aspect of the enterprise that he, Strasberg, and Miss Crawford were embarked upon. He spoke again and again of the demoralized state of the American theater and of the plight of the actor in that environment. He spoke of the possibilities of the performer as a true creative artist, trained under the new methods emanating from Russia, and performing plays relevant to the society about him in a theater whose every element was integrated aesthetically into one organic whole. He spoke of devotion to an ideal of theater which would answer to the spiritual needs of its audience. It is no wonder that it was said of Clurman that he talked the Group Theatre into existence.

Clurman and Strasberg were looking for actors who had not only the basic acting abilities that would make possible a workable permanent ensemble, but those in whom they recognized a potential for growth in the kind of theatrical environment they were proposing. They wanted performers whose character and spirit ensured an idealism kindred to their own. There were to be no stars in the new theater. Katharine Hepburn, who came to one of the Steinway Hall meetings, was a notable example of someone who decided she did not want to join the new organization precisely because she felt her destiny—stardom—lay elsewhere.

During the winter of 1930–1931, they carefully made their choices of company members. Some of the actors, such as Phoebe Brand and Dorothy Patten, they knew through the Theatre Guild. Others they met through the Friday meetings or by catching their performances in shows. They went to see Sandy Meisner in Maxwell Anderson's *Gods of the Lightning* at the Provincetown Playhouse, for example, and were introduced to Robert Lewis, who was also in it. Lewis remembers Strasberg asking, "What were you trying to do?" in a tone of voice that suggested he hated the young actor's performance. Lewis was, nevertheless, invited to the meetings at Steinway Hall, and he and Meisner ultimately became members of the Group.

While Lewis and Meisner were essentially novices, as were many of the young actors who were chosen, some of the original Group members were already established in their careers. Morris Carnovsky, for one, had worked quite successfully for the Theatre Guild. Stella Adler, a daughter of the famous Jewish actor, Jacob Adler, had already made her own mark in the Yiddish theater; and Franchot Tone was in great demand in the commercial theater as a young leading man.

In subsequent seasons new performers were added to the theater's roster. Elia Kazan, fresh out of Yale; Jules Garfield (later to become the movie star John Garfield), and others, such as Karl Malden and Martin Ritt, all started their careers as Group actors.

It was Miss Crawford who persuaded the Theatre Guild to release Paul Green's *The House of Connelly* to the new theater group being formed by Clurman, Strasberg, and herself. She also raised several thousand dollars, including a thousand from the Guild itself, to get the group started in earnest during the summer of 1931 (Maxwell Anderson and Eugene O'Neill each gave a thousand to the cause). The actors and directors of the new organization began functioning as a theater in Brookfield Center, Connecticut, a summer-camplike site five miles from Danbury, which Miss Crawford had found for the group. They lived rent free in several houses on the property, one of which had a big kitchen and dining room where the company ate their meals together; the actors paid ninety dollars apiece for the summer's supply of food. A big barn served as a rehearsal hall. There, work on the Group Theatre's first production began, and Strasberg launched his effort "to make of the twenty-eight actors an 'artistic organism' with its own special character and aims." [22]

The Group's first summer rehearsal period at Brookfield Center was similar to the Moscow Art Theater's experience in Pushkino, the summer resort some twenty miles from Moscow, where Stanislavski and his actors prepared for their premiere season in 1898. Like the Russians, who were setting out to revolutionize the theater in their country, the members of the Group were a disparate set of individuals come together to find a common aesthetic and social basis for creating a viable and significant artistic enterprise. Mixing hard work with play and socializing, the young company discussed their plans and hopes, explored new relationships, rehearsed their play, and were alternately worried about the realities of the coming fall and exhilarated by the headiness of being part of something new and vital. Their activities that summer set the foundations for America's first important ensemble theater.

According to Strasberg, it was Clurman who insisted that Strasberg direct their initial production, thereby assuring that the new approach to acting would become the hallmark of the Group. The goal of that first summer's work was to achieve "a unified approach to performance" by grounding the actors in the fundamentals of the Method as received by Strasberg from his studies at the American Lab and developed by him at the Chrystie Street Settlement House. Those actors who had little or no background in Method training were given instruction by Clurman, while Strasberg brought the various elements of the Method to bear on the rehearsal work for *The House of Connelly*.

Clifford Odets would recall some thirty years later how "getting a part in the Group Theatre meant that you would learn what the hell the technique was about. There weren't too many technique classes, and the only way we could really learn and get the benefit of Strasberg's training was to get a good part. In that way he would work with you solo, he would work with you in pairs. This was a very important reason for getting a good part. . . . If you wanted to find out what this was all about, you had to tiptoe around and listen with one ear, and make believe that you weren't listening. Those actors who had the good parts got the real and best benefits of Strasberg's training, and the others did not; that's all." [23]

The important elements of that training that received special emphasis at this time were improvisation and affective memory. Improvisation was employed by the Group in several forms: the actors were given situations analogous to those in the play which they had to enact extemporaneously; this allowed them to discover and explore behavior they could not preconceive. They also improvised on the text of the play itself, using their own ad-lib speech rather than the author's lines; this allowed them to develop their belief in what they were enacting and to break a sometimes slavish adherence to verbal patterns. Eventually, the improvisations got so close to the situations in the play that the actors unconsciously started using the author's language. Some of the improvisatory exercises were intended to create a proper background reality for the performances. When word got around that actors were improvising doing farm work in the basement of their theater during the New York run, there was much kidding about "those crazy Group people digging potatoes in the cellar." Nevertheless, improvisation, in all its forms, was to become very popular with Method practitioners in the years ahead.

The specific procedure by which "an exercise in affective memory" was carried out was as follows: the actor would choose a fairly potent real-life emotional experience to "work on." (In Strasberg's subsequent classroom teaching the actor was told to limit himself to events that had taken place at least seven years earlier. Under no circumstances was he to try to use a recent experience or one that still had a conscious effect on him. In the Group productions, however, any and all experiences were drawn upon.) After a period of concentrated relaxation, he began to recollect the experience by recapturing the sensory elements that accompanied it. Step by step, Strasberg would ask him, "What do you see before you? What do you feel underneath your feet? What do your clothes feel like on your body? Does the air have a particular smell? Is it warm? or damp?" and so on. Eventually the reexperiencing of the sensory life surrounding the event would release the accompanying emotion.

If the actor tried to approach the emotion directly, however, it would not come forth. Emotion, Strasberg explained, can only be approached indirectly through the memories of sensory stimulation encoded with it. Once the actor successfully stimulated the desired emotion through the exercise, he was able to gain greater and greater control over it by repeating the sequence of sense memories till ultimately one or two sensory keys could release the emotion when and as he needed it. What originally took more than a half hour of concentrated effort to accomplish could eventually be achieved in about sixty seconds, "the golden minute," as it came to be called. When the actor wanted to experience a certain emotion at a particular point in the play, he would begin to prepare for it one minute before he reached that moment. With proper preparation and practice, he could bring the desired emotion into play, performance after performance.

For the Group actors, the first effect of discovering this procedure "was that of a miracle," according to Clurman.

Here at last was a key to that elusive ingredient of the stage, true emotion. And Strasberg was a fanatic on the subject of true emotion. Everything was secondary to it. He sought it with the patience of an inquisitor, he was outraged by trick substitutes, and when he had succeeded in stimulating it, he husbanded it, fed it, and protected it. Here was something new to most of the actors, something basic, and something almost holy. It was revelation in the theatre; and Strasberg was its prophet.[24]

The effort invested in preparing the company during that first summer of the Group's existence had telling results. A performance style unique in the history of American theater was achieved. "The Group people had succeeded in fusing the technical elements of their craft with the stuff of their own spiritual and emotional selves." Under the directorial guidance of Strasberg, they created a genuine ensemble piece characterized by the honesty and sincerity of its execution. When *The House of Connelly* opened at the Martin Beck Theatre on September 23, 1931, it was received enthusiastically by the New York critics. Adjectives like "luminous," "tremulous," and "pellucid" were used to describe the performance; comparisons with the work of the Moscow Art Theater were drawn. Even among those for whom the production had its drawbacks, there were words of praise and encouragement. The eminent drama critic, Stark Young, said,

There was not an instance of stage cheating for effect, or of hollowness; there was no forcing, no individual grabbing of the scene; you felt the play free of tampering or intrusion. The promise that lies in such an attitude is obvious; the very genuine welcome given . . . to the Group's first venture rested basically on that.[25]

The first summer-training program's emphasis on truth of emotion was followed, in the second season, by experimentation in "theatricality and clarity of interpretation." Among the variety of exercises aimed at stimulating the actors' mental, physical, and emotional agility were single-word improvisations such as the one Strasberg still recalls as an early "playwrighting" effort of Clifford Odets. Given the word *America* to enact, the then actor-member of the Group thought a minute and began. "He went to sleep. He awoke suddenly, looked at the alarm clock (imaginary) and then began frantically to dress. He then rushed into an imaginary subway into which he crowded. He next entered an office, hastily took off his hat and coat, sat down at his desk, lit a cigar, and then—leaned back in his chair, put his feet on the desk, and placidly smoked on with nothing to do." *America.*[26]

There were also improvisations in which two people were given three unrelated words, such as *nose, sing,* and *beer,* which they had to incorporate logically in a dramatic situation they were given one minute to prepare. Poems were "performed" in contexts not necessarily related to their original meaning for the purpose of demonstrating how the import of words could be changed or affected by different given circumstances or characterizations. A Group favorite, and an especially hilarious example of this exercise, was Robert Lewis's version of Walt Whitman's "I Sing the Body Electric." As he recited this joyously exultant hymn of praise to the human body, Lewis shivered and squirmed ecstatically in the character of a meek little clerk bravely enduring a very cold shower.

Strasberg had his actors create dramatic scenes inspired by pieces of classical music and famous paintings. A Brahms quintet suggested a child's death during an operation. The drawings of George Grosz served as the basis for an entire pantomime conceived and directed by Art Smith.[27] Gibberish exercises, in which the actors improvised without the use of real words, helped release emotion that was felt but could not be expressed freely. Strasberg also made special use of Ouspenskaya's exercises in animal characterization to help develop his actors' concentration, observation, and imagination.

In subsequent seasons these and similar exercises were regularly introduced into both the training and production work of the Group. While rehearsing *Men in White* during their third season, for instance, the actors who were to play doctors and nurses improvised two operating-room scenes to help get their creative juices flowing. The first was performed in somber slow motion to the accompaniment of Beethoven's Seventh Symphony. The second was played as a frenetic, *commedia dell'arte*-style romp, with the actors accidentally sewing up instruments inside the patient and so on, to the galloping rhythms of Offenbach's *Gaité Parisienne*. At the same time, the performers, always interested in thorough research, also visited hospitals where they observed actual medical procedures firsthand.

Many of these exercises were incorporated into the acting-training programs of those Group members who subsequently started classes of their own. Some fifteen years later a good deal of this work was to characterize the initial training at The Actors Studio.

Much of the exploratory work of the summer of 1932, especially the experiments in theatricality and the development of the imagination, reflected the growing influence on Strasberg and the Group of Eugene Vakhtangov, the Russian director and theorist whose theatricalism appealed to the Americans. They in fact preferred his ideas on stylization to Stanislavski's purely realistic approach to production. Most important for their work, Vakhtangov showed that theatricality and Stanislavski's approach to the actor's reality are not incompatible.

Vakhtangov's reconciliation of his own highly theatrical visualizations with Stanislavski's insistence on true inner experience was of critical significance to Strasberg, who felt his own artistic interests could well be served by such a synthesis. Strasberg always considered his own productions less "purely realistic" and more poetical or heightened in their realism than Stanislavski's. For that reason he felt a strong affinity to the general thrust of Vakhtangov's ideas, though his staging for the Group did not reflect the more obvious theatrical elements in Vakhtangov's work.

Vakhtangov's so-called "second formulation," Strasberg believes, supplied practical and theoretical solutions to the problem of how to get the actor to be truthful and theatrical at the same time. This recasting of Stanislavski's basic question for the actor facing a role from "What would I do if I were the character?" to "What must I do to make myself behave as the character?" offered the performer an approach to whatever reality was required of him. It allowed the actor to find the stimuli that would bring him up to the necessities of the part—including the director's theatrical conception of it—rather than bringing the role down to the dimensions of his own personality. In getting his Chrystie Street actors to think of themselves as priests or nuns, Strasberg used this technique to create the "heightened" behavior he wanted in his production of Racine's *Esther* at the SAD.

Vakhtangov argued that the actor's theatricality must not be imposed from without. It arises when the actor is properly stimulated, properly motivated. It must always be justified inwardly, rooted in the actor's true experience. This is what Vakhtangov meant (as reported in the words of his disciple, B. E. Zakhava):

To create and not be oneself is impossible. It is essential not to distort oneself on the stage, inasmuch as the actor retains his own personality on the stage. You must remove whatever is superfluous as far as the character goes and not add what you do not possess. You cannot seek the character somewhere outside yourself and then fit it on—you must make it up out of the material which you yourself possess.

The actor's "material," his unique individuality, was of paramount importance to Vakhtangov. Strasberg's own guiding principle in actor's training, from the earliest days of the Group to his current activities at The Actors Studio, is summarized in Vakhtangov's admonition on the subject (again, in the words of Zakhava):

The liberation and disclosing of the individuality; this must become the principal aim of a theatrical school. A theatrical school must clear the way for the creative potentialities of the student—but he must move and proceed along this road by himself; he cannot be taught. The school must remove all the conventional rubbish which prevents the spontaneous manifestation of the student's deeply hidden potentialities.[28]

This translation of Zakhava's book was done especially for the Group by Mark Schmidt, a sometime political anarchist who worked as a dishwasher at the Group's summer headquarters in Connecticut. Strasberg commissioned him to translate the Zakhava volume as well as a number of other Russian texts, including selections from Vakhtangov's diary and several works on Meyerhold. Every day at sundown, just before dinner, Schmidt read aloud from the Zakhava book to the Group members who gathered around. By summer's end he had translated the whole thing in this manner. Selections of what he had read were put down for permanent reference. Schmidt translated others' works as well. The Group hoped to publish some of these translations, but actually distributed only two of them.[29]

Strasberg's work with the actors was intense and demanding. Now in his early thirties, his private and professional personalities had begun to gel into the characteristics that would identify him throughout his life. A short man with a high forehead and already thinning hair, he had an often impassive though intelligent face with expressive eyes behind round glasses—all contributing to an impression of studiousness. In social situations, Strasberg was a quiet, at times eerily nonverbal person. One wondered at the man's reticence. Was it the result of a deep-seated and uncontrollable shyness or of a calculated need to keep others off guard about his state of mind—or both? In the public arena, when discussing theater ideas or answering questions on topics that interested him, a different persona emerged. He would become positively garrulous. When he was directing or training performers, all traces of shyness or taciturnity were replaced by a strongly assertive certainty, forcefully, even fanatically expressed.

His authoritative temperament could be very intimidating. There was something in him of the Russian ballet master who terrifies his dancers. After a rehearsal, for instance, he might say to an actor through clenched teeth, "How many times have I told you to relax! RELAX!!" The tempestuous anger and self-assured insistence on the correctness of his ideas rubbed some people the wrong way.

Albert Dekker once tried to explain to Strasberg that his actors could not hear what he was trying to tell them when he got so angrily emotional with them—that though they would like very much to do what he wanted, they could not understand, through the storms of his temper, what he was after. Strasberg says that Dekker's remarks made a strong impression on him, but the occasional tantrum remained a part of his personality. Both he and Clurman, according to the latter, could be quite arrogant at times and display an "appalling lack of grace" in dealing with the company.

But the effect of the work and the growing assurance of the company also made Strasberg something of a hero to his players. Morris Carnovsky remembers the young director's "curious priest-like quality" during rehearsals for *The House of Connelly*. "I recall him in that ugly yellow slicker that he wore. He looked as if that were his priest's uniform. He'd walk through the rain in that. He was fanatically absorbed in his work. And this was good—very moving." [30] During the early years of the Group, the actors responded very positively to his strengths—to his unique insight into their problems, to his nurturing care of their talents, and to the dramatic results of the procedures he demanded of them.

As the public response to those results heightened, the Group began to enjoy success, both critically and, with Sidney Kingsley's *Men in White* (1933), financially.* Strasberg was immensely interested in the developments in the Russian theater, which during the twenties and thirties was the most dynamic and innovative in the world. When Sidney Kingsley decided to reward Strasberg for the success of *Men in White*, Strasberg's wife, Paula, suggested a trip to Russia to study the theater and meet the personalities he had been reading about.** In May of 1934, Strasberg set off for the Soviet Union, and was followed shortly thereafter by Kingsley, Clurman, and Stella Adler.

* The MGM film version of *Men in White* was directed by Boleslavsky in 1934.
** Strasberg's first wife died in 1929; he married Paula Miller, an original member of the Group, in 1934.

While there, he met with Vakhtangov's widow—the Russian director had died in 1922 at the age of thirty-nine—and saw her husband's famous production of *Turandot*. (He had already seen Vakhtangov's equally famous staging of *The Dybbuk* when the Habimah Theater visited New York in 1927.) He also met many of Russia's leading theater people, including Meyerhold and Okhlopkov, visited classes and workshops, and saw a number of productions at the Moscow Art Theater, at Meyerhold's theater, and elsewhere.[31] Oddly enough the one person he might have been expected to seek out—Stanislavski—he avoided.

The reason for this, as he explained years later, was the state of the work at Stanislavski's theater. "I went to see the Moscow Art Theater and I was angry because there in a production of *Vaskryesyénye* (*Resurrection*) was a leading actor who in the middle of the performance looked out towards the audience. If I had been Russian, I would have gotten up on the stage and killed him. But I was American, so I had to be quiet. I saw other things on the stage which I did not like." Upset as he was, he knew he could not avoid being critical of the situation if he met Stanislavski.

With Meyerhold, on the other hand, he felt free to ask probing questions. Not only had he seen the great director's productions, which he thought were brilliant, but he had seen the classroom work in Meyerhold's famous system of bio-mechanics for the actor, with which he was not impressed. "I wasn't afraid to ask Meyerhold, 'What's the matter, don't you want your actors to experience?' He said, 'Yes, I do.' I said, 'Why don't they?' He said, 'They're bad actors.' I didn't answer that. He was wrong, but. . . . In other words, with Meyerhold I felt free. He was the greatest genius I've met— probably the greatest genius that the theater has ever had, certainly as a director (and greater, in that respect, than Stanislavski). Nonetheless, I was not of his school, so it didn't bother me. Stanislavski I had a different feeling about. All my work was inspired by the ideas of Stanislavski. If I had gone to see him, I would have had to say something about what I had seen on the stage of the Moscow Art Theater. And I couldn't do that to Stanislavski." *

* When Strasberg told this story to some Russian theater people on a recent trip there, they commented that he should have gone to see Stanislavski anyway, because at that time the Russian master himself was distressed by what was happening at the MAT and probably would have agreed with Strasberg's criticism. Strasberg, therefore, now regrets the lost opportunity.

Stella Adler, however, was not so reluctant to seek out Stanislavski, and her meeting with the famous Russian led to one of the most controversial episodes in the history of the Group—a confrontation between Strasberg and her some months later. An actress with a decided theatrical flair, Miss Adler had always felt somewhat out of place amongst the mostly "untheatrical" personalities in the Group. And though she herself had studied with Boleslavsky and Ouspenskaya, she was not happy with the thrust of Strasberg's work, which she thought dwelled too much on the actor's personal emotion. She believed that a lot of what he did came from his need to force something interesting out of the basically untheatrical and inexperienced young actors in the company.

When she and Clurman met Stanislavski in Paris late in 1934, she confided to the Russian director that she had become disenchanted with her work as an actress and that she feared his System was the cause of her unhappiness. Stanislavski, who was in the French capital recuperating from an illness, promptly told her, "If the System does not help you, forget it. But perhaps you do not use it properly." He then offered to work with her on a scene from *Gentlewoman*, one of the Group's unsuccessful productions in which she played the title role, an aristocratic wife of an American governor. For five weeks they worked together, conversing in French, for several hours a day. Stanislavski emphasized the importance of *actions* and *given circumstances* with her. " 'For emotion,' " he told her, " 'I search in the *given circumstances* [the particularities of each of the play's situations] never in the feelings. If I try and do the psychological, I force the action. We must attack the psychological from the point of view of the physical life so as not to disturb the feeling. . . . *In each psychological action there is some physical element.* Search for the line, *in terms of action*, not in feeling.' " [32]

When she returned to the Group, she brought with her a chart of the System which Stanislavski had outlined for her.[33] She announced that the company had been misusing the "affective memory" exercise, which Stanislavski now recommended only as a last resort, and that the given circumstances and action, according to the Russian theorist, should be given primary attention. Strasberg was angered by her report and her charge of misuse of the work, and concluded that either she had misunderstood what Stanislavski had told her or that the Russian master "had gone back on himself."

Miss Adler insists her account of her work with Stanislavski was accurate, that in fact she had taken a secretary with her to each session with him, and that the secretary's notes, verbatim quotes of what he said, specifically identified and corrected the misinterpretations and misemphases in Strasberg's work.[34]

Stanislavski's own recollection of his Paris sessions with Miss Adler does not fully clarify matters. He describes "a completely panic stricken woman" clutching at him and begging him to save her from the effects of his System. He had to work with her, he says, "if only to restore the reputation of my system. I wasted a whole month on it. It turned out that everything she had learnt was right." On the face of it, this would seem to indicate that her accusations of misinterpretation were somewhat exaggerated. Affective memory, after all, was a good part of the "everything" she had learned under Boleslavsky and Ouspenskaya. Stanislavski, however, goes on to say that he stressed what he terms "the through-line action and task" in his work with her, calling it "the crux of the whole system." And this appears to tally with Miss Adler's insistence that his emphasis was on the given circumstances and action above all else.[35]

It seemed to Strasberg that the charges of mistaken emphasis were totally unfounded. "We did emphasize the inner reality. And this was the particular characteristic of our work which excited people: the strength of the emotional intensities, the almost volcanic eruptions. But we had never not included the strong element of actions. We used actions. We used given circumstances. We used everything of that kind." He came ultimately to explain Miss Adler's encounter with Stanislavski in terms of her "mistaken idea of her own problem," which, he says, had nothing to do with the general problems of the Group.

Strasberg did not believe Miss Adler's work in *Gentlewoman* had been a failure. Nor did he believe her feelings of unhappiness about her acting had anything to do with a mistaken use of affective memory. She never had a problem inciting emotion, he says. In *Gentlewoman* "It was the problem of clarifying and defining the precise emotional thing I wanted to get from her—not which she wanted to get." The directorate of the Group—Strasberg, Clurman, and Crawford—felt that John Howard Lawson's play needed a more sophisticated treatment, a performance on a "lighter level," and one less heavily emotional than that of previous Group plays. "I didn't want

Stella's emotionalism. To put it quite simply: Jewish emotionalism. As a result, in that particular play, with her I worked on absolutely nothing. Her first reading was all I wanted. If she felt ill at ease, it was because she was not being permitted to do what she liked or wanted to do. I had to fight with Stella. I remember telling her, 'Godammit, if you cry, I'll kill you!' " The implication is clear: faced with an actress of this particular temperament and talent, Stanislavski would naturally respond by playing down the element of emotion to stress the more "objective" elements of action and given circumstances. As if to underscore the point, Strasberg notes that when she left the Group to appear in plays directed by Tyrone Guthrie and Max Reinhardt, the critics took issue with her "loose emotionalism"; her performances were "too emotional," they said.

Strasberg's protestations on the matter were of little effect at the time, however, and his subsequent analysis of events does not alter the fact that many members of the Group company responded very favorably to Miss Adler's announcement. Her report was, in fact, a watershed experience for the Group. "The emphasis which had been put very strongly on the conscious manipulation of the actor's exact emotion was abandoned by most of the actors. The Stanislavski system was from then on reinterpreted by pressure coming from his own statement," she would write years later.[36]

Strasberg takes issue with this claim, arguing that there was little or no actual change in the work habits of the Group. He especially denies Clurman's statement in *The Fervent Years* that he "decided to take advantage of the suggestions furnished by Stella's report, and to use what he could of the 'innovations' in Stanislavsky's method." He states emphatically, "I made not the slightest change in my work!" There is no question, however, that the continuing disagreements between the various practitioners of Stanislavski's ideas in this country date from this episode.*

Strasberg was, of course, annoyed and hurt by the company's response. Up to this point he had had the actors' unquestioned support in artistic matters—Clurman speaks of their "adoration" of the director in the early years. Now he was open to challenge.

---

* Some forty-five years later, Strasberg and Miss Adler would still be disagreeing, and with unabated vigor and vitriol. See Suzanne O'Malley, "Can the Method Survive the Madness?" *The New York Times Magazine*, October 7, 1979, pp. 32–34, 36, 39–40, 139–41.

The mid-thirties witnessed endless temperamental wranglings within the Group. For Strasberg the climax of these internecine quarrels came when his role in the Group (and those of his fellow directors) was harshly evaluated by the Actors' Committee, which had been formed to win the performers a greater voice in the organization. While acknowledging him and his method of work as "the greatest artistic force in the American theatre during the last five years," the document drafted by the committee early in 1937 went on to describe his once necessary "great courage, his doggedness, his arbitrariness, his need to be right, his cold scorn of artistic compromise, his clannishness, his removal from life, his hysterical force (used as a threat) and above all the brute domineering of his will" as "unhealthy." [37]

The tone of the actors' evaluation did not sit well with Strasberg. The criticism was severe and Strasberg was highly sensitive to its tone of censure.

As it turns out, the Actors' Committee criticism of Strasberg and his fellow directors was part of a political strategem instigated by a secret Communist cell in the Group to gain influence over the organization. Elia Kazan revealed this many years later when he discussed how he behaved "treacherously" to the Group (his own word) as a member of that cell and how he quit the Party when it ordered him to participate in a strike aimed as a takeover of the theater troupe by its membership. [38]

The committee criticism brought to a head Strasberg's growing disillusionment with the Group that ultimately led him to submit his resignation from the organization in the spring of 1937. Cheryl Crawford, who was similarly disturbed by problems with the Group, as well as by the criticism and the lack of cooperation she had encountered, had resigned just before he did. The committee spoke of her having submitted to "six years of dirty jobs," which the actors appreciated, but also noted that she behaved "as a disappointed artist . . . a 'martyr' to the Group. . . . She never stops trying to impress people with her own importance, the work she is doing, how what other people receive credit for doing is really her work. . . ." [39]

In the letter to Clurman announcing his decision, Strasberg remarked that from his point of view, "the Group had been a success, but his resignation was prompted by the feeling that the members of the Group had destroyed its leadership."

Throughout this stormy period in the Group's history, relations had grown strained among the three leaders, especially between Strasberg and Clurman. The latter was put off by Strasberg's touchiness, and his refusal to deal with any criticism of his role as artistic director. Strasberg, for his part, was upset over what he called Clurman's "somnambulism" and by what he felt was Clurman's failure as managing director to shield him from the Group problems that affected his work as artistic director. Miss Crawford apparently sided with Strasberg. Clurman accepted both their resignations "with a kind of friendly fatalism, and no argument." [40]

Years later, according to Strasberg, someone who had been involved with the Group's behind-the-scenes political machinations let slip to him that he was not supposed to have resigned when he did. His leaving evidently threw a monkey wrench into the Communist cell's plans to take control of the organization. When pressed for further explanation, Strasberg's interlocutor quickly changed the subject.

Strasberg worked extensively over the next decade as a Broadway director, while Miss Crawford established herself as an independent producer. They were to collaborate on several productions over the years, the first being *All the Living* by Hardie Albright in March of 1938. Strasberg also continued his lifelong teaching career.

Clurman stayed with the Group Theatre and continued as its sole head for the remaining four years of its existence. Though he had been criticized by the Actors' Committee for his failures as managing director ("Harold really works only under the spell of inspiration, crumbling just before rising to heights"), it felt he was still the logical person to head a restructured theater organization. The report said, "He is still the clearest and the most whole of the three directors, and in him the Group Idea still flowers the most." He initiated the following season auspiciously with a production of Clifford Odets's *Golden Boy,* and directed all but four of the organization's subsequent plays, which included three more by Odets, who had become famous as *the* Group playwright. Two plays by Robert Ardrey and one by Irwin Shaw were directed by Elia Kazan, who up till then had been an actor-member of the Group; William Saroyan's *My Heart's in the Highlands* was directed in a notable production by another Group performer, Robert Lewis.

Elia Kazan, or "Gadge" as he was nicknamed because of his fondness for gadgets, had come to the Group Theatre in 1932. A Greek born in a small suburb of Istanbul, Turkey, he was brought to America at four and grew up on the Upper West Side of Manhattan and in New Rochelle, New York. He attended Williams College and the Yale School of Drama, where he studied theatrical production and took a seminar in playwrighting with the famous George Pierce Baker during the very last year of that eminent teacher's career. He wrote a number of plays at Yale and acted in several classics—as Wagner in Marlowe's *Dr. Faustus*, Pylade in Racine's *Andromaque*, and Solyony in Chekhov's *The Three Sisters*, among them.

As a Group actor, he made a tremendous impression in three Odets plays: *Golden Boy, Paradise Lost*, and *Waiting for Lefty*. The fiery intensity of his performing, an emotional forcefulness that came from his natural "pent-up anger," gave his portrayals of the gangster roles in the first two plays an arresting authenticity. When he appeared in *Lefty*, many in the audience thought he was a real cab driver off the streets. In other roles he was less good, according to Harold Clurman, who directed him in a number of plays. "When he had to play anger or hurt, anger from being a suppressed character, he was excellent. He also knew how to take direction. When the part was within the compass of his ability, his own directorial head made his performances, his response as a director, first class." He considered himself "a very limited actor. . . . I didn't have much range. I was like an instrument with only three or four very strong notes." [41]

Despite this self-estimate, Kazan's dedication to his acting while he was still pursuing it was exemplary; it was typical of the earnestness with which he approached all creative endeavor.

I worked like a maniac. First of all I took the Stanislavsky training with the utmost seriousness. I did all the physical work, gymnastics, acrobatics, dancing. I worked much harder than actors work today. I did sensememory every day. You feel an orange and when you 'peel' it without touching it, you actually feel how the peeling feels to your fingers; I became very good at that. Then I took singing and speech lessons because I spoke like a New York street kid, very slangy. I thought of the roles mostly psychologically. I analysed the main drive of a character and from the main drive there were stems, the 'beats', that would build up the whole part. I understood how to divide a part into various tasks. I took innumerable notes, like I have all my life.[42]

This was the sort of devotion to craft he would come to expect from the young actors who turned to him for guidance in the years ahead. It was a dedication and discipline inspired and encouraged by his involvement with the Group Theatre.

But acting was not properly his métier, as he saw it. Performing often made him ill at ease. So although to many it looked as if he had a promising acting career ahead of him, he deliberately cut it short. He has noted, incidentally, that Brooks Atkinson's review of his performance in *Five Alarm Waltz* played no small part in his decision to quit.

As for Mr. Kazan, he is getting to be a self-conscious actor with purple patches and many little curlicues on the side. Cast as the mad genius of the play, Mr. Kazan has to act several scenes costumed in a pair of drawers, and it is pleasant to observe that he has a nice little thicket of black curlicues smack in the middle of his chest. Since nature gave him those, he is entitled to them and is herewith handsomely congratulated. But what worries this art lover are the little fancies in his acting style that look as if they had come out of a book. Mr. Kazan's acting in this drama is studiously spontaneous.[43]

Kazan was especially furious about the "thicket of black curlicues" gibe and decided there and then that he would never allow himself to be insulted in that way again. After that production he simply withdrew from performing and never acted again. His attention turned fully to directing, which had always been his first love, and he went on to make his many outstanding contributions in that field.

A native New Yorker, Robert Lewis started out to be a musician. After City College, he attended the Juilliard School of Music, where he studied cello and piano and took courses in composition and theory. When the opportunity arose, he switched to acting, making his first appearance with the Civic Repertory Theatre in *The Would-Be Gentleman* in 1929. He joined the Group during its first season—the youngest of the original members—and appeared in many of its productions.

His acting had a "stylistic" quality to it, by all reports, and he was encouraged in this, according to Strasberg, but never at the expense of inner reality. He was affectionately labeled a "theatrical Trotskyite" by his colleagues. By taste and temperament, he was much more drawn to what Vakhtangov called "fantastic realism" than most of his associates in the Group, though there were stylized elements in many of the Group's productions, most notably in *Johnny Johnson*. In 1934, when Strasberg and Clurman were in Russia, Lewis did an experimental production of Samuel Ornitz's *In New Kentucky*, a poetic play about a strike, which had "Vakhtangovian" qualities. Strasberg felt it was as good as the Vakhtangov productions he saw in Russia. When Clurman decided to present Saroyan's *My Heart's in the Highlands* as an experimental Group production, it was only logical for him to choose Lewis to direct it because of that play's poetic and fantasy elements. The production proved to be a critical success and one of the highpoints of the Group's attempts at theatrical stylization.

During the 1937–1938 season, Lewis set up a small Group Theatre school to train promising actors who might eventually be absorbed into the parent company. The idea was to prepare young performers in such a way as to avoid the problems outside actors, unfamiliar with the Method, often encountered when joining a Group production. This Group "Studio" had Lewis, Meisner, and Morris Carnovsky teaching the fundamentals of the Method to both scholarship students and paying pupils, while special instructors in fencing, movement, and speech rounded out the training program. The original plan was to organize the work on the basis of plays the Group was interested in exploring. The Studio's students were to be assigned parts in these plays and instruction was to center on various components of acting as they arose in conjunction with the student's particular roles in specific plays. To this end, playwrights were to be invited to participate in the work of the unit. It was hoped the enterprise would provide a constant stream of new acting talent and an experimental testing ground for writers.

Unfortunately, the Studio lasted only a single season, despite the fact that financially it was modestly successful. It failed primarily because the Group did a good deal of touring and was away from New York for long periods. Even so, when time permitted, Kazan, Lewis, and others offered classes for local students while on the road. Ten years later, however, they were to come together once again to establish another studio—The Actors Studio—the workshop for actors that was to have such an unmistakable impact on the American theater.

The Group Theatre went out of existence on January 4, 1941,

with the closing of its final production, Irwin Shaw's *Retreat to Pleasure*. The organization's last few seasons were filled with tensions, fallings-out, and recriminations; an air of "dreariness and discouragement" surrounded its dissolution. There was an attempt to lure Strasberg back during this period in the hopes he could ignite again some of the heady enthusiasm of the early years, but he was unwilling to return unless matters were "clarified and corrected," and so the effort came to nothing. At one point it looked as if the last official Group play would be Odets's *Clash by Night*, directed by Strasberg. But the production's major backer, Billy Rose, did not wish to share billing with the Group, and so the organization ended its life denied the sentimental appositeness of bidding farewell with a play by *its* playwright.

During the ten years of its lively career, the Group was subject to a fair share of hostile criticism. There were charges of clannishness, intolerance of criticism, mystical reverence for Stanislavski, poor judgment in the choice and execution of plays, and inadequate business sense—all trotted out to explain why the Group had not succeeded, after such an arduous and dedicated struggle, in establishing itself as a permanent institution.

But all such criticisms do not explain the Group's demise. (The reasons for that are complex and include the continuing unavailability of good plays and the sheer exhaustion from the relentless struggle to survive in an economically unresponsive environment. They are, properly, the subject of another book.) Neither do they gainsay the Group's greatest achievement: that it demonstrated the nature of a true theater—a theater that is founded on an idea, served by a working technique that makes it possible for that idea to be created on stage, and embodied in a permanent company of people who share a common appreciation of that idea, and who therefore stay together over a long period of time, working and building as a unit, to see that idea flourish.

The miracle of enduring ten years in an indifferent and often hostile commercial theater environment is evidence in itself of the virtues of tenacity, loyalty, and selfless devotion to an ideal and a dream. Aside from the creative talent it introduced and nurtured, the Group represented and still represents a serious and idealistic effort to "make of the theater an art," in every sense of that term. Its purpose, in

Clurman's words, "was artistically and culturally sound . . . to make the production of stage plays actually mean something in the lives of the participants."

For the players involved, this meant caring about "the individual actor's total personality." The performer's development was of critical concern. The nature of the acting method he was being trained in required his using not only his histrionic talent, but his actual experience, that is, his emotions, impulses, and intuitions. The actor's personal problems, as far as they might interfere with his growth as an artist and craftsman and thereby affect the life of the theater, had to be comprehended and dealt with. "Our personal approach to the actor, then, did not consist in an immodest prying into succulent privacies, but was an attempt to get to the fundamental realities that affected him," Clurman explained.[44]

There were criticisms of the Group's approach to acting, especially from the point of view of its effect on the performers themselves. Such misgivings were summed up in Laurette Taylor's remark "Why must they make acting a malady?" There were accusations that the theater induced neurosis in its members, or attracted the unbalanced, and that the actors in their tendencies to emotionalism and "hysteria" distorted art and verged on pathology—criticisms that would be leveled at the Group's spiritual inheritors some fifteen years later.

(During the forties, when they were working together on the film *Dragon Seed,* Katharine Hepburn said to Robert Lewis, "You know you and Gadget Kazan were the only two who were mean enough to come through those whole ten years in the Group Theatre completely untouched." Lewis retorted, "You're absolutely right, Katharine. Outside of three complete nervous breakdowns, it didn't touch me at all.")

Various Group members, several of them prominent teachers of acting in their own right, were critical of Strasberg's emphasis on emotional memory then, and have remained so to this day.

Sanford Meisner recalls that "the Group took introverted people and intensified their introversion. . . . The result was that many, many young actors . . . were damaged by the approach." Stella Adler agrees "that the work was unhealthy. There was a certain stress on the use of the actor's personal emotion which landed them in the booby-hatch and shattered them. . . . You couldn't be on the stage thinking of your own personal life. It was just schizophrenic." Phoebe

Brand (Mrs. Morris Carnovsky) remembers that "confusion was one of the terrible things we suffered from." [45]

Strasberg acknowledges the pressures placed on the actors but points out that many of the young performers were raw and inexperienced and had to be molded into a functioning ensemble in a very short period of time. "In later years," he explains, "we didn't work that deliberately any more, only when there were problems." Was the pain, the trauma, and the confusion worth it? Strasberg believes that the results spoke for themselves: the creation of a troupe of actors whose work together was critically hailed as a landmark achievement in the history of the American theater.

Clifford Odets spoke in no uncertain terms about what was accomplished. "I don't think in our day you will see a company like that, and I don't think, still, that in our day anyone could put together such a company but Lee Strasberg. It was Lee Strasberg's baby and he was one hundred percent responsible for it. Later with this perfected tool, this ensemble, this acting company, anybody could direct them who had a common lingo and a common frame of reference. It was very easy for Harold Clurman to direct *Awake and Sing* or *Golden Boy* with this company that Lee Strasberg had put together. I could have directed it. Any actor could have directed it by that time. Lee Strasberg has never gotten enough credit for that." [46]

To the general public and the critical establishment at large, the Group's acting was a revelation and a consistent pleasure. The reviewers often criticized the Group's productions for dramaturgic shortcomings, but the acting company itself was invariably cited as the finest in America.

The loss of the Group in 1941 was deeply felt by its actor-members throughout the forties. As a theater organization, it had cultivated respect for the actor, created conditions for the continuity of his development, prompted feelings of belonging, and fostered a sense of dignity, of dedication, and of creative artistry in him. It had brought together a diverse set of people, and through shared experiences had given them a common outlook on theater and performance —the Group Theatre heritage. Among the Group veterans were those who, in an attempt to carry on that heritage, founded The Actors Studio before the end of the decade. Ultimately—perhaps inevitably—many former members were to play a role, large and small, in the history of that spiritual offspring of the Group.

CHAPTER 2

Birth of
The Actors Studio:
1947–1950

THERE IS A PARADOX in the fact that Lee Strasberg, the individual most closely identified with The Actors Studio and the man who, in the course of things, would achieve world renown as its guiding spirit, played no part in its founding in 1947. Strasberg's delay in coming onto the Studio scene, which will be examined in the chapter that follows, was the result of his perplexing relationship with Elia Kazan, his onetime Group Theatre student and colleague, who had matured into *the* American theatrical wunderkind of the forties. It was Kazan who, in answer to a felt need, decided to create the new workshop.

The Actors Studio was born out of Elia Kazan's desire to rekindle the flame of idealism and devotion to craft embodied in the concept of "the Group Theatre tradition." During the decade of the forties, even as he developed into one of America's foremost theatrical directors, Kazan sustained a sense of loss for that period of creative ferment with the Group that he has characterized as "the best thing professionally that ever happened to me." [1] He missed the feeling of the continuity of work, the ongoing training that having an artistic home such as the Group had made possible.

In the seven years after the Group folded, Kazan's directorial career was astonishing. Among the dozen plays he staged between 1942 and

1947 were *The Skin of Our Teeth* (1942), *One Touch of Venus* (1943), *Jacobowsky and the Colonel* (1944), *Deep Are the Roots* (1945), *All My Sons* (1947), and *A Streetcar Named Desire* (1947) —this last having gone into rehearsal the very week the Studio began its operations. And in motion pictures, after an auspicious film-directing debut with *A Tree Grows in Brooklyn* in 1945, he won an Oscar as best director for *Gentlemen's Agreement* in 1947 and the New York Film Critics Award of 1947 for both *Gentlemen's Agreement* and *Boomerang*.

Having had to direct many different kinds of players during these years, from Broadway stars such as Helen Hayes, Mary Martin, Tallulah Bankhead, and Fredric March to the nonprofessionals in his documentary short, *People of the Cumberland*, Kazan learned to accommodate himself to each actor's particular talent and personality and to ease the fears of those who thought of him as ". . . the young Stanislavsky . . . coming around and trying to tell us how we should act." [2] He was aware that an experience as passionate and exclusive as that which the Group had afforded could result in a dangerously narrow approach to the art of acting, and sought to avoid that trap. Years later he would say about the same acting tradition, "I've never thought of The Actors Studio as intellectually insular or special in its methods. I've always thought the methods could be applied in some degree or other to every sensitive person, every sensitive actor."

On the other hand, whatever Kazan achieved as a director was inevitably accomplished in spite of the mélange of acting styles and abilities he had to contend with. Under the typical commercial pressures of the New York theater, he was unable to use actors to their fullest potential, or to create the kind of ensemble playing he had participated in with the Group. There was neither time nor place to explore and experiment with the actor. Kazan had to make do.

Moreover, as a former player himself and always a deep admirer of that calling, Kazan believed that the actor and his art were grossly undervalued in the American theater.

No one can appreciate what the Studio means unless he can recall what the actor was in the Broadway Theatre before the Studio existed, a part of a labor pool, his craft scoffed at—you either had it or you didn't in those days, talent was a kind of magic, mysterious, inexplicable elite.

The fact that a soul could be awakened to its potential was not recognized then. Or that acting could be studied as a course of training, not only voice and make-up and stage deportment, but the actual inner technique itself. . . .

The great body of the profession, like the longshoreman on the water-front, shaped-up every morning, hoped to be lucky, made the rounds, waited for a phone call, lived on the curb, had nowhere to come in out of the rain.[3]

In 1947 Kazan, by now a powerful and influential force in the American theater, decided that he, personally, would have to do something about the situation of the American actor. He had come to realize that if he was to serve his own creativity to the utmost on future projects, he himself would have to turn out a whole generation of actors. He decided to establish a "farm" where he could cultivate a new crop of performers trained in the techniques he had learned in the Group. (A number of early members recall the Studio being set up, in part, as a "pool" or "stable" of actors for Kazan's productions.)

In addition, Kazan wanted to invigorate the young American actor with a new sense of dignity and respect for his profession—to get him, as he put it, "out of that goddamn Walgreen drugstore" (a performer's hangout, which, for Kazan, was a symbol of artistic time-wasting: a place where players waited passively and unproductively for news of auditions while sharing each other's fleeting companionship). He wanted to give the actor a kind of artistic home-land by creating a place, a player's place, where the actor could meet with his fellows to develop his craft and deal with his artistic problems in a serious and sympathetic atmosphere. In later years, he would say of the Studio that it came to represent for the actor what Israel represents for the Jew.[4] The Actors Studio was Kazan's way, in the words of Hamlet, of "see[ing] the players well bestowed."

Harold Clurman claims it was he who first suggested the idea for a studio to Kazan. During their association on the production of *All My Sons*, Clurman proposed establishing a paying school that would have a regular contingent of ten or twelve scholarship students. Kazan liked the idea, according to Clurman, but then proceeded to develop a plan without him. He feels that Kazan forgot about him because Kazan felt a certain intellectual and emotional rivalry with his former teacher (their producing partnership did not last beyond *Truckline Café* [1947]). Clurman says that Kazan's decision not to include him in his plans for the workshop hurt his feelings somewhat and Clurman told him so. Kazan, for his part, recalls none of this, and denies getting the idea for the Studio from Clurman. In any case, Kazan conceived of the project as a noncommercial venture from the outset.

Kazan's account of how he went about organizing the Studio is at variance with published accounts of his having discussed it with Cheryl Crawford in a Greek restaurant. "We didn't decide in any restaurant," he insists. "That was her version of it. I can only give you mine. Everybody remembers it differently. I remember talking to Bobby [Lewis] first. And then I remember going up to Cheryl's office and proposing it to her there and she, of course, went for it. Maybe we had dinner in a restaurant, or lunch. . . . It was simple; it wasn't a difficult thing to organize."

Cheryl Crawford's "version" of the Studio's founding over food, if true, would have resonant historical affinities with the beginnings of the Moscow Art Theater and the Group Theatre. Stanislavski made his first plans for the Moscow Art Theater at a restaurant called the Slavyansky Bazaar.[5] In *The Fervent Years,* Harold Clurman mentions his meeting with Lee Strasberg at Child's restaurant during which they held preliminary discussions of the plan that ultimately became the Group Theatre. Miss Crawford recollects meeting with Kazan on April 17, 1947, at a Greek restaurant which no longer exists, on West Fifty-ninth Street. During the meal, they reminisced about the Group and observed how sad it was that there was no opportunity for talented young actors to experiment in their work and to explore their craft. In his remarks during the opening session of the 1972 season of the Studio, Strasberg wryly wondered aloud about the possible significance in the fact that these three organizations had all started in restaurants.

In the years after she had left the Group, Miss Crawford had pursued an ambitious producing career on Broadway. Several of her productions were unadulterated flops, including plays by Dorothy Thompson, Marc Connelly, and Sir James M. Barrie—this last, her revival of *A Kiss for Cinderella* (1942) directed by Lee Strasberg. But her presentation of Lenore and William Cowen's *Family Portrait* (1939), a play about Christ's mother and supposed brother, starring Judith Anderson, was a critical success—except with the Catholic Church, which banned the play—though not a financial one. She produced, as well, three outstanding musicals during the forties. Her

1941 revival of Gershwin's *Porgy and Bess* was a tremendous success and ran, off and on, for four years. In 1943 she presented Kurt Weill's *One Touch of Venus* and in 1947 had another long-run hit with *Brigadoon.*

Despite the mixture of well-produced and not-so-well-produced projects, Miss Crawford's activities in the years between 1937 and 1947 continued the high-minded impulses that had characterized her work with the Theatre Guild and the Group. She consistently sought to involve herself with quality projects, if not always profitable ones, and her record as a producer was, on the whole, a distinguished one.

During the mid-forties Miss Crawford demonstrated her continuing concern and struggle to break out of the usual Broadway production mold with two highly idealistic theatrical ventures. That they both were ultimately ill-fated takes away nothing from the value and accomplishments of the enterprises. In 1946, under the auspices of the American National Theater and Academy (ANTA), she was instrumental in the founding of the Experimental Theatre. It was to be a showcase for actors and playwrights, and a platform for theatrically ambitious, but otherwise "noncommercial" plays. In its first season the Experimental Theatre put on five dramas for five performances each at the three-hundred-seat Princess Theater and won the Sidney Howard Memorial Award as the season's most important development in the theater. A year later, shortly after she had seen The Actors Studio get under way, Miss Crawford was to become involved in an acrimonious controversy over the Experimental Theatre's choice of plays and its "exploitation" of such stars as Charles Laughton and John Garfield and such well-established directors as Lee Strasberg. It seems that some theater folk expected more radical "experimentation" with repertoire and casting from Miss Crawford.

Before the Experimental Theatre's founding, in 1944, she had also launched the American Repertory Theatre with Eva Le Gallienne and Margaret Webster. She acted as managing director for five of its productions at the International Theater before the organization folded in the spring of 1947.

Her experience with the American Repertory Theatre was very much on her mind as she discussed the situation of young actors with Kazan that April 17 afternoon, as she has remembered it, in the Greek restaurant on West Fifty-ninth Street. There were three talented young actors who had worked for her in the repertory company whom she thought would be ideal for the project Kazan outlined to her: they were Julie Harris, Eli Wallach, and Anne Jackson. Kazan, she recalls, mentioned, in addition, three young actors in his production of *A Streetcar Named Desire* whom he wanted involved in his project: Marlon Brando, Kim Hunter, and Karl Malden. And here, unfortunately, her account of the meeting with Kazan runs into trouble.

Kazan's production of *A Streetcar Named Desire*—which was to feature Brando's superb, torn-T-shirted portrayal of Stanley Kowalski—a performance that would become emblematic of The Actors Studio approach to acting—went into rehearsal on October 1, 1947, and did not open in New York until December. So Kazan could not have discussed Brando, Hunter, and Malden as if they had been appearing in the play the previous April—some eight months earlier! But this is precisely how Miss Crawford recalled the meeting to a *New York Times* reporter in 1973.[6] When questioned on the discrepancy, Miss Crawford acknowledged that she had probably melded her memory of the 1947 meeting with that of a later 1948 meeting with Kazan about the Studio. This does not invalidate her contention that there was a meeting at which plans for the Studio were discussed, but it does throw into question Miss Crawford's recollection that she was approached about the project before Robert Lewis was.

It would be unfair to overemphasize the significance of such slips of memory, however, although it does indicate the *Rashomon*-like difficulty one encounters when trying to sort out the truth about certain events in the Studio's past. All the major figures involved in the history of the Studio admit to uncertainty about some of the facts concerning the early years. In cases where there are no objective data with which to measure one "version" of an incident against another, there is no alternative but to acknowledge that the point is at issue. The problem of gauging "historicity" within the Group Theatre tradition, of which The Actors Studio is a part, is exemplified in Miss Crawford's reaction to Clurman's *The Fervent Years*:

You want my opinion? It wasn't altogether that way. At the time I had stopped reading Harold's book I'd gotten to around the middle of it and I threw it over into the fireplace because I didn't agree with a number of things he said in factual matters. . . . Two years later when I was able to finish it, I appreciated all the wonderful and good things about it and just gave up on some of the facts because I might have been wrong too. . . . But it seemed to me he had certain ideas about exactly what went on that were in total contrast to my memories. Whose memory is right and whose is wrong nobody will ever know till I write my memoirs about the Group. If I do, then we can compare them.

To which Clurman replied:

As for whether my facts are right or wrong, Lee Strasberg once said: "If everybody in the Group wrote a book it would always be a different book." And that is as it should be.[7]

Strasberg himself also takes issue with *The Fervent Years*. While admiring much about the book—he says he was very moved and excited by its vitality and impact—he insists that many of Clurman's statements are incorrect and were never checked.

Robert Lewis, at the time Kazan contacted him in the spring of 1947, was enjoying his own success as the director of the Lerner and Loewe musical *Brigadoon*. After directing several other productions in New York—among them *Heavenly Express* (1940), which he staged while still a member of the Group, *Five Alarm Waltz* (1941), and *Mexican Mural* (1942), which he also produced—Lewis had made his Hollywood movie debut as an actor in *Tonight We Raid Calais* (1943). While in California he also appeared in *Dragon Seed* (1944), *Son of Lassie* (1945), *Ziegfeld Follies* (1946), and *Monsieur Verdoux* (1947), and directed a production of Obey's *Noah* at the Actors Laboratory Theatre. Just before joining forces with Miss Crawford on *Brigadoon*, he directed *Land's End* (1946) in New York.

Lewis's account of the start of The Actors Studio is in substantial agreement with Kazan's. The two of them had long been close, intimate friends who were deeply fond of one another and who admired each other's work. They had lived together and had shared the same dressing room during many years of the Group Theatre. Kazan broached the idea of the Studio to Lewis one afternoon as they strolled in Central Park. They discussed who should be involved with the new organization and mentioned several familiar names from the Group. Cheryl Crawford was a logical choice to be the new outfit's business manager, and Kazan subsequently discussed it with her—presumably in that Greek restaurant on West Fifty-ninth Street.

Lewis and Miss Crawford were immediately receptive to Kazan's ideas and the three began organizing a fall opening for the work-

which Kazan directed. When the Studio received its charter as a nonprofit corporation from New York State in January 1948, she, along with Fitelson, was one of the five signatory corporate members. (The others, of course, were Kazan, Lewis, and Miss Crawford.)

During that first week at the Union Methodist Church, Lewis conducted a kind of general orientation for his group. On Monday he discussed why the actor should become familiar with the rules of his art—how, in fact, the theater compared with other arts as to "rules" and "forms." Wednesday was given to a discussion of the actor's "intention" and how characterization should grow out of intentions. On Friday he discussed the rehearsal period; the following Monday, he spent on the selection of plays. By Wednesday of the second week his students were ready to work. Among the very first scenes presented—in various stages of preparation—at the Studio were Tom Ewell and Jane Hoffman in *The Adding Machine*, David Wayne and John Forsythe in *Another Part of the Forest*, Stephen Elliott and Anne Jackson in *They Knew What They Wanted*, Kevin McCarthy and Elizabeth Ross in *Love on the Dole*, and Jay Barney and Joy Geffen in *One Sunday Afternoon*.[10]

Busy as Lewis's class was at that first location, it was not until the move to the dance studio on East Fifty-ninth Street that the real work began in earnest. A number of the actors, including Marlon Brando, presented their initial scenes there. The first ongoing project at the Studio was also begun on East Fifty-ninth Street with the continuing work of E. G. Marshall and Herbert Berghof on Kafka's *The Trial*. Nancy Walker came to the Studio a couple of times while it was on the East Side and wanted to join, but Lewis felt she was already a complete talent and did not need the Studio. He had definite ideas, just as Kazan did, about whom he wanted in the Studio. Early in 1948, he would go so far as to reconsider a number of his original selections and take appropriate action.

In class, Lewis was effervescent and witty. Like his mentors, Clurman and Strasberg, however, he was also somewhat garrulous. He became annoyed when he thought someone was not paying attention to what he was saying. Once, noticing that Marlon Brando seemed not to be listening, Lewis interrupted himself to ask: "Marlon, what was I saying?" Brando looked up from the newspaper he was reading and immediately shot back: "You stepped in what?" silencing the director for the moment. Another time, Tennessee Williams was caught whispering during one of his visits to the class. "If you want to talk, I'll leave," Lewis told him. Williams began to apologize, but Lewis was adamant. Either he or Williams would leave. The playwright, somewhat abashed, got up and left. As a teacher, Lewis was always ingratiating and sympathetic to his students; his criticism of their work has been described as strictly "supportive." But he expected reciprocity from the class in the form of respect and affection and became unhappy if he felt these were not forthcoming. He grew particularly upset whenever attendance was down, on which occasions he threatened to quit. But the actors, who were genuinely fond of him, managed to persuade him to return.

Kazan's and Lewis's classes were quite dissimilar. They dealt with different material (primarily scenes with Lewis and exercises with Kazan) and gave particular emphasis to different elements of technique. Despite their generally acknowledged agreement on the larger principles of the actors' art and their common roots in the fertile soil of the Stanislavskian and Group traditions, each man brought his unique experience, personality, and artistic interests to bear on the work. Neither one represented himself as teaching *the* Stanislavski Method. In fact, although there was much talk in both classes about the Group, there was comparatively little reference to "the Method" or to Stanislavski. In one class, Lewis took pains to explain, the Lewis method was being taught; in the other, the Kazan method.[11]

Kazan had had a good bit of experience in teaching actors, mainly with the New Theatre League, during the thirties. His approach to the subject, in both its specifics and its intensity, reflected his own strenuous efforts to become an actor with the Group. He was very strict with his young actors, demanding of them the seriousness and dedication he had brought to his own acting. He was adamant about people really working: if you did not work, you were out. He insisted on the promptness and preparedness of his students. The door was closed at eleven o'clock, and the actors had to be there, ready to present a scene or exercise on demand.

Most of the new members of Kazan's class were strangers to each other. By way of breaking the ice at the first class meeting, Kazan asked each of them to respond to the person sitting next to them and to whom they were being introduced by describing instantly what animal that person reminded them of. When Nehemiah Persoff was introduced to Joan Copeland, for instance, she remembers "blurting out, with my usual tact, 'a baboon'!" He was then obliged to be a baboon. When the tables were turned, and he was asked to describe her, he quickly and pointedly said, "a cat!" Meowing and preening seductively, she proceeded to create herself as a cat. They became and have remained close friends from that introduction.

Whenever Kazan had to miss a class for professional reasons, his associate, Martin Ritt, would take over the session. Ritt was thoroughly familiar with Kazan's procedures and with the special talents and shortcomings of each member of the group. In the sessions he conducted, he put a special emphasis on "sensory work." Actors attempted to recall specific sensations and to re-create them imaginatively. These included everything from the "feel" of familiar objects to reexperiencing a complex "overall state" such as drunkenness. A typical exercise would be to thread an imaginary needle with imaginary thread—something Julie Harris was very adept at—working not for the mimetic action of threading per se, but for the "sense memory" of the process. Ritt defined the work of Kazan's class as "exercises in imagination, concentration, faith, and a sense of truth—all calculated to make the actor a pliant instrument." [12]

Working with Kazan was continually exciting; his adrenaline never stopped pumping and the actors too were energized by his intensity. He constantly challenged the spontaneity and sensory awareness of his actors, exposing them to many of the exercises he had learned in the Group Theatre. He would toss a set of keys at a student and tell him to improvise with them. They could become medals or fingernail files—anything that came into the actor's mind on the spur of the moment. In a similar "object exercise," he would ask someone to take a hat and create a bird with it, a Vakhtangov procedure that Strasberg too had used with his Group actors. On occasion he would turn the whole class into a menagerie, the animal exercise (which he had introduced at the first session) being a powerful imaginative tool. James Whitmore once created what everyone sensed, from the way he moved, the way he held his hands together, was a seal. The class agreed that his was the most successful rendering of an animal to date. Whitmore, however, was crestfallen. When Kazan asked what was the matter, the actor dolefully explained he was a dachshund.

Kazan also had the actors imagine themselves objects such as a telephone book or a melting wax statue. He once called on several of them to create brief scenes using three hand claps as a logical part of the action. He would give the actors three arbitrary movements and ask them to justify their use during an improvisation. Similar to this was the three-word improvisation which, as with so many of these exercises, was straight out of the work of the Group. Vivian Nathan recalled how she and Anne Hegira were once assigned *red, soup,* and *line.* "You had to go out of the room—you had a minute—and you had to make up a story and act out the story with those three words in it." Other examples (from Lou Gilbert's notebooks) were *agent, hospital, lemondrops* and *necktie, summer, wristwatch.*

There were also one-word improvisations to test the actors' spontaneity. Kazan once shouted "Israel!" to Don Hanmer, who immediately got up and climbed onto a chair where he crouched cautiously as it slowly became apparent he was carrying a gun. Gibberish exercises, which can facilitate expressiveness by forcing the actor to discover ways to communicate his thoughts and feelings through nonsense syllables rather than actual speech, were also used. The one exercise notably absent from Kazan's practice—an absence that reflected his response to Stella Adler's Group Theatre confrontation with Lee Strasberg and which dated from that time—was affective memory.

Most important of all, perhaps, were the so-called "action" exercises. Crucially central to Kazan's work with actors both on stage and in film is his emphasis on the character's objective in a scene: what the character wants and why he wants it.[13] In the terminology of the Method this objective or intention of the character is often called his "action." When the actor fully understood what he wanted in the scene, went the rationale for this approach, when he could practically taste his "need" and tried to "go for it," his imagination would release in him all sorts of creative impulses that would lead him to discover appropriate physical and emotional behavior for his character.

Kazan would give his Studio actors one or more lines to learn and then ask them to think up twenty or so different "actions" to play while speaking them. For instance, "How are you? Imagine finding you here," might be played with the action "to belittle," or "to frustrate," or "to sympathize," and so on.[14] Actors also had to memorize a poem or a nursery rhyme and then figure out ten different actions to "enact" them with. In more complex improvisations Kazan set up given circumstances within which the various actions were to be played out.

Julie Harris once did an improvisation with James Whitmore in which she had to pawn something because she desperately needed money. Kazan explained that she had purposely gone to a strange part of town to transact her business. She took a few moments to prepare and was so totally absorbed in the reality of the situation that when Whitmore said "Hello, Julie" as she entered the door, she was completely thrown. All she could think was, "How did he know me?"

Relations between the director and his students were warm and affectionate. Kazan felt he had a wonderful group of people to work with. "They were all fresh to it. It was a rekindling of something that everybody thought had died and had disappeared . . . and some special fervor about a start . . . there was something especially wonderful about the beginning of it." Kazan openly displayed his affection for his "kids." (Some years later Molly Kazan was overheard criticizing her husband for still using the term. "What are you always calling them 'kids' for? Heavens, some of them are thirty-five!") He liked to put his arm around people as he walked by and create a general sense of "togetherness." He was unusually sensitive with actors; he was at ease with them and in turn he put them at ease. According to Vivian Nathan, "You never got the sense that anything you did was foolish or stupid." His students adored Kazan. Many began to imitate his rough-and-tumble ways, walking and talking like him and trying to be the way they thought he would like them to be. Something of a personality cult developed around him as certain actors unconsciously strove to emulate his style.

In Lewis's class, the established actors were trying themselves in unfamiliar roles, including parts they would not normally be considered for in the commercial theater. Eli Wallach, for instance, who was playing The Duck and The Two of Spades in the American Repertory Theatre production of *Alice in Wonderland* at the time, worked on the character of the doomed young writer, Treplev, in Chekhov's *The Sea Gull*. Tom Ewell, caught up in the long-run *John Loves Mary* in which he had been giving a prize-winning performance, made a memorable impression during the Studio's first year as Lennie in a scene from *Of Mice and Men*. The opportunity to try his hand at such serious roles—he also worked on Oswald from

Ghosts and Mr. Zero from *The Adding Machine* at about the same time—meant a great deal to Ewell because he had become categorized as a comedian. "The audience cried," he recalled years later. "No one had ever cried at me before." [15]

At the same time Marlon Brando was making Broadway history and establishing the Method actor "prototype" with his performance as Stanley Kowalski, he was cultivating totally contrasting aspects of his talents at The Actors Studio. A former star pupil of Stella Adler's, his most memorable work that first year was as the Archduke Rudolph Maximillian in a long scene from *Reunion in Vienna* with Joan Chandler. He played the Alfred Lunt role in high style, having rented a beautiful costume for the occasion and presenting himself "replete with pencil-thin moustache, long cigarette holder, sword, and Hapsburg accent." [16] Resplendent in this outfit, Brando sat down at one point in the scene—with a ball going on in the next room—and removed his boot, revealing a sock with a hole in it and his foot sticking out "just as dirty and crummy as could be." It was a funny and telling moment that brought the character, a former nobleman now reduced to driving a cab, vividly to life. Also, during the course of the scene, impulsively and totally unrehearsed, he poured some champagne down Miss Chandler's bodice as she screamed bloody murder. By all accounts it was a hilarious performance.

Lewis asked Brando to repeat the scene as part of an affair to raise money for the Studio and to get certain people interested in the organization. Brando declined but offered instead to organize the event on his own. That spring The Actors Studio held the first of a long string of "survival" benefits. Brando put together a unique entertainment, which included a stand-up comedienne he knew who worked in a Greenwich Village nightclub, him himself playing drums for some dancer friends from the Katherine Dunham group, and a selection of Charlie Chaplin movies.

Brando made his presence felt in whatever project he chose to participate. A year or so later, when the advanced class was doing *Uncle Vanya*, he volunteered to play Serebryakov in a scene from the first act of the play. Everyone else had a big part in the piece, but as the professor, Brando simply had to enter with the others and busy himself with his books. As soon as he walked in, his coat slung over his shoulders and laden down with reference books and notebooks, he established the character of the self-absorbed professor in lifelike detail. Much of the scene was played with his back to the audience. Vivian Nathan remembered, "The conversation in the scene was going on, but your eye went to him because he had done his homework. The others were busy being languid as usual in Chekhov, while he was in thought. He adjusted his pince-nez, reached for one of his books, and you saw that he had to check something he knew was in this second book. As he took a pencil and paper the book dropped. Then he tried to reach for it and he couldn't and another book dropped . . . that was what everyone watched."

During the early years, Brando did several improvisations of the kind in which the actors are each privately given an "action" to play in opposition to one another. The resulting conflict becomes, ideally, a lively dramatic encounter. Often, however, this sort of "improv" bogs down in an "ineluctable force versus an immovable object" stand-off. In one such improvisation, Rudy Bond played an old-time actor who has been given a first-floor dressing room. Brando played a leading man assigned to an upstairs dressing room who wanted, as his "star's prerogative," to dress downstairs. His objective was to get Bond out of the dressing room. After a great deal of haggling dialogue, of insistence met with resistance, Brando suddenly picked up Bond and bodily carried him out of the room, much to the amusement of the class.

Alan Schneider recalls an improvisation in which he played a guard in a concentration camp where Brando and David Wayne were prisoners. Their task was to break out and Schneider's was to stop them. "Marlon was marvelous . . . he beat the shit out of me and, really, I thought he was going to kill me. I was scared. I had glasses on. But then after the improvisation . . . he came over to me—he was so gentle—and apologized in that kind of quiet manner." At another session, Brando was supposed to be returning to his apartment where he had hidden some drugs. Eli Wallach was told he was an FBI agent who had been assigned to find the narcotics in Brando's apartment. He said to Brando, "Give me a minute to walk around the room, then you walk in." When Brando entered he looked at Wallach and said, "Who the fuck are you?" Wallach, shocked at the language—not usual on the stage at that time—said, "What?!" Brando repeated the question. Wallach sputtered something about the super having let him in to look at the apartment, which he was interested in renting. Brando's language got cruder and cruder. Wallach said, "Just a minute." Brando pushed him and said, "Just get out." Wallach said, "Don't push, don't push." Brando continued the stream of threat and invective, and kept pushing him. Wallach resisted and Brando picked him up and threw him out of the room, slamming the door behind him. Wallach opened the door to get back in; he was furious and really ready to kill Brando. But Marlon was laughing. So was the class—uncontrollably. In the post-scene discussion, Wallach was criticized for not finding the narcotics.

Kazan once set up an improv in which Brando was to try to seduce a girl by passing himself off as a serious painter who wanted to do her portrait. Brando was wildly and hilariously inventive as usual; he even used a foreign accent to achieve his goal. Kazan did not critique the scene but asked the class, "Can anyone do it better?" Anthony Quinn, who attended Studio sessions though he was never listed as an official member (he was to work with Kazan and Brando on *Viva Zapata!*), came forward. "I can," he said. After some whispered directions from Kazan, he proceeded with the same improvisational situation. Totally different in color and temperament—he was more menacing and threatening, for one thing—his performance, to the delight of his audience, was equally as impressive as Brando's.

In addition to the acting classes, students also studied speech with Edith Stebbens and dance and movement with Anna Sokolow, a rigorous taskmaster who managed to infuse her actors with the confidence to perform various physical feats that initially they felt were beyond their capacities. "The floor is your friend," she would note emphatically. The work in her sessions included contraction-and-release exercises, "action" movement exercises—walking while trying to listen to a bird singing, for example—and the use of famous paintings as conceptual and compositional starting points for dance movement. Kazan, who had always deeply respected the dancer's discipline—he had had some dance training back in the thirties and had even performed with Jerome Robbins at one time—also participated in these sessions with his actors. Robbins, himself a member of Lewis's group, also gave occasional dance classes at the Studio.

Miss Sokolow directed an experimental production of William Saroyan's *Elmer and Lily* at the Studio which integrated acting, movement, and music. Kazan brought Saroyan to see his one-act play and the playwright was delighted with it. For Miss Sokolow it was a major step forward in her dance work, and she credits the origin of her abiding interest in what she calls "total theater" pieces to her experience with that Studio project. Her activity with the Studio actors also served as the basis for an entire choreographic play called *Rooms*. This piece, about people living in little rooms in the loneliness of the big city, though first conceived as a project for actors, went on to earn itself a reputation as something of a breakthrough in modern dance. It is still performed today.

To round out the Studio program and expose the membership to a variety of theatrical experiences, the directors occasionally invited prominent theater figures to speak at the workshop. Thornton Wilder, Robert Edmond Jones, Moss Hart, Robert Morley, Charlie Chaplin, Richard Rodgers, Aaron Copland, Harold Clurman, Leonard Bernstein, Lawrence Langner, and Stark Young were among the actors, authors, composers, directors, and designers who spoke to the classes in the early years.

The honeymoon atmosphere that prevailed at the Studio during the first months of its existence was abruptly dispelled in late December 1947 when a large number of people were dropped from Lewis's class. Many of the founding members, having gotten into the Studio, had never really participated in the work there—as if to have been accepted was sufficient fulfillment of their actor's ego (a not uncommon phenomenon throughout the Studio's history); their complacency made it difficult to schedule scenes for each session. Others who had participated, however, were soon found wanting by the Studio heads. Just before Christmas, it was decided by Kazan and Lewis that there were too many actors in the latter's group for it to function effectively, so during Christmas week those who had not shown real interest and those who, it was felt, were not up to snuff were sent letters disinviting them.* It was a very traumatic experience for the people involved and, in addition, angered and disillusioned several of those who had not been asked to leave.

Early in 1948 further adjustments were made in the membership as various people were dropped or drifted away from both

* The complete list of people who were removed from membership (from a comparison of lists in the Cheryl Crawford Files, NYPL-LC) is as follows: Jay Barney, John Becher, Philip Bourneuf, Peter Cookson, Stephen Elliott, Robert Emhardt, John Forsythe, Joy Geffen, Anne Jackson, Sidney Lumet, George Matthews, Patricia Neal, Ty Perry, Frances Reid, Kurt Richards, Elizabeth Ross, Julie Warren, Mary Welch, and William Woodson.

classes.* Some of those let go, including Anne Jackson, Patricia Neal, John Forsythe, and Mary Welch, were brought back to the Studio in subsequent years. But these expulsions had repercussions insofar as the disquiet they caused led ultimately to the establishment of a life-member policy (once a member, always a member) several years later.**

At least one actress refused to be "pruned," and her arguments for not being dropped spelled out the dilemma of those who were. Joan Copeland was called in to speak with Martin Ritt, who was given the task of explaining to those being asked to leave the reasons why. Ritt, trying to be kind, told her that the Studio was not serving her. Staunchly, Miss Copeland insisted on talking to Kazan face-to-face on such an important matter to her. She told Kazan that before coming to the Studio she had had a certain foundation to her work. Wrong as it might have been, it had given her the confidence to perform. Now, just exposed to the ideas of the Studio, she was in a transition stage—between two stools, as it were. Having given up the "crutches" she was used to, she now would be crippled if she were not allowed to continue to learn to walk anew. There was no turning back. Therefore, she said, she insisted on staying on, and did.

The high point of the year for Lewis's class came in the early spring of 1948. After months of scene work and various preliminary explorations and experimentations in character study during which Lewis managed to dispel much nonsense about the Method, he decided it was time to embark on a full-scale project that would probe the actor's problems in depth and provide an opportunity to test his students at real ensemble playing. The approach was to be an unhurried, deliberate investigation of the material selected. The play he chose was Chekov's *The Sea Gull*.

In the first stage of the project, the actors spent two months reading and rereading the play—nine or ten times in all. None of the parts were cast at the start. The distribution of roles was kept flexible from session to session so that everybody could try whatever they wanted; the actors would come in and say, "I haven't read Kostya," or "I didn't do Nina." By the last of these sessions everyone had read

* Dropped from Kazan's group: Dorothy Bird, Betsy Drake, Peg Hillias, Robin Humphrey, Alicia Krug, and Pat McClarney. From Lewis's group: Henry Barnard, George Keane, Peggy Meredith, Beatrice Straight, and John Straub.

** The comings and goings of members during this period makes it impossible to promulgate a single definitive membership list for the Studio's early years.

every part. Lewis used these readings to give a very clear analysis of Stanislavski's ideas and to explore everything possible about the play and about the process of working on a play.

When the actors were thoroughly aware of the acting and interpretive problems, Lewis cast the play as he saw fit, then rehearsed and staged it in three weeks. Montgomery Clift was originally cast as Treplev, but had a disagreement with Lewis and withdrew from the production. Clift, whose relationship to the Studio was tentative at best, later portrayed Treplev for the Phoenix Theater in a production of *The Sea Gull* that also featured Maureen Stapleton in the role of Masha. This Off-Broadway presentation, which opened May 11, 1954, was totally independent of the Studio project.

Henry Barnard took over Clift's role. Other members of the cast were David Wayne (Medvedenko), Maureen Stapleton (Masha), Thelma Schnee (Arkadina), Joan Chandler (Nina), George Keane (Trigorin), Herbert Berghof (Dorn), Michael Strong (Shamrayev), William Hansen (Sorin), and Mildred Dunnock (Paulina). Karl Malden was the stage manager. The play was presented twice at the Studio (at 1697 Broadway) for members and friends. The public and the press were not invited, as the Studio considered the production a private exercise (although Lewis himself had higher hopes for it). For those who saw it, it was one of the memorable events in the Studio's early history.

To bring to a close their first season of work together, Kazan had been casting about for a full-scale project for his own group. He was looking for a play with a large number of young parts that would give his actors a variety of characterizations to deal with. Molly Day Thatcher, Kazan's wife, suggested a first play by Bessie Breuer, a writer whose reputation at the time was based on some short stories and two novels, *Memory of Love* (1935) and *The Daughter* (1938). Miss Breuer's play about the problems of a group of battle-fatigued fliers and the women who loved them seemed a perfect choice. Set in a small café on an island off the Florida Gulf Coast near a hospital for convalescing air force combat crews, *Sundown Beach* had a cast of thirty characters, representing, in the author's words, ". . . every kind of man who had psychiatric wounds, from an illiterate hillbilly to the most literate intellectual."

Kazan's actors gathered in the downstairs lobby of the Ethel Barrymore Theater (where *Streetcar* was playing) to meet Miss Breuer and to hear the play read to them by the director. Kazan spoke the lines so simply and convincingly that at one point, when he said: "Anybody got a cigarette?" Miss Breuer went out and got him a cigarette, forgetting that the line was in her own script. Familiar as he was with every one of his students, Kazan had decided on exactly whom he wanted to play each part. Some of the actors were initially disturbed by the casting: Anne Hegira did not want to play a woman of forty; Julie Harris did not think she should play a hillbilly girl, seeing herself as a femme fatale. Once the work got under way, however, the wisdom of Kazan's choices became evident—especially in the case of Miss Harris, who was to distinguish herself with a touching performance as Ida Mae.

The next meeting of the class at the Studio's new headquarters on Broadway and Fifty-third Street began many weeks of concentrated rehearsal of the play, including a great deal of improvisatory work. As it became apparent the play was turning into something special under the ministrations of its young cast, a plan was prepared for presenting *Sundown Beach* commercially. Miss Breuer recalls Kazan telling her, "Every day now for weeks we've been working on your play. I have not found a single impure word in it. It has been a wonderful experience for me. I'll bring it to Broadway no matter what."

Since most of the cast members were unemployed at the time, and therefore available, it was decided to tour the play during the summer and to bring it into New York at the beginning of the following theater season. Kim Hunter rehearsed the play and eventually played for a week that summer during her vacation from *Streetcar*, but was replaced when she had to return to the Williams play, first by Louisa Horton and then by Phyllis Thaxter. Steven Hill quit the cast of *Mister Roberts* and Edward Binns quit *Command Decision* to be in the Studio's first production. Kazan would not allow Rudy Bond to leave *Streetcar*, however, and Jocelyn Brando remained with *Mister Roberts*.

Miss Breuer's play, originally called "Sons of Icarus," went through extensive revision, including the title change. Unused to the exigencies of writing for the theater, the author had composed her play with the expansiveness of a novelist. Kazan demanded greater concision of her, and she wound up trimming more than a third of her original manuscript. Molly Kazan worked with her on the editing of it. The published edition of the play includes a sizable portion of the original draft as an appendix to The Actors Studio version of the script.[17] Miss Breuer was also prevailed upon to incorporate some new scenes for members of the group who did not have enough to do in the play. One such example is the scene in the third act written for Vivian (Firko) Nathan, who played Helen. " 'Gadge' forced me and forced me to develop the people," she recalled. "He forced the third act on me at gun's point. Within two days I had the scenes."

The play was produced under the auspices of Louis J. Singer, while Kazan and Miss Crawford contributed their directorial and organizational services and helped to raise money. The three of them decided to present the show at a couple of summer theaters as a sort of try-out before bringing it to Broadway.

The owners of the Westport Playhouse were not eager to book *Sundown Beach* because no one in the cast was a "name." Despite the absence of stars, however, Westport made more money on the Studio production than anything else they did that summer. On the first night the lights blew out, and part of the show was played by flashlight and candlelight. Nevertheless, the critical and public reception for the play was unusually enthusiastic. Similar critical enthusiasm plus highly favorable word-of-mouth when it ran from June 28 to August 28 in Marblehead, Massachusetts, resulted in the production's being moved to Boston for an unanticipated two-week extension of its summer run. The critical response in Boston was equally auspicious; *The Boston Globe* even commended the play in its editorial pages. A notable exception, however, was the reviewer for *The Christian Science Monitor*, who complained about the actors' tendency "to mumble their lines"— perhaps the first such criticism leveled against Studio members.[18]

Oddly enough, after such a fine reception out of town, when *Sundown Beach* came to Broadway as the first production of the 1948–1949 theatrical season, it was received very coolly by the critics. The opening at the Belasco Theatre on September 7, 1948, was, in fact, a critical disaster.[19] Much of the blame was leveled at Miss Breuer's script, which the reviewers compared to the ill-fated *Truckline Café*, the Maxwell Anderson play produced the previous season (also at the Belasco) by Kazan and directed by Harold Clurman. The critics dwelt on what they considered Miss Breuer's failure to integrate her various story lines. Brooks Atkinson said the play gave ". . . an impression of breathlessness as though it were running very fast to stay in the same place throughout the evening." [20] While most of the reviews praised individual performances, the acting as a whole was also found wanting, as was Kazan's direction. It was, to say the least, a stupefying reception after the glowing praise of the summer tour.

Just before the opening in New York, Kazan had redirected the production to reenergize and tighten it up. In a letter to Miss Crawford, Miss Breuer had expressed her pre-Broadway concern over the variableness of the previews: "When Gadge is away the performance falls to pieces and is like children reciting . . . the moment Gadge appears it's as if they were puppets and he held the strings and he was their voice." In retrospect, Miss Crawford believes that Kazan redirected the production to the point where "It got the actors nervous, and they pushed too hard." Atkinson also faulted the "aggressive direction," which was "full of violent physical interludes that [had] no particular meaning," for helping to foster a high-strung and self-conscious performance in which "most of the actors [were] tense and rigid, and strain[ed] after effects they [did] not wholly understand." [21] In addition, many of the actors seemed to be particularly upset because Kazan was absent on the opening night. He was staging *Love Life* in Philadelphia and did not return for the occasion. Some of the actors felt it was as if he had deserted the company. As one of them put it, "Daddy had left. Daddy wasn't there. The whole thing became frenetic, wild, and hysterical without Kazan's protective presence."

Several theater critics commented on how the Studio production echoed the strengths and shortcomings of the earlier Group Theatre. Atkinson, discussing what he called the overtraining of the young company, observed that "the performance of 'Sundown Beach' was a public exhibition of technique under pressure, like some of the Group Theatre's overwrought works." [22] A notion that the Studio was becoming the inheritor of the Group Theatre tradition not only in spirit, but in practice, had arisen in theatrical circles as soon as production plans for the Breuer play had been announced. At that time Clifford Odets was reported to have asked, ". . . isn't it a bit early to be handing over the mantle of the Group Theatre to Studio, Inc.?" He also announced that he and Harold Clurman had plans along the same lines. Kazan, for his part, publicly denied that the Studio was "hankering after the mantle of the Group Theatre" and welcomed the possibility of a Clurman-Odets studio. The course the Studio was to take in the years ahead would show that Kazan was not, as a matter of fact, thinking of it as a theater-in-the-making.

Sundown Beach closed after seven performances. Posted on the callboard beside the closing notice was a note sent by Kazan from New Haven, where *Love Life* was then in tryouts: "We had a wonderful year. No one can take that away from us. No one can take the future away from us either." To the company his message seemed a promise of things to come—that the Studio would continue to produce plays. But such was not to be the case. A second production announced in March of 1949—*Battleship Bismarck* by Maurice Valency, to be directed for the Studio by Martin Ritt—never got off the ground. Kazan, it soon was to become apparent, had thought of *Sundown Beach* as an isolated project and not as part of the Studio's general evolution into a producing organization.

During the summer of 1948 a deep personal rift developed between Lewis and Kazan that ultimately led to the former's resignation from the Studio. The "cover" story at the time and the explanation of events given in various publications since is that the two directors reached an artistic impasse over the future of the Studio. In these accounts Lewis supposedly wanted the workshop to develop into a theater while Kazan wanted it to remain a workshop.

None of this is true. The two men were always in fundamental agreement about aesthetic questions involving the Studio, though they may have differed over particulars. Neither of them ever *planned* for the Studio to become a theater; they were both very busy with successful directing careers at the time, and felt no need to build a theater organization. Lewis resigned as the result of a falling-out with Kazan over the manner in which his associate took over the direction of *Love Life*, the Kurt Weill–Alan Jay Lerner musical, which Lewis himself at one time planned to stage.

Lewis had mostly enjoyed his first year at the Studio, but there had been some clouds on the horizon. The director was generally well liked by his actors, but his occasional arrogance and authoritarianism did not always sit well with them. For one thing, members resented his not allowing them to express their opinions of each other's work after a scene was presented. The lack of absolute approval of his conduct of the class—the actors' fondness for the man notwithstanding—as well as the periodic slackening of attendance by the members rankled with Lewis and made him occasionally unhappy.

Sometime in the spring he wrote a letter to Kazan expressing his hurt and disillusionment and his desire to quit. At that time Kazan persuaded him to reconsider. Several months later, however, matters took a turn for the worse when it was announced that Kazan was to direct *Love Life*.

Lewis had brought *Love Life* to Kazan several months earlier to get his opinion of the musical's merits. At the time Lewis and Miss Crawford were considering a production of the property, to follow their successful collaboration on *Brigadoon*. Kazan's initial reaction was less than enthusiastic and shortly thereafter, partly in response to his friend's opinion, Lewis decided to drop the project. Later on, when Kazan was announced as the director of the show, rumors began circulating that he had feigned disliking the musical in order to secure it for himself. Angry and upset by the rumors and by a letter in which Lewis expressed his dismay at the manner in which Kazan had dealt with him, Kazan wrote a detailed reply to Lewis, which he ended with an appeal to his friend to stay with the Studio. But Lewis, though he himself denied the rumors of Kazan's ostensible duplicity, could not forgive Kazan's treatment of him.

Instead of personally coming to him to explain his decision and to ask his blessing, Kazan had flown off to Florida and let a trembling Miss Crawford break the news to Lewis over the phone. Lewis found this unacceptable behavior between close friends. He felt that all Kazan had to do was to call him and say, "Bobby, I've changed my mind. Now, do you really still not want to do it?" And Lewis would have said, "No, God bless you. Go ahead and do it." And that would have been the end of it.

By the testimony of many people who have known the director, Kazan's cavalier treatment of Lewis was not uncharacteristic of the man. He sometimes hurt people in his struggle for success. Lewis felt that one could not teach integrity and honesty to one's students and behave in life as Kazan had—walking over people to get on with his career. (Cheryl Crawford, upset by the breach, expressed regret at what had happened in a letter to Lewis that included an apology for her own "damned human defects I'm still working on. . . .")

The announcement of Lewis's resignation from the Studio appeared in *The New York Times* the following week, August 4, 1948. The item included his denial that there had been a quarrel between himself and his codirectors.

Lewis's class at the Studio was naturally disturbed by the turn of events. They met to discuss Lewis's resignation and their own future. Thelma Schnee read a letter from Lewis in which he sent the members greetings and announced that he was going to set up his own Studio. He invited his former students to join him, but only one or two seemed interested. They were mainly concerned not with their former teacher but with the future of the group and with the continuation of their work. After airing all their complaints about the unit's procedures to date, they outlined their ideas as follows:

a. Return to thorough review of *fundamentals*.
b. *Scenes* based on this work.
c. Class criticism of scenes.
d. One-act plays directed by several class members.
e. . . . Develop directors in the studio among themselves.
f. . . . Find a new play and have the Studio produce it as we are doing with SUNDOWN BEACH.

They also discussed the possibility of the two classes working together, at least on occasion. They expressed the hope that Kazan would remain actively committed to the Studio, despite his growing involvement with other things. Finally, they deliberated about possible teachers for the group. Harold Clurman, Sanford Meisner, and Lee Strasberg were among the candidates about whom the members frankly expressed their approval or reservations.

Responding to the advanced group's desire to have the Studio produce a play for them, Kazan approached Harold Clurman with the idea. The actors had suggested him as a possible director. Clurman said he would think about it, although, privately, he had already decided that he did not want to have anything to do with Kazan after the way he had been treated by him when the idea of the Studio originally arose. Many of the actors in the group wanted Clurman to replace Lewis, and a delegation of them came to him with the request that he take over. But Clurman declined. A notable exception to those advocating bringing in Clurman was Marlon Brando. Evidently, the experience of being directed by Clurman in *Truckline Café* had not been a happy one for him.[23]

Less than two weeks after Lewis's departure, Meisner and Strasberg, both of whom would become Studio teachers during the 1948–1949 season, had their first official contact with the workshop, participating in a production conference for a new television series The Actors Studio was embarking on—a series that was to prove a landmark in the history of televised drama.[24] At that August 12 meeting plans were laid for the first program to be directed by Martin Ritt and the second and third by Meisner and Strasberg. Meisner did indeed direct the second show for the Studio that September, but Ritt's participation did not come until later, and Strasberg's involvement in the series went no further than that first meeting.

The idea for a television show had been suggested to Kazan by Dorothy Willard, who persuaded him that a series emanating from the creative forces in the Studio and bearing the imprimatur of the workshop would be an excellent means of gaining support for the organization. The Studio was to receive 10 percent of the gross monies paid for the dramatic series. This income was enough to see the entire Studio through the two seasons of the telecast with enough left over to carry it through the fall of 1950.

Originally scheduled to begin broadcasting Sunday, August 29, The Actors Studio television programs did not get under way until September. The first of them was Tennessee Williams's one-act play, *Portrait of a Madonna*, starring Jessica Tandy and directed by Hume Cronyn. A foreshadowing of his then current hit, *Streetcar*, it had originally been done at the Actors' Lab in Hollywood in 1946. Miss Tandy had played the central character, Miss Lucretia Collins, a figure resembling Blanche Dubois in certain respects, in that California production. In fact, she was first considered for the part of Blanche when Kazan heard reports of her performance in the earlier role. Her television portrayal, warmly applauded by the critics, got the Studio's series off to an auspicious start. (The second program, directed by Sanford Meisner, was *Night Club*, which aired on October 3, 1948. Among those in its cast were Maureen Stapleton, Cloris Leachman, and Lee Grant.)

The Actors Studio television series, a pioneering experiment in national "coaxial-cable" broadcasting, produced fifty-six shows that received consistently excellent reviews. Primarily adaptations of short stories, each program was rehearsed by the Studio members at the workshop for two weeks before being broadcast live. The Studio provided not only the acting and the directing talent but the stage managers as well, among them Lou Gilbert, Martin Balsam, Alan Schneider, and Richard Boone. A few of the programs were directed by non-Studio figures such as Norris Houghton, and included non-Studio actors such as Robert Morley and Dennis King.

Most of the shows were directed for the Studio by David Pressman, Martin Ritt, and Daniel Mann. ABC assigned Ralph Warren and then Alex Segal to do the television directing. When the series was switched to CBS in its second year, Yul Brynner, then a staff director there, handled several of the programs. CBS had picked up the show after it finished its splendid first season by winning the Peabody Award. The citation for this distinction read:

To "Actors Studio" for its uninhibited and brilliant pioneering in the field of televised drama. "Actors Studio" guided by John Steinbeck, Elia Kazan, and Cheryl Crawford, and produced by Don Davis had presented one act plays, short stories, and sketches, whose acting, direction, lighting, and production show the highest degree of skill and resourcefulness. In the opinion of the judges, "Actors Studio" is the first to recognize that drama on television is neither a stage play nor a movie but a separate and distinct new art form.

(John Steinbeck, at the time a vice-president of World Video, Inc., the firm that produced the Studio programs, had been named as "literary adviser" to the series, but he actually had nothing to do with the production of the teleplays.)

Actors Studio TV came to an end in March of 1950. In the spring of the following year, an attempt was made to revive it. The new program, which was to feature original scripts written especially for the series by, among others, Clifford Odets, Tennessee Williams, Arthur Miller, and Joseph L. Mankiewicz (who had won an Oscar that year for *All About Eve*), never got beyond the talking stage. With the conclusion of its brief adventure into television production, the Studio ended the only period of sustained financial stability it was to know for the next fifteen years. Among the young performers Actors Studio TV helped introduce to American television were Martin Balsam, Richard Boone, Mildred Dunnock, Tom Ewell, Lee Grant, Julie Harris, Kim Hunter, Cloris Leachman, E. G. Marshall, Kevin McCarthy, Nehemiah Persoff, William Redfield, Eva Marie Saint, Maureen Stapleton, Jo Van Fleet, Eli Wallach, and David Wayne.

With the resignation of Lewis during the summer of 1948 and the swift opening and closing of *Sundown Beach* on Broadway that September, the members of the Studio faced an uncertain second season. The advanced group, still leaderless, continued to cast about for a teacher who would help implement the ideas they had discussed at their July meeting. Kazan's group saw less and less of him since he had gone into production with *Love Life* and Martin Ritt had more or less taken over the class. Both units were still hopeful that the Studio would continue producing plays.

Kazan called a meeting at the beginning of the second year to explain fully what he had in mind for the Studio. Though he understood that many of the actors really did not want just to take classes, he made it clear that they were not going to be turned into a company. The Studio was going to remain a workshop, a talent pool, and a place where actors could come and do whatever they wanted. There was an implication that individual projects might occasionally evolve into a production, but, Kazan explained, the Studio was not going to have a company; it was not going to become a theater. Needless to say, many of the actors were deeply disappointed.

Kazan also announced that he had persuaded Joshua Logan to take over the departed Lewis's class for several months. Up to this point, the class had been using some of its own members—mainly William Hansen and Herbert Berghof—to lead the group on an alternating basis. In line with his desire to open up the Studio to other creative minds, Kazan planned to invite a variety of guest teachers over the coming season. Moreover, he asked Sanford Meisner to establish a third class at the Studio which would include newcomers Meisner would bring in. He also began trying to persuade Lee Strasberg to become involved with the workshop. Strasberg, very hesitant at first, eventually agreed to participate on a limited basis in the fall of 1948. Despite Strasberg's presence at the Studio during the closing year and a half of the forties, the very special nature of what his involvement with the workshop portended for the organization and, through his work there, for the American theater as a whole, would not become fully manifest until the early fifties.

Joshua Logan, at his first meeting with the advanced class, gave a preamble about his trip to the Soviet Union in 1931 when he met Stanislavski, how he had been exposed to the Method, and how he was not such a "commercial" director. He also reminisced about his first theater and the young actors, including Henry Fonda and Margaret Sullavan, who had worked with him there. His Studio group wanted him to direct them in a project, so he started out on some Tennessee Williams one-act plays, including *The Strangest Kind of*

Romance with Eli Wallach and a reading of *Twenty-Seven Wagons Full of Cotton* with Maureen Stapleton.

Eli Wallach also directed Miss Stapleton, Margaret Phillips, and Anne Jackson (later Mrs. Wallach) in Williams's *Hello from Bertha* for Logan. They rehearsed for about ten days before presenting the one-acter. The morning of the performance, Wallach stepped before the curtain to make a few introductory comments. He said, "I directed this play because I'm interested in prostitution." He got a laugh. So he said, "No, seriously . . ." and went on to explain how he had been involved with the United States Army's V.D. unit during the Liberation after World War II. He told of raiding whorehouses in North Africa and flying a secret mission to Berlin, right after it fell, to discuss venereal disease with various army units. After about fifteen minutes of this, he said, "And now the play!" Logan said, "The hell with the play. Go on with the sex lecture." The three actresses were so furious with Wallach that when the curtain went up, they did nothing he had directed them to do. "It was such a trauma, I haven't directed since," he has noted ruefully.

Logan's work with the Studio actors was not terribly fruitful either, unfortunately. It became apparent within a short time that he really was not conversant with the Method, that he did not know what to do with the actors in this exploratory situation, and that he was nervous and ill-at-ease because of it. He remained at the Studio for only a couple of months.

When Logan departed, Kazan asked David Pressman, who was then Meisner's assistant at the Neighborhood Playhouse, to take over. He codirected the advanced group for a while, but was most heavily involved with the production of The Actors Studio TV series, for which he directed twenty-four shows. Pressman was followed by Daniel Mann, who worked steadily with the Studio actors both in class and in the TV series (he directed nine of the shows) until he achieved an outstanding success with his direction of *Come Back, Little Sheba*. After that, his involvement with the Studio decreased markedly.

The various teachers who taught at the Studio over the three-year period between the fall of 1948 and the fall of 1951 brought with them actors they had worked with or students from their private classes. Richard Derr, for instance, was invited by Joshua Logan, Rod Steiger by Daniel Mann, and, among others, Richard Boone, Lee

Grant, Gene Saks, and Jo Van Fleet by Sanford Meisner.[25] Other prominent actors who joined the Studio during this time were Jean Alexander, Beatrice Arthur, Barbara Baxley, Lonny Chapman, Salem Ludwig, Lois Nettleton, Alfred Ryder, Eva Marie Saint, Frank Silvera, Kim Stanley, Jan Sterling, Ray Walston, and Dennis Weaver.[26]

In the fall of 1951, Kazan and Miss Crawford decided it was time to put an end to the coming and going of various interim teachers and to consolidate all the acting classes under a single instructor. For three years there had been not only the periodic substitution of teachers, with their contrasting approaches to acting training, but a constant shifting of units between teachers and of members from unit to unit. The result was a loss of continuity in the work with individual actors. The ostensible virtues of drawing on a diversity of teaching talent had degenerated into the very real drawback of unfocused and uncommitted work by directors whose primary interests lay outside the Studio. The time had come to give the organization a greater uniformity of purpose and direction. The man chosen to bring order and a new seriousness to the training at the Studio was Lee Strasberg.

From September 27, 1948, the day he conducted his first class at the Studio,* Lee Strasberg worked there continuously, sharing Kazan's group at first and then coexisting with Daniel Mann, for much of the time, as one of two principal teachers. Strasberg took over when Mann decided to leave the Studio to follow his directorial ambitions, after the success of *Come Back, Little Sheba*, and when the last of the "interim" teachers, David Alexander, departed in the fall of 1951. Given the title of "Artistic Director of The Actors Studio," Strasberg initiated the course of work that was to make the still relatively unknown Studio a cynosure of the American theatrical landscape during the decade of the fifties and an object of national and international interest and controversy to this day.

---

* Lou Gilbert's notebooks give this date with the first entry of Strasberg's name. The earliest existing list of his class is "Strasberg and Advanced Class, November 26, 1948," Archives.

CHAPTER **3**

Strasberg
Takes Over:
1951–1955

THE LATE THIRTIES and the following decade had not
been kind to Lee Strasberg in his effort to establish himself as an important theatrical director. In the thirteen years between his departure
from the Group and his assumption of the leadership of The Actors
Studio, Strasberg had directed a total of sixteen plays, only a handful
of which could clearly be called critical successes.[1] And of these, by
Strasberg's own account, only one, Hemingway's *The Fifth Column*,
had been commercially profitable.

It should be pointed out, however, that the brunt of the adverse
criticism of most of the plays Strasberg directed during these years
was leveled at faulty dramaturgy rather than at production values. On
a number of occasions, in fact, despite critical reservations about the
play itself, Strasberg received fine personal notices for his work. For
example, in his review of *All the Living*, Cheryl Crawford's first independent, post-Group production, Brooks Atkinson, after noting that
the play's plot was "poorly proportioned" and "nebulous in details,"
observed:

. . . the performance under Mr. Strasberg's versatile direction is one of
the foremost achievements of the new theatre. It is a perfectly composed
portrait with several lines of motion, swinging from the general to the
particular with no break in the rhythm; it has depth and scope and audi-
ble excitements.[2]

[77]

Of *Clash by Night*, which he faulted for Odets's "maundering and wordy" second act, Atkinson wrote, ". . . the whole thing is beautifully acted and produced under Lee Strasberg's direction." [3] And finally, in evaluating Hemingway's *The Fifth Column*, which he considered a flawed but commendable play, Atkinson said, "There has been no more vital writing this season. Nor has there been a more stirring performance than the one Lee Strasberg has directed on the Alvin stage." [4]

There were quibbles expressed about Strasberg's work on other of the productions, however. And none of the twelve plays he directed in the six years after he left the Group succeeded in galvanizing or advancing his career. He left New York for the West Coast in 1944, burdened with feelings "of discouragement and lack of direction."

Strasberg's three-year stay in Hollywood, during which he directed screen tests for Twentieth Century-Fox while learning the film business, failed to open any new doors. In later years he would sum up that period as "an unfruitful but nonetheless educational experience." By the spring of 1947 he was back in New York, trying to find a place for himself in the theatrical ferment of the postwar years. Cheryl Crawford, seeing he needed the money, invited him to coach the sixty actors in the cast of *Brigadoon* on a once-a-week basis. The classes were held at the Ziegfeld Theatre, where the musical was playing, and consisted mostly of the dancers and singers of the chorus. Miss Crawford brought in Julie Harris, Anne Jackson, and Eli Wallach from the American Repertory Theatre to participate.

Strasberg also began planning an unusual and controversial project to develop young writers for the stage and screen. In an article in *The New York Times*, he explained how this service to playwrights would help them select interesting themes and situations ". . . for which [their] ideas and talents are suited, and then proceed in this creative collaboration to the solution of all of the dramaturgic problems." [5] This enterprise, which he planned with Anderson Lawlor and for which he envisioned a capitalization of $150,000 from some thirty investors, never got off the ground.

Strasberg's most important activity during the late forties, and the one which would ultimately be recognized as his greatest contribution to the American theater, was his training of actors. In addition to his private acting classes and such special arrangements as the coaching of the cast of *Brigadoon,* he also served on the faculties of both the American Theater Wing and the Dramatic Workshop.

Strasberg's influence on American acting had grown steadily since his days with the Group, especially as those who had worked and studied under him, then and later, moved out into the theater world to teach and influence others in their turn. His thirty-four-page essay, "Acting and the Training of the Actor," had appeared in John Gassner's *Producing the Play* at the beginning of the decade.[6] This article was one of the earliest attempts to delineate an American version of the Method, and it helped to establish Strasberg's authority in the field. When *Acting, a Handbook of the Stanislavski Method,* a collection of influential acting articles of the thirties compiled by Toby Cole, appeared in 1947 with an introduction by Strasberg, it was as if to suggest once again his special preeminence in the field of acting training.[7] "More or less behind the scenes in the forties, Strasberg became very much the man of the hour," Paul Gray wrote in his "Critical Chronology" of the Stanislavski influence in America.[8]

In the summer of 1948 a small committee from the Studio's "Lewis Unit" (Thelma Schnee, Fred Stewart, Michael Strong, and Eli Wallach) called on Kazan to ask him to help them find a permanent replacement for their recently departed teacher. Strasberg inevitably came under consideration as a logical successor to Lewis. "I was looking around for someone who was by nature a teacher," Kazan recalls, "and I knew who I had in mind: Lee Strasberg. It took me a long time to get Strasberg involved; he hesitated, he backed off, he qualified, he did everything in the world to try and get out of it. I just persisted." [9] Some knowledgeable observers felt Strasberg resisted Kazan because he was resentful and even somewhat skeptical about the Studio owing to the fact that he had not been asked to be part of it from the beginning.

Without question, given his qualifications, Strasberg would seem to have been a natural choice to have worked with Kazan on founding The Actors Studio. In the light of Kazan's later efforts to involve Strasberg in the organization and of his frequently acknowledged enthusiasm for Strasberg's unique qualities as a teacher,[10] the question arises: why had he not included his former mentor in his original plans for the Studio? The answer appears to be that Kazan, despite a tendency to focus in retrospect only on his positive feelings about

Strasberg, had always had reservations about some aspects of Strasberg's teaching—especially about the emphasis put on the actor's personal experience as tapped by means of affective-memory exercises.

Robert Lewis recalls that Kazan, even during the period he was trying to recruit Strasberg, continued to have mixed feelings about the man.

Kazan opposed Strasberg right from the beginning. When they had to bring in a teacher they tried Meisner, Logan—anybody but Strasberg. But Gadge always accommodated himself and got Lee to teach—beginning with history of theatre. Gadge thought a lot of Lee's techniques were strange and he always complained to me. But once Lee got in at the Studio an attempt was made to put him on the map.[11]

Lewis is mistaken in his impression that Strasberg came to the Studio only after Meisner and others had been there for some time. In fact, Strasberg was at the Studio at the very start of its second season (September 27, 1948). Strasberg shared Kazan's group at the same time Logan taught the advanced group and Meisner had his own, separate group. But as far as Kazan's feelings about Strasberg's approach to acting were concerned, his account is confirmed by Strasberg himself.

Gadge was not too sympathetic to my coming in because he never really understood what it was I did in the Group Theatre from the training point of view. . . . My impression was at that time and on a later occasion that he wasn't either too aware or convinced of the significance or value of the work.

For his part, Strasberg was concerned less about Kazan's ambivalent feelings toward him than about getting involved with an organization that was not committed to becoming a theater. "I said, 'For me, something like this is the basis for the building of a theater. Otherwise it has no purpose.'" Nevertheless, by late September 1948, Kazan succeeded in persuading him to take part in a limited capacity. Strasberg agreed to participate as one of several teachers, with the clear understanding he was keeping his options open. "I said, 'I don't want to assume any official position because I don't know that I'm interested in it. I don't know that you are interested in what I have to give.'"

Strasberg had other reasons for resisting Kazan's attempts to get him to make a deeper commitment to the Studio. For one thing, he was determined not to get sidetracked from the main line of theater—professional production. His mind was full of all the plays he wanted to stage; his real ambition was to resuscitate his quiescent directorial career. In January 1948 he had directed his first play since his return to New York, Jan de Hartog's *Skipper Next to God*. Produced by Cheryl Crawford as part of the ANTA Experimental Theatre series, it was a critical success for Strasberg and the first of three plays that reunited him with John Garfield, the fiery young leading man of the Group Theatre. Only a few months after he began working at the Studio, he was once again busy directing Garfield in Clifford Odets's *The Big Knife*.*

In his first year with the Studio, Strasberg shared Kazan's unit, working without pay, as did all the teachers. It was understood that he would continue to teach at the American Theatre Wing and the Dramatic Workshop as well. During this time, Kazan began a process of disengagement from the Studio, which was to accelerate as time went on. The era of his single-minded devotion to teaching at the workshop had really ended after its first season. At least part of the reason for his detaching himself, apparently, was Kazan's shock and disappointment at the outcome of *Sundown Beach*, whose failure had made him doubt his ability as a teacher. But after staying away from the Studio for most of the 1948–1949 season, he returned to continue an active involvement into the mid-fifties. Still, by the second season, he was seeking to shift the burden of the teaching to other shoulders—mostly to Strasberg's shoulders.

I was directing plays and movies both, in those years; I didn't have time to go teach, and didn't have much interest in it after a while. I wasn't a particularly good teacher. I would be very good some days and then on other days I would find the work tedious and get through it as best I could.[12]

Strasberg brought a new seriousness to the work at the Studio. He was not particularly delicate about rooting out dilettantism where he found it. Nor did he pull any punches about what he felt were shortcomings in the teaching of the Method by his colleagues, including Kazan. If Kazan had reservations about some of Strasberg's procedures, Strasberg in turn was critical of Kazan's training work

* Of his work in this production, Brooks Atkinson, *The New York Times*, February 25, 1949, p. 27, said: "Lee Strasberg, working in a minor key, has designed a beautiful performance that has spontaneity and tension at the same time. Although he does not force it, it is never colorless or tepid."

with the actors. For one thing, he felt Kazan emphasized "actions" out of proportion to other elements of the Method, such as sensory work. In his determination to set things right, Strasberg, according to some, seemed to want to show everyone that they knew nothing about the Method.

His attitude toward the Studio actors when he first arrived was "let's see if you really can act . . . let's see if you know anything." His first sessions were violent ones, his reaction to the level of work more often than not a caustic fury. It was reported that he seemed to have tantrums after every scene. The Studio was changing: an atmosphere of challenge had replaced the familial cordiality of the first 1947–1948 season with Kazan. Strasberg, more sure of himself as a teacher—and certainly more dogmatic in that capacity—than Kazan, brooked no contradictions and invited no opinions on acting theory. He was there to tell the actors what was what, and he expected them to adapt themselves to his ways. Some Studio members felt he was unduly severe with the class, although most of them quickly came to appreciate his unusual perceptiveness and his uncanny ability to limn, with almost X-ray precision, their essential strengths and weaknesses.

Throughout his career, Strasberg had what might be called a "jeweler's eye" for talent. Even discussing great actors of the past, he was able to conjure up the special flavor of their various acting qualities through a sympathetic and insightful penetration to the heart of their work. Combining a theater scholar's discernment and a great acting teacher's sensitivity to the most elusive historical clues to performance, he had a unique facility for evoking landmark characterizations (such as Edmund Kean's Shylock) while evaluating them critically at the same time. In class, this genius for crystallizing the essential features of the actors' instruments and work habits became an invaluable tool in nurturing those young performers who would emerge as leading players during the fifties.

However, one use of Strasberg's ability to crystallize problems and prospects for the actor did not find favor. At the end of each of the first few seasons, it was Strasberg's custom to give a summation of every actor's work. He would go through the whole class in open session and evaluate each person's progress during that year. This procedure made many of the actors nervous and uncomfortable. It ceased, according to several of the Studio members who were there, the year Marlon Brando read a newspaper throughout Strasberg's commentary on his work.

In his second year of teaching in the Studio's fourteenth-floor headquarters at Fifty-third Street and Broadway, Strasberg was officially listed as part of the "new guiding directorate" of the organization. In February 1950 Strasberg received his first fee from The Actors Studio. Although it had always been Kazan's intention that the teaching would be offered gratis, he was sympathetic to Strasberg's financial situation (Kazan and Miss Crawford could afford to contribute their services at the time) and agreed to the Studio's providing him with a salary. Strasberg and May Reis, the secretary, became the only salaried personnel in the Studio's early years. In various letters soliciting contributions during this period, however, the fact was emphasized that all staff members but two contributed their services. Over the years, the monies due Strasberg were paid to him very erratically. On numerous occasions he received only part of his fee because of the Studio's condition of never-ending financial crisis.

During the 1950–1951 season, even as he shared teaching duties at the Studio (still at 1697 Broadway and Fifty-third Street) with Daniel Mann, Strasberg's directing career reached a critical stage. The previous season it had nearly foundered after a grimly disappointing experience with Alexander Knox's melodrama, *The Closing Door*. In January 1951 Strasberg's long-contemplated presentation of Ibsen's *Peer Gynt* opened with John Garfield playing the title role. It was an unfortunate production for both actor and director. There were a few approving reviews, but the majority of critics found the production earthbound and lacking in lyricism, and Strasberg himself came in for harsh words. This was to be the last production Strasberg would direct on Broadway till the advent of The Actors Studio Theatre some thirteen years later.

The following fall, as the Studio's fundamental worth and promise became more and more apparent to Strasberg, he decided to make a greater commitment to it. By the opening of the Studio's fifth season, 1951–1952, he assumed the title of artistic director. All other acting teachers had departed, and he alone defined the course of work and determined "artistic policy." Kazan, though he founded the Studio, was no longer its shaper. He had, in effect, "given" the workshop to Strasberg.

Kazan held no regular classes at the Studio after 1951, although he did return, impressively, from time to time, to set up experimental projects, to lend support, or simply to observe. He was responsible for several projects of note in the early fifties. The first was an attempt to explore Act One of Ibsen's *Hedda Gabler* from three distinct interpretive approaches, each to be performed at a separate session. He assigned these to different directors. Marlon Brando staged his *Hedda* in the context of a decadent southern environment. His sympathetic heroine was played by Thelma Schnee. Brando went to great pains with the project, even to the extent of helping build the set and painting it himself. Bert Conway's *Hedda*, featuring Kim Stanley, was set in a militaristic milieu, where her behavior was ascribed "to the psychological factor that her father had wanted a boy when she was born." Steven Hill's version, with Jo Van Fleet, based Hedda's behavior on sexual frustration.

Kazan also devoted six months to the intensive investigation of how to deal with a song on stage, using given circumstances. He asked his actors to bring in a scene that would make its dramatic point using only the words of a song as its text. Karl Malden sang "Some Enchanted Evening," not as a romantic lover, but as a janitor sweeping out a deserted theater and amusing himself with the sound of his own voice in the empty hall. June Havoc, while singing "Tea for Two," played a woman frustrated with her life and her worthless husband, who one morning makes herself absolutely charming and sweetly brews him a nice cup of breakfast coffee with poison in it.

One of the most fruitful examples of what was achieved in that class was a scene done by Jo Van Fleet, working with a simple nursery rhyme. She came on stage with a basket full of children's toys which she scattered all over the floor. As she started singing, she began gathering up the playthings and it became apparent in the course of her song that she was putting away the toys of a child who had died. For many, it was an overpowering performance.

Especially noteworthy among these early-fifties projects was Kazan's work on Tennessee Williams's *Ten Blocks on the Camino Real*, the original, one-act version of his full-length *Camino Real*. Kazan sought to find the key to the right style for the play by bringing a different directorial approach to each of the several scenes he was experimenting with. Eli Wallach, who played the leading role of Kilroy, recalls the ingenious strategy the director used to elicit the dramatic confrontations he strove for: ". . . he instructed me to go on stage to make friends. 'I can't tell you how to make friends,' he said. 'Just do it.' He then instructed the other actors to reject me—renounce me. This game, this pitting of actor against actor within the circumstances of the play, is what makes Kazan brilliant." [13]

Wallach was performing in *Mr. Roberts* at the time he worked with Kazan on the *Camino* project. They would rehearse after the show till one or two in the morning. Kazan said things like, "Run up the side of the wall." Wallach protested, "Gadge!" Kazan told him, "Chaplin did it." So Wallach would figure a way to run up the side of the wall. Tennessee Williams was astounded when he saw a performance of it.

After receiving suggestions from the playwright and others, Kazan proceeded to work further on it. As a result of what he had seen at the Studio, Williams expanded the one-act into the full-length play that was taken to Broadway in 1953 with a large contingent of Studio people in the cast.* When the play was later published, it carried a dedication to Kazan.[14] "It never would have been done," Kazan recollects, "except that I showed it to Williams at the Studio."

It was also Kazan who threw the Studio and the rest of the theater and film world into turmoil on April 12, 1952, when *The New York Times* carried a news item about his "friendly" testimony before the House Committee on Un-American Activities and a statement in the form of a paid advertisement in which he defended his actions.[15]

In the late forties and early fifties, during the period of the cold war and the vehemently anti-Communist tenure of Senator Joseph McCarthy, theater artists with a history of radical or "progressive" sympathies were faced with a grave dilemma. Scores of prominent actors, directors, and writers were called before the House Un-American Activities Committee (HUAC) to testify about their involvement with the Communist party and its various "front" organizations. Those who refused to cooperate in the committee's investigations were threatened with blacklisting or, worse, imprisonment. The most painful and distasteful aspect of these proceeding was the pressure put

---

* Joseph Anthony, Martin Balsam, Aza Bard, Barbara Baxley, Michael V. Gazzo, Mary Grey, Salem Ludwig, Vivian Nathan, Lucille Patton, Nehemiah Persoff, Fred Sadoff, Henry Silva, Frank Silvera, David J. Stewart, Jo Van Fleet, and Eli Wallach. Brooks Atkinson, *The New York Times*, March 20, 1953, p. 26, said: "It was played with great skill and ingenuity. . . . As theatre work, the production and performance are superb."

on those testifying to implicate others. The struggle to avoid what many perceived as moral perfidy was a treacherous one. Some succumbed, some resisted. In either case, careers were ruined and lives were shattered.

Kazan, at the height of his career as a film and theater director, was a prize catch for HUAC because he agreed to speak freely about his past. What upset and angered Kazan's friends and associates both in and out of the Studio was his naming of names in his disclosures about Communist attempts to infiltrate the Group Theatre in the mid-thirties. At his first appearance before an executive session of the committee on January 14, Kazan had declined to identify Party associates. But at a subsequent appearance on April 10, again in executive session, he presented an affidavit to the investigatory unit which included a list of one-time members of the Group's Communist cell. Among those named were: Phoebe Brand (Mrs. Morris Carnovsky), Morris Carnovsky, Paula Miller (Mrs. Lee Strasberg), Art Smith, Lewis Leverett, Tony Kraber, J. Edward Bromberg, and Clifford Odets. In a letter to the committe Kazan stated, "I have come to the conclusion that I did wrong to withhold these names before, because secrecy serves the Communists, and is exactly what they want."

Reaction to Kazan's testimony was outspokenly hostile. Many of his best friends cut their ties with him. They would pass him on the street without acknowledging him, or even cross the street to avoid him. The label of "stool pigeon" was bandied about. Kazan, who noted at the conclusion of his testimony that a copy of his affidavit was placed with Spyros P. Skouras, president of Twentieth Century-Fox, was accused of trying to save his career no matter what the cost. Even among those of his oldest acquaintances who refrained from condemning his behavior publicly, there were many who believed his decision to testify was less the result of his desire to make a symbolic demonstration of his anticommunism (which is how he explained his actions), than of the fact that he had "too much to lose" by not testifying. Many years later Kazan was to observe most revealingly, "I commit myself all the way as a person who wants to survive somehow, by any means!" [16]

Nevertheless, Kazan has always insisted that his actions were ideologically motivated—a product of his anti-Stalinism and of his conviction that the Communists' conspiratorial use of people had to be exposed. In retrospect, he does admit to an ambivalence about the naming of names. On the one hand, he feels that what he did was "repulsive." But he has also stated that the testimony he gave, provoked by his antipathy to Communist goals, was justified at the time, and that it has long since been validated by revelations of "what the Soviet Union has done to its writers, and their death camps, and the Nazi pact and the Polish and Czech repression. . . ." [17] It should also be pointed out that there were people who were sympathetic to Kazan's situation and who supported his actions—even among those directly affected by his testimony. Clifford Odets and Paula Strasberg, warned by Kazan of his intention to testify, told him they thought he was doing the right thing and gave their permission for him to name them.[18]

Kazan's testimony had its repercussions at the Studio. A number of people simply dissociated themselves from the workshop. May Reis, for instance, a great admirer of the director until that time, left in disillusionment after five years as the Studio secretary. She subsequently became secretary to Arthur Miller and Marilyn Monroe. Brando is reported to have said, "I'll never work with that sonofabitch again!"

He did, of course, in *On the Waterfront,* released in 1954. Lou Gilbert tells a story of snubbing Brando at the Studio shortly after it was announced he would be working with Kazan again. Gilbert said to him, after first greeting him enthusiastically, "Oh, remind me, I don't want to talk to you." Brando asked, "Why?" Gilbert said, "No, no, I don't want to talk to you." Brando left, abashed. Gilbert, realizing that his hostile behavior toward Brando was uncalled for, rushed after him only to have Brando yell at him on the street to leave him alone or he would kill him. Gilbert subsequently wrote Brando several letters by way of apology, but received no reply. Morris Carnovsky, one of those who had not given Kazan permission to name him, confronted Lou Gilbert about Gilbert's continuing to attend the Studio. On the other hand, there were many Studio figures who were quietly supportive of the director—not the least of them, Lee Strasberg.

The dilemma of how to respond to the situation resulted in a meeting at the Studio. There were those who felt some public stand against the director was called for. Kazan's position was that since he had never questioned what any of the members' politics were in determining who was to become a member—or for any other reason

—their response to his behavior should be strictly a private matter, and should not interfere with their commitment to the Studio. The outcome of the debate was a decision that the Studio would not be political.

Ironically, although its officers and members thought of the Studio as nonpartisan and nonpolitical, the outside world tended to look on the workshop as a "left-leaning" organization. Despite the fact that their opinions spanned the political spectrum from conservative to liberal (and beyond), members were often warned not to include the fact of their membership in their "bios" or in theater programs—especially when sending such information to the two major television networks, CBS and NBC—because the feeling in the business was that the Studio was "leftist." Members were deeply concerned about the threat of blacklisting during the McCarthy years, as they had good reason to be. *Red Channels*, one of the publications involved with blacklisting, would make a point of a performer's Actors Studio membership. A number of Studio actors were in fact blacklisted for varying periods during that time.

The Studio, despite the fact that it has never taken a political stance nor made any ideological pronouncements, was to feel the effect of this "leftist aura" as late as 1968. In September of that year, Shelley Winters wrote to Howard Hughes requesting his financial support for a Studio in dire need. Miss Winters reports that Hughes had been ready to give the Studio fifty thousand dollars a year for ten years until "someone told him the Studio was 'Communist'."

Kazan kept away from the Studio during the spring of 1952. His feelings about the atmosphere there are expressed in a letter to Cheryl Crawford written later in the year.

About the Studio, I've alternated and wavered. Some days I've felt like withdrawing finally and completely. But that has been seldom and only when I felt most sensitive to the rejection and bitterness growing out of my 'stand' and reaching me in rumbles and rumors.

I dont want to do anything destructive. I want to do something good.

On the other hand I cant—no one could—work with unfriendly people. There are some. How many I dont know. How it will go from now on, no one can guess. I dont feel anymore like working there this minute, than I did all spring when I stayed away. However one must count on the future with confidence rather than vengeance, and I know, irrespective of how active I am, the studio is tremendously important. And as an expression of what is best and priceless in Lee, I couldn't do anything but help it.[19]

The bitterness of certain members toward Kazan never completely disappeared. For others who were there at the time, the anger evolved into "mixed feelings" or was tempered by a process of reconciliation over the years. Robert Lewis, who had despised Kazan for testifying, had long rehearsed what he would say to his former friend and colleague if he ever ran into him. One day, some years later, he was walking past the ANTA Theatre on the other side of the street when Kazan popped out of the theater building. Their eyes met and they screamed "Juicy!!" at one another as they ran with outstretched arms to embrace. ("Juicy" was their mutual nickname in the Group Theatre.) All of Lewis's prepared statements went out of his head. Deeper feelings of affection reasserted themselves as the two men were moved to find each other again after not having spoken for years. They have remained close friends.

For many members, especially those who came after 1952, the whole issue became moot, and was overshadowed by the director's dynamic artistic reputation and his continuing contribution as a guiding and supportive force at the Studio. Despite his less active involvement after the early fifties, his name was still something to conjure with and his presence, whenever he attended sessions, gave a fillip of excitement to what happened there.

It was, in fact, Kazan's involvement with the Studio during the early fifties, limited as it was at times, that gave the organization its *réclame*. By mid-decade he had become an enormous force in both theater and film; whatever he touched as a director seemed destined to flourish. Among his achievements, for many of which he won awards, were *Death of a Salesman* (1949), *Tea and Sympathy* (1955), and *Cat on a Hot Tin Roof* (1955) for the stage, and *A Streetcar Named Desire* (1951), *Viva Zapata!* (1952), *On the Waterfront* (1954), and *East of Eden* (1955) for the screen. Strasberg himself has stated on numerous occasions that, historically speaking, the reputation of the Studio was made not by Strasberg, but by Kazan, through his distinctive use of Studio people in his films and stage productions. It was Kazan's name that drew the most talented young performers in New York to the Studio, and for good reasons.

For the actor, contact with Kazan promised not only inspiring artistic stimulation, but the real possibility of overnight stardom.

Hundreds of actors tried to get into the Studio each year. Between the fall of 1948 and the spring of 1951 alone, over two thousand performers auditioned. Of these, thirty or so were accepted, putting the total membership in the fall of 1951 at approximately eighty-five members. Approximation is unavoidable because the records of membership are hopelessly confused for the first eight years of the Studio's existence. For one thing, members were listed on the basis of their active participation, so the lists fluctuate as people come and go. In addition, the status of certain actors originally brought in by Meisner, Mann, and other teachers was challenged and a number were dropped.*

An attempt was made to straighten out what Kazan called "the muddled state of Studio membership" at the beginning of the fifties. Several categories were defined: members—recognized as such by all concerned; provisional members—"who have never actually been accepted as such but whom we regard as good Studio material and who are, so to say, working their way towards membership"; and guests—people who were brought in as observers and whose status was to be reviewed at regular intervals. Every actor who attended Studio sessions at the time was reconsidered in terms of these categories and those peripheral cases who did not "fit in" were asked to audition for membership *pro forma* (and to be judged accordingly) or to leave.

However, there were continuing adjustments in the membership rolls as certain members and "guests" continued to be dropped for nonattendance or, since the Studio was gaining more and more recognition, as various actors applied for reinstatement. Anthony Quinn and Dorothy McGuire were two such "guests" dropped in October 1953. Only after the Studio came to rest permanently in its present home on West Forty-fourth Street was the policy of life membership firmly established (and that of "provisional membership" abolished), and not until the formation of The Actors Studio Theatre in the early sixties was a complete and accurate listing of life members finally compiled.

* May Reis estimated that there were "approximately" ninety-two members at the end of 1949. Existing lists from the spring and fall of 1951 vary in count from eighty-two to eighty-five members.

During the fifties there were two ways to become a member of The Actors Studio. The standard procedure for admission, the one still followed to this day, was the two-part audition, open to any and all applicants over eighteen years of age. Young aspirants would first register for the periodic preliminary auditions. If the actor had no training at all, it was explained that the Studio was not a school for beginners and one of several training places might be recommended to him; but he was not prevented from auditioning if he wanted to. He was told to prepare one five-minute scene with a partner (no monologues). A contemporary piece was suggested, something the actor could do simply and easily, featuring a character close to himself in age, type, and experience. He was told that the judges would try to estimate his native talent, his use of himself in a part he felt close to, and not his verbal or physical skills as an actor. He should therefore avoid the special complexities of Shakespeare or "period" drama.

In the long history of the Studio auditions, a great variety of audition material has been used. Besides the usual scenes from contemporary plays of each decade—a good deal of Odets, Williams, and Miller during the fifties, plus Albee during the sixties and Pinter during the seventies—candidates have presented dramatizations from modern novels and short stories by such writers as Irwin Shaw and William Saroyan, original scenes written for the occasion, and improvisations. Resourceful actors, determined to make an impression, were often unabashed in their inventiveness. Two auditioners once presented an improvised scene designed to satirize the traumatic and humiliating experience of having to audition before a panel of Studio members. In the course of their carrying-on, one of the actors gave a fairly convincing rendition of a heart attack. But evidently it was not convincing enough, as they were not admitted.

A number of actors indulged in seminudity at auditions, according to Miss Crawford. "I suspect that they wished to show us how free and uninhibited they were. We certainly witnessed a good number of bare breasts and jock straps." [20]

The preliminary audition was given before three or more judges, selected from an audition board appointed by Strasberg. If the candidate's scene partner also wanted to be considered for membership, he simply had to so inform the Studio secretary the night of the audition. (Studio members have partnered scenes on occasion.) The actor was notified within a week of the results. If he failed to pass, he was told that he might audition again—as often as he would like, in fact—but that there must be a year's lapse between auditions. If he passed, it was arranged for him to return with the same partner and the same scene for presentation before Kazan, Miss Crawford, and Strasberg.

A representative example of the whole audition ordeal was related by Earle Hyman at a 1977 "Salute to The Actors Studio" at Florida State University. In a narrative reminiscent of many members' experience, he described how he and his fellow auditioner sought to pick a scene to satisfy the Studio's panel of judges.

The first time around, having heard that the judges were impressed with highly emotional scenes, he and his partner went all out "spilling their guts," yelling and screaming at one another. The audition committee was unimpressed. On their second attempt, having been informed that the Studio was interested in work with "objects," they turned on more radios, smoked more cigarettes, and handled more props than you could imagine possible in five minutes on stage. They were encouraged to try again—but with a simple scene.

Hyman, making a clean break, asked another actress—one with whom he was romantically involved—to work with him on a scene from a short story that paralleled what the two of them were going through in real life at the time. Removing the "he saids" and "she saids," they performed the dialogue from the story and made no effort to get worked up about the situation. Nor did they attempt "to show off their ease at being 'natural' on stage." Hyman, in fact, felt that "nothing happened" in the scene in which two people who are in love with one another, but know there is no future in their love, sip wine and talk about everything except being in love. The scene was so "undramatic" that he did not expect to get into the Studio the third time around either. But he did.

When Strasberg introduced Hyman and the other new members that season (Geraldine Page was in the group), they were duly applauded by those who knew how difficult it had been getting there. Strasberg said, as he would in the future on many similar occasions, "Enjoy it. It may be the last time you'll ever hear applause again in the Studio." [21]

The other means of admission during the fifties was a procedure by which "actors of a certain status in the professional hierarchy" could be voted in as active members of the Studio. These individuals were first granted three months' observer privileges, during which they were expected to present work, their "observerships" being extended on the basis of their participation. Those whose work showed progress could be admitted directly to official membership.

On a number of occasions over the years, actors (and nonactors) have become members of the Studio by invitation. Aside from the original Robert Lewis group and those who came with Mann and Meisner and were asked to remain, such individuals as Roscoe Lee Browne, Dane Clark, Tamara Daykarhanova, Rita Gam, Burgess Meredith, Sidney Poitier, Paula Strasberg, Anna Mizrahi Strasberg, and Franchot Tone have been voted directly into membership by the Studio's directorate or by Strasberg himself. In the early sixties several actors who performed with The Actors Studio Theatre were similarly admitted.[22] Various directors and playwrights, including Frank Corsaro, Martin Fried, Jack Garfein, Michael V. Gazzo, Charles Gordone, Israel Horovitz, Arthur Penn, Eleanor Perry, Frank Perry, Sydney Pollack, Mark Rydell, Alan Schneider, and John Stix, have also been granted membership on the basis of their contributions to the life and work of The Actors Studio, as have certain other nonperformers, such as Liska March and Carl Schaeffer.

During the 1970s Strasberg brought in a number of prominent performers: Zoe Caldwell, Jill Clayburgh, Robert De Niro, Robert Duvall, Lainie Kazan, Barbara Loden, Michael Moriarty, Jack Nicholson, and Carroll O'Connor.

But those admitted by invitation, whether because of their standing in the profession or years of devotion to the Studio, have been comparatively few. The means by which the overwhelming majority of actors became members, including the most famous "names" associated with the Studio during the fifties, was the Studio audition. Paul Newman auditioned as Val Xavier in a scene from *Battle of Angels*. Ben Gazzara, who first auditioned for Daniel Mann, passed his "final" with a scene from Odets's *Night Music*. Kim Stanley got in with *Bury the Dead*. Anne Bancroft did a scene from *Two for the Seesaw* with Studio member Kevin McCarthy while she was appearing in the original Broadway production with Henry Fonda. Steve McQueen used a scene from *A Hatful of Rain*. Rip Torn adapted a passage from *The Grapes of Wrath*. Joanne Woodward used *The Rainmaker*. And Geraldine Page passed her audition with *Awake and Sing*.

Usually the Studio would dissuade the applicant from presenting an original scene of his own "and testing his writing ability when he is auditioning as an actor" (as it stated on one of the audition-instructions sheets). But on occasion such material served the auditioner admirably. James Dean and Christine White were outstandingly successful in an original scene written by Miss White for their Studio audition in 1952. The two performers had perfected the piece, which dramatized a nighttime encounter on a beach between an intellectual drifter and an aristocratic southern girl, over a period of several weeks. They rehearsed in Central Park to get the proper out-of-doors atmosphere, with Dean stopping total strangers and asking them to watch in order to test the response to their work. They rewrote and rewrote, going over their lines in taxis and in bars. On the night of their audition, despite Dean's inability to see anything without his glasses, they made an extraordinary impression.

Strasberg recalls the impact of that joint audition after twenty-two years. "It seemed simple, easy, believable. [It had a] wonderful quality. Very much what we would like to see from people when they come to us." It was an auspicious start for the young actor, who, in that early summer of 1952, was destined to become an epitome of The Actors Studio/Method actor in the mind of the general public. Unfortunately, in terms of his actual work at the Studio, it was also an unfulfilled promise.

It is one of the larger ironies of the history of The Actors Studio that James Dean, the young actor whose name comes so readily to mind whenever the Studio is mentioned and whose style of acting the world has taken as a definitive creation of that institution, was very inhibited there and worked very little in class. It is a rare Studio member who can recollect a scene in which James Dean appeared. Strasberg, who recalls his audition so readily, can remember nothing specific of the actor's work from the time Dean became a member until his death three years later. In Strasberg's opinion, Dean's work during the period of his membership never again matched that audition.

It was my feeling that he didn't go far enough. It seemed to be, as with many other people, that he was not using enough of himself. He continued on the same level and I always looked for the things that will open up more. My impression is, that while the work continued, it did not make any progress that I remember or was aware of.

During the three years he was a member, Dean's television and stage career and the three motion pictures that brought him international fame kept him busy. But there were other reasons why he worked so infrequently at the Studio. His first scene as a member was not received very well. Dean and Miss White had rehearsed an original comedy sketch called "Abroad," which they had written together. They intended to perform this piece about two young people planning a trip to Europe as their initial work at the Studio. An older member to whom they had shown it, however, discouraged them from presenting it. Instead, Dean chose to work on a scene from the novel *Matador* by Barnaby Conrad. He dramatized a chapter from the book in which the matador prepares for his final bullfight. The scene was an internal monologue in which he tried to convey the man's emotions without words. Dean, who was passionately interested in bullfighting, worked hard on the matador's ritualistic preparations, using only a few props: a statue of the Virgin, a candle, and the matador's cape. He changed the scene more than a dozen times in rehearsal, and on the morning of the performance, he walked off stage before finishing what he had planned to do. His work provoked a long and penetrating critique from Strasberg. Dean listened impassively, but the color drained from his face. When Strasberg had concluded his remarks, the young actor slung his matador's cape over his shoulder and silently walked out of the room. It was a long time before the highly sensitive Dean, deeply upset by the criticism, ventured to do a scene again.

It was Frank Corsaro who eventually persuaded Dean to return to the Studio. The actor was playing a small mime role in Corsaro's production of *The Scarecrow* at the Theatre De Lys, when the director suggested he make his peace with Strasberg. Dean did return, but only half-heartedly. He took part in some improvisations that Corsaro supervised at one point and, in response to a visit to the Studio by some members of the Kabuki Theater, worked up some of his own improvisations based on Japanese forms. He also played the small role of Starkson in *End as a Man* when it was first rehearsed at the Studio.

Jack Garfein remembers him studying the recorder at the time and playing duets of baroque music with William Smithers during breaks in the rehearsals. Dean once confided a harrowing story about his family and the miseries of his life in New York to Garfein as they walked toward the Royalton Hotel in Midtown. Garfein was horrified and very moved until they reached their destination and Dean began to smile. His narrative had been a hoax, a kind of acting exercise at Garfein's expense, and Dean was very pleased with its effect on his listener.

Dean had plans for several projects: to work on a stage western with Lonny Chapman; to play Woody Guthrie, with whose music he was quite taken; and to do Lorca's *Blood Wedding* in great style. But none of these ideas were realized, and he actually presented few scenes. Most rewarding for him, perhaps, was his work on Chekhov's *The Sea Gull* with Joseph Anthony. Dean played Konstantin Treplev, and according to Anthony "totally identified with the character, a fellow wanting to be a writer, on the outs with society, and in trouble with his family." Among the Method techniques he used was "substitution." He told Anthony that in order to make real for himself the character of his theatrically flamboyant mother, Arkadina, he filled his mind with images of Stella Adler during the scene. Strasberg thought the work was "lovely." [23]

But much of what he attempted at the Studio still provoked criticism. When Fred Stewart asked him to play Pierrot in a production of Edna St. Vincent Millay's *Aria Da Capo*, for instance, he did some imaginative experimenting with *commedia dell'arte* elements, working from the classic Jacques Callot drawings of *commedia* figures. Strasberg was not enthusiastic and told Dean that he wanted him to work on material that was closer to him. His often pained and intimidated expression made plain his agony at being "excoriated" publicly. For the most part he was a loner and rather reticent at the Studio. Many remember his silent observation of the sessions in which others took part. Kazan, who came to dislike Dean intensely after he worked with him in *East of Eden*, described how the actor sat "in a sort of poutish mess in the front row and scowled . . . you know, active narcissistic and so on." A more benign recollection stresses the young actor's inner magnetism, which made people want to watch him. Strasberg has an image of him scrutinizing a scene like a mole, sitting there with a quizzical look on his face, as if to say: "Is this going to work?" or "I'd like to believe, but can I do it?"

Evidently Dean did value his exposure to the acting experiments and criticism at the Studio, even if his own work there was a painful experience. ". . . the Studio makes you develop motivation," he once explained. "It makes you work from the inside out. . . . [Hollywood will] permit you to be a good actor, . . . but you really have to *want* to be one. And that desire I get from the Studio. . . ."[24] He acknowledged his respect for Strasberg's teaching in an interview in *The New York Times*, calling him "an incredible man, a walking encyclopedia, with fantastic insight." This did not necessarily mean that he fully understood what Strasberg's teaching was all about. His explanation of what acting meant to him is perhaps more a clue to his cinematic persona and to his sense of fatality than it is to what was being taught at the Studio:

To me, acting is the most logical way for people's neuroses to manifest themselves, in this great need we all have to express ourselves. To my way of thinking, an actor's course is set even before he's out of the cradle.[25]

It should be pointed out that this kind of thinking about acting is not altogether unusual among certain Method actors—even among Studio actors. The excitement generated by the "freeing" aspects of Method training sometimes leads to distortion in a performer's work—especially when the individual in question lacks discipline, guidance, and an overview of the totality of acting. Such notions as "acting as an expression of neurosis" or "feeling is everything in acting" do not accurately represent the teaching of The Actors Studio, but are, rather, the result of a little learning being a dangerous thing.

A year after Dean's tragic death in an automobile accident in September of 1955, Strasberg wept at the Studio as he discussed the loss of the twenty-four-year-old actor whose last motion picture, *Giant*, had just been released.

I hadn't cried when I heard of his death; Jack Garfein called me from Hollywood the night it happened, and I didn't cry. It somehow was what I expected. And I don't think I cried from that now. What I cried at was the waste, the waste. . . .[26]

In the summer of 1956, Arthur M. Loew, Jr., contributed one thousand dollars toward the establishment of The James Dean Memorial Fund at the Studio. Its purpose was to help actors who were "broke." At first the board of directors wanted to keep the fund secret, presumably so that actors would not come to depend on it, but would be helped through it only in real emergencies. But Loew wanted actors to know they were getting help from James Dean, indirectly, and insisted on the public announcement of the fund's existence. In time others contributed to the fund, which lasted well over a decade and helped many members, providing minor loans and in one case supporting a famous performer through a lengthy breakdown.

As the Studio's reputation in theatrical and film circles grew, it began to draw interested onlookers, curious to see what all the excitement was about. The "guest" actors who came to observe and work at the Studio included such figures as Shelley Winters, June Havoc, Dane Clark (all of whom later became members), Dorothy McGuire, Hurd Hatfield, Anthony Quinn, Yul Brynner, and Zero Mostel. They were followed by many other Hollywood and European "stars" who made it part of any trip to New York to see what was going on at the Studio. It got to the point where the members began to object to the "too much casual dropping in" of Hollywood celebrities.

Studio actors sometimes found it difficult to do the very personal, even intimate work in front of the visiting strangers. It was hard enough among one's own friends and colleagues, but visitors made the actors even more self-conscious. Michael Wager, for example, was once in the middle of a relaxation exercise, trying "to strip himself" in order to release the necessary emotion for a monologue from *The Three Sisters* he had been struggling with. Strasberg was leading him through it step by step. At the very moment he was feeling most vulnerable and most awkward, he looked up and saw Gerard Phillipe, an actor whom he hero-worshiped, sitting in the audience. He cringed inwardly as he thought to himself, "Oh shit, what must he think. . . ."

Visitors also included directors from many parts of the United States and from Holland, Italy, France, Israel, and other countries. Numerous theater artists came to speak as well as to observe. Demonstrations for the membership were given by the Kabuki company and by Jean-Louis Barrault's acting troupe when they were playing in New York. Interestingly enough, the only theater figures strictly barred from attending the acting sessions were the producer, the casting director, or any individual in an immediate position to give actors work.

Certain producers and directors such as Herman Shumlin, Roger L. Stevens, and William Wyler were welcome to attend the Studio at their pleasure, but not when they were actively casting plays or films. Charles Chaplin visited the Studio in February of 1950, around the time he was searching for a young woman to play the lead in his upcoming film, *Limelight*. A special arrangement was made for him to interview a number of Studio actresses outside the usual workshop schedule. He was especially interested in Cloris Leachman and Phyllis Ann Love, whom he arranged to screen-test on a subsequent visit to New York, when he was able to attend the sessions and speak to the members. The role, of course, finally went to Claire Bloom.

When Mrs. Samuel Goldwyn, who had given the Studio a substantial donation, wanted to attend the acting sessions and "see the people," Strasberg asked, "What for?" She told him, "Well we're casting now. It'll be good for the people." He told her, "You can sit outside in the hall and watch the people. But I'm sorry, I cannot let you into the place. I cannot let the people get the feeling that they're being watched for casting. I cannot permit this kind of thing in any way to contaminate [the work]." He explained that the pressure on the actors was great enough without exposing them to the need to make an impression on people who might help their careers. It would remain a cardinal principle that the work at the Studio was exploratory, experimental, process work and not preconceived, auditionlike "performing."

Even so, it was not always possible to say no to certain prominent film and theater people. On one occasion, when he was working on two monologues from Ghelderode's *Escurial*, Lou Antonio received what he considered puzzling criticism from Strasberg, such as: "Usually your work has more reality . . . in the past you've been . . . it's more usual for Lou's work to be . . ." It was a kind of apologetic, almost protective criticism. Antonio could not figure it out until he thought to run downstairs and ask the Studio secretary, "Who's here today?" She answered, "Carlo Ponti's in the back row." On another occasion Antonio got a screen test and a film role from John Frankenheimer, who watched him do a scene from Camus's *Caligula*.

Many actors were later cast in films and plays by a silent guest who had seen some of their work at the Studio. On occasion it was by means of fellow actors: Shelley Winters saw Dennis Weaver do a scene from Tennessee Williams's *27 Wagons Full of Cotton* and was impressed enough to recommend him to the talent department at Universal Pictures, which led to his signing with that studio in 1952 and, ultimately, to his co-starring on the television series "Gunsmoke" some three years later.

Sometimes graduation to a stage or screen role could be achieved through the teachers themselves: Eli Wallach was cast in *Mr. Roberts* by Joshua Logan on the basis of his work in Logan's class. And Wallach's work with Kazan on *Camino Real,* both at the Studio and on Broadway, was the result of the director's having seen his performance in class. Though Kazan frequently used Studio people, on occasion some specific classwork by an actor revealed new promise that the director immediately perceived. Geraldine Page, for example, was cast in Kazan's production of *Sweet Bird of Youth* on the basis of a scene at the Studio from *Mourning Becomes Electra.* Her performance in that piece revealed to him that Miss Page could play roles far removed from the spinsterish Alma type with which she had become identified in *Summer and Smoke.*

Other times casting was brought about through visitors. One of the numerous instances of this was Eli Wallach's being cast in *The Rose Tattoo* on the basis of Tennessee Williams's having seen him in the *Camino* project at the Studio and the playwright's subsequent recommendation.

Even so, the ever-present possibility of advancing one's career by being seen at the Studio, while undeniably a part of the excitement of being involved with the workshop, was never a primary objective of working there. The idea of using the Studio to showcase one's talents was anathema both to Strasberg and the members. In fact, many members objected to any hint of pressure to produce "interesting" results. It undermined the very nature of a safe place in which one could explore one's craft freely, with minimum fear of the inevitable risk of failure, that the workshop represented.

One of the special advantages of the Studio was that it offered the actor a protective environment in which he could take the time to find his way into a role without worrying about anyone's preconception of it, including his own. Strasberg infused the actors with the confidence to trust in their uniqueness. Vivian Nathan responded, when asked what she personally felt was of most value in Strasberg's teaching: "He taught me not to be afraid of *my* Mary Tyrone in *Long Day's Journey into Night.* It's my Mary. I'm not following in anybody's footsteps. The thing of value is that you find who *you* are.

If I tread this land, this scene, this particular place, it is mine. It is my view. It doesn't matter who was before me, who held this or did that. . . . It's only the doors to your own soul that have to be opened."

Preconceptions of an actor's "commercial type" were also set aside, albeit temporarily, to allow the performer to explore what his special uniqueness could bring to a role. Maureen Stapleton, categorized as an "earthy" type, tried her hand at S. N. Behrman's *No Time for Comedy*, the sophisticated humor of which she felt was "far from her." Anne Bancroft and Kevin McCarthy sang their way through *My Fair Lady*. Eli Wallach worked on a number of roles he would never be cast in commercially, including the valet Jean, opposite Anne Jackson's Miss Julie, and Hamlet in a memorable closet scene opposite Mildred Dunnock.

The Studio also allowed the actor to investigate basic approaches to the work on a play. At one experimental extreme, Lonny Chapman, an actor/playwright/director, sought to evolve a play or theater piece directly from the work of the actor rather than from a preexistent script. He would set a scene or situation—a smoky bar, for example—and ask the actors to improvise, always starting from the senses and seeing where the sensory elements took the actor. Then he would call in a playwright to observe the improvisations and to work up a script from the actors' inventions. Unfortunately, in the effort to avoid any preconceptions—Chapman did not even want to start with a theme—the work tended toward a certain vagueness, which was Strasberg's criticism of it.

A more common experiment was the actors' attempt to work on a play without a director, a procedure that has been employed a number of times over the years. One of the highlights of the work done when the Studio was located at Fifty-third Street was a presentation of O'Neill's *Desire Under the Elms*, featuring Richard Boone, Vivian Nathan, Jo Van Fleet, and Jo Anthony. In that project, the actors never rehearsed together. Having only established a physical setting in common, they prepared individually and privately, and then confronted each other for the first time at the session, adjusting to each other on the spot. The *Uncle Vanya* project in which Marlon Brando played Serebryakov, Herbert Berghof played Vanya, and Steven Hill played Astrov was another, earlier, such experiment. The actors in that case similarly agreed that they would not tell each other anything, except to use the house, a setting by Boris Aronson, as a sensory point of departure. The purpose of not discussing anything in advance was that there would be no preconceived staging but, rather, a true encounter of the characters taking place. When it was shown at the Studio, the response was highly enthusiastic. It was then suggested that they get a director to finish it. Martin Ritt worked with the actors for a week and, according to Berghof, "the whole thing fell apart."

On the other hand, a project that began with actors working among themselves and which then came to fruition under a director was Tennessee Williams's *The Rose Tattoo*. Many aspects of this Broadway production were first explored at the Studio. Directed by Daniel Mann, it brought to prominence Maureen Stapleton and Eli Wallach, who had first come to the attention of Williams and Cheryl Crawford at the workshop. Fittingly enough, the world premiere of the motion picture version of the play was the occasion for the Studio's second annual benefit.

The first film benefit for the Studio had been Kazan's *East of Eden*, released a year earlier in 1955. That film, too, had its origins in a project presented at the Studio—at least obliquely. Lonny Chapman, Will Hare, Janet Ward, Walter Matthau, and Pat Hingle, among others, had worked on a dramatization of the first part of Steinbeck's novel. The author came to see the project at 1697 Broadway and shortly thereafter decided that the portion of the book he would dramatize for the film was the second half.

Actors worked on a wide variety of projects at the Studio during the early fifties. A large segment of Brecht's *Mother Courage* was shown there. Schnitzler's *Reigen (La Ronde)* was adapted and produced by Thelma Schnee, John Stix, and Curt Conway, among others. The entire J. D. Salinger novel, *The Catcher in the Rye*, was translated into a full-length play by Fred Sadoff, who played the lead, cast, directed, set, and lit the whole production. Other projects included two additional Sadoff experiments, *Toulouse-Lautrec, His World* and James Thurber's *The Thirteen Clocks*; Lonny Chapman's productions of T. S. Eliot's *Sweeney Agonistes* and his own *Saddle Tramps*; and Fred Stewart's presentation of *The Farmer's Hotel* by John O'Hara.

Of all the Studio projects in the first half of the 1950s, two were of special significance: Calder Willingham's *End as a Man*, directed by Jack Garfein, and Michael V. Gazzo's *A Hatful of Rain*, directed by Frank Corsaro, both of which later became Broadway hits. The projects were particularly noteworthy because they dramatized Studio work at its best. For the first time, the special talent of Studio actors, nourished by the unique teaching of Strasberg, was exposed in the public arena to the surprise and delight of both critics and theatergoers. The success of these plays intensified interest in the Studio and in the distinctive brand of emotionally volatile acting that characterized the work of its members. What is more, their success seemed to confirm the efficacy of the Studio training and the possibilities for fruitful collaboration between playwright, actor, and director in the Studio environment.

Calder Willingham had dramatized *End as a Man*, his novel about life in a southern military academy, in 1951, four years after the book was published. With a running length of nearly five hours, the original script had met with no response from commercial producers and had lain in the author's drawer for over two years. After Willingham and Jack Garfein met by chance at a party, Willingham agreed to let the twenty-four-year-old director try his hand with it as a workshop project. Garfein, who was observing at the Studio, asked Strasberg for permission to work on the play as an official project. With Strasberg's approval he began rehearsals at the Studio's headquarters, then on the fifth floor of the ANTA building at 245 West Fifty-second Street.

In casting the play, Garfein chose from among the younger, unknown members because the more established Studio actors—those with Broadway and film credits—were neither responsive to the project nor to the idea of working with a novice director. Garfein says he sensed a subtle snobbishness among the old-guard members toward the new arrivals, and it seems perfectly natural that the older performers would be somewhat discriminating about which time-consuming ventures they would get involved with.

The Studio setup, which mixes older and younger or experienced and neophyte members in one working unit, has its supporters and detractors. While it goes without saying that beginning actors enjoy many benefits from interacting with and learning from those whose careers are well under way, there are those who have felt that the amalgamation of Lewis's advanced group with Kazan's neophytes was the root cause of some of the workshop's subsequent problems.

For one thing, many of the Studio's most famous actors ended their active involvement because they got tired of seeing the same fundamental acting problems being dealt with over and over again. And while they were willing to submit themselves to critical comment from their peers, they found it difficult to accept the same from "greener" members with whom they did not share the same sense of collegiality. It got to the point during the fifties where Paula Strasberg suggested to her husband that he form a "Golden Unit" that would be restricted to the more prominent members of the workshop. After deliberating over the idea for a while, Strasberg decided it would not be in the best interests of the Studio.

Among the young actors Garfein chose for his *End as a Man* project were Ben Gazzara, who at the time was working as an elevator operator at *The New York Times*, Albert Salmi, working as an usher at the Alvin Theater, and such similarly struggling thespians as Pat Hingle, Arthur Storch, Paul Richards, William Smithers, and James Dean.

Rehearsals usually ran from 10:00 P.M. until two in the morning because of the Studio's busy schedule. Kazan, seeing the Studio lights on at two-thirty one morning, went to check who was on the premises at such an ungodly hour and was astonished to find Garfein and his actors rehearsing. Visibly impressed with their devotion to their work, he told them, "You're going to be all right."

For three months the actors searched for ways to find the behavior for the young cadets they were playing. The company went so far as to visit West Point and hold military drills for themselves. Improvisations were set up that sometimes spilled over into their real lives. One afternoon after a long day's rehearsal, Ben Gazzara began taunting Arthur Storch about a personal matter as they sat with some of the other cast members in a local coffee shop. Storch reddened and became deeply upset under the merciless teasing until his fellow actors pointed out that Gazzara was baiting him in this real-life situation only to give both of them an actual taste of the bully-victim relationship that existed between their characters on stage.

After weeks of intensive work, Garfein scheduled a run-through to which he invited the playwright. The work of the actors and director so inspired Willingham that he earnestly began to apply himself to revise his drama to make it more playable. In a single night he rewrote the entire first act and set about to trim down the script to three hours in performance time. On a production budget of fifty dollars, the play was finally presented at the Studio for three performances in May and June of 1953. It was received with acclaim.

In the demonstrable enthusiasm of the entire Studio family for the project, one thing became clear: any snobbishness and standoffish-ness—real or ostensible—toward newer members was quickly dissi-pated by fine work. Garfein came to realize, as have most members over the years, that no matter how interestingly you might comment or criticize in class, no matter how bright you were, what finally counted and broke down barriers was the work you did on stage.

Word quickly got around that the project was something special and several producers showed up at the third performance to look it over, which made Garfein both excited and nervous. Kazan, also on hand, noticed the effect of the presence of the producers on the young director, took Garfein aside, and said to him, "What are you doing with those people? Now listen you! One thing: don't be im-pressed with people! I'm seeing you being impressed. What are you impressed by? It's the work that matters!"

Kazan's admonition was very much to the point, because several producers expressed an interest in presenting the play commercially. With typical Broadway logic, however, each wanted to recast the entire production with established actors. Garfein was adamant: any production of *End as a Man* would keep its original company intact as long as he had anything to do with it. Claire Heller, highly en-thusiastic about the work that had gone into the Studio project, offered to finance a modest production of the play on Garfein's terms.

The day after the third and final performance, Willingham wrote to Strasberg to express his gratitude for the "invaluable experience" of working on his play at the Studio. He also revealed his doubts about agreeing to the five-thousand-dollar production at the Theatre De Lys that Miss Heller had offered him as a result of the Studio presentation. Willingham explained his feelings about the play's com-mercial possibilities and wondered if he should not hold on to it till a "regular Broadway production" could be realized. (When he orig-inally read the script, Strasberg reportedly told Garfein, "This is Broadway material. I don't understand why nobody has done it.") Evidently, Willingham was convinced not to wait, because a month later *End as Man* was booked for a September 15 premiere at the little theater on Christopher Street.

The Theatre De Lys in Greenwich Village was a regular home for Studio members during the summer of 1953. Immediately preceding the arrival of Willingham's play, another project involving a large number of Studio personnel had finished a limited engagement there. This was Terese Hayden's special summer series of four plays, which began its run at the very time *End as a Man* was being shown uptown at the Studio.[27] Though not an official Studio project, the series was very much a part of the Studio experience. Cheryl Crawford even gave Miss Hayden permission to rehearse her plays in the Studio's rooms. Featuring such players as Patricia Neal, Eli Wallach, Anne Jackson, Leo Penn, Rebecca Darke, Salem Ludwig, Bradford Dillman, Albert Salmi, and David J. Stewart, under director Frank Corsaro, each of Miss Hayden's productions ran for one week to good notices.

Terese Hayden, a theater woman whose accomplishments included helping to found the Equity Library Theater and creating the *Players' Guide*, had been an active observer at the Studio from its inception and was to become an official member a decade later. Stuart W. Little, in his documentary history of the Off-Broadway movement, *Off-Broadway: The Prophetic Theater*, notes that her summer series was historically important because it induced "actors of solid reputation to appear off Broadway for the first time in any numbers. Within a repertory framework established actors were able to do plays and take parts they would not ordinarily have had a chance to perform in the context of their commercial careers." [28]

There were no players of "solid reputation" in *End as a Man* when it began its run at the Theatre De Lys on September 15, 1953. In fact, only one of the actors was known at all—Frank M. Thomas, a veteran of early television and of numerous westerns. Today his is probably the most obscure name in that company of what one newspaper reviewer at the time called, "one of the most fascinating displays of unknown talent . . . ever seen."

When the show was being prepared for its Off-Broadway debut, a couple of cast changes were made because some of the actors had other commitments. Mark Richman joined the company, and Anthony Franciosa, who was working as a short-order cook at the time, took over for James Dean in the small part of Starkson. Dean, in the meantime, had just won his first Broadway role in *The Immoralist*.

As the play neared its opening night, Garfein was faced with a phenomenon that other Studio members would experience in similar situations in the years ahead: the Studio's leaders—Strasberg in particular—were not about to risk the workshop's reputation by appearing to officially endorse or sponsor the public presentation of a project developed there—though they were perfectly willing to share in the credit for a work that was well received.

Strasberg had encouraged the project during its development at the workshop, but he was unwilling to put the Studio's name on the line by officially linking it with the commercial production of *End as a Man*. None of the Studio leaders, in fact, came to the opening. Garfein, following the precept that a director must do everything to foster the confidence and creative spirit of his actors, assured the company that Strasberg was behind them so that they would be up to the opening-night performance. He even took an ad out in the show's program thanking The Actors Studio for making the production possible. After the reviews came out, the Studio feelings in the matter changed, and Garfein was voted in as an official member.

The opening night of *End as a Man* marked the first time that first-string reviewers covered an Off-Broadway premiere. The overall reaction to the production was distinctly favorable, though many critics noted structural flaws in the play's second act. The response to the acting, however, was unqualified praise. The production made a star of Gazzara, whose portrayal of the calculatingly sadistic Jocko De Paris received special notice. The critical acclaim, however, was as much for the ensemble work of the actors as for individual performances. Stark Young, who saw the play in December, was moved to communicate his enthusiasm in a letter to Jack Garfein.

I must write you at once how very heartening last evening was: the admirable and human and imaginative directing; the fine spirit among the acting; and the more than often absorbing writing. I hope from this you will go on into other significant productions and that those actors will have opportunities with you or elsewhere that will allow them to exercise the same spirit and conscience. I was very much impressed not only with the living stage quality achieved but also with the mutual exchange among the characters. A great deal that our Broadway theatre needs and needs badly is illustrated or embodied in the whole occasion of *End as a Man*.[29]

Young saw the play at the Vanderbilt Theater on Broadway, where it had been shifted in mid-October as a result of its success. There, and later at the Lyceum Theatre, it continued its run for 148 performances. Work on the production had continued during its Off-Broadway run. Both Kazan and Clifford Odets came in to make suggestions about the direction and the play's structure before its Broadway opening. While it played on Broadway, rehearsals with the actors continued to keep it fresh and alive. When William Smithers and Albert Salmi left the show, indignant at Gazzara's getting star billing, they were replaced by Anthony Franciosa and Mike Kellin. But the fabric of the ensemble playing, the distinctive nature of the work, was not disturbed because of the continuing care with which rehearsals were conducted.

Later in the run, when the play was a success, there was a strike by the actors who wanted to be paid more than their Actors' Equity minimum salaries. It was soon resolved. James Dean, who had closed in *The Immoralist* by then, offered to take over Gazzara's role during the brief strike. Gazzara heard about it and never forgave Dean, who later tried to get the part in the film version as well.

Soon after, Gazzara began receiving offers from Hollywood, a number of them channeled through Strasberg, but turned them down in favor of continuing his work at the Studio. At the time, he explained his decision as a case of self-interest rather than as a grand gesture toward the Studio. "When I work with Strasberg here, I receive a more permanent value. I'll be better off becoming a real good actor for the rest of my life than zooming around in Technicolor as long as my profile holds up." [30] Kazan, shortly thereafter, in 1955, cast him as Brick in the stage production of Williams's *Cat on a Hot Tin Roof*. Two years later, he made his film debut in *The Strange One*, the motion picture version of *End as a Man*, also directed by Garfein. Sam Spiegel, the producer of the film, originally wanted Kazan to direct it; but Kazan declined, and insisted that it was Garfein's work. Six of the nine other Studio members of the original Off-Broadway cast were also used in the movie, which was billed as "the first picture filmed entirely by a cast and technicians from The Actors Studio, New York."

Gazzara, Franciosa, and Paul Richards, three of the actors who appeared in *End as a Man*, also participated in what is perhaps the single most famous project in the Studio's history, *A Hatful of Rain*. An electrifying instance of what the Studio was capable of, this production more than any other dramatized the virtues of the close cooperation that playwright, director, and actors achieved in the Studio work process, and provided grounds for the expectation of outstanding things to come. At the same time, the true nature of that work process and its relationship to Michael V. Gazzo's play has never been clearly understood.

The conception and development of Gazzo's drama have long been misrepresented in accounts and articles about the Method and the Studio that touch on his play. Almost from the beginning, the play was thought to have been improvised into existence, Gazzo simply having set down the words of actors ad-libbing situations he set up for them. When the play was produced in 1955, the publicity and local word-of-mouth certainly gave that impression. Given the background of certain Studio experiments—Lonny Chapman's, for example—and the special association of improvisation with the Studio in the public mind, the notion that the actors created the play, though understandable, is, nevertheless, unfounded. Gazzo, for his part, has denied on numerous occasions such an account of the play's origins.[31] In rightfully asserting his sole authorship, however, he has sometimes given the impression that improvisation played no role whatsoever in the work on the play. This also was not the case, as improvisations *were* used. They were not used to create the play, but they were used to help bring it to life.

The whole enterprise began when Frank Corsaro happened to drop in at the Studio one afternoon while Gazzo, Anthony Franciosa, Henry Silva, and Paul Richards were working on a scene entitled "Pot," which Gazzo had written. The piece was about a group of dope addicts trying to cope with one another, and the actors were evidently having difficulties. Corsaro, noticing that they "were sitting around looking rather dazed," asked what was going on. When they showed him the script and told him what they were trying to do, he became fascinated with the problem and its possibilities. He and the actors improvised on the scene for about two weeks, after which they presented it at the Studio. The effect of their "brilliant improvisation" was tremendous. They were encouraged to continue working on it.

Corsaro was convinced that there was a full-length play in the material and told Gazzo so. The playwright, primarily because of the improvisations the actors had done around the scene, agreed there indeed seemed to be a play. According to Corsaro, the two-week experiment "opened up a series of avenues" for Gazzo. After they sat down and discussed the possible ramifications of the material and what it suggested to them both, Gazzo went off to write the play, and soon had a rough outline of it.

It is at this point, many people have assumed, that Gazzo simply recorded the two weeks of improvisations, which is not true. According to Corsaro, who became the play's official director, those improvisations were purely exploratory and opened up the playwright's imagination to possibilities. The play's dialogue and its dramatic structure were basically his own; only a few of the play's lines were originally improvised by the actors and taken over by the playwright. In Gazzo's words, the play was "written by the process of getting up around six o'clock in the morning, sitting and smoking to a background of jazz, and using the fingers and mind."

Once the outline of the play was complete, Corsaro and his actors, now including Ben Gazzara, went ahead and spent their time building up a series of improvisations creating the lives of the characters up to the point where the play began. "At that point," Corsaro remembers, "we took the script and began to inject it with our own explorations. And Mike then watched very carefully and it was interesting what evolved. But essentially, it was his material and the adjustments he made were adjustments that would ordinarily happen—only under these circumstances, slightly more extraordinary."

As a result of the showing at the Studio, several producers became interested in the project. According to Corsaro, Jay Julien was chosen because he seemed more than sympathetic; he seemed willing to continue the project on the basis on which it had been started. Less than a year after Julien took up the option, on November 9, 1955, the play opened at the Lyceum Theatre to critical acclaim. In the cast were Frank Silvera, Ben Gazzara, Shelley Winters, Henry Silva, Paul Richards, Harry Guardino, Anthony Franciosa, Steve Gravers, and Christine White. Ironically, the very scene out of which the play evolved had to be trimmed down before the show opened in New York. According to Shelley Winters, it became apparent in New Haven that even though that particular scene was marvelously written and performed, "the whole play stopped, and for forty minutes they had a scene about junkies. They had to cut it down to fifteen minutes because it stopped the thrust of the play." Miss Winters was the last of the principal actors to become involved with the production. During the period of work on the play, her role had been played by Carroll Baker and Eva Marie Saint, among others. Miss Saint would reclaim the role in the film version of the play.

One of the most arresting qualities of the Broadway production of *A Hatful of Rain* was its unusual vitality. Brooks Atkinson called it a "brilliant Actors Studio job," marked by "living characters in an authentic environment." [32] Strasberg cited "the process by which the play was helped into being" for giving "each moment the character of life." [33] The performers sought to continue that process through a constant effort to keep the play fresh by keeping themselves on the *qui vive*. Their ensemble playing allowed for a continuing openness to momentary inspiration so that each performance was different, unique.

During the time *A Hatful of Rain* was being rehearsed at the Studio, the workshop was in cramped quarters on the top floor of the ANTA Theater on West Fifty-second Street. The Studio had moved to the top floor of the ANTA after four years (April 1948–June 1952) in its headquarters at the CBS Building, at Fifty-third Street. Through the generosity of Roger L. Stevens, the Studio occupied the old Theatre Guild rehearsal rooms in what had once been the Guild Theatre.* Corsaro and his actors booked space when and where they could, but the competition for rehearsal time from various other projects, classes, and individual actors created havoc. Strasberg found it necessary at one point to send a memo to Corsaro, admonishing him about monopolizing the precious rehearsal space: a similar problem had forced the actors in *End as a Man* to rehearse after midnight. At the time, there was no question of the Studio's moving to larger quarters. The financially strapped organization was fortunate to be where it was and to have whatever room it had.

No doubt the workshop would have liked to have stayed on there, but when the ANTA Theatre was remodeled in the summer of 1954, it was forced to leave. Suddenly there was no place to prepare scenes or work on projects, nor would there be for an entire year. The

---

* It was here that *End as a Man* and *A Hatful of Rain* were first presented to the membership. The Studio spent two theatrical seasons (September 1952–August 1954) in this, the fifth meeting place of its first five years. The following recapitulates those earlier locations: (1) The first meeting of the Studio on Sunday, October 5, 1947, at the Old Labor Stage on West Twenty-ninth Street and Broadway; (2) beginning that week, regular sessions in a rented hall in the old Union Church on West Forty-eighth Street; (3) in January 1948 classes held in a dance studio on East Fifty-ninth Street; (4) in April 1948, the move to the CBS Building at 1697 Broadway.

membership had to hunt around for rehearsal room the following season because the Studio decided, as a temporary expedient, to rent space only for class sessions twice a week. From October 1954 to June 1955, the workshop bided its time in its temporary home at the Malin Studios on West Forty-sixth Street (1545 Broadway, Room 610) while plans were laid for bringing the years of wandering to an end.

The idea of a permanent home for the Studio had been brewing for a long time. Strasberg explained what it would mean to the organization: "It's having a place where you can laugh together. In Europe the theatre has a café life, a restaurant life, a place where people can meet, play with ideas. You'd be surprised at the close relationship between creativity and *Kaffeeklatsch*. Seriously. That's why it's so important for the Studio to have its own building: to have a place not only for work, but for just getting together, for hanging around, for fooling around with concepts, all the things you can't do when you're *not* working, and have no time to do when you *are*." [34]

As the Studio became busier and the limitations of space became a problem, the need for suitable permanent lodgings intensified. In the summer of 1952 there had been negotiations to buy the Old Slavic Hall at 347 East Seventy-second Street, but an agreement was never reached. The loss of the ANTA headquarters prompted an earnest search. John Stuart Dudley, a lawyer friend of Kazan's, and Fred Stewart scouted around for a location. In "Hell's Kitchen," they found the old church building the Studio was to occupy to this day.

Soon efforts were under way to raise the money to buy and refurbish the new home. Among themselves, the members collected twelve thousand dollars on an initial pledge of a hundred dollars per member. Seed money in the amount of ten thousand dollars was pledged by Roger L. Stevens and Kazan. Most important, Jack Warner generously offered the Studio the entire proceeds of the New York premiere of *East of Eden*.

Kazan's *East of Eden*, featuring Studio members James Dean, Julie Harris, Jo Van Fleet, Barbara Baxley, Lois Smith, and Lonny Chapman, opened at the Astor Theater on March 9, 1955. The first in a long series of large-scale Studio benefits, it was organized by Morton Gottlieb, who arranged for support from a large contingent of society women under the honorary chairmanship of Mrs. Averell

Harriman and for a phalanx of celebrity ushers, including Margaret Truman and Marilyn Monroe. Concerned that people did not like to contribute a lot of money just to see a movie—"The Actors Studio wasn't even a *disease*," he pointed out—Gottlieb also arranged for a gala evening of free entertainment at an after-theater party held at the Sheraton Astor Roof. Carol Channing sang "Diamonds Are a Girl's Best Friend," accompanied by composer Jule Styne (Gottlieb had tried, but failed, to convince Miss Monroe to join in the number); Harold Arlen performed a piano medley; Howard Dietz and Arthur Schwartz sang a song composed especially for the occasion; and a relatively unknown Sammy Davis, Jr., made a smashing debut before the many gathered celebrities who had never heard of him before. The entire evening, before and after the screening, was broadcast over television and radio, creating a good deal of publicity for the Studio. The benefit, however, raised much less than the forty thousand dollars it was expected to. The members themselves raised the bulk of the money needed to make the down payment and begin renovations on the almost hundred-year-old church at 432 West Forty-fourth Street.* A variety of benefits over the years eventually

* The new home of The Actors Studio had been erected in 1858. In January of that year, the trustees of the Seventh Associate Presbyterian Church (founded in 1856) bought the property on the south side of West Forty-fourth Street, between Ninth and Tenth avenues, and shortly thereafter began construction of a church building. Sometime during its first years, its name was officially changed to the West Forty-fourth Street United Presbyterian Church in the City of New York.

According to the Reverend Edward Radcliff, whose ministry there lasted from 1925 through early 1931, the church's congregation was composed of people of Scottish and North Irish heritage who "brought with them the narrowness and conviction reflected in the terrible conflict in Ulster today." Pastor Radcliff had run-ins with the militantly anti-Catholic Orangemen, who wanted to use the church for their meetings.

After helping to celebrate the church's seventy-fifth anniversary in March 1931, Pastor Radcliff departed and was replaced by Dr. J. Campbell White. This new minister had grandiose plans for building a fourteen-story "skyscraper church" that would include the church proper, a settlement house, a Bible school, and various meeting rooms and apartments for resident students. To this end, he mortgaged the West Forty-fourth Street Church to buy the four-story tenement immediately to the west of the church. Within a short time, thanks to the precariousness of finances during the Depression, the mortgage was foreclosed and the property passed to the former owner of the building next door. The church continued to function for another decade, however, until at last, after eighty-four years, it succumbed to the thinning of its congregation's ranks. The final service of the West Forty-fourth Street United Presbyterian Church was held on November 1, 1942.

Over the next few years the building was shared by three congregations, one Greek, one Italian, and one Spanish. In June 1946 the American Theatre Wing made it possible for the Studio to pay off its mortgage and take full possession of the building.

In the course of the spring of 1955, extensive renovations were undertaken on the two-story Greek Revival building with its brick-bearing wall structure and its wood-beam and wood and cast-iron column construction. Individual members contributed their money and their labor to repaint, carpenter, and otherwise refurbish the interior of the church. A "Buy a Brick for a Buck" campaign was started to finance the work. On the lower floor a central staircase was removed and the space reapportioned to provide offices, a reception area, a Green Room, a small library, a kitchenette, and, in the rear, a rehearsal room. A new stairway was installed over one of the adjacent alleyways. The 37-by-55-foot main sanctuary on the upper floor was redesigned by Peter Larkin into a spacious performance area surrounded by a horseshoe balcony and rows of folding chairs facing the rear wall stripped to its red-brick surface. Larkin's design gave the room an aura of classic American simplicity, the kind we associate with a New England town hall or an old meeting room or courthouse.

By the fall of 1955 the Studio was prepared to move into its new headquarters. There was a sense of occasion as the organization, embarking on its ninth season, gathered for its first session there on October 14. Strasberg, taking in the renovated structure, congratulated the members on their achievement. Over the years there would be many occasions when he would pause to comment on the building's conduciveness to creativity—on its feeling of order, simplicity, and beauty. He and Kazan spoke of their plans and hopes for the workshop. That afternoon there was a strong awareness of how far the Studio had come in its first eight years, with its achievements, its growing recognition, and its potential for the future. Invigorated, optimistic, and secure in its new home, The Actors Studio felt well on its way to becoming an institution.

---

leased the church and started a school for war veterans returning to the theater. (Strasberg taught there during this period.) The Wing's Professional Training Program held on to the building for five years, moving on to new quarters in September 1951. The property was then taken over by the National Amputation Foundation to house a national rehabilitation center for American war amputees. Four years later, on February 16, 1955, The Actors Studio signed contracts for the purchase of the building from the National Amputation Foundation and later that spring took possession of its first permanent home and its headquarters to this day.

CHAPTER 4

The Studio in
the Spotlight:
1955–1959

U<small>P TO</small> 1955, the Studio's reputation had been growing steadily in professional and artistic circles, but the workshop was still relatively unknown to outsiders. The publicity attending the move to its permanent headquarters on West Forty-fourth Street helped change all that. The world began to take notice. Within a few years, this initial curiosity would be transformed into raging controversy, and the terms *Actors Studio* and *the Method* would be bandied about as many came to consider the workshop and the acting technique to be *the* theatrical phenomenon of the fifties. About the upsurge of this popular recognition and the ascendancy of The Actors Studio actor, Harold Clurman wryly observed, "It's a little embarrassing that, now that the Group has been dead for seventeen years, it's a commercial success."

Domestic interest in the Studio was fed by a constant stream of feature articles in magazines and newspapers.[1] Columnists did their share to keep the public abreast of the latest goings-on at the Studio. Celebrity "drop-ins," meaning Studio visits by such personages as Grace Kelly, Joan Crawford, Jerry Lewis, Helen Hayes, or Laurence Olivier, were always good copy. A notoriety of sorts began to develop around the workshop as visitors offered their opinions about what they had seen and heard there. While defending or attacking the Studio, these guests (and sometimes the members themselves) inevitably related some choice anecdotes about the workshop. These stories and commentaries were picked up by others, who had never been to the Studio, and were repeated and enlarged upon by them with varying degrees of awareness of the facts.

On occasion the Studio itself contributed directly, if unintentionally, to its growing fame. The organization's third annual benefit on December 18, 1956, for example, took place amidst a controversy with the Roman Catholic Church. Once again elaborate publicity was created around the event, and once again the event was the premiere of an Elia Kazan film—in this case *Baby Doll,* featuring Studio members Carroll Baker, Eli Wallach, Karl Malden, Mildred Dunnock, and Lonny Chapman in the major roles. As a letter from the Benefit Committee stated, it was to be "a real Actors' Studio affair." The provocative production of Tennessee Williams's first original screenplay, set in a decadent and rather degenerate southern milieu, aroused the moral indignation of the Catholic hierarchy. On the Sunday before it opened, Cardinal Spellman, who reportedly never saw the picture, took the dramatic step of denouncing *Baby Doll* from the pulpit of St. Patrick's Cathedral and warning Roman Catholics against seeing it.

The next day, the mayor of New York, Robert F. Wagner, publicly protested the use of his and his wife's names on the list of sponsors which had appeared on The Actors Studio Benefit letter. The Studio apologized for the inadvertent error, explaining that the names had appeared on some old stationery printed for previous occasions when their use had been authorized. In the meantime, this embroilment with the religious and political leaders of the city naturally provided considerable publicity for the film, just about guaranteeing the success of the benefit. The premiere, attended by a number of notable, non-Catholic religious leaders like Rabbi William F. Rosenblum of Temple Israel and the Very Reverend James A. Pike, dean of the Cathedral of St. John the Divine, raised approximately forty thousand dollars.

The Studio, however, had never intentionally courted the mounting domestic fame and notoriety. In fact, as the media's interest threatened to disturb the essential privacy of the work there, the Studio instituted a policy of discouraging publicity. Many requests for interviews, feature "spreads," and even television program "tie-ins" were turned down or ignored. At one Studio benefit Kazan said, "The Actors Studio is clean. It originated with one purpose: no one gets in except through audition and a desire to work and want to be in. We didn't start to have publicity. The world is full of publicity, too much publicity. We wanted to stay simple. We wanted to do what we came together to do: work."

Leo Shull, the publisher of *Show Business*, suggested various means for improving the Studio's relationship with the press. In conversations with Strasberg and in a memorandum he sent to him, he discussed the idea of annual open-house meetings as a means of enlisting "the sympathetic cooperation of the press" and creating allies among newspapermen. He argued that the Studio, as it grew into an institution, would have to "explain its work, disclose its aims and report its progress." The alternative, he pointed out, would be a continuation of the misunderstandings and unfair criticism that had already begun to develop. As it happened, no action was taken on his suggestions.[2]

Foreign interest in the Studio, however, was a somewhat different matter. The Studio's leaders seemed more receptive to international excitement over the organization's emerging role on the American theatrical scene. Through institutions such as ANTA, playwrights, actors, directors, singers, and dramatic critics from around the world were privileged to observe sessions at the workshop. During the 1959–1960 season alone, the Studio played host to visitors from Argentina, Brazil, Costa Rica, Denmark, England, Finland, the Netherlands, Norway, the Philippines, Portugal, Sweden, Venezuela, India, France, Israel, Ireland, and Greece. Representatives of various European publications, Radio Free Europe, and the United States Information Agency were welcomed to publicize the Studio abroad.[3]

Underlying the policy of encouraging international interest was the directors' desire to legitimize the Studio as an institution by earning foreign recognition of the workshop's importance to the future of the American theater. The Studio therefore responded with special interest to an inquiry from Kenneth Tynan, who was seeking the workshop's cooperation for a major television program about the Method for England's Independent Television. With Penelope Gilliatt as writer, and featuring interviews, discussions, and filmed segments of actual Studio work especially arranged for the program, the nearly two-hour broadcast was to be the first European attempt at a close examination of the "new" American acting phenomenon. As with many other projects in which the Studio was involved, the Tynan program was to prove highly controversial.

The program opened with a dialogue: actor Brian Bedford suggesting that the Method could inject a new vitality into the English theater and actress Yvonne Arnaud disagreeing completely. By way of clarification, the viewer was next taken to The Actors Studio itself, where Geraldine Page, on film, worked on a scene from *Miss Julie* for which Strasberg had suggested certain improvisational approaches. The artistic director then analyzed where he felt she had succeeded and failed, following which, Lenka Peterson performed a "private moment"—one of Strasberg's highly controversial innovations in acting training. This exercise, designed to help the actor feel "private in public" by having him create behavior he would normally stop if intruded upon, can often be statically realistic, but it can also be emotionally charged. In this case, Miss Peterson behaved as if she were at home, alone; after due preparation, the rather gentle and soft-spoken actress turned on some Hungarian music and proceeded to perform a wild and tempestuous Gypsy dance. After the dance, Miss Peterson, who loves circus clowns and clowning, practiced some pratfalls. It was a funny "private moment."

A discussion on those two pieces of work and on the Method in general followed. Taking part were a cross-section of American and English actors, including Rex Harrison, Robert Morley, Wendy Hiller, Orson Welles, Eli Wallach, Kim Stanley, and others. In addition, there were interviews about the Method pro and con, with Tennessee Williams, Arthur Miller, Peter Ustinov, and Strasberg himself. These latter parts of the program set up the nature of the disagreements over such issues as language, emotion versus meaning, professional discipline, and the relationships among playwright, actor, and author. But these exchanges were essentially surface and inconclusive.

Except for Robert Stevens, who had recently been playing the title role in John Osborne's *Epitaph for George Dillon*, and Kenneth Haigh, who created the role of Jimmy Porter in *Look Back in Anger*, both of whom spoke strongly in favor of the Method, the English actors were critical of the Studio procedures and techniques and a little supercilious in expressing their opinions. After Strasberg's segment, Morley commented, "That man uses twenty words where one would do." Miss Hiller asked, "Wasn't it true that The Actors Studio was a workshop for out-of-work actors?" After the show, Kay Kendall half-apologetically told Eli Wallach, "We English are so square, we have to smuggle our tits past customs!"

The Studio actors were on the defensive throughout and not so coherently persuasive as they might have been. The result was an entertaining television program, but one that did not dispel certain basic misunderstandings about the Studio's work. The Studio would always have sympathetic theater friends in England, but this program did not contribute much to its recognition with the theater-conscious English public.

The Actors Studio and the Method of course had been known in England long before the Tynan telecast. All the films featuring Studio members were well known, and there had been a great deal of discussion in theatrical circles about what was happening on the New York stage. Earlier that very season in London, the English had gotten a potent taste of the Studio influence at its best when Kim Stanley appeared as Maggie in *Cat on a Hot Tin Roof*. But one figure in particular had aroused special curiosity about the strange American acting "school" because of her international prominence and the glamour associated with her name. Two years earlier this actress had been the object of extensive publicity in England during her filming of *The Prince and the Showgirl* with Laurence Olivier. The fact that such a luminous star had been attending sessions at The Actors Studio, and that Paula Strasberg, the wife of the artistic director of the workshop, was her acting coach on the film, drew attention to the organization, as her attendance at the workshop, several years earlier, had aroused American curiosity about it.[4]

Marilyn Monroe generated publicity wherever she went, and her involvement with the Studio was grist for the publicist's mill. "Everybody wanted to know what the Actors Studio was that the phosphorescent Marilyn should be concerned with it," said Harold Clurman.[5] She had become involved with the workshop when the move to West Forty-fourth Street was being planned, but her name really became associated with the organization during its first season in the new headquarters. Over the years her presence there played a large part in its growing fame. Ironically, however, she never did become an official member.

Miss Monroe's interest in what the Studio had to offer was genuine and deep-rooted; it had been foreshadowed at earlier stages of her career. At the very beginning of her work in films in 1947, she had been a student at The Actors Lab in Hollywood. There, under Morris Carnovsky and his wife, Phoebe Brand, Miss Monroe had first encountered the Group Theatre kind of training. The experience had had no visible effect on her talents at the time, but it did bring her face to face with some of the basic problems she was to struggle with over the years—her difficulty in concentrating and relaxing.

The artistic leaders of the Studio were not the first to respond to the qualities which they felt made Miss Monroe an actress of unusual potential. In 1951 she became a student of Michael Chekhov, and during her course of study with him played Cordelia to his King Lear in Hollywood. Chekhov considered her an actress of unusual sensitivity. He decried the waste of her talent in insignificant parts and predicted that her great promise would be fulfilled in screen roles of increasing depth and dimension.

In New York, three years later, Cheryl Crawford met Miss Monroe for the first time at a dinner party, and the actress, by now an established movie star, spoke of her ambition to become more than a Hollywood personality. Miss Crawford suggested The Actors Studio and a meeting with Strasberg. Kazan, who had known the actress in California, also recommended that she study with Strasberg and arranged a meeting. Before long, she began private lessons in Strasberg's home.

After this preliminary kid-gloves treatment to reassure her, Miss Monroe began to attend Strasberg's private classes at the Malin Studios and to observe at the Studio.[6] She soon presented her first piece of work in the private classes: Molly Bloom's monologue from James Joyce's *Ulysses.* Encouraged by her progress, she subsequently worked on Brieux's *Damaged Goods* with Delos V. Smith, Jr., on Lorna from *Golden Boy* with Phillip Roth, on Holly Golightly from *Breakfast at Tiffany's* with Michael J. Pollard, and on Blanche from *A Streetcar Named Desire* with John Strasberg.

At the Studio, Miss Monroe was shy and diffident. Delos V. Smith, Jr., who was an official Studio observer as well as a family friend of the Strasbergs, would pick her up and bring her to the Studio and sit beside her during the sessions. Afterward they would go on to Strasberg's private class, returning to the Studio for the five o'clock sessions of the Playwrights Unit on Mondays and of the new Directors Unit on Wednesdays. Earnest in her desire to learn and grow as an artist, Miss Monroe would sit quietly among the Studio members and eagerly absorb the work going on. In Strasberg's words, "She had a luminous quality—a combination of wistfulness, radiance, yearning—that set her apart and yet made everyone wish to be part of it . . ." [7] Roy Schatt's photographs of her at the Studio are startling confirmation of that description. Sitting there, with no special makeup and no special lighting, she stands out from the group as if a nimbus shone about her.

Even so, her diffidence had a practical effect in her reluctance to perform. When she had gained a certain confidence through her work in the private classes, Strasberg asked her to prepare a scene for the Studio itself. Alan Schneider suggested she try Sabina from *The Skin of Our Teeth*, but after some thought she decided against it. She considered doing Grushenka from *The Brothers Karamazov*, but that, too, was set aside. When Strasberg asked Maureen Stapleton to work with her, the two actresses selected a scene from Noel Coward's *Fallen Angels*. After two weeks of rehearsals, they decided, in Miss Stapleton's words, "that they didn't have the facility one should have for playing Coward's two 'ditsy' broads." Miss Stapleton suggested they try something else, and they finally settled on Eugene O'Neill's *Anna Christie*.

Miss Monroe worked diligently on the role of Anna Christie. Over the next several weeks, she studied the play with the help of Arthur Miller, whom she was to marry some months later, in June of 1956, in a wedding ceremony at which Strasberg was to give her away. They analyzed the text together and even acted out sections, with Miller taking the part of Old Chris. She was plagued with fears about remembering the lines, never having had to learn so many at one time as a movie star. Helpfully, Miss Stapleton suggested the old device of writing out the lines in longhand. But the closer they came to the performance, the more she would forget, so Miss Stapleton recommended leaving the script on the table during the scene. Should she "go up," she would have it there to consult. Miss Monroe demurred, "If I do that now, I'll do it the rest of my life." When they finally performed the scene, she was word perfect; it was the first time they had gone through the entire piece without a single mistake.

Miss Monroe took a special interest in the physical production of the scene. From her film experience, she knew a great deal about lighting and sets and was very careful about how they were arranged. Moreover, she brought empty bottles and all sorts of props from her apartment for the scene. The performance date was canceled again and again because of last-minute "nerves," but finally set in February of 1956. The two actresses wrote other people's names in the Studio scene book so that the session at which they performed would not turn into a circus, but it was nonetheless crowded with curious members. Before the "curtain" they eased their nerves with coffee laced with Jack Daniel's.

Most of the onlookers were genuinely impressed with Miss Monroe's sensitivity, but felt that Miss Stapleton, who says she herself "was a wreck," acted at less than top form because of her concern for the painfully nervous actress. Strasberg angrily disagrees with this assessment and insists Miss Stapleton was excellent. Those Studio members who say otherwise, he argues, are expressing a certain prejudice against Miss Monroe, whose presence in the workshop they resented. By claiming that Miss Stapleton did less than her best because of her worry over her partner, they are seeking to qualify Miss Monroe's achievement. "Maureen did as well as she could do," Strasberg explained. "Marilyn did as well as she could do. Marilyn's quality on the stage . . . was phenomenal. I'm sorry. I've seen Jeanne Eagels, and I've seen Pauline Lord, and I've seen Laurette Taylor, and her quality on the stage was unbelievable." In his expert opinion, Miss Monroe stole the scene from the highly talented Miss Stapleton by virtue of the delicate tremulousness of her acting. He was very gentle with her in his analysis of the work and praised her courage for making the effort of appearing in public before such a highly critical audience for the first time.

The scene from *Anna Christie* was the only work Miss Monroe ever did at the Studio, but her involvement with and support of both the workshop and Strasberg were to continue and to grow. In 1959 there were plans for a television version of Somerset Maugham's *Rain* with Strasberg directing her in the Jeanne Eagels role. The playwright was quite thrilled with the idea of Miss Monroe playing Sadie Thompson, but unfortunately the project never materialized.

Around the same time, the actress demonstrated her feelings about Strasberg and the Studio by contributing ten thousand dollars to the organization to allow him to make a theatrical research trip to Japan. "His study of the work of the Japanese theatre is important and necessary for the members of the Actors Studio," she explained.* It would not be her last gift to either Strasberg or the Studio.

---

* Financial problems and other pressing obligations forced him to abandon his plans for the trip. He would finally visit Japan during the 1970s.

The notion of sending Lee Strasberg off to Japan to study its theater for the benefit of The Actors Studio—and, by extension, for the benefit of the American theater as a whole—was consonant with what Miss Monroe and others saw as his emerging role as a combination teacher/scholar/theoretician/innovator on the American theater scene. His "deep and unique contribution" in that respect was first acknowledged publicly by Kazan, who wrote warmly and enthusiastically of his mentor/colleague at the time of the campaign to buy the Studio's new home. Reviewing Strasberg's work up to that time, Kazan stated that "the Studio is the present and most complete expression of his genius for enlarging the horizons of creative people." He further declared, "The final fact is that our whole theater would have been less vital and less ambitious without the influence of this one man who has given so quietly and so unceasingly to so many people, because it is his nature to study and to think and to teach." [8]

Strasberg's intellectual activities during his years with the Studio also contributed significantly to his reputation as an *homme du théâtre*. In 1953 he was invited to prepare articles on David Belasco, Michael Chekhov, Mrs. Fiske, and others for the prestigious *Enciclopedia dello Spettacolo*.[9] Four years later, he wrote the introduction to a new edition of Diderot's *The Paradox of Acting* and William Archer's *Masks or Faces?* and was given the signal honor of composing the article on acting for the *Encyclopaedia Britannica*, replacing in part Stanislavski's own essay on directing and acting.[10] On June 28, 1957, he proudly read his three-thousand-word entry to the members of the Studio, noting what he had been forced to leave out as he went along. That same day, Henry A. Kissinger wrote to Strasberg to express his delight at the artistic director's acceptance of an invitation to address the Harvard International Seminar, of which Kissinger was the executive director. (Strasberg made a good enough impression to be invited back by Kissinger the following year.) There were to be many such invitations.

Strasberg was keenly aware of his and the Studio's evolving role. From the time the Studio moved into its new home, there had been continuous soul-searching about how best to implement the potential of the workshop, how to extend its functions so as to guide it along the most productive channels, how, in short, to turn it into a vital and enduring institution. As the primary creative force behind the Studio, Strasberg had many ideas he hoped to realize in that direction.

One of these was in the area of publishing. Strasberg had long been interested in writing a history of the Method and of editing and collaborating on various books on the theater. Such projects seemed terribly elusive until the end of 1958, when Ivan Obolensky, of McDowell, Obolensky, Inc., entered into negotiations to start an extensive publishing program with Strasberg and the Studio.

There was an excited exchange of ideas. Strasberg proposed a first English translation of the complete works of Stanislavski, but that idea was abandoned after some opposition from Elizabeth Reynolds Hapgood, translator of the existing American editions.[11] An entire "Actors Studio Series" was projected, with volumes on the Method from both a historical and theoretical point of view. Strasberg was particularly excited about a companion "International Theater Series" that was to consist of several histories of the theater, to be written by outstanding theater scholars and edited by himself. Strasberg had long felt that "purely academic" history of theater was insufficient. He proposed to ask various questions of the participating scholars so that they could address themselves to actual "practitioner" considerations. He would serve as the catalyst, injecting himself into the work in an effort to stimulate his collaborators to search for the problems that they themselves might not be interested in. One area he thought to have closely examined was the question of how professional acting got started.

Sadly enough, the Obolensky publishing program never got beyond the letter-writing stage. Money was lacking and the epistolary enthusiasm petered out. It was soon replaced, however, by plans for a new venture, a "Weidenfeld project," which got as far as the drawing up of a contract for a six- to eight-volume theater history with the Strasberg-as-catalyst format. This latter undertaking seemed so promising that Strasberg discussed it eagerly and at length with Studio members, something the highly cautious artistic director normally would not do. It must have been somewhat embarrassing for him when the whole enterprise collapsed from indecision and inaction.*

There were a number of other projects that did not work out for the Studio during the late fifties. Any one of them might have

---

* Strasberg has projected volumes that have not been forthcoming on other occasions, as well. During the late thirties, for example, he promised "a full-length critical study of the history of the development of the art of acting," which was never written. See *Theatre Workshop* 1, no. 2 (January–March 1937): 94. He is currently working on two books he hopes will finally see print.

had enormous influence on the future of the organization. The State Department approached the Studio about preparing several plays to tour Europe and Russia in repertory. Negotiations were started on behalf of the project by the National Arts Foundation in September 1955. Plays were discussed, Studio members were approached, but matters never developed any further. Both the ABC and CBS networks proposed to establish working relationships with the Studio, either of which would have given the workshop national exposure and an assured income. The offers, unfortunately, came to nothing.

Working relationships between the Studio and at least two major schools were also up for consideration during this period. In 1959 Archibald MacLeish, whose play *J.B.* had been directed by Kazan the previous year, discussed with the director the possibility of the Studio taking charge of the theater activities at the new Loeb Drama Center at Harvard University. Much more promising, however, was an affiliation that David O. Selznick tried to establish between the Studio and Brandeis University in Waltham, Massachusetts. Selznick's plan was to have the Studio actively organize and supervise the school's complete theater arts program with Kazan and Strasberg serving as supervising directors. As part of the arrangements, the Brandeis drama students were to be allowed to observe at the Studio, and the workshop was to provide both the faculty and guest lecturers, including major names in the American theater, to the university. When it seemed that such an ambitious program would not work out, Selznick suggested the Studio establish a permanent summer theater festival in Waltham. None of these ideas came to fruition.

The main reason for the failure to realize any of these projects was that the Studio by its very nature was not set up to follow through on the various proposals. In a word, it was a cottage-industry arts organization being asked to function as if it were an institution richly endowed with funds and staff.

There is another more subtle consideration, too: Strasberg and his colleagues were not in fact especially eager to widen the operating base of the workshop. A board of directors, for instance, might have been brought in to develop the organization into a major artistic force, but such a step would have meant going "public" in a way that was anathema to Strasberg and his associates. The artistic director in particular wanted to be answerable to no one, and on the several occasions when proposals were introduced to broaden the Studio administrative structure, Strasberg made it clear that he would leave if his authority were compromised.

Moreover, while Strasberg had very real, if not precisely defined, aspirations for the growth of the Studio, Kazan and Miss Crawford did not seem to fully share his ambitions; nor did they feel any urgency to apply their productive talents toward the realization of those ambitions. The artistic director, for his part, was not essentially an initiator. Strasberg functioned best when ideas were presented to him for consideration, clarification, or development. His very real contribution to the Studio was his time, his advice, and his teaching genius. If others did not create opportunities and supply the active ingredients, namely, cash and entrepreneurial know-how, to see them fulfilled, his special talents could not do so. Even with projects that were most personally important to him—those publishing ventures, for instance, which would have been such a happy extension of his fundamental nature and interests as scholar, bibliophile, and pedagogue—he was unable to *make* things happen on his own.

The result was that while Strasberg had hopes for the evolution of the Studio, he and his associates nevertheless proceeded cautiously with a kind of wait-and-see attitude. Unable or unwilling to define and implement a specific program for the workshop's future, Strasberg, as artistic director, took what might be characterized as a "reactive" stance, watching for various developments to come to a head while taking little or no definitive action to help them along. Or, conversely, he allowed himself to be carried along with plans that failed to satisfy him fully.

This latter phenomenon is illustrated with regard to the Studio's experience in theatrical production during the fifties. Not since the end of the first season had the question of the workshop's role vis-à-vis production come up for serious attention. The success of *End as a Man* and *A Hatful of Rain* thrust the whole question center stage once again. "How," it was asked, "can the Studio properly involve itself in the production of projects emanating from the workshop without threatening the developmental work of the actors?" The feeling among the directors was that the Studio should profit financially from such productions while assuming a responsibility for their quality. The situation was complicated because the Studio leaders were not prepared to commit the workshop to becoming a full-scale producing unit with a regular seasonal schedule as part of the New York commercial theater.

There had been continuing pressure from within the Studio to expand to the point where involvement with productions was commonplace. Most of the members were strongly in favor of a theater evolving out of the workshop, but their eagerness was met with caution, tentativeness, if not outright resistance, by the directorate. When Liska March was approached by three businessmen who wanted to give her $150,000 to start a small Actors Studio theater, she brought the idea to Lee and Paula Strasberg. She was told to forget about it: they had bigger ideas than that.

Strasberg was opposed to anything "small-scale" when it came to the public presentation of plays under the Studio's banner. While Kazan seemed to be somewhat in favor of the members having a sort of Off-Broadway outlet where the project work of the Studio could be shown, the artistic director felt "that the Studio name and the Studio effort must be completely official and authoritative— otherwise it is dangerous to the work." He was not going to support a setup that, he said, would simply mean using the Studio as a showcase. His feelings in the matter were colored by an unmistakable concern for his personal prestige. "I am not willing my name, and my authority, and my responsibility to it. If we do anything as The Actors Studio, it has to bear not the stamp of the individuals of The Actors Studio, but the stamp officially of those people who carry the official responsibility for the Studio, which means the directors."

Yet the prospect of a large-scale theatrical venture was contemplated with a certain trepidation. Those in charge, having been through the experience of the Group Theatre with all its problems and its ultimate collapse, were loath to move until they felt the time and conditions were propitious. "Certainly while the vista intrigues us," Strasberg said in his remarks concluding the Studio's 1956–1957 season, "the responsibility slightly, not exactly frightens us, but nonetheless appalls us. We're not easily frightened. We bear up. But it is not a light goal or task to undertake. So I frankly do not quite know what is to happen."

By 1958 the directors finally seemed to have discovered a way to reconcile Strasberg's hopes for a large-scale, "authoritative" Actors Studio theater and the members' desire for a smaller-scale outlet for the experimental project work. A program encompassing two theaters was planned. In the larger theater, fully professional presentations, which would be advertised, worked on, and considered as official Actors Studio productions, would be put on. Two plays in which the Studio was interested, Archibald MacLeish's *J.B.* and Michael V. Gazzo's *Night Circus*, were considered as strong possibilities for this major part of the project. With Kazan responsible for this "first theater of The Actors Studio," Strasberg agreed to cast his vote for the "second" theater, which would showcase Studio projects at the Bijou Theater, and which would proceed with a production of Sean O'Casey's *The Shadow of a Gunman*.

The Studio directorate were especially keen on making their theatrical debut with the MacLeish play. Strasberg felt very strongly that Kazan should do the play as part of his own progress as a theater artist. He believed Kazan could provide "the vitality, the veracity, the aliveness, the vigor, the theater enthusiasm, which plays like that need." Moreover, it would demonstrate the Studio's range and versatility in dealing with nonnaturalistic drama. It would be an excellent opportunity to show how a Studio artist could avoid the pitfalls of turning such a play into a "rather pageant-like, rather pictorial, rather verbal" production. Gazzo's *Night Circus*, on the other hand, would be a highly suitable second entry, representing the kind of realistic play that could be brought to life most fruitfully through the work processes of the Studio. And though it needed revision, it was felt that Kazan could easily carry it off.

Then the directors discovered they did not have access to the MacLeish play after all. By the time the Studio expressed interest in presenting it—Kazan had been a little hesitant at first—the rights had already been assigned to Alfred de Liagre, a friend of MacLeish's. Though the Studio would have been willing to coproduce the play, there was no reason for de Liagre to enter into such an agreement. He had Kazan as director and could use whomever he wanted from the workshop membership.

This left only the Gazzo play, which Strasberg was reluctant to present as a first choice. He was concerned that without the balance of the MacLeish play, *Night Circus* "would only continue the kind of image [of the Studio], not that which we wish to undo, but which we wish to redress. We want to give a true image of ourselves. This is one side of our work. But by doing it as a first thing, it would seem to accept the emphasis that other people have put upon our work."

In any case, Kazan suddenly decided that Gazzo's play was not in condition to be done, and that the author was rushing into production. (In his introduction to *Famous American Plays of the 1950s*, Strasberg said of the play: "In its original version, it contained some excellent scenes, but even more original was its effort to capture the sound, smell, and rhythm of a jazz world. Somehow, this was lost in the final version. The ear for fresh and colorful dialogue remained, but separated from an environment which could give it life [i.e., the Studio, in which the playwright's earlier *A Hatful of Rain* was nurtured], it seemed overblown and forced.") Jay Julien wound up producing it without the Studio, with Frank Corsaro directing. Starring Ben Gazzara and Janice Rule, it quickly opened and closed at the Golden Theatre in December of 1958. Thus, the Studio was left with no play for its "first theater" and only the "second theater," Bijou project on the horizon.

Word that The Actors Studio was about to embark on the production of plays occasioned a good deal of interest in New York theatrical circles. Rumors about the workshop's negotiating for the Bijou Theater began in mid-June of 1958. Cheryl Crawford and William H. Fitelson, her attorney (and a member of the Studio board), quickly denied them, explaining that the Studio itself was not going into commercial production. This would have threatened its tax-exempt status under its New York State charter. The Bijou Theater was being leased to a corporation wholly owned by Miss Crawford and Joel Schenker, her business partner in the venture. The producers planned to put on a variety of plays, it was announced, a number of which would be cast exclusively with Actors Studio members.

Miss Crawford had become friendly with Schenker, the president of the Webb & Knapp Construction Corporation, in 1956. She brought him to observe at the Studio, and they soon formed a theatrical partnership. In 1958 they took a year's lease on the six-hundred-seat Bijou and raised $150,000 to produce three plays there. The plan was for the Studio to receive 20 percent of the profits with the actors working at lower salaries than usual and with no star billing. The first production scheduled was the O'Casey play.

The Shadow of a Gunman has been worked on as a project since

February 1955. For two months, under the direction of Jack Garfein, the actors, with familiar intensity, rehearsed as many as six nights a week, often from 8:00 P.M. to two or three in the morning. There was a conviction that they were involved in another "major" Studio event. In April the play was put on for three performances before Studio members and friends. It was well received. Then, after looking around for a potential Broadway producer, Garfein went off to make the movie version of *End as a Man*. At the same time, Kazan came to feel that The Actors Studio itself should do the play. And so Miss Crawford came into the picture.

The road to Broadway, however, was not to be smooth. Strasberg wanted the production recast with stars. He suggested Garfein get in touch with Rod Steiger and Geraldine Page. Garfein demurred, agreeing to replace only one leading actor: the role of the young girl would go to Susan Strasberg. He insisted that, aside from certain character people who were necessary to the play but not available among the Studio membership, all the actors who had played major roles in the Studio project should do so on Broadway. It was "the work that counted," not the stars. Strasberg reluctantly agreed, but was upset about it because he felt that the well-known actors of the Studio could best reflect the work of the Studio, an opinion he still holds.

As an Actors Studio production, *The Shadow of a Gunman* came under the watchful eye of the workshop's leaders. When Kazan and Strasberg saw the show in rehearsal, they felt it was in appalling condition—lifeless and tepid. In an ordinary commercial situation, Garfein, who had returned from filming *The Strange One* to direct the play, might have been fired at this point. Under the circumstances, however, there were certain obligations to support the work. And though the leaders felt the production was terrible as it was, they did not think it irretrievable. Since Kazan could not actively participate in rectifying the situation because he was in the midst of directing *J.B.*, it was decided that Strasberg would come in the following day to discuss with Garfein what had to be done to save the show. If they succeeded in overcoming the production's problems, the show would open. If not, not.

When Strasberg arrived the next day, Garfein, who had not expected him, asked him not to interfere with the rehearsals for fear it would demoralize the actors and hurt the show. Strasberg angrily departed. When previews started the following Friday, there were still severe problems with the production. Kazan and Strasberg decided that if certain improvements were not immediately realized, the show should not open. Garfein felt the Studio's moving in at this point was a usurpation of his authority. Strasberg argued, with justification, that the director had agreed to work under the aegis of The Actors Studio, and that "what the Studio is responsible for, the Studio has authority over."

What followed was as unpleasant a falling-out as any in the annals of the New York theater. Garfein offered to buy out the production, but Miss Crawford refused his offer and told him either to agree to Strasberg's coming in or to accept the closing of the show. At Kazan's suggestion the director invited Strasberg in as his teacher and friend to "advise" on the presentation. When it became clear to him that more than advice would be forthcoming—that Strasberg was in fact going to direct the actors—Garfein resigned from the play and placed the matter in the hands of his lawyer.

Rehearsals were called off and the opening postponed. Then a compromise was eventually worked out. Strasberg stepped aside, and Garfein, who was to continue directing the play, promised to retain the changes Strasberg had made in his daughter Susan's scenes. The Studio, represented by Miss Crawford, was still in fact the producer, but before the show opened, The Actors Studio name was removed from the marquee. On opening night Mrs. Sean O'Casey lavished praise on the production and some of the reviews were quite favorable. Brooks Atkinson, in *The New York Times,* called the performance "masterly."

But the ill-will between the director and the Studio leaders was not to abate. The producers reasserted their control over the production once it was apparent it would have a "run." Garfein was barred from the theater and any further contact with the cast. Strasberg came in to work with the actors. Despite the favorable reviews, he was displeased with the presentation—as were a good many people in and out of the Studio—and, agreeing with the negative criticisms from various quarters, tried to remedy its shortcomings.

When challenged with the production's shortcomings by Studio critics, however, Strasberg responded with characteristic defensiveness. Despite the fact that the Studio's name went back on the marquee the morning after the reviews came out, he told the National

Theatre Conference of 1958, "In the production of *The Shadow of a Gunman* there are eleven people in the cast.* Four people are members of Actors' Studio [*sic*]; six people are non-members of the Actors' Studio [*sic*]; and one other member is caught in between. That is Susan Strasberg, who may have the talent of the Actors' Studio, but does not have its training. That is the make-up of the cast. Yet when the production is done, everyone here blames it on Actors' Studio." [12]

Around this time, Garfein heard that Paula Strasberg had told the drama editor of *The New York Times* that Garfein had not directed the production at all—that Lee Strasberg had directed it. When the matter was referred to Brooks Atkinson, he said he knew Strasberg's work and that it was Garfein's work in *Shadow* that he had reviewed. But Garfein was understandably distressed.

The young director faced yet another upset when several members of the *Shadow* company asked him to return to the Studio, which he had avoided once the trouble began. They tried to persuade him to accept Strasberg's taking over, but Garfein felt betrayed by his "weak-willed" actors. (Except for Bruce Dern, who wrote him a letter expressing his indignation at the way Garfein had been treated, he would call them all "quislings.") He thought it ironic that having fought to keep them in the production, they were now too scared to take a position in support of their director.

Not long after, the unpleasantness of the whole episode was capped when Garfein, who originally came to America as a survivor of Auschwitz and Bergen-Belsen, heard through Calder Willingham and Carroll Baker (Mrs. Garfein at the time) that Paula Strasberg was telling people that she did not believe Garfein had ever been in a concentration camp.**

For three years Garfein and the Strasbergs did not speak to one another, though they lived in the same building and often encountered each other in its elevator and lobby. It was not until the aftermath of Marilyn Monroe's death in 1962 that Mrs. Strasberg, in a mood to make amends for past unpleasantness, called one night

* William Smithers, Gerald O'Loughlin, Bruce Dern, Daniel Reed, Susan Strasberg, Stefan Gierasch, Zamah Cunningham, Arthur Malet, Katherine Squire, George Mathews, and James Greene.

** In 1963, Daniel Stern published *Who Shall Live, Who Shall Die*, a thinly disguised novelization of Garfein's story, centering on the struggle over *The Shadow of a Gunman* and touching on the director's childhood experience as a Nazi prisoner.

and said she thought they should make up. She expressed how badly she felt at what had happened and invited the Garfeins to have dinner with her and her husband. The two couples toasted their reconciliation with some champagne Miss Monroe had given Strasberg. Several years after that, Garfein was to play a central role in the creation of The Actors Studio's West Coast branch in Los Angeles.

The Shadow of a Gunman earned no money for the Studio. Neither did the "non-Studio" production of Norman Corwin's *The Rivalry*, a play about the Lincoln-Douglas debates starring Richard Boone. (Though Boone was a Studio member, this production had nothing to do with the original plan to feature Studio-created projects at the Bijou Theater. It was for all intents and purposes an independent commercial presentation, though Miss Crawford still planned to pay the Studio a percentage of any profit the play made.) The third play, Orson Welles's *Moby Dick,* was never realized. A final component of the Bijou venture that also failed to materialize was a projected Sunday evening series of special events.

An entry in that series that Miss Crawford was especially eager to present was Edna St. Vincent Millay's *Conversation at Midnight,* as arranged and directed by Eli Rill. This Studio project, featuring Don Fellows, John Harkins, Dick McMurray, Gerald O'Loughlin, William Smithers, and Arthur Storch, had created quite a stir at the workshop when it was first presented in June of 1958. Miss Crawford, in fact, had hoped to give it a full-scale Off-Broadway production.

To expedite matters, she went up to the Millay home at Steepletop in the Berkshires to talk to Norma Millay, the poet's sister, about a possible production. She invited Miss Millay to come to New York to see the play at the Studio and introduced her to Thornton Wilder and Archibald MacLeish, who were also attending the performance. Miss Millay was furious with the presentation because there were cuts and rearrangements in the material. She wanted it done exactly as written, or not at all. Miss Crawford and MacLeish took Miss Millay to Thornton Wilder's apartment in the Algonquin Hotel to try to persuade her otherwise, but she stubbornly refused to consider the matter despite the fact that Wilder and MacLeish were "madly enthusiastic" about the Studio production.

Miss Crawford was similarly frustrated with another Studio project, presented just a month earlier: Fred Stewart's *A Memory of*

Living, a pastiche arranged from the poetry of Edgar Lee Masters, Robert Frost, and Carl Sandburg. Prepared over a period of two years, this project—the first such large-scale production in the new West Forty-fourth Street home—featured two dozen Studio members re-creating the life of an American village sometime in the last century. It was set in a cemetery in which all the characters were entombed in a monumental pyramid; one by one they came to life and told their stories, before returning to their graves. Miss Crawford wanted to develop the project into a full-scale production, but was stymied by Robert Frost, who objected to having his verse used with that of other poets.

In addition to her producing efforts and her administrative responsibilities at the Studio, Miss Crawford also found time to hold an occasional seminar in theatrical production. These usually lasted about a half-dozen sessions and were attended by a wide variety of interested students ranging from Lucille Lortel and Toby Cole to Steve McQueen. (In recent years, Miss Crawford has taught a regular course in theatrical production at Hunter College in New York.) She also gave several lectures about the Russian theater based on her 1935 visit to the Soviet Union with Harold Clurman as part of her contribution to the educative process of the Studio.

Various other Studio members made similar contributions from time to time by organizing and teaching classes in their "specialties." Viveca Lindfors, for example, conducted a workshop in Strindberg's plays at one time, while Michael Wager ran a Shakespeare scene-study group. Despite the jokes and criticisms about mumbling and inarticulateness at the Studio, speech has not been totally ignored there. Edith Stebbens taught a speech class in the first year, and Mildred Dunnock did the same during the early fifties. Later on, Liska March brought in Alice Hermes, one of the most promising figures in the field, who was active at the workshop through 1970. Nevertheless, it is true that interest in each of these speech classes, while high and widespread at the start, eventually petered out—a phenomenon peculiar to all of the special offerings introduced at the Studio.

Over the years, the workshop set up classes in fencing, jazz dance, Yoga, T'ai Chi Ch'uan, and other assorted disciplines. Occasionally, Strasberg objected to some of these when he felt they were inimical to the basic approach to acting represented by the Studio. He has never approved of ballet training for the actor, for instance, because he believes such body work unavoidably entails a particular style of expression, that it "sets forms" rather than preparing the individual generally for any physical task he might be required to execute. In fact, it was on this very point that he *did* support the introduction of T'ai Chi Ch'uan instruction; he feels that the Chinese dance training is excellent preparation for flexibility and expressivity in movement.

Strasberg, always wanting to operate on the highest level, sought to bring in major theatrical figures to lecture and teach at the Studio. Gordon Craig, who had so inspired the artistic director in his youth, was invited from England, but was unable to make the trip. Others, such as the critic Stark Young, did visit the workshop.

Strasberg, in introducing and praising Young, explained how the "qualities and merits" of the evanescent art of the theater lived on only in the writing of certain perceptive and creative critics, of whom the eminent American theater chronicler was a rare and unique representative. Young, who was very touched by his reception at the Studio, remembers that during the artistic director's remarks all he could do was "stand there like an idiot and smirk." [13]

When it was decided during the first year on West Forty-fourth Street that the actors should have some body training, the man Strasberg selected was no less a personage than Étienne Decroux, the famous mime and teacher of Marcel Marceau. Kazan managed to solicit a twenty-five-hundred-dollar contribution for the purpose from Samuel Goldwyn, who wrote to the director, "I feel as you do about the importance of body work to give the actors grace and proper movement. . . ." Decroux arrived in New York in October of 1957, and, after an initial series of six lectures to the membership and invited guests, spent the next eight months giving classes at the workshop. The Studio also presented him in a public lecture on "The Art of Mime" at the Morosco Theatre on February 3, 1958.

The most tangible and long-lasting of the Studio's innovations during the fifties, however, was not the supplementary courses for the members, nor the tentative forays into production, but the long-heralded and twice prefigured Playwrights Unit, established during the 1957–1958 season.

Clifford Odets had made the first attempt to set up such a unit seven years earlier, when, in March of 1951, he gathered a group of writers for three months of biweekly meetings at the fourteenth-floor Studio headquarters on Fifty-third Street. Odets, whose play *The Big Knife* was directed by Strasberg in 1949, had frequently come to observe the work at the Studio. On one occasion he and Strasberg arranged a sort of experiment/demonstration for the members. Three actors were handed scripts for a domestic scene involving an aunt, an uncle, and a grandfather. They were given time to think about the scene and to discuss it among themselves, after which they read the scene to the class. Then Odets came forward and said, "Let me play something for you." He turned on a tape recorder and the members heard the same scene as it had really happened. In preparation for a writing project, the playwright had secretly put a tape recorder underneath his own kitchen table and recorded a real conversation between his aunt, grandfather, and uncle.

The playing of the tape demonstrated to the surprised actors the unexpected vividness and variety of the actual scene as compared with the acted version. Though the Studio members had read the scene "very nicely, very simply, very well—and seemingly logically and sincerely," in Strasberg's words, they had flattened it out a little to get a sense of the reality and a feeling of naturalness. The real scene had a surprising "fullness of excitement, vividness of response and sudden poetic leaps of expression." Strasberg recollected several years later that "The way in which [Odets's] uncle could switch from some ordinary remark to (*shouting passionately*) 'TEN YEARS OF MY LIFE!' and back to (*chattily*), 'Well, I mean, she's an idiot,' was fantastic. This was dialogue spoken by an ordinary man with an accent and a choked voice, but that ordinary voice became so vivid and expressive through the coming together of emotion and sound and meaning that it was thrilling. It would be flabbergasting to hear that tone on the stage." [14]

Playwrights were very eager to work with Odets. *The Country Girl* had opened the previous November and was in the fourth month of its run at the Lyceum Theatre at the time he was forming his unit. Over three hundred scripts were submitted to him when his plans for the group were announced. Odets read every one of them and personally chose the writers who would study with him. For three humid spring months, from late March to late June, he diligently and punctually arrived at the Studio twice a week for an intensive and incisive seminar in the craft of dramaturgy.

In his early meetings with the group, he gave the writers exercises in the form of situations they had to dramatize. For instance: "A man gets up in the morning, discovers that ten dollars is missing from the wallet in his pants pocket and by nightfall he and his wife have decided on a divorce. Write it in one scene." Generally, though, the writers brought in material they had already completed, each session being devoted to a particular playwright's work. At first, Al Saxe, Odets's right-hand man in the class, would read the members' work aloud, much to the discomfort of the writers. Apparently his voice was neither pleasing nor properly dramatic. William Gibson insisted on reading his own script, and pretty soon all the plays were being read by the authors themselves, though Odets, on at least one occasion, did the honors for one of them.

After listening to the writers' evaluation of a fellow member's work, Odets would launch into an almost line-by-line analysis of the script. His approach was very technical, and he was especially capable of helping writers to develop a sense of structure in their writing. He stressed the psychological veracity of character as it related to the dramatic movement of the play, and was adamant about removing deadwood from a script. If a line did not reveal character, advance the plot, or somehow relate to the author's central theme, it was to be excised.

A good many of the playwrights were young, idealistic, and socially conscious, all of which was reflected in their writing. They tended to criticize one another's work from the point of view of its political content. Some of them felt a necessity to challenge Odets, who they believed had abandoned his early idealism for the materialistic success of Hollywood. Tempers occasionally flared. Looking as though he were in ill health or just plain cold—he wore a big scarf to class—Odets would at times launch into a diatribe with familiar Group Theatre "vigor." He would defend his outbursts: "Do I seem angry? I'm not angry. I'm just interested." Inevitably some of the young writers responded hostilely and found the older master "severe and rather sour."

But he was also much loved by a good number of the writers who found him "patient and maternal." He had a wonderful sense of humor, and there was much laughter in the class. He was also exceedingly generous with his students, arranging for batches of tickets to shows for them and spending many hours with them individually out of class. (Sessions at the Studio sometimes ran more than four hours.) A number of his students became very close to him and continued to consult him regularly on the progress of their work. William Gibson, who went on to write such Broadway hits as *Two for the Seesaw* and *The Miracle Worker*, considered Odets one of the two best talkers he ever listened to and said of his unit, "I never learned so much, so fast, in my life," a sentiment echoed by other members of the group. The unit, unfortunately, did not continue into the following year, during which, among other things, Odets was called to appear before the House Un-American Activities Committee two weeks after having been named in Kazan's affidavit.

Almost four years passed after the demise of Odets's class before the Studio made a second attempt to start a writer's group in the spring of 1955. Then, in the wake of the workshop's move to the church on West Forty-fourth Street, Kazan felt it was time once again to try to realize the natural integration of the dramatist into the life of the Studio. He invited Robert Anderson, whose *Tea and Sympathy* he had directed two years earlier, to form a Playwrights Unit at the Studio's new home as part of the expansion and "institutionalizing" of the workshop's activities. Despite some good work, there were problems with this Unit from the beginning. The hope was to develop the writer's theatrical sensibility, to impress on him that the drama was more than a branch of literature. Few of the writers really understood the special nature of the Studio's methodology and its possibilities for the playwright. Anderson, whose background was essentially academic, was himself not really conversant with the sort of process that had made *End as a Man* and *A Hatful of Rain* possible. He was unable to coordinate the work of the playwrights, actors, and directors into a unified effort. As a result, despite certain amounts of stimulating intellectual discussion, no real progress was made toward inculcating a working technique that would richly draw on what the Studio had to offer—a goal, in fact, that would continue to elude the Unit throughout its history. Anderson left within a year.

Kazan had apparently anticipated these problems at the very time Anderson's group was being formed. With remarkable prescience, he outlined the necessities for an effective Playwrights Unit in a letter to Strasberg, undated, but probably written around 1955 (now in the archives), in which he related how he had approved a list of writers Anderson had submitted to him only to have had second thoughts about the whole project. He explained why the Studio "should interest itself in only a limited number of playwrights" who would "be chosen by the same unarticulated measures by which we choose actors or directors. . . . They should be representative of the same impulse in Art which makes us select over and over again . . . the same kind of actors." In his view, the Studio should not be running a play writing course, but should fully integrate the writers into the Studio activity. He told Strasberg that he planned to work with Anderson when he returned to the city the following January. "I should say that my job should be first of all to make them more Theatre people, less literary people. And secondly, to make them feel, to the best of my abilities, the impulse in art, and Theatre art, to which the Studio belongs. . . . Finally it is important that the equivalent be found for the playwright to the way we have worked with actors. This work with themselves and through themselves is the big contribution we can make to playwrighting [*sic*]."

But Kazan was not able to get back to work with the playwrights until more than a year later than he anticipated, by which time Anderson had long since been gone. Following Anderson's departure, the Unit was broken up into a variety of special sessions with such people as Harold Clurman, William Inge, Strasberg, and sundry directors (Frank Corsaro, among others) monitoring the class. After two consecutive seasons of this, the group "sort of dribbled away," in Corsaro's words.

In the middle of the 1957–1958 season, Kazan finally established the Playwrights Unit on a more or less permanent basis. First he selected a number of directors and asked each of them to bring in a writer with whom he wanted to work. Kazan, according to his wife, the author Molly Day Thatcher Kazan, "had come to believe that the single most important relationship in our theatre is that between the writer and his director. When that relationship is full and fruitful —not placid and not necessarily harmonious but alive and close— then the play has its best chance." It was this combination of writers and directors that was to give the Unit its "dynamic"—"The clash, the contrast, the contribution of the two crafts which have kept the Unit, whatever its faults, kicking and alive. It is this concept which makes it unique among playwrights' groups." [15]

At the beginning of the following season, Kazan found he was too busy to continue his active leadership of the Unit. William Inge and Molly Kazan were asked to take over. The bulk of the responsibility fell on Mrs. Kazan's shoulders, since she was familiar with the Unit, with the Studio, and with Strasberg's teaching. Inge moderated many of the group's sessions that year and shared the crucial choice of new writers with Mrs. Kazan, but as a practicing writer jealous of his time, his commitment never went much beyond this, although he was to remain actively involved until the spring of 1960. At Mrs. Kazan's suggestion, Arthur Penn was invited to share in leading the Unit. He picked new director-members for the group, with Strasberg's approval, and provided a welcome balance to the temperaments of the other two leaders. In the long run, however, his participation was also severely limited by his own successful career as a director.

Molly Kazan and Inge had increased the membership of the Unit when they took over in 1958. The idea of directors bringing in writers was set aside because they "occasionally got enthusiastic about relatively unpromising writers, whom they had no way of comparing to other candidates." The focus shifted to seeking out a variety of writers rather than only those who shared, in Kazan's phrase, "the same impulse in Art." The only criterion for membership became talent. Writers submitted examples of their work—scenes, short stories, a chapter from a novel, or a sample of poems—and were selected accordingly. Michael Wager, who served as Mrs. Kazan's assistant and as play-reader for the group, brought authors and directors together for the work in the Unit. The sessions, which had been held in the ground-floor rehearsal room at the back of the Studio, were moved upstairs to the main room. The time of the meetings was also shifted from the evenings to Tuesday afternoons, making it possible for many more actors to participate in the Unit's work. This last was very important, since the Unit's leaders wanted to move away from staged readings of the plays under consideration, which had more or less been the procedure under Kazan, to full performances with as much of a physical production as the Studio could offer.

The evaluations after the scenes could be quite lethal. At first, non–Playwrights Unit members of the audience were asked to leave the room for these postmortems. But Studio actors objected to this policy and were eventually allowed to remain, although not to comment on the work. The performers in the plays presented, however, were sometimes invited to contribute to the discussions.

Though Kazan's vision of a writers' group that would be thoroughly integrated into the Studio methodology was far from realized, the Playwrights Unit was a vitally functioning segment of The Actors Studio by the 1959–1960 season. The membership included many prominent names: James Baldwin, Lorraine Hansberry, Arthur Laurents, Norman Mailer, and Edward Albee. Among the works presented for examination during that year were Howard Sackler's *Jersey Jim and Mr. Welk*, directed by Alfred Ryder and featuring Zero Mostel and Arthur Storch; two plays by Molly Kazan, *Rosemary*, directed by Gerald Freedman, and *Paradise Hotel*, directed by Frank Corsaro, with Anne Bancroft, Eli Wallach, Piper Laurie, Billy Daniels, and Clifton James in the casts; the first presentation of Norman Mailer's *The Deer Park*, directed by Corsaro, with Anne Bancroft, Patrick O'Neal, and Kevin McCarthy, among others; and the American debut of two of Albee's plays, directed by John Stix: *The Zoo Story*, with Lou Antonio and Shepperd Strudwick and *The Death of Bessie Smith*, with Margret O'Neill, George Gaynes, John McCurry, and Harold Scott. The decade ahead would witness further changes in the makeup of the group, both in leadership and in membership, but the activity of the Unit would continue right into the seventies.

The primary enterprise of the Studio, of course, remained the two weekly acting sessions presided over by Strasberg. The procedure would remain the same for almost twenty-five years: Every Tuesday and Friday, shortly before eleven, members congregating in the reception area on the first floor would begin filing upstairs to take seats in the three sections of tiered platforms abutting the playing area. In the front row of the center section, a wood and canvas director's chair with the name "Lee" painted on it would sit waiting for the artistic director to take his place. At its left would be a low table with a tape recorder, a windup alarm clock, and an index card with the scenes scheduled for the day.

Shortly after eleven Strasberg would enter the room, drape his coat over the back of his chair before sitting, and proceed to read off the title of the first scene. The lights would go off. The actors might begin immediately or, more usually, would start after several minutes in preparation. Often, the first pair of players to work on any given morning would have been on their set, relaxed and in concentration well before the beginning of the session. The actors usually rehearsed their scenes for a long time before presenting them, but not always. On occasion they might be trying an improvisation to create the life of their characters in the moments before or in between the written scenes of the play. Or they might attempt various exercises to help deal with an "instrumental" problem, such as an inability to express certain feelings, that they wanted to resolve. The nature and extent of their preparation varied according to the circumstance.

The scene or exercise might run under ten minutes or as long as an hour. When it was over, the lights would come up, the actors would by way of unwinding place a couple of chairs at center stage and begin to explain what they were working for—what they were trying to accomplish, with Strasberg occasionally asking a question to clarify a point. The work in such sessions has precise objectives. The actors try either to overcome a recurring problem or to extend themselves into unfamiliar areas. Their explanation of what they were aiming at provides the framework for the subsequent discussion of the work and the extent to which it has succeeded or failed.

Strasberg's characteristic approach to evaluating the actor's work was developed from his reading of Trotsky and Lenin during the twenties. Trotsky wrote that the way in which you judge something is to ask, "What did you expect, and what did you get?" Lenin, in one of his letters responding to a village's appeal for aid, brushed aside the emotional and generalized language of entreaty and asked such definite questions as, "How many people do you have? How many guns do you have? How many guns do you need? How many bullets do you have? How many bullets do you need?" This dramatized for Strasberg the importance of critically evaluating creative problems by reference to specific detail. He urged the actors to steer clear of the general, the rhetorical, the discursive in their explanations. "Give me the facts," he would tell them.

After the actors had spoken their piece, Strasberg would turn to the audience and ask, "What would you say?" The members would offer their observations and suggestions, Strasberg sometimes challenging a remark he felt was out of line. When everyone had his say, the tape recorder would be turned on by the Studio stage manager sitting next to Strasberg, and the artistic director would begin a lengthy and detailed analysis and assessment of the work. At approximately noon, the second scene would be presented in precisely the same manner. By shortly after one o'clock the session would be over.

The value of Strasberg's teaching had long been appreciated in theatrical circles, but its full significance was not publicly acknowledged until Kazan wrote about it in an article for the *New York Herald Tribune* in February of 1955. Hailing his colleague as "that extraordinary and unique phenomenon: a born teacher," Kazan went on to say, "Like all great teachers, he is abidingly concentrated on his subject and on his students, and he never ceases to learn from both. Teaching is his way of life: explaining, guiding, scolding, waiting, analyzing, reading, reexplaining, listening, studying, encouraging, repeating, discovering." The effect of Strasberg's teaching over the years, Kazan concluded, has been wider and deeper than has been realized. "The final fact is that our whole theater would have been less vital and less ambitious without the influence of this one man who has given so quietly and so unceasingly to so many people, because it is his nature to study and to think and to teach." [16]

This same man, who on more than one occasion has been called "probably the greatest American teacher of acting in our time," [17] was, nevertheless, a continuing focus of controversy and criticism throughout the Studio's heyday. The reasons for this are complex, stemming partly from Strasberg's personality, partly from misunderstandings of his ideas, and partly from his own failure to present his ideas in a sufficiently lucid and cogent manner.

Strasberg's shyness sometimes caused awkward moments for members and guests who took his occasional reticent blank looks as signs of irritation or arrogance. Even those who knew the man well were sometimes caught off guard. "People used to come out and say, 'He hates me,' and I'd say, 'Now why do you think that?'" recalls Geraldine Page. "'Well, I went up and asked him something and he looked at me like he'd never seen me before and didn't know who I was.' And I would always patiently explain to everybody that he is pathologically shy, this man. He can be the warmest person when he's sitting in his chair and you've done a scene. When you're talking about work, the communication is monumental. Then after class, you say, 'Oh, Lee,' and he gives you this completely blank look.

Social he can't be. It's nothing personal. It's just his problem. One time I was explaining this, and I had somebody fairly convinced, and we went back over to the Studio after lunch. For some reason, Lee was still there, and as we went in I said, 'Hello, Lee.' And he gave me that blank look. And I said, 'I wonder what I've done.' They howled at me then." [18]

Then there was the hypersensitivity to criticism that Strasberg first manifested during the Group Theatre days. Simply put, Strasberg is not able, perhaps does not want, to recognize his faults sufficiently. Harold Clurman, who has known him for some fifty years, says that this is Strasberg's major failing. "Maybe inside he does, but he pushes it away. He flares up as if you scratched him. He can't bear to be scratched and he does not wish to see his own limitations. Everyone has limitations. As a matter of fact, one's limitations are part of one's growth. He doesn't like to recognize his limitations, I think. And he has limitations, which is nothing against him because you always have to judge a man by his strengths and not by his limitations."

Criticism of Strasberg, or even resistance to his will, can arouse a formidable adversary posture in him. He explodes with rage. Clurman reports that Strasberg has always had some difficulty expressing adverse criticism calmly. "I once said, 'If you have something to criticize me for, say it calmly, because when you get excited and loud and violent, one doesn't hear what you are saying. One only hears the anger. One doesn't hear the point.' And he then said, 'I can't. I can't express myself easily, frankly . . . reveal myself quietly.' "

Taken all together, the oversensitivity to criticism, the temperamental outbursts, and the shyness merge into a strangely contradictory picture: this great teacher of the art of acting, which is an art of communication, appears to have enormous difficulty communicating effectively. Strasberg's tendency to loquaciousness, in light of that image, is only an added paradox.

"I went to a party and heard Lee Strasberg talk for three hours in one sentence," Maxwell Anderson once remarked. Strasberg's penchant for talking at length is well known among theater people. His discursiveness has often served to obfuscate a telling observation he wished to make, and put off people in the process. It has been suggested by detractors that the introduction of the tape recorder at the acting sessions in 1956, with all its implications of speaking for posterity, has played a part in encouraging Strasberg's volubility. Harold Clurman has observed that Strasberg tends to make very good points when he lectures, "but then he tends to dissipate the effect by overelaboration. Perhaps this is the result of the situation at the Studio. As a director one's observation must be lucid and to the point. But in the context of the Studio where Lee has the time to be expansive, he tends to go on and on." Clurman himself is, of course, no piker when it comes to the "gift of gab." Anderson reportedly once said of *him*, "At first you wished Harold would finish talking, then you wished that he would just finish a sentence." Clurman's favorite riposte, and one perhaps that Strasberg could use as well, is, "A friend of mine by the name of Goethe once said, and I remember it well, that 'Everything has already been said, but since nobody listens, you have to say it all over again.'" Paul Zindel, the Pulitzer Prize–winning author of *The Effects of Gamma Rays on Man-in-the-Moon Marigolds*, tells a tale of his successful use of Strasberg's brilliant but lengthy explications to deal with his tax problems. He had been keeping a day-to-day diary of expenses for income-tax purposes when he discovered, to his great delight, that by interlarding his daily financial entries with copious notes of Strasberg's talks, he could profitably confuse the Internal Revenue Service at his annual audit.

Finally, however, and in addition to the real and ostensible shortcomings of Strasberg's personality and manner, there are the misunderstandings of him by others that must to a large extent be held accountable for the controversy surrounding the man and his work. Strasberg has argued, with considerable justification, that theater people who have observed at the Studio have often failed to make a distinction between a personal reaction to the work and a judgment made on the basis of knowledge of its intentions and methodology.

Studio members, for instance, have been aware that Strasberg deals with the individual actor on a cumulative basis. When he offers a suggestion, they understand that he is responding not just to the work of the moment, but to everything he knows about that actor. What members learn from his commentaries is similarly cumulative, and they are careful, therefore, not to put a wrong emphasis on any of his specific observations. On the other hand, a onetime guest—to cite one out of many such possible examples—might be put off by Strasberg's harping on the need for greater emotionality from Actor A, unaware that at the following session he might rip into Actor B's excessive emotionality. The members know that Strasberg is not advocating greater or lesser emotion per se, but rather that each actor realize the nature of his individual emotionality as it affects his total expressivity as a performer. That same onetime guest, however, may depart with a partial view of Strasberg's work, and in passing on his impressions, will create yet another distortion of what the Studio represents.

Strasberg has complained that guest actors, directors, and writers are quick to demand that the drama critic who judges one of their plays not limit himself to the expression of his own subjective reactions, but that he include an objective account of the play, of the author's intentions, and so on. Yet when these visitors, in turn, become critics of the work at the Studio, they fail to take account of the rationale behind the Studio's approach to the art of acting. They often refuse, for example, to comprehend the relationship between the human problems and the artistic progress of the performer, whose very humanity—psychology, memory, feelings, physicality, etc.— is the material out of which he creates a character. They often misconstrue the fundamental work on the actor's instrument and criticize the Studio approach for being "too personal" and the "Method actor" for being overly subjective, even narcissistic.

The whole issue of "immodest prying" into the actor's "succulent privacies," as Harold Clurman put it, dates from the days of the Group Theatre. During the fifties, when Strasberg made a point of bringing his readings in psychology to bear on his teaching, he was whimsically referred to as a "poor-man's psychiatrist" in his private classes. But the idea that he was actually practicing a form of psychotherapy with the Studio actors is apocryphal. Celeste Holm once quipped that Strasberg "was good for actors working through their oedipal problems," but the fact is he was very tentative with his mental scalpels and on many occasions would tell a performer: "I'm not your analyst . . . you don't work that out here."

There were times when out of private concern for a particular actor, he would discuss his psychological problems with him, and, more often than not, would suggest that the actor seek professional help. But these matters were never broached publicly at the Studio itself. Moreover, it was not a general policy of Strasberg's to recommend psychoanalysis to all Studio members as a matter of course, despite his belief that the knowledge of oneself it can offer is of value to an actor.

That psychoanalysis over the years became an important factor in the lives of many Studio members is much more the result of the popularity of that discipline during the fifties and the natural inclination of actors of sensibility to seek out the help it could provide than of an actual necessity arising out of the nature of the Studio work.* There were, in fact, many actors who were reluctant to undergo psychoanalysis in the belief it would disturb their creative functioning. Marlon Brando mentioned this fear when he discussed his own analysis in an interview with Truman Capote.

I was afraid of it at first. Afraid it might destroy the impulses that made me creative, an artist. A sensitive person receives fifty impressions where somebody else may only get seven. Sensitive people are so vulnerable; they're so easily brutalized and hurt just because they *are* sensitive. The more sensitive you are, the more certain you are to be brutalized, develop scabs. Never evolve. Never allow yourself to feel anything, because you always feel too much. Analysis helps. It helped me.[19]

It was Brando who sent James Dean to an analyst when he realized how troubled the younger actor was. "And at least his work improved. Toward the end I think he was beginning to find his own way as an actor," he recalls. The fact that Dean went into analysis is interesting in light of the fact that what Brando and others had feared would happen to them at the hands of an analyst, namely a dangerous tampering with their creative mechanisms, was what Dean felt he had experienced all too traumatically when he presented his first scene at the Studio. After that ordeal, he told a friend, "I don't know what's inside me. . . . I don't know what happens when I act—inside. But if I let them dissect me, like a rabbit in a clinical research laboratory or something, I might not be able to produce again. They might sterilize me! That man had no right to tear me down like that. You keep knocking a guy down like that and you'll take the guts away from him. And what's an actor without guts?"[20]

Dean was not alone in having suffered from the harsh, probing criticism meted out at the Studio. A number of actors had similar experiences and reactions. When Strasberg severely criticized Mil-

* Kazan has been psychoanalyzed twice. Strasberg has never been.

dred Dunnock after she did a scene from *Auto Da Fé*, she stayed
away from the Studio for three years. Julie Harris recalls getting
feverish after the classes with Strasberg, "sometimes even ill." The
artistic director's rigorous attacks were a constant source of controversy. One member spoke, half-sarcastically, of "the annual ingenue
breakdown." Though never viciously intended, his fault-finding as-
sessments could be shattering to fragile egos. Almost protectively, it
became a custom for actors to buoy each other up. On the other hand,
by the late fifties, with members themselves becoming rather severe
about one another's work, many Studio actors came to feel that the
Studio was no longer a place where one was "safe" or "free to take
chances," but that it had become a testing ground where one had to
prove oneself.

Certainly the view that Strasberg was excessively harsh was not a
universal opinion, as the personal accounts of a score of actors whom
Strasberg helped during this period affirms. Shelley Winters, for one,
observed:

Despite everything that you hear about Lee, he's very kind. He's only
tough with people who can take it and who are successful. I've never
seen him clobber somebody who isn't strong enough to take it. In my
own early days at the Studio, he was very kind to me. Now he'll get
very tough if I'm lazy or I won't work, and he'll criticize me in the
areas where I need it very sharply and question me if I've achieved it.[21]

For many actors, Strasberg's rigorous and demanding approach
was exactly what they sought. Tamara Daykarhanova, a veteran of
the Moscow Art Theater and herself an acting teacher of standing,
said of the artistic director in February 1955, "I learned *a lot* from
Lee Strasberg. For me he is *The Teacher*—most inspired, a real
'talent and its errors detector.' *Nothing* in your behavior on the stage
escapes him! I have a tremendous admiration for Lee. . . ." Five years
later, Eli Wallach, who described himself as a "thorn in Lee Strasberg's side for a good many years, and a man who said [Strasberg]
practiced psychiatry without a license," declared of the Studio and
its artistic director: "I come here for a very specific reason, a very
personal reason. Lee Strasberg represents to me an outlook, a conscience, a way to work, a constant finger pointed at me, and I've had
the taste of the cup of success. And I must say it tastes kind of flat.
I'm trying to find a way to flavor it. He knows the formula to flavor

The Group Theatre company posing for photographer Ralph Steiner's Rodin-inspired mock improvisation, "The Thinking Actor," at Green Mansions, New York (summer 1933). Left to right, front row: Sanford Meisner, Morris Carnovsky, Walter Coy, Alan Baxter; second row: J. Edward Bromberg, Mrs. Art Smith, William Challee, Ruth Nelson, Gerritt Kraber, Russell Collins; third row: unidentified apprentice, Art Smith, Eunice Stoddard, Dorothy Patten, Cheryl Crawford, Clifford Odets; fourth row: unidentified apprentice, Grover Burgess, Lewis Leverett, Robert Lewis, Herbert Ratner, Alexander Kirkland; fifth row: Helen Thompson, Margaret Barker, Elia Kazan, Luther Adler, Stella Adler, Paula Miller (Strasberg); top row: Paul Morison, unidentified apprentice, Virginia Farmer, Phoebe Brand (Carnovsky), Mab Anthony, Alixe Walker, Harold Clurman, Lee Strasberg.

The Group's founders: Harold Clurman, Cheryl Crawford, and Lee Strasberg (1933).

Elia Kazan and Robert Lewis in *Waiting for Lefty* (1935).

Marlon Brando as
Stanley Kowalski, with
Karl Malden, Jessica
Tandy, and Kim
Hunter, in *A Streetcar
Named Desire* (1947).

Elia Kazan surrounded by cast members of *Sundown Beach* on the lawn of the Westport Country Playhouse (1948). Left to right, front row: Joan Copeland, Michael Lewin, Treva Frazee, Kathleen Maguire, Don Hanmer, Ira Cirker; second row: Steven Hill, unidentified, Nehemiah Persoff, Edward Binns—partially obscured by Lenka Peterson, Cloris Leachman, Kazan with his hand on Kim Hunter's shoulder, playwright Bessie Breuer, unidentified, Vivian Firko (Nathan); in the rear: Martin Balsam, Robert F. Simon. The child, Ralph Robertson (with his mother), played Julie Harris's son.

Above: Julie Harris and Steven Hill in *Sundown Beach* (1948).
Below: Pat Hingle, Ben Gazzara, and Arthur Storch in *End as a Man*
(1953).

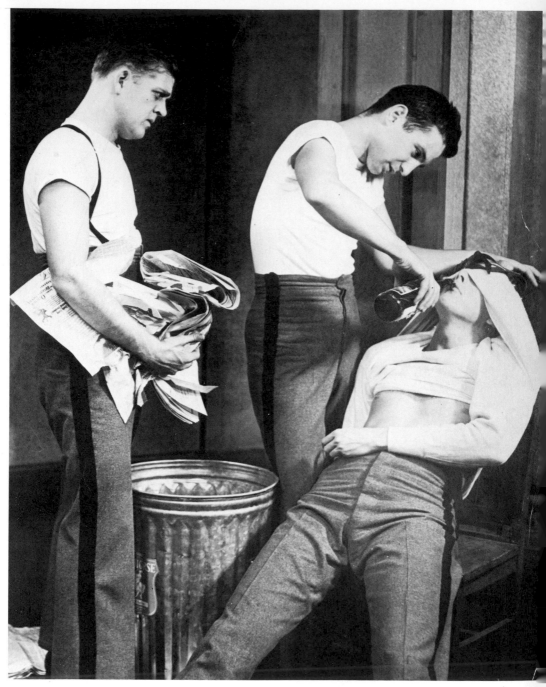

Pat Hingle, Ben Gazzara, and Albert Salmi in *End as a Man* (1953).

Ben Gazzara and Elia Kazan discuss rehearsals of *Cat on a Hot Tin Roof* (1955) in Child's restaurant, a popular Studio hangout during the Malin Studios period. Kazan cast Gazzara in the role of Brick in Williams's play as a result of seeing the young actor's work at the Studio.

Below: Anthony Franciosa, Frank Silvera, Shelley Winters, Harry
Guardino, and Ben Gazzara rehearsing *A Hatful of Rain* (1955).
Right: Brando off-camera during the shooting of *The Wild One* (1953).
The dungarees and leather, like Kowalski's torn T-shirt, were to become
iconographic of "Method" acting.

ROY SCHATT

James Dean with the bullfight cape he used in his first scene at the Studio.

ROY SCHATT

MILTON H. GREENE

Above: Marilyn Monroe, in the
third row, is an attentive listener
at a Studio session held at the
Malin Studios during the 1954–
1955 season. Strasberg, holding a
newspaper, is at center.
Right: Marlon Brando and
Marilyn Monroe pose together
in a rare publicity shot for an
Actors Studio benefit to raise
funds for the new Studio
building.

Strasberg discoursing at the Studio.

SYEUS MOTTEL

Above: Members of The Actors Studio Theatre's Production Board
announcing plans for the presentation of *Strange Interlude* (1963). Left to
right: Anne Bancroft, Frank Corsaro, William Prince, Edward Albee, Pat
Hingle, Geraldine Page, Rip Torn.
Below: Ben Gazzara, William Prince, Pat Hingle, and Geoffrey Horne look
on as Geraldine Page and Betty Field rehearse a scene from Act III of
Strange Interlude (1963).

Below: Julie Harris, Lee Allen, Tim Everett, and Iggie Wolfington in *Marathon '33* (1963). Bottom: James Baldwin and Burgess Meredith working on *Blues for Mister Charlie* (1964).

Frank Corsaro (right) directing Paul Newman, Joanne Woodward, and
James Costigan in *Baby Want a Kiss* (1964).

Above: Kim Stanley (Masha) comforts Shirley Knight (Irina) as she weeps in Geraldine Page's (Olga's) arms in a moment from *The Three Sisters* (1964).

Left: The party scene from Act I of the Studio Theatre's production of *The Three Sisters* (1964). Clockwise around the table, from the left: Kevin McCarthy, Geraldine Page, Albert Paulsen, Robert Loggia, James Olson (partially blocked), Kim Stanley, Shirley Knight, Luther Adler, Gerald Hiken, Barbara Baxley, Brooks Morton; standing downstage: David Paulsen, Tamara Daykarhanova.

Above: The Actors Studio West, at 8341 Delongpre Avenue just below
the Sunset Strip, converted from the garage on the William S. Hart
estate in West Hollywood, California.
Below: Rod Steiger rehearsing a play with Patrick McVey and others
for the Studio's Playwrights Unit.

Above: Fred Stewart leading the festivities in the Studio's annual Christmas Mummer's play, *The Masque of St. George and the Dragon*.
Below: Al Pacino, Robert De Niro, and Robert Duvall speaking with Carl Schaeffer at an Actors Studio party (1978).

THE CHARLES MACARTHUR CENTER
FOR AMERICAN THEATRE

Above: Strasberg giving a lecture-demonstration to a student audience at the Florida State University School of Theatre, Tallahassee, during "A Salute to the Actors Studio" weekend (January 14–16, 1977) at which he was awarded an honorary doctorate. Seated behind him at far left are Studio members and associates, including, from the left: Kevin McCarthy, Anna Strasberg, Jack Garfein (holding coffee cup), Harold Clurman, Joan Copeland (leaning forward), Paul Zindel, David Garfield, Earle Hyman (hand to face), and Susan Strasberg. Right: Christopher Walken in a Studio project.

SYEUS MOTTEL

Right, from top to bottom:
Ellen Burstyn, Estelle
Parsons, Eli Wallach
moderating sessions at the
Studio.

Below: Al Pacino playing third base for
The Actors Studio softball team in the
Broadway Show League competitions.

IRA MAZER

IRA MAZER

HENRY GROSSMAN

Above: The founders of the Group Theatre and The Actors Studio reunited at a 1978 Studio benefit: Strasberg, Crawford, Kazan, Clurman, and Lewis.

Below: The Founding Father and The Guiding Spirit (1978). Clurman looks on as Kazan and Strasberg celebrate their forty-six-year association.

HENRY GROSSMAN

it. And I think, damn it if I'm going to go elsewhere if I can't find that flavor. . . ."

For Maureen Stapleton, who worked to counter excessive emotionalism at the Studio—playing, in her words, "a gland, not a woman"—Strasberg's criticism was salutary no matter what the quality of her work at any given time. "What's great about the Studio is I can take a scene, any scene, and just do it, good or bad, hot or cold, and take my lumps. I'll find out something. Maybe I'll find out why I couldn't do it." [22]

Eva Marie Saint, who came to the Studio a "tense, self-conscious and painfully shy" actress, credits Strasberg with "liberating" her.[23] Anne Jackson, who has called him "a saint for actors," says that Strasberg was instrumental in overcoming her terror of taking direction and advice.[24]

With Geraldine Page, Strasberg worked on controlling vocal and behavioral mannerisms. As she prepared to work on the role of Clytemnestra in Giraudoux's *Electra* for her first scene at the Studio, he instructed her to hold on to a stationary pole and warned her: "I want you to stand still and talk loud. No gestures, no line readings." [25] She suffered this insistence and many others over the years and was rewarded by learning "to differentiate between her real talent and the banalities of personal habit." [26] In the process, of course, she emerged as one of the finest talents ever associated with the workshop.

Kim Stanley, regarded by many theater people as the outstanding American actress of her generation, worked with Strasberg for fifteen years at the Studio. She credits him with curing her of some very bad habits, such as her overeagerness to be liked by the audience. "I had an acute case of the 'cutes,' which Lee helped cure me of," she notes. When she was asked to play Millie Owens in William Inge's *Picnic*, she worked on the role at the workshop under Strasberg's supervision. During the late fifties, when she was consistently being cast in realistic and pathetic roles, he insisted that she work on comedy so as to avoid the pitfalls of self-imposed stereotyping. In fact, for the first eight months or so that she was in the Studio, he told her he wanted her to work on nothing but high comedy. This infuriated the actress, who wanted to explore all the great emotional roles and did not feel comfortable doing comedy, which is exactly why Strasberg pushed her in that direction. Early on at her audition, he had sensed her strong emotionality; it was something, as she herself put it, "she walked in the door with." In order to expand her talent, she had to plumb unfamiliar waters. With some resistance, a lot of trepidation, and not much pleasure, she worked on a number of comic scenes, including *Red Peppers* with Nehemiah Persoff and, in the role of Gwendolyn, on the garden scene from *The Importance of Being Earnest*. Sometime later she came to appreciate what Strasberg had done for her. "It broadened my whole base, and not only in obvious ways. I would never have been able to do Chekhov, to find the humor in his plays, for instance, without that work." Her estimation of the artistic director, given at the end of the decade, was high indeed: "Each person Strasberg works with comes out a much broader, fuller, deeper person because Strasberg is interested not in exploiting talent but in nurturing it and making it grow. . . . He made it possible for the whole world to open up for me. I'd feel that's what I want, that's what I've always felt. It was like coming home." [27]

The Studio as a home was a notion that pleased Strasberg. The idea of a family of artist members with the artistic director as the paterfamilias was eminently preferable to the concept of the Studio as a temple with the actors as communicants and Strasberg as the celebrant. This latter image had gained currency in the popular press, where Strasberg was often referred to as "the high priest," "guru," "pope," or "rabbi" of the Method and the Studio was pictured as a shrine or church to which the faithful eagerly flocked. The facts that the workshop headquarters had once been a church, that Strasberg usually wore a clerical-looking dark suit and shirt, and that talk of the Method and "Methodism" had a quasi-doctrinal ring to it only served to reinforce the religious imagery. Accusations of religiosity were leveled at Studio members, who provoked non-Method actors with their "dogmatic arrogance." [28] Celeste Holm, herself a member of the Studio, spoke of the "cabalistic pomposity" of the actors there, while Julie Harris explained that she ended her active participation because she did not like the true-believer aspect of the place. Various journalists complained of the workshop's growing "cultism," complete with "arcane lingo" and passionately defended "revealed truth."

The "home and family" image of the Studio, on the other hand, prompted criticism of the actors' "clannishness." A typically deprecatory anecdote illustrating this point tells of a young Studio actor involved with a war movie listening to the film's technical adviser telling war stories. The speaker, a five-year veteran of front-line action, tried to describe the special closeness of the soldiers at the front: "You know that the man next to you might be the one who can save your life in a few moments or he might be dead. I have never felt such a wonderful spirit." The Studio actor reportedly rejoined: "That's how all of us at the Studio feel." [29]

Moss Hart once told Miss Holm that he would never hire more than one Studio actor at a time because they tended to form cabals. The idea that Studio members found it difficult to work with non-Method actors, and vice versa, was reinforced by such incidents as Kim Stanley's quitting O'Neill's *A Touch of the Poet* during its run because of the dissension among the performers. (Miss Stanley claims she left the show because Eric Portman manhandled her in their scenes together.)

Much of this was a distorted and exaggerated misreading of simple youthful enthusiasm for high-minded aesthetic values and the perfectly natural camaraderie of those sharing ideals. The fervor of such idealism undoubtedly occasioned lapses in humility, tact, and simple courtesy—a phenomenon not so unusual in any artistic discipline that takes itself seriously. Nevertheless, the view of goings-on at the Studio as eccentric and recondite was more a question of "good copy" than a sensitive and insightful analysis of the workshop's reality.

A general portrait of the Studio actor as a "crazy, mixed-up kid" of the "dirty fingernail school of acting" became commonplace during the fifties. He was seen as a rebel against refinement, decorum, and gentility, who, in his nonglamorous approach to acting, was attempting to appear "proletarian."

Kazan has said, "What counts in the Method is the revolt against the heroic, romantic, rhetorical theater." [30] The rejection of refinement, decorum, and gentility was another step along the road to greater "reality," "truthfulness," and directness of expression. As Clurman put it, "These young actors fear nothing so much as any identification with the stuffed shirt." [31] In the public mind, of course, the prime symbol of the Studio actor was always to be the torn T-shirt and its prototype, Marlon Brando as Stanley Kowalski—or, alternatively, Brando as the leather-outfitted motorcyclist of *The Wild One.*

Much was made of the Studio actor's "costume" during the fifties. That many members chose to wear casual dress was considered either quaintly bohemian or a calculated attempt to offend taste. From a representative feature article:

"Members of the Actors' Studio . . . tend to dress more or less alike. The men usually show up wearing blue denims or chino pants with T-shirts and lumberjackets. The actresses go in for plain blouses and skirts, and spurn the glories of make-up and salon coiffures. No matter what her income bracket may be, an actress would not be caught dead wearing a mink coat to the Studio." [32]

These neat generalizations, however, are belied by the very pictures that accompanied the article, showing actors wearing jackets and ties, and actresses in a variety of dressy outfits and makeup. This type of journalistic exaggeration was typical of the failure to underscore the individuality of Studio members as to tastes, outlook, interests, and talent. The repeated references to Studio attire especially irritated Strasberg, who explained that many actors dressed casually for economic reasons. He took delight in pointing out, however, that when Rod Steiger became a Hollywood star, he still chose to wear jeans—only now made to order and furnished with silver buttons.

There were also attempts to define a "Studio mentality." From the same article:

Studio actors seem to be serious intellectuals who like nonobjective paintings, the quartets of Bartok, and the poems of Yeats, T. S. Eliot and Dylan Thomas. They are interested in philosophy and religious mysticism. They can discuss the theories of Existentialism readily. By and large, they profess to be uninterested in money or success.

Strasberg has said, "If they were anything, they were *not* intellectuals." Serious, however, they were.

Their "seriousness," high though it was, often invited mockery. There was the time Geraldine Page's work on a scene from *Mourning Becomes Electra* was ruined by an overzealous young actor who ate the crucial prop candles she had prepared for herself while he was frenziedly crawling around, breaking bottles, and otherwise acting up a storm during his part of the session.

Then there was Albert Salmi's work on *Hamlet*. The actor entered and recited, "O that this too too solid flesh would melt, thaw and resolve itself into a dew! . . ." Suddenly he stopped and said, "Oh, sorry, Lee. That's not the speech I wanted to do. God, I'm all mixed up," and quickly exited. A moment passed, and he returned with a doll which he held before him and which he instructed, "Speak the speech, I pray you, as I pronounced it to you, trippingly on the tongue; but if you mouth it . . . Ah Christ!" He dropped the doll and apologized anew. "That's not the scene I wanted to do. Jesus, I don't know what's wrong with me." He exited again only to enter a third time angrily remonstrating with himself. "O what a rogue and peasant slave am I! Is it not monstrous . . ." And again he stopped short, looking totally lost. "I really don't know what's gotten into me. . . ." As he started to exit yet one more time, Strasberg, exasperated beyond endurance, shouted after him, "Albert! What are you doing!" Salmi answered, "Well, Hamlet's crazy, so I'm playing him crazy."

There were also accounts of violence and uncontrolled aggressiveness at the Studio. Dane Clark once referred to the Studio as his "Stillman's," meaning the place where, as an actor, he could "work out." There have been occasions, however, where Studio members have gone beyond the bounds of the sort of sparring one might consider proper to a performers' gymnasium, and have actually provoked fights with fellow actors "to get something going." During one of the sessions at which they worked on Strindberg's *The Stronger* in 1961, for instance, Anne Bancroft and Viveca Lindfors had an all-out "fight to the death." According to Cheryl Crawford, they really went at it, crying and screaming as they scratched and mauled one another. When Madeleine Sherwood tried to intervene, Strasberg said, "Stay out of it! Stay out of it!" "That was a fight! Two washerwomen couldn't have done that well." Studio detractors, of course, offered this and similar isolated episodes as typical of what went on at the workshop.

Studio actors were frequently held up to scorn for their conduct during rehearsal and performance. The actor's "preparation" was a frequent object of derision. The need to take time to relax and make contact with some inner process, perhaps a sensory exercise, struck certain directors and fellow actors as an indulgence bordering on the fetishistic. These scoffers were not impressed with the explanations of how this strange offstage behavior helped make it possible for the actor to create the emotional fireworks that thrilled audiences.

A favorite joke was built around the Method players' passion for analyzing their every act on stage: George S. Kaufman tells a "bothersome actor" to cross the stage and hold for four "beats" before speaking his next line. "What's my justification for holding four beats?" the actor asks the director. "Because I tell you to, that's why!" Kaufman screams in reply. Or a typical variation: "What's my motivation for moving on that line?" inquires the actor. "Your paycheck!" snaps the director. These actors' interjections were considered disruptive and unprofessional, except perhaps by those few responsive directors who tolerated such "difficult" behavior because they understood it was the result of the performer's caring about what he was doing. The opposite was all too often the case, even among some "non-Method" directors who should have known better. Before they started rehearsals for *Major Barbara*, Charles Laughton quite genially but firmly said to Eli Wallach, "I don't want any of that Stanislavski shit from you!"

Undoubtedly there were instances where Studio actors, out of an inappropriate devotion to their own sense of integrity, were uncooperative and insensitive to the feelings of fellow actors, directors, and even playwrights. Various stage and film actors complained of Studio people refusing to stick to the lines in rehearsal and leaving their fellow performers to find their cues by guesswork. There were even accounts of actors so caught up in their preparation or "inner work" that they missed cues.

On occasion they simply got carried away. One early incident during the Studio's very first season involved Eli Wallach, who was taking Strasberg's class with the cast of *Brigadoon* as well as working in Robert Lewis's unit at the workshop and appearing on Broadway in Katharine Cornell's 1948 production of *Antony and Cleopatra*. Wallach played a messenger who appears in Act II to inform the queen that Antony has married Octavia. One day he heard Strasberg give a lecture on "action." "If you go on stage to do something, do it!" Strasberg exhorted his actors. Wallach was so stirred by the talk, he could hardly contain himself at that evening's performance. He rushed into the theater and hurriedly put on his costume, makeup, and sword. He was so worked up by Strasberg's words that he could not wait to give Cleopatra the news of Antony's marriage. But Shakespeare wrote several long speeches for Cleopatra before the messenger reveals his message. Wallach would say, "Madame . . ." and Miss Cornell would reel off several lines of poetry. He would repeat, "Madame! . . ." and again she would speak at length. Finally, unable to contain his pent-up enthusiasm, he abruptly exclaimed, "Madame, would it please you hear me?"—and cut a good number of Miss Cornell's best lines. The astonished actress hauled off and hit him, then swept off stage. Wallach went to Strasberg's next class and said to him, "What the hell kind of Method is that?!" Strasberg told him, "Wait for your cues!"

Studio actors were also accused of a tendency to confuse the preparatory, exercise work of the workshop, which aims to develop the performer's technique, with the exigencies of production, which call for less self-consciousness and greater attention to the effectiveness of the performance. Many were reproached for their neglect of vocal technique and their shortcomings in the area of physical expressivity. Tyrone Guthrie wrote, "The Method-ists overprize the Search for Truth as opposed to the Revelation of Truth. They have neglected the means of communication." [33]

This notion of the Studio actor as inarticulate, self-absorbed, and intractable was to a large extent influenced by Marlon Brando and James Dean. In the public mind these were the quintessential Method actors—intense, instinctive, rebellious. Their unique portrayals of the tough yet somehow sensitive loner struck a sympathetic chord in the sensibilities of young actors, who came to interpret the mannerisms of their characterizations in such films as *A Streetcar Named Desire, On the Waterfront, East of Eden,* and *Rebel Without a Cause* as the essentials of a new, "truthful" acting style. In his article on acting in the *Encyclopaedia Britannica,* Strasberg said, "So strong was the fusion of performer and role that many of the traits of the character were confused with those of the actor and led to serious misunderstandings."

Brando, especially, served as a model for these young theater people. The sheer brilliance of his portrayal of Stanley Kowalski in *Streetcar,* with its intuitive and impulsive aliveness, its defiant and impudent sexuality, were irresistible to them. They saw in the character's toughness and coarseness an assertion of reckless independence; in the actor's technical achievement, the possibilities of creative conquest. This combination of aggression and sensitivity, of potency and skill, made Brando *the* exemplary artist-rebel of the day to his young admirers.

Ironically, Brando did not think he was right for the part of Kowalski at the outset. Kim Hunter recalls him saying during the early rehearsals, "They should have got John Garfield for Stanley, not me; Garfield was right for the part, not me." Garfield, who was offered the role but turned it down, would no doubt have brought a brute-strength "rightness" to the role. He would not, however, have had the undertow of emotional sensitivity that gave Brando's performance its special distinction. (When James Dean worked on some scenes from *Streetcar* some years later, his interpretation of Kowalski was reportedly "more sensitive and more ironic" than Brando's.) This unique juxtaposition of the tough and the sensitive, which Brando was to articulate more fully in *On the Waterfront*, was especially appealing to the young actors who strove to emulate him.

"I'm not flattered when I hear of young actors who copy me," Brando said. "If it's true and they do, I think it's bad. But then everyone has a choice of whom he will copy." [34] James Dean was repeatedly, perhaps unfairly, accused of copying the older actor. After the opening of *East of Eden*, Brando remarked that Dean was "wearing my last year's wardrobe and using my last year's talent in the movie."

"When a new actor comes along he's always compared to someone else," Dean replied to those accusing him of imitating Brando. "Brando was compared to Clift, Clift to someone else, Barrymore to Booth and so forth. . . . I can only do the best job I can. . . . People were telling me I behaved like Brando before I knew who Brando was. . . . I have my own personal rebellions and don't have to rely on Brando's. . . . Within myself are expressions just as valid. . . . And I'll have a few years to develop my own—what shall I say?—style." [35]

The Brando imitators were not Studio members. Such "copying" was frowned upon at the Studio, where each actor's individuality was the measure of all things. Ben Gazzara, who was irritated by comparisons of himself with Brando, declared, "People who imitate Marlon are just punks. Lee would not let anyone get away with that. It would destroy an actor's integrity." The Brando image was most potent among aspiring actors, any of whom could label themselves "Method actors" and be accepted as part of the Studio phenomenon. And this has been the source of much of the misunderstanding surrounding the Studio. Outside observers, journalists, and others who failed to distinguish between the activities of the workshop and the behavior of the hundreds of young actors making claims to Method discipleship, helped to obscure the true nature of the Studio's strengths and weaknesses.

Though the offensive incidents ascribed to Studio members were always among the more delectable morsels of theater gossip, in light of the actual attitudes and practices of the workshop's individual members, it is apparent that the objectionable elements were blown out of proportion and unfairly taken for the norm. Moreover, much of what was ascribed to the workshop and to its members was in fact the doing of that large variety of "Method" practitioners, both teachers and performers, who had no connection with the Studio.

Certain Studio actors, to be sure, committed transgressions at various times. There have been misguided attempts to use workshop exercises—usually techniques improperly digested—in production situations; Studio actors have pleaded personal comfort ("I can't do that; I just don't feel it!"), challenging their directors and resisting the requirements of the play; Studio actors have been found wanting in the performance of "classical" roles.

But these were isolated and individual shortcomings, related to particular actors in particular circumstances and not to all Studio members as a matter of course. Studio actors have been as variable in their strengths and weaknesses as any other group of actors. The workshop emphasis has always been on individual development. Not all the actors have done the same exercise work in their training; not all use precisely the same Method elements in their performances. Consequently, the enormous variety of acting qualities and individual temperaments defy propounding a generalized Actors Studio stereotype. As Kazan put it, at the Studio "there's no rubber-stamping. Geraldine Page doesn't act like Julie Harris. I don't direct like Arthur Penn."

In critical accounts of Studio work, objectionable instances were rarely balanced by references to positive accomplishments. As one among many such possible examples, Strasberg once cited a television review by Jack Gould, in which the writer criticized the speech of the young Steve McQueen, whom he held up as an illustration of bad Studio acting, while at the same time applauding the performance of Studio actress Vivian Nathan, whom he neither named nor identified as a Studio member.

At the Studio, all such shortcomings were discussed frankly. Many actors who had trouble being heard or speaking clearly were repeatedly reminded to work on these problems. Strasberg expressed his indignation in very plain language at actors who dropped into casualness or who resisted a director because they did not "feel" like doing something. Both he and Kazan taught, as a matter of principle, that the learning process and the production process were never to be confused. "Sure, when we teach at the Studio we try to develop the actor psychologically," Kazan has said. "But if I direct a play, then it's the play that counts and the individual actor is no more than a means."

The overwhelming majority of Studio actors are reasonable and pragmatic in putting to use what they have learned at the workshop. Maureen Stapleton's quip, "Method, schmethod, the audience has to hear you," is a representative sentiment.

The publicists' stereotype of the Method-mumbler aside, there is still a distinguishable phenomenon that can be identified as "Studio acting." It is a mode of performance readily differentiated from typical English or French acting. It is unconventional, deeply felt, and psychologically detailed. It is more impulsive than calculated and more openly emotional than intellectual. It has idiosyncratic qualities, which at their worst fall into mannerism and at their best create the effect of unique, living individualities.

It was this singular kind of acting, with all of its emotional richness and visceral appeal, that stirred such enthusiasm for the work of the Studio actor and created the unflagging interest in the activities of the workshop during the fifties. "Like it or lump it, the Actors Studio has literally given birth to the clearest, most carefully defined, most virile approach to the player's craft that the American theater has produced," was how Walter Kerr summed up its impact. "If it has partial roots in the Stanislavski-born, and Group Theater–nourished, techniques of the Thirties, it has gone well beyond them: from low-keyed naturalism into open fire, from prosy accuracy to ranging and even rhythmic power. It has evolved a 'right' pattern for the plays of Tennessee Williams, Arthur Miller, and William Inge—who are, after all, our best young playwrights." [36]

The relationship between the plays of the forties and fifties and the kind of acting that developed to "service" them is well worth noting. The fact that the Studio was originally set up as a stable for Kazan's productions (with Strasberg training the horses), and that Kazan's work with the plays of Miller, Williams, and Inge, with their emphasis on psychological and emotional elements, required a certain kind of training and not another, to some extent explains the kind of training that was developed. The market conditioned the preparation.

Studio training was a reflection of Kazan's and Strasberg's tastes in acting, as was their selection of the membership itself. Kazan referred to this in his letter to Strasberg, previously quoted, about the proposed Playwrights Unit, headed by Robert Anderson. "The playwrights should be chosen by the same unarticulated measures by which we choose actors or directors," he wrote. "Our taste—who we are—functions here, and it must function with playwrights. They should be representative of the same impulse in Art which makes us select over and over again . . . the same actors and the same kind of actors."

The Studio emphasis on the actor's individuality, and the profound exploration of that individuality, is—Strasberg's teachings aside—very much related to Kazan's own view of the art of acting and to his own pragmatic mode of casting and working with actors. For one thing, he does not place a high value on versatility in acting. He prizes, as he puts it, "the penetration of a talent, the depth, the degree to which the artist in any field is able to reveal his or her particular experience . . . the important thing is how much an actor is able to illuminate a part, how deep he or she is able to go; how much they are able to show you about the content of their roles. This is more important than versatility." [37]

It was to serve the "classic" American drama that Kazan proposed establishing The Actors Studio as the resident company in a kind of national theater. Throughout the fifties such a project was much talked about among the workshop's directors, especially by Strasberg, for whom it was a very special ambition. Kazan had always had mixed feelings about the Studio's going into production, but he too eventually got caught up in Strasberg's vision. As early as 1953, for instance, Kazan wrote to Miss Crawford, "I think the best thing we can do with the Studio is to start to turn it slowly into something like an English Club theatre, or Old Vic. Let's do it. That would be exciting. Lee is very excited about it."

The Bijou project, with its controversial *Shadow of a Gunman* presentation, had been a first, and half-hearted, attempt precisely in that direction. The failure of that initial foray into theatrical production was a setback, but only a temporary one. The effort to find the Studio's proper fulfillment continued as the directors and members debated the workshop's ultimate orientation throughout the decade. At the closing session of the 1958–1959 season, the discussion centered on the question "Whither the Studio?" Was there or was there not to be a theater in the future?

At the October 6 opening session the following fall, Strasberg spoke of a turning point in the activity of the Studio. He explained that up to then the workshop had been recognized, not so much by its work, but as a symbol or inspirational idea of the actor's craft and of what the theater should aspire to. It was now time for the Studio to fulfill its potential and assume a role at the very forefront of the American theater. The need for a fresh impetus had been building for some time and steps were being taken to start the Studio on its new path.

Earlier that spring the Studio directors had hired Gordon Rogoff, a cofounder and former editor of the English theater magazine, *Encore*, to serve in a newly created position of "Administrative Director." His job was to act as a "full-time coordinator of activities and general spark plug," while working to raise money for the expansion the Studio contemplated. When Rogoff joined the workshop in May of 1959, Kazan presented him with a six-page proposal for the Studio's future. It spelled out a wide range of development to be undertaken in two phases. The first of these was a three-year plan to increase Strasberg's involvement to the point where he could devote his full attention to the workshop and give up his private teaching. The much busier schedule of Studio activities was to include an expanded Playwrights Unit and a new Directors Unit. The second phase, to run concurrently with the first, was to lead the Studio toward production. In Kazan's words, Rogoff was brought into the organization to be the "maniac . . . who will in fact PUSH US TO DO WHAT WE WANT TO DO (even in spite of ourselves)." [38] The ultimate goal toward which the Studio was to be "pushed" was the creation of a theater.

In his proposal to Rogoff, Kazan had written that the Studio "should use the next three years to create a repertory of at least two productions which will be emblems of what we can do, what we in-

tend to do and what our Theatre Ideal is, described in stage terms
.... These will ARM us.... We can then truly know, as will everyone else, that we exist as a Group Theatre ... the Actors' Studio as
a Group Theatre."

Rogoff, unfortunately, found his situation at the workshop frus-
trating in the extreme. He tried, unsuccessfully, to promote an
ANTA-sponsored Actors Studio tour and other theatrical activity.
He also failed to raise funds for the workshop, a job for which he
was temperamentally unsuited, but one, nevertheless, he had been expected to perform. His main unhappiness, however, was his inability
to deal effectively with Strasberg, whom he came to consider an obstacle rather than an aid to the accomplishment of Kazan's stated
goals, and this finally led him to resign. Several years later, in an article written for the *Tulane Drama Review,* he publicly—and, in the
opinion of many, quite cruelly—excoriated Strasberg as a theatrical
menace and the reason for the Studio's failure to develop into a major
producing organization.[39]

Strasberg was to have run-ins with other ambitious individuals who
joined the Studio with visionary plans and copious energy. They too
would come up against his resistance—a puzzling and stymieing
cautiousness and unreadiness that many of those who know him well
have attested to. For his part, Strasberg vehemently has rejected any
such characterization of his behavior, of course, and has ascribed his
actions to considered and invariably astute judgments of persons and
situations. In any case, there is no doubt that he wanted the Studio to
become a theater, and there was one major effort to move the workshop in that direction on which he was to pin many of his hopes.

In the spring of 1956 Kazan had begun an exploratory correspon-
dence with the trustees of the newly conceived "Lincoln Square
project" (as Lincoln Center was called at the time) about the possibilities for the Studio's participation as the theater component of that
cultural enterprise. Writing to John D. Rockefeller III at that time,
Kazan had proposed a repertoire of American artists appearing in
American drama. "Our fundamental intention would be to make our
people and the world aware and proud of the work and importance of
the American Theatre—its plays, its craftsmen, their techniques and
their talents." Several letters discussing questions of repertory and the
design of the proposed theater as well as the Studio's potential involve-

ment were exchanged over the next few years, and Kazan and Miss Crawford were eventually invited to join the Center's advisory council on drama.

On October 21, 1959, Kazan was officially announced as "an associate in the development and direction of the Lincoln Center Repertory Theatre." The Studio's long-cherished dream of becoming a producing organization seemed on the threshold of fulfillment. As Strasberg indicated in his remarks opening the season, the coming year portended a significant turning point in the life of the workshop. As the plans for expansion proceeded apace and the possible link with Lincoln Center was in the offing, it seemed quite clear that the organization would not long remain "a force without a face." Having become a world-famous institution by the end of the fifties, the Studio appeared destined finally to emerge during the following decade in its definitive form as a "true ensemble," which would create for America a national theater.

CHAPTER **5**

Stanislavski and The Studio: The Method Controversy (A Digression)

meth·od/'meth-əd/ *n* . . . 4 *cap* : a dramatic technique by which an actor seeks to gain complete identification with the inner personality of the character being portrayed — usu. used with *the* [1]

THE ACTORS STUDIO holds a special distinction in the history of the performing arts in twentieth-century America: that of having been the center of a controversy over a *means* of aesthetic creation. Major battles have been fought over the ends of art, over the forms and contents of rival systems, but never has the United States witnessed the sort of conflict over the methodology or techniques of an art like the one inspired by the Method.

The turbulent notoriety of the Method during the 1950s was instigated in large part by the uninformed critical commentary which held the acting technique up to scorn as artistic mumbo-jumbo, responsible for all the histrionic excesses of the period. This notoriety was also of course fanned by the fierce advocacy of the Method's supporters, who were often fervent in its defense without adequate knowledge of its true nature. As a fashionable subject vividly highlighted by the publicity that surrounded the Studio, the Method was much discussed but little understood.

There were, and continue to be, several aspects to the Method controversy. On the one hand, there are the critics who argue that the Method as a *means* has led to a certain *end*, namely a particular acting "style" (often characterized as "introverted" or "naturalistic"). These critics are countered by the practitioners who argue that the Method is *not* inevitably linked to one performance style—it has seemed so only because of the kind of plays the Method has been applied to—but that it is, rather, an organic approach to acting basic to all types of theatrical production. On the other hand, there is the internecine quarrel among champions of various interpretations of Stanislavski's theories as to what the Method properly consists of. In other words, there has been criticism of the Stanislavski Method per se as well as criticism over how it has been interpreted in America by particular actors and teachers.

Stanislavski first consciously defined his Method during a vacation in Finland in 1906, eight years after founding the Moscow Art Theater and long after that organization's reputation for fine ensemble acting had been established. (The MAT's celebrated Chekhov productions had all been created before the Method was formulated.) Despite the integrity and seriousness with which he had pursued artistic excellence during the early 1900s, and despite his success at overcoming the cruder aspects of nineteenth-century acting and staging with his subtler, more realistic, and more emotionally true theatrical productions, Stanislavski found himself in a quandary. The joys of performing had begun to pale for him after all those active years of producing, directing, and appearing in his theater's repertory. He had come to feel that all the artistic experience he had accumulated along the way did not provide him with a foundation for future growth. For all his experimenting with new forms and new concepts, he could not sort out what was of permanent value to him from what was merely meretricious. The acting was still hit or miss. Sometimes a performance soared; at other times—all too frequently, alas—it would be leaden. Although he did valiant battle against what he called acting "stencils" (clichés), Stanislavski felt he was still relying on tricks. And this undermined his creative self-esteem.

In this mood of self-critical bewilderment, he sought to investigate the reasons why his performing had become lifeless and empty to him, and, through a careful analysis of everything he had learned about the subject, to discover some basic truths that would remedy his situation. He launched a systematic examination of the phenomenon of creativity in acting and began to define certain principles that he believed made it possible.[2]

He studied the acting of his contemporaries and the writings of the great actors of the past, searching for the common elements that made their highest creative achievements possible. He pinpointed the necessity of establishing a Creative Mood in which the actor could effortlessly tap his inner resources in order to create at will. To bring about the Creative Mood, he concluded, the actor must practice relaxation and concentration, and develop his sense of belief and feeling for truth on stage. Truth was to become the touchstone of his aesthetic philosophy. "You may play well or you may play badly," he would quote the great Russian actor Shchepkin, "the important thing is that you should play truly." [3]

Around 1909, Stanislavski outlined a first draft of his Method or System, and tried to introduce its concepts into the rehearsal work of the MAT. He met enormous resistance from the veteran actors of the company until the success of his production of Turgenev's *A Month in the Country* (1909), in which he first used some of his new techniques, convinced many of them of the Method's worth. In the wake of that success, Nemirovitch-Dantchenko, Stanislavski's partner in the founding of MAT, insisted on establishing Stanislavski's procedures as the basis for working on all future MAT productions.

Nevertheless, it was difficult fundamentally to change old attitudes and habits within the company, so Stanislavski formed the First Studio, where his theories could be explored without prejudice by the younger members of the MAT. Here, under Leopold Sulerjitsky's supervision, Vakhtangov, Michael Chekhov, Boleslavsky, Ouspenskaya, and many others studied and experimented with the Method. Their productions of *The Good Hope* and *The Cricket on the Hearth* established the efficacy of Stanislavski's ideas, finally dispelling, in the process, the MAT company's resistance to the Method. (*The Cricket on the Hearth*, in particular, Stanislavski found "unusually moving." He considered the production a major artistic achievement and had nothing but praise for the young actors who, under Sulerjitsky's ministrations, played with "heartfelt" emotional richness.)

Stanislavski continued to develop his System throughout his life. In the early stages he was heavily influenced by Yoga and conducted experiments in which his actors attempted to "radiate 'prana rays'" to the audience. Around 1914 he began to introduce new techniques for stimulating the actor's emotions (including the affective-memory exercise) based on his reading of the French psychologist Ribot. In later years he became familiar with the work of Pavlov, with whom he corresponded, and made adjustments in his methodology as a result.

With the publication of *My Life in Art* in the United States (1924), as well as many articles by former members of the MAT and various theater commentators, Stanislavski's ideas—at least particular aspects of them—began to be widely disseminated. But with the lack of a thoroughly systematic exposition of the theory and technique involved, the System/Method was absorbed piecemeal abroad, and those who applied it did so with a limited knowledge of the complete practice of its creator.

By Stanislavski's seventieth birthday in 1933, his System, as it had come to be known, was being used throughout Russia and the rest of the world, albeit in a profusion of adaptations and interpretations. Stanislavski, looking over the diversity among his followers in the MAT and its daughter theaters, observed: "People may say that what united my comrades in art, my pupils, and those who share my ideas . . . is the 'Stanslavski System.' What system? By now, in every theatre that has sprung from the Moscow Art Theatre, this system has been transformed into something different, new, even contrasting." [4]

While welcoming the diversity of approach, "providing only that what [the actor] does is justified from within and in accordance with the eternal laws of nature which are binding on all," Stanislavski was nevertheless concerned with the possible harm that could be caused by "the twisted interpretations put on my so-called 'system' which, in the way it is presently being taught, can put young actors on quite the wrong path."

The question of the distortion or misinterpretation of his ideas arose continually throughout Stanislavski's life and was partly due, on the one hand, to his continuing development of his theory and practice, and, on the other hand, to his reluctance to publish anything like a definitive account of his System/Method along the way. After his death, when everything he had to say had been said and all his books had been written, those who had been closest to him, even his own pupils, went "their separate ways artistically . . . using his legacy differently, each according to his own individuality and interests." [5]

As early as 1919 Eugene Vakhtangov was decrying the misrepresentation of Stanislavski by Michael Chekhov, who like himself had been a founding member of the First Studio. In his article, "To Those Who Write about the Stanislavsky System," Vakhtangov dismisses F. F. Komissarzhevsky's criticism of the Method as uninformed, and scolds Chekhov for attempting to discuss the practical application of the Method instead of waiting "until Stanislavsky's book is published and from it learn what Stanislavsky wants to say and how he says it." [6]

The irony is that none of the Stanislavski books published during his lifetime ever did clarify the practical applications of the Method. Vakhtangov, who was said to have understood the essence and implications of the System/Method better than his teacher, himself made innovations in the technique, theoretically in his "formulations" and practically in his highly stylized approach to theatrical staging. But Stanislavski, despite a period of strong disagreements with him, ultimately approved Vakhtangov's work, both as a director and as a teacher, and acknowledged him as his "dear friend, beloved disciple . . . only heir . . . and . . . creator of new principles of the revolutionary art." [7]

It was, in fact, under the guidance of Vakhtangov that the Method was most devotedly and fruitfully utilized. Stanislavski told Stella Adler in 1934 that the Method had never been fully practiced at the MAT. Only in the Studios, he noted, and particularly by Vakhtangov —initially at the First and later in the Third Studio—was it consistently employed.

The version of the Method that came to America was, as noted earlier, that of Stanislavski via Vakhtangov and Boleslavsky. It was based on the working procedures of the First Studio, which had achieved such satisfying results in the productions of *The Good Hope* and *The Cricket on the Hearth*. Like Stanislavski's colleagues and pupils in Russia, Strasberg too found his own special emphases and developed his own innovations as he put into practice what he had learned from his teachers.

In using the techniques he inherited and those he himself developed, Strasberg never represented himself as a spokesman for the Stanislavski System. Nor did he try to pass off his own work as Stanislavski's. In fact, the Russian master's name was rarely mentioned during the early years of The Actors Studio. It was not until approximately

1955, in response to the publicity growing around the Studio and the journalistic habit of invoking Stanislavski's name, that Strasberg began to talk in terms of the System and the Method.

Though, as far back as the Group Theatre, Strasberg and his actors had spoken of the Method, the use of the term with those overtones of cultic significance it developed during the early fifties originated outside the Studio. According to Strasberg, "We would simply say 'a method' or 'Stanislavski's ideas' or 'Stanislavski's method,' because work in a studio is done very unsystematically. . . ." [8] There were also reasons why Strasberg emphasized the word *Method* rather than *System* in his discussion of the technique:

"System" seemed to me to suggest that there was a clearly defined way of telling an actor how to act in every situation. Actually nothing in Stanislavski tells him what to do. It only tells him how he may go about finding what to do, and what he finds to do may differ from actor to actor. Therefore I use the term "method" because it seemed a better description of what is a creative rather than an imitative process. [9]

This usage also reflected Strasberg's reluctance to accept all of Stanislavski's ideas as a kind of "package deal." Stanislavski was not an infallible oracle whose every statement was true, per se. What was true was what worked. He explained his reasoning in a letter to Christine Edwards, the author of *The Stanislavsky Heritage:*

I do not believe that anyone but Stanislavsky himself has a right to talk of the Stanislavsky System. I have therefore stressed the use of the word "Method" as against "System" to suggest that while we obviously are influenced by Stanislavsky's ideas and practices, we used it within the limitations of our own knowledge and experience. . . .

By saying that the Group Theatre used an adaptation of the Stanislavsky Method, we mean that we emphasized elements that he had not emphasized and disregarded elements which he might have considered of greater importance. Also, that in experimenting with some of the ideas propounded by Stanislavsky, we came to conclusions and practices of our own which he might not have agreed with. Personally, I am critical of the way in which Stanislavsky used his own work in some of his productions, and therefore, I could not subscribe to many of the basic essentials of the ideas which he made use of. . . . In other words, while it would be true to say that we try to make use of the basic ideas of the Stanislavsky System, we do not feel it necessary to be limited just to those ideas or procedures that Stanislavsky himself used, nor would he necessarily agree with whatever is done in his name.

I therefore feel it both theoretically wise and practically sound to talk of the work done by the Group Theatre and the Actors Studio as being an "Adaptation of the Stanislavsky System." The "Method" is therefore our version of the System.[10]

The Method, as developed by Strasberg over the years, begins with two fundamental elements of the System, which Strasberg considers among Stanislavski's greatest and most essential discoveries: relaxation and concentration.[11] On many occasions Strasberg has said that tension, which he defines as the expending of unnecessary energy in the human body, is the actor's occupational disease. Before the actor can think or feel, much less create imaginatively on stage, he must be free of tension.

To promote relaxation, Strasberg has the actor sit in a chair and proceed to find a position in which, if he had to, he could fall asleep. The actor uses a straight-back or folding chair rather than something more comfortable, because the unyielding chair represents the sort of obstacle to being at ease on stage which he must learn to overcome. The stage is full of uncomfortable, inconvenient, and disconcerting conditions and a performer must relax and function in spite of them. After shifting his body around for a while, searching out areas of tension, the actor focuses his attention on relaxing various muscle groups, particularly those associated with mental tension, such as the areas of the temples, the bridge of the nose leading into the eyes, the thick muscles of the jaw leading into the chin, and the neck muscles. If the actor feels some emotional disturbance during the process he opens his throat and permits a sound from deep in the chest to come out, to make sure the emotion is not blocked. The relaxation period may take twenty minutes or more before the actor's relaxation is tested by the teacher, and he is then permitted to proceed with various exercises or scenes.

In order to develop concentration, the actor, in Strasberg's methodology, must go through a series of exercises in handling imaginary objects through sense memory. At first he tries to re-create a morning drink—coffee or orange juice—by trying to recapture the sensory stimuli of the feel of the cup or glass, its shape and weight, the odor and taste of the liquid, and so on. From there, he proceeds through a graduated sequence of "objects," including applying makeup or shaving; feeling sharp pains, tastes, smells, extremes of heat and cold; experiencing "overall sensations," such as sunshine, snow, or a shower; and working to re-create a place. The personal-object exercise, which focuses on the re-creation of belongings that have special significance to the individual, such as childhood toys or mementos from loved ones, is also part of this sequence and usually activates a noticeable emotional response in the actor. After working his way through all of these exercises singly, the performer repeats them in increasingly complex variations of twos, threes, fours, and so on, sometimes combining them with an animal exercise as well.

The point of this work with imaginary objects is not to suggest them through mime, nor to just pretend that they are there, nor to simply picture them in the mind's eye, but to recapture their reality through the mediation of kinesthetic sensory data to the point where a physiological reaction takes place. The memory of a lemon's sensorial elements, for instance, can provoke actual salivation. All of these exercises (and several of those described later) come under the Stanislavskian rubric of "the actor's work on himself" and are intended to develop not only the performer's concentration, but his awareness, sensitivity, imagination, and expressiveness as well.

While he works his way through these exercises, the actor also prepares scenes, gradually learning how to integrate the sensory study with his performing. For scene work, the player selects specific sensory tasks to fulfill in order to create those effects he wants in his performance. This practical application of the work with sensory objects falls under the heading, "the actor's work on the role."

The work with imaginary objects is crucial to the creativity of the actor, according to Strasberg. Obviously, the ultimate range of imaginary objects that a performer must create on stage is enormous. It may include physical objects, overall sensations, mental or fantasy objects, situations, events, relationships, and other characters. If the actor is to fulfill his acting task, which might be defined in part as the imaginative and truthful response to imaginary stimuli, he must be well grounded in the simplest sense-memory work. For this reason, Strasberg rejects exercises in concentration and imagination that use real objects. His insistence on the inefficacy of using real objects is in fact a bone of contention between him and other Method teachers. "The ability to create and to respond to imaginary objects and circumstances" is fundamental, he believes, to the argument that the actor is a *creative* rather than an *interpretive* artist.[12]

Strasberg feels he has gone beyond Stanislavski in his efforts to help free the actor to be more expressive. Over the years he has developed a number of exercises and procedures for unblocking feelings and emotions that the actor is experiencing internally but not manifesting externally; for deepening the intensity of the actor's response; and for avoiding cliché behavior and seeking out fresh colors from the actor.

One of the procedures standard to all these exercises is the "speaking out" of problems. As the actor works on a scene or exercise, he often encounters an inner turmoil of confused motives, fear, tension, distracting feelings, and so forth. Strasberg has the actor talk out loud about these "instrumental difficulties" which beset him as he works. By airing disturbing experiences, the actor avoids repressing them, which would only aggravate matters, and takes control of his situation—in effect neutralizing the difficulties. This then clears the way for him to create those experiential realities, which otherwise would be blocked, that he needs for his performance.

The procedure demonstrates the use of the actor's "double consciousness," that is, his ability to be "in" and "out" of the play at the same time. Strasberg, like Stanislavski before him, holds that the performer must be both actor and observer. In the words of Tommaso Salvini, "An Actor lives, weeps, laughs on the stage, but as he weeps and laughs he observes his own tears and mirth. It is this double existence, this balance between life and acting that makes for art." [13]

In the gibberish exercise, adopted from Boleslavsky and Ouspenskaya, two people play a scene using nonsense sounds instead of words. It is designed to wean actors away from the cliché handling of lines by forcing them to communicate intensely through vocal inflection and nuance. It demands a great deal of concentration and ingenuity, not to mention intuitive grasp, to successfully transmit and receive intentions, feelings, and even thoughts, without the intervention of words. The effort exerted often frees a person to express with greater emotional openness and physical demonstrativeness what they are having difficulty communicating on a literal level. Strasberg first tried the exercise on an actress in the Group Theatre who was having precisely that problem. He has used it ever since to get the thoughts and feelings the actor is really thinking and feeling into the actor's tone of voice so as to endow that tone with unexpected colors and expressiveness.

One of the most fruitful exercises for liberating the expressive impulses of the actor is the "song and dance," a procedure Strasberg discovered while working with some singers and which he developed over a period of five years. There are two parts to the exercise. First, the actor sings a song he is thoroughly familiar with, one tone at a time, while standing still and relaxed and concentrated on what he is doing. As he sings, he makes eye contact with his audience and tries to be aware of his inner tensions, feelings, and impulses. In the second part of the exercise, he begins to move or dance in a succession of patterns and rhythms, singing each note of the song in short, impulsive bursts, with Strasberg often calling for the change from one movement and tempo to the next.

During the exercise, strange things start happening to the performer: nervous tics and tremblings run through his body; tears or laughter, or both, often begin welling up inside him. He soon becomes aware of the conflict between his will to control his body and the natural impulses that seek to evade that control. The exercise teaches the actor to make contact with these impulses and sensations and allows him to let them manifest themselves more readily than he was formerly able to. It trains "the actor's peculiar ability to be free and yet to will the freedom," according to Strasberg.

Of all Strasberg's innovations, perhaps none has been so misunderstood and so misrepresented as the "private moment." Ever since its conception and development around 1956–1957, this procedure, which was intended to help the actor achieve deeper levels of concentration on stage, has been the object of much reckless speculation and gossip of the "immodest prying into succulent privacies" sort. It has been characterized by its detractors as some kind of "sinister" indulgence in sexual or scatological display, exhibitionist in motive and potentially dangerous to sensitive actors.[14]

The private moment was devised by Strasberg in response to his rereading of Stanislavski's remarks about the actor's needing to be "private in public." Its purpose was to help actors inhibited by the presence of the audience to confront this difficulty and overcome it by enacting a moment of real privacy in front of people. In private, people do things unself-consciously that they could not do in front of others: they talk to themselves or to plants, hold imaginary dialogues with other people, sing or dance with abandon, give vent to strong emotions, and so on. The actor preparing the exercise was instructed to create sensorially the environment in which he felt securely alone. He was even allowed to bring in some familiar objects from home to flesh out this environment. And then, once he achieved a sense of privacy, he was told to try to recapture the reality of his private behavior—some activity he would stop immediately if someone entered his room—and to allow himself to deal with the particular feelings and sensations that would normally cause him embarrassment if observed by others.

Most private moments are actually rather mild affairs. What one person feels very private about, another might feel quite open about. Some actors, for instance, are terrified of singing in public, though they may do so freely at home behind closed doors. For them, an appropriate private-moment exercise would be to create a sense of privacy on stage that would allow them to sing freely. Other people are meek and shy in public, but quite bold and dramatic in the privacy of their room. The exercise would allow them to prevail over their inhibitions and enter entirely new areas of expression. In addition, the fact that people are often quite dramatic and theatrical in private makes the exercise an especially useful tool in staging certain special moments such as soliloquies, monologues, and other instances when a person is left alone on stage, according to Strasberg.[15]

The private moment, Strasberg also points out, is not for every actor. If a performer is totally uninhibited on stage, there is no point to his doing the exercise. Many Studio members have never performed one; others have been dissuaded from doing them. During the late fifties and the sixties, on the rare occasion when a Studio actor proceeded to remove all of his clothes, Strasberg would take him to task for indulging in a meaningless exhibition, and tell him to keep away from the exercise. It was obvious that for these actors, who were usually not even properly relaxed or concentrated, these ultimate moments of privacy were not truly *private*.

Studio actors were expected to uphold basic standards of good taste in their efforts to be honest and personal during these exercises. But of course these standards changed over time. With the liberalization of screen and stage mores during the seventies, elements of nudity in the private moment, which would not have been tolerated earlier, were allowed on occasion, though never in an atmosphere of flippancy or sensationalism.

The private moment is undoubtedly the most notorious of Strasberg's innovations in acting training, but another aspect of his teaching has been even more fundamentally criticized: his emphasis on affective memory. Strasberg has been accused of stressing affective memory at the expense of practically every other element in the Stanislavski System. This item seventeen on the System chart that Stella Adler brought back to the Group Theatre from her meeting with Stanislavski was a subject of contention for the Russian master as well, for *he* was criticized for *his* emphasis on it.

On more than one occasion Stanislavski defended the role of affective memory as basic to all the actor's creative work. Some of his Russian colleagues argued that the actor's extensive reliance on what is essentially his personal experience would limit his creativity to the range of that experience, restricting him to only those roles that were consonant with his particular character and personality. Stanislavski answered that, on the contrary, one's affective memories were like primary colors: they could be re-created in multifarious combinations of hues and tints to provide the actor with any reality he wanted.[16]

The same criticism was to crop up again with reference to Strasberg and the Method approach in America, as commentators complained that the stress on "feeling the part" produced actors with a narrow scope and an apparent inability to play many of the established classics.

It was argued that the emphasis on affective memory led some actors to depend on it excessively and to misuse it. Even theater people generally sympathetic to the Method pointed out that danger. Actors would hang on to the emotions aroused by the exercise at all costs, and in the process isolate themselves from any real interaction with other players on the stage. Their performances featuring these solipsistic self-indulgences might be interesting, but were usually detrimental to the play. Other actors would use the exercise as a substitute for the emotionally releasing abreactive processes of psychoanalysis, a sort of "private therapy." Still others would feel threatened, perhaps actually harmed, by some of the more powerful, near hysterical emotions provoked by the procedure.

Strasberg has contended that the misunderstanding or misuse of affective memory by individual actors is not the result of the emphasis on it, but rather a case of a little learning being a dangerous thing. Many of these performers have not studied the procedure under proper supervision, nor have they trained themselves to use it in an integrated overall acting technique. Strasberg has continually warned actors against making hasty generalizations about the Method and trying to use what they have learned prematurely. Even at The Actors Studio the training in the technique is not systematic, but piecemeal and occasional. And while the procedure is carefully explained and placed in its proper perspective whenever it is dealt with there, not all the members maintain the continuity of training and the professional discipline that would make the technique of real value to them.

Affective memory is by no means an indulgence of Strasberg's. It is an absolute necessity to his concept of acting as the creation of real experience in response to imaginary stimuli. For him, it is the only way to bring emotion under control and harness it so that it can be at the service of the actor's will. Even so, Strasberg does not advocate emotion for emotion's sake. Most of the psychological harm and creative frustration actors have suffered in straining for feeling is the result of their misusing the affective-memory procedure by going directly for the emotion, or by trying to hold on to it at all costs. Strasberg teaches that emotion must be approached through the mediation of sensory stimuli, and that even when the actor begins to experience the emotion, he continues to focus his attention on the kinesthetic elements while letting the emotion run its course. Eventually, the repeated work with the sensory stimuli establishes a conditioned reflex whereby the merest suggestion of key sensory elements sets off the emotion. His approach to emotion and emotional control is not of the psychoanalytical school of Freud, according to Strasberg, but of the behavioral school of Pavlov.[17]

As it developed, Pavlov played an important role in Stanislavski's evolving theories during the 1930s. The physiologist was very interested in Stanislavski's work and asked to see a manuscript copy of *An Actor Prepares* while it was being written. The two corresponded up to the time of the scientist's death in 1936, and it is reported that Stanislavski began using various physiological terms at rehearsals during this period. It was under the influence of the Russian physiologist and of materialist psychology in general that Stanislavski evolved the culminating form of his System: the Method of Physical Actions.

A procedure that ostensibly revolutionized the Stanislavski techniques that preceded it, the Method of Physical Actions operates on the premise that all behavior is "psychophysical," and that if an actor selects appropriate physical actions and executes them with full belief and logic in the playing of a scene, he will automatically elicit an emotion in the process. In the light of Stanislavski's long search for a workable approach to the actor's creative mechanism, it was a significant shift from the so-called "line of inner action" to the "line of physical actions." Though both Strasberg and the proponents of this "final" method claimed to reflect the stimulus-response theories of Pavlov, the advocates of the Method of Physical Actions were to prove among the most vocal critics of The Actors Studio "distortion" of the System, especially vis-à-vis the emphasis on affective memory as opposed to physical action.

Stella Adler's 1934 report to the Group Theatre about her meetings with Stanislavski, during which he explained to her the centrality of "actions and tasks" to his theory, was certainly an indication of where the Russian master was heading at the time. But the precise nature of the changes he was broaching was yet to be clarified, and there were to be four more years during which he would solidify the approach that would formally be tagged "the Method of Physical Actions."

The publication of several books by Stanislavski, including *An Actor Prepares* (1936) and *Stanislavski Produces Othello* (released posthumously in 1948), revealed his explicit call for approaching the emotions through physical actions. But the first of these volumes had also emphasized inner processes and had included a lengthy discussion of "Emotion Memory" and its importance, so that it was not absolutely clear whether his ideas on physical actions were simply cumulative additions to his earlier theories or a radical departure from them.[18]

Finally, with the publication of Stanislavski's complete works in Russian and their translation into German, there began a debate over the relationship of the Method of Physical Actions to the System as a whole. A number of theater scholars argued that the Method of Physical Actions was a revolutionary change in Stanislavski's procedures. Strasberg, in his 1957 article for the *Encyclopaedia Britannica*, challenged this evaluation:

Some have interpreted this as a reversal of his previous methods. Actually, it was intended not to rule out or contrast with but to serve as a life belt by means of which the previous preparation and work on a role could be securely held.[19]

It was not until the winter of 1964, when members of the Moscow Art Theater came to America to conduct a series of lectures and discussions, that the subject at last received a full airing here.[20] The Moscow Art Theater seminars were attended by a large number of American theater people, including members of The Actors Studio. Through their translators, the Russians discussed the evolution of Stanislavski's ideas and the Method of Physical Actions in great detail. The Americans were particularly interested in the status of affective memory in the final version of the Stanislavski System. The Russians tried to explain how Stanislavski had abandoned the affective-memory-exercise approach to emotion long before his death in 1938 in favor of the physical-actions approach, which he called "the result of my whole life's work," though he continued to speak of affective memory as the fundamental source of the actor's emotional life on stage. "Was this not a contradiction?" the Americans might have asked.

The confusion on this point has its source in a problem of terminology. The phrase *affective memory* (or, alternatively, *emotion memory*) has been used to describe two distinct concepts: the *phenomenon* of affective or emotion memory, that is, the capacity of the mind to store emotional experience and the accumulated wealth of such recoverable emotional experience itself, as opposed to the affective memory *exercise*, by means of which specific emotional components of this "storehouse" are directly tapped through sensory-recall techniques. It was the *exercise* that critics denigrated when they spoke of the "misuse of affective memory." The *phenomenon* of emotion memory was never challenged. Stanislavski's "final" theory simply argued that properly chosen and executed physical actions would somehow subconsciously connect with the actor's memory of affect and safely release the appropriate emotion as necessary.

But, the question remains, did the Method of Physical Actions actually accomplish what was claimed for it? Stanislavski evidently felt that it did, and a slew of Russian theater practitioners have, since his death, continued to proclaim its unique efficacy and value.[21] The historical record, however, apparently tells another story.

Stanislavski worked on his new method with the younger members and students of the MAT; as happened earlier in his career, the veterans of the company rebelled against his innovations. Significantly enough, Stanislavski never tested the Method of Physical Actions on himself in production, as he did with his earlier procedures. Nor did he complete his experiment of testing the efficacy of the method in the production of *Tartuffe,* which got under way in 1937 and was completed only after his death. His limited attempts to use aspects of the method in his penultimate production of Bulgakov's *Molière* were likewise inconclusive, as the play was a failure. Despite Stanislavski's assertions about his new technique, and despite all the attempts by Soviet historians and theoreticians to play up the final and absolute efficacy of the Method of Physical Actions, there was no definitive proof while Stanislavski lived that the method could create the kind of living experience on stage that its proponents said it could.

Strasberg has argued that to this day there has been no dramatic evidence that the Method of Physical Actions does, in fact, arouse emotion as it is supposed to. And if the application of the procedure is any test, the moribund reputation of the Moscow Art Theater, which under its former director, Kedrov, was run with an extreme emphasis on the "final techniques," might indicate that the Method of Physical Actions is a procedure that has not lived up to expectations.

The polemics of the advocates of Stanislavski's final teaching—and one can only speculate on how the Russian master would respond to whatever has been achieved artistically by those who promote his later ideas with such missionary zeal—cannot obscure one crucial historical fact. It was the transfigured acting of the Moscow Art Theater of the 1920s and before—the period of the now "discredited" earlier Stanislavski techniques—that so inspired the world and so revolutionized theatrical performance.

Despite the insistence of its advocates that the Method of Physical Actions is *the* definitive and immutable solution to the problems of acting, despite even Stanislavski's assertion that it is the fulfillment of his life's work, there have been good reasons for the relative indifference to the technique as a total approach to performance and for the continuation of individual applications of the System. In American professional circles not the least of these reasons has been the absence of any truly outstanding actors who have been trained in the procedure.

In America, Stanislavski's ideas are taught in a variety of adaptations, the most well known being Strasberg's at The Actors Studio with its emphasis on sensory and affective elements. Other teachers in the Stanislavski tradition, most notably Stella Adler, Sanford Meisner, and Uta Hagen, have been successful and influential in their own rights; the many talented and successful actors who were trained by each of them is evidence of that. (Many Studio members have studied with one or more of these teachers, too.) But Strasberg's unique approach, antedating all the others, has been spotlighted through his association with The Actors Studio, and has undoubtedly been the most famous and most influential over the long term.* Consequently, much of the general criticism that is leveled at the shortcomings of Method training is implicitly aimed at Strasberg and the Studio.

When the *Tulane Drama Review*, for instance, published a two-issue examination of "Stanislavski and America" in the fall and winter of 1964, the second issue included several articles that, implicitly and explicitly, were aimed at debunking Strasberg. One of these, Gordon Rogoff's "Lee Strasberg: Burning Ice" piece, was, in many respects, an *ad hominem* attack on the man.[22] The preparatory notes for that issue, which are on file in the offices of *The Drama Review*, reveal the negative predisposition on the subject of Strasberg. Despite this tendentiousness, Theodore Hoffman, associate editor on the first issue who was not involved with the second, wrote in his introduction to the project that "the Group and Studio experience, however inadequate and aborted, generated most of the worthwhile theatre we possess. It can weather the withering tongue of controversy, fulsome tribute, and the malpractice of *faux devots* and imitators. . . . Lee Strasberg is the touchstone of our mid-century theatre, possibly its most significant thinker." [23]

Other critics disagreed, seeing him as responsible for whatever was

---

* As if in recognition of this, in January 1963 Strasberg was sent to Moscow for a three-week visit as America's representative to the Stanislavski Centenary.

wrong with the American theater. "Strasberg has been the interior decorator of a crumbling structure whose foundations he has done nothing to change," said Robert Brustein.[24] Many of these critics felt that Strasberg's Method training perpetuated an acting style suitable to only one kind of production style: realism—"contemporary" realism, to be precise. Similar fault had been found with Stanislavski during his long career, but, as Strasberg's critics pointed out, at least Stanislavski and the Moscow Art Theater worked within the classical repertory. Even the great Russian experimenters, Vakhtangov and Meyerhold, these critics noted, used classic texts in their work. It was true that the American Method had helped create outstanding productions of Odets's, Miller's, and Williams's plays, but what of the rest of the world literature? Michael Redgrave summed it up this way:

I think the present manifestation of the Method is admirable for certain kinds of realistic plays, but I think the onus of the proof of Mr. Strasberg's theory rests with him and that he and his disciples must produce professional productions of plays from Shakespeare, Restoration Comedy, or, say, Giraudoux or almost any of the later French playwrights.[25]

The complaints against Method training inevitably revolved around the emphasis on the inner technique. Stanislavski in *An Actor Prepares* had stated that "the fundamental aim of our art is the creation of [the] inner life of a human spirit, and its expression in an artistic form." The critics argued that at the Studio the second half of that statement was being grossly neglected. When Robert Lewis gave his memorable series of lectures on the Stanislavski System in the spring of 1957 in an attempt to clear the air of the misunderstandings that surrounded the subject, he underscored the lack of theatrical expressivity in the work of many Method devotees.[26] Though he did not name them, the implication was clear that he included Strasberg and the Studio among those who gave only token recognition to the development of the actor's voice and body. Without the proper training in the external elements of the System, went Lewis's message, Method actors would never be able to play the classics. They would never develop the necessary style.

For Strasberg, such criticism has always been beside the point. While he acknowledges the importance of voice and body training, for him the first essential of acting is the training of the imagination to respond to imaginary stimuli in order to create whatever reality in whatever "style" the actor, the director, or the play calls for. Strasberg insists that style is simply an expression of content, the play's content. It is not an acting technique, nor a special way of performing, but a "heightened reality" that is achieved through finding the subtext for a play that allows the actor to respond as he must. The creation of a style is the result of the kind of procedure Vakhtangov used in his production of *Turandot*, where the actors played performers putting on a play, in order to justify inwardly the theatricality he wanted. But first and foremost, the essential thing for him is "the human being and his living presence," whose reality is the same in all plays from all times. That is why he rejects the idea that there is a Method style or that the Method is useful only for contemporary realistic plays.

In fairness to Strasberg, it should be pointed out that he constantly cautions young Studio actors against the sort of naturalistic slouch that became part of the Brando-Dean image. Such casualness, he warns, is not to be equated with being real on stage; it "is only the pose of reality." Over the years, he has particularly enjoyed helping actors explore the great roles in dramatic literature, and has said that for him "the most interesting things in the Studio have been where the people have worked on Shakespeare and have come through with fabulous investigations of situations."

He is proud to point out that more Studio actors have worked on such parts as Hamlet, Richard III, Lady Macbeth, and Juliet than on any single character in contemporary drama. More scenes of Shakespeare have been done at the Studio than those of the next four most frequently performed playwrights *combined* (Chekhov, Williams, O'Neill, and Strindberg). From a very long list of scene work, there were Paul Newman as Petruchio, Bruce Dern as Henry V, Geraldine Page as Lady Macbeth, Rip Torn as Macbeth, Al Pacino and Ron Leibman as Richard III, Christopher Walken as Iago, Barbra Streisand—in her single appearance at the Studio—as Juliet, and Kevin McCarthy, Michael Wager, Alfred Ryder, Roscoe Lee Browne, and Estelle Parsons(!) as Hamlet, to mention only a few. (Most of these people worked on a variety of Shakespearean roles, as have dozens of other Studio actors over the years.)

But all this work in class and all the professional efforts of individual Studio actors with the classics notwithstanding, and despite

Strasberg's doctrinaire theorizing about the illimitable applicability of the Method approach, the truth is that the American Method simply does not have a record of accomplishment in the production of noncontemporary plays. Elia Kazan stated it quite directly in the early seventies when he said, "We have not solved the classical acting problem. I failed with it." Is this inherently the fault of the Method? Not so, says Strasberg, who ascribes this failure primarily to the general and crucial lack of intensive training over an extensive period for most American performers. "There is no real training today for the actor, in The Studio or anywhere else," Strasberg has admitted. "The actor there comes in contact with a certain directed stimulus, but there is no consecutive and systematic adherence to a routine as a result of which the actor can become skillful and able easily to accomplish the kind of things that craft or technique would make it possible for him to do." [27]

The Method, in other words, never having been "methodically" or thoroughly inculcated, has never been truly tested; neither in the classics nor, for that matter, in the more experimental modern drama. For this reason, one has to take on faith that, above and beyond its known virtues, the Method can accomplish all that Strasberg says it can. Unfortunately, polemical posturings, however persuasive, are no substitute for demonstrable proof. This is perhaps the greatest irony emanating from Strasberg's work at the Studio. By its very nature the Studio has failed to test the full possibilities of its actors and its Method. Two two-hour meetings a week with Strasberg (cut down to one a week by 1978) can hardly serve to train anyone in depth. Since there are no requirements to sustain membership once one is admitted, Studio actors are not obliged to work with any regularity, to study the basic elements of technique with any consistency, or to develop the full range of their creative equipment (including voice, speech, and physical agility) to any established standard. And, by and large, they do not. In any given season, most members do far more observing than acting at Studio sessions. The individual's work there is, for the most part, sporadic and haphazard.

What the Studio does offer is a very limited service to members who feel they have specific problems they want to deal with. Strasberg is truly at his best analyzing matters for them and suggesting ways to solve their difficulties. Depending on the intelligence, the dedication, and the courage of the individual actor, his advice can be very valuable and has proven so. But often the actors are not clear about how to extrapolate these encounters with Strasberg to their work as a whole. As for those who are observing the work: young new members have been advised to wait a year, studying the way Strasberg subtly handles each individual performer, before speaking up to criticize or even comment on what they see. It is so easy to misconstrue what goes on at the Studio that without careful and continuing attention, misconceptions and misapplications of the Method inevitably result.

Members' explanations of how they actually work and how they interpret Strasberg's teaching are surprisingly varied. Those who use Strasberg's techniques precisely as he would want them to are few and far between. Many Studio members have conceded that they do not consciously or consistently use sensory exercises, affective memories, or other Method elements, and Strasberg has criticized a number of famous Studio members for not really being masters of Method technique.

Each Studio member seems to internalize Strasberg's teaching as best he understands it, subjectively transforming it into his own way of working and usually using what he has absorbed more instinctually than consciously. Though the actor can pick up important information from observing and working at the Studio, what he learns, being to a great extent piecemeal and discontinuous, winds up being integrated into his consciousness in a highly random, unstructured manner. The whole process may point him in the right direction and stir in him a good deal of creative enthusiasm, but it does not necessarily make him an accomplished artist. This is what Strasberg means when he says that the Studio provides its members with only "a certain directed stimulus" (as opposed to a totally designed training experience).*

The lack of systematic and thorough training in the Method at the Studio has been responsible for many of the workshop's shortcom-

---

* It was precisely in order to provide an environment for such continuity and work in depth that he decided to establish his schools, the Strasberg institutes in New York and Los Angeles, in the early seventies, Strasberg has explained. Entirely independent of the Studio, though the two are sometimes confused, the Lee Strasberg Institute was to absorb more and more of Strasberg's attention during the seventies as he came to feel that it was there, where his ideas were being systematically and intensively inculcated and verified, that the Method was being most consistently and properly utilized.

ings and has contributed to much of the misunderstanding that plagues Strasberg and the organization. It has also contributed to the impression that Strasberg and the Studio are not primarily interested in producing well-rounded actors, but only in servicing the narrow-gauge, close to "type," careers of stars-in-the-making. Some of Strasberg's public statements seem to verify these perceptions, unfortunately. The fact that what he intends to say is often simply misconstrued does not help matters. In an article for *The New York Times* in September of 1956, for example, Strasberg wrote that "the simplest examples of Stanislavsky's ideas are actors such as Gary Cooper, John Wayne, and Spencer Tracy. They try not to act but to be themselves, to respond or react. They refuse to say or do anything they feel not to be consonant with their own character. They have no conscious theories; they try to be simple and honest. This is what lends their work a peculiar sense of authenticity, even at moments of technical insecurity." [28] There was a flurry of protest from outraged readers. Howard Lindsay wanted to know if Strasberg was promoting "personality" actors, who play themselves rather than the author's character? What about the intent of the playwright? Was this another confirmation of Method distortion? [29]

By referring to Cooper, Wayne, and Tracy, Strasberg was trying to upset the notion that the Studio and the Method had a corner on talent or that "Method acting was in a cubby hole somewheres. People got together and practiced some kind of magic and they came out Method actors." It was the same point Stanislavski constantly made: that he did not *invent* anything in the way of acting techniques; great actors of past and present used these procedures without a conscious or systematic awareness of them. Strasberg was certainly not holding up Cooper and Wayne as ideals of great acting, but was simply suggesting that in their own way they practiced what he has elsewhere called "the primitive form or exaggerated form of Stanislavski, insofar as they always remain only themselves, which is Stanislavski's first stage of work." He even went on to say in the *Times* article that the proper understanding and study of the Method techniques "might serve to enlarge the scope of these same actors who otherwise tend to develop only one facet of themselves."

This kind of misunderstanding might have been avoided if there had been some comprehensive presentation of Strasberg's ideas with which to examine and clarify matters. No one who was familiar with his position on the Vakhtangov "second formulation" could think he was advocating bringing the character down to the size of an actor's personality. Michael Chekhov, in his book *To the Actor*, quotes Stanislavski's admonition to him to "Organize and write down your thoughts concerning the technique of acting. It is your duty and the duty of everyone who loves the theater and looks devotedly into its future." [30] It is the Studio's and the Method's loss that Strasberg has not yet done so.

At the present time, Strasberg is working to finish a book he hopes will finally state his case clearly and unequivocally. If such a book had appeared years ago it might have helped demystify the Method and the Studio and perhaps eliminate some of the confusion and controversy that have dogged them for so long.

The controversy over the Method was at its most intense during the fifties, subsiding somewhat during the sixties except for the arguments over the Method of Physical Actions. (The occasional private and public flare-ups between Strasberg and Miss Adler are evidence that the internecine dissension among Method-ists still smolders, however.[31]) In the late sixties far more radical acting approaches were to become the fashionable sources of conversation and polemic. As the Method passed out of this period of active controversy, its use continued unabated, while its true nature—both strengths and limitations—was more generally recognized and accepted. From the perspective of theater practice, after all, the Method was essentially a technique (a "set of tools," as Strasberg put it) and not the be-all and end-all of acting. The words of Stanislavski, as recorded posthumously by one of his directors, put the subject into perspective:

Besides the method, actors must have all the qualities that constitute a real artist: inspiration, intelligence, taste, the ability to communicate, charm, temperament, fine speech and movement, quick excitability and an expressive appearance. One cannot go very far with just the method.[32]

CHAPTER **6**

Kazan Departs:
1960–1962

"**A**LTHOUGH WE HAVE NO FORMAL NATIONAL THEATRE as such in this country," declared *The New York Times* "Topics" editorial of May 14, 1960, "in a way the Actors Studio has become that, for it has been demonstrating since its inception that there is indeed an American style of acting."

Thus began a salute to the Studio from one of New York's leading institutions—an instance of recognition that in its special way made The Actors Studio "official" at last.

"The American actor," the editorial stated, "responds . . . to a naturalism based on the creativity of the individual and this is why the method has become the dominant school of American acting, with the Actors Studio its symbolic as well as actual fountainhead. It thrives here because it fits the American character." [1]

This welcome gesture at the beginning of what was to prove a tumultuous half decade for the workshop was occasioned by an unprecedented event in the Studio's history: the opening of its doors to the general public for "An Evening of Scenes from Studio Work." A special benefit to raise money for a projected building fund, the affair consisted of three performances of scenes worked on in class by some of the more illustrious members of the Studio, including Jo Van Fleet and Alfred Ryder in Tennessee Williams's *I Rise in Flames, Cried the Phoenix;* Eli Wallach and Anne Jackson in Sean O'Casey's *Bedtime Story;* Lee Grant in Dorothy Parker's *Glory in the Daytime;* and, as the *pièce de résistance,* Anne Bancroft and Kevin McCarthy in Lerner and Loew's *My Fair Lady.*

During the preceding fall, at another fund-raising party which brought in over thirty-five thousand dollars to the Studio, the directors had initiated a "Friends of The Actors Studio" committee, the first of a number of such groups that were to be formed in the years ahead. The idea was that these "Friends" would make substantial contributions to keep the Studio afloat, and, in return, would be invited to participate in various Studio functions, including special lectures, receptions for visiting artists and theater companies, and special performances.

The first of these special performances was a presentation in 1959 of two one-act plays, Tennessee Williams's *The Night of the Iguana* and William Inge's *The Tiny Closet.* Both plays had been presented by Studio actors Vivian Nathan, Rosemary Murphy, Arthur Storch, Patrick O'Neal, Lou Antonio, and Joanne Linville at the Spoleto Festival in Italy during its second season the previous summer. For the performance at the Studio in the autumn of 1959, the cast, under the direction of Frank Corsaro, performed a version of the Williams one-act play that the author had revised after Spoleto. Williams attended the Studio presentation and subsequently expanded the piece into the full-length play which Corsaro and a mostly different cast took first to Florida and then to Broadway, where it opened on December 28, 1961. (During the third Spoleto Festival, in the summer of 1960, another group of Studio performers, Jo Van Fleet, Alfred Ryder, and Tom Milian, under the direction of Eli Rill, performed two one-act plays of Williams's—*The Lady of Larkspur Lotion* and *I Rise in Flames, Cried the Phoenix*—and a single one-act play of Meade Roberts's, *Maidens and Mistresses at Home at the Zoo.*)

Despite the appeal of such events as the public showing of work-in-progress on *Iguana,* and the spring presentation of experimental scenes, however, the Studio was not able to keep the Friends committee alive beyond its first season. (Regrettably, the workshop has never enjoyed steady financial support from any one group of people.) Annual benefits therefore continued to be the main source of income well into the seventies. Non-Studio celebrities often generously contributed their services to these gala affairs. In 1961, for instance, Mike Nichols and Elaine May participated in a spoof on auditioning for the Studio at the benefit held in the ballroom of Roseland Dance City. They were joined by Mary Martin, Henry Fonda, and Nancy Walker, under the direction of Joshua Logan.

The Friends committee of 1960, short-lived as it was, did perform the valuable service of raising enough money to help the Studio realize some of its plans for expansion. There were finally funds to get the long-awaited Directors Unit under way and to begin enlarging and reorganizing the Playwrights Unit. Strasberg declined to select the members for the new directors group, and so Gordon Rogoff interviewed the more than two hundred young aspirants who were interested in becoming part of the new Unit, whittling down the choices to the approximately eighty-five members and fourteen observers whom Strasberg approved and met with for the first time on February 25, 1960.[2]

Directors had played an integral role in the life of the Studio from the beginning. As early as 1949, Gene Frankel, John Stix, and Alan Schneider had been designated official director-observers. It was not a privilege easily earned. Strasberg's policy was that all potential director-observers had to have solid production credits. Jack Garfein, who had studied in Strasberg's directing class at the Dramatic Workshop, remembers coming to his mentor with reviews of a television show he had directed that said the production had had the excitement of the early Group Theatre. It was not enough. Strasberg told him, "You have to direct something in the theater." Garfein, desperate to become an official observer, arranged to stage *Camille* for the Equity Literary Theatre just so Strasberg could see it. Strasberg, genuinely and generously interested in dedicated and ambitious young talents, attended a performance and admitted Garfein to the Studio. Subsequently, a number of director-observers, including John Stix, Frank Corsaro, and Garfein, were voted into membership.

In late 1957 Garfein organized a group of young directors who met with Strasberg on and off during the spring season of 1958, but this arrangement, like a similar one set up by John Stix in the early fifties, lasted only briefly. It was only in February of 1960 that a Directors Unit as a continuing part of the Studio's operations was firmly established.

The rationale for the creation of the Directors Unit was to provide these theater artists, like their player-colleagues, with "a place to come in out of the rain," an environment in which they could freely explore and expand their talents. The Unit was not intended for beginners, nor was it conceived as a school for directors. It was not a forum for showcasing directorial talent; as with the acting, there was no emphasis on final results. It was a place that offered a sense of continuity and collegial encouragement in the *process* of working.

Strasberg operated from the premise that many directors are not really aware of or sympathetic to the actor's problems. It became one of the purposes of the Directors Unit to familiarize the young directors with the Method approach to working with the actor, as well as with what Strasberg calls the "basic procedure" for attacking a play, namely, visualizing it, analyzing the text, and translating it into the kinds of directions that facilitate the actor's responding as the director requires. It was Strasberg's aim to make directors more willing to trust the creative ideas of the actor and to see what the actor could contribute before the director imposed his will.

On various occasions Strasberg recalled how Stanislavski's own directorial procedures had evolved in this respect. During the earlier part of his creative life, Stanislavski had been heavily influenced by the "despotic" approach to directing of Ludwig Chronegk, who headed the troupe of the famous Duke of Saxe-Meiningen. In emulation of the "producer-autocrat" Chronegk, the Russian master would give his actors detailed directions about every aspect of their performances. To illustrate Stanislavski's crippling imposition of his own preconceptions on a role, Strasberg quoted Stanislavski's notes for the scene of Nina's first meeting with Trigorin in the prompt copy for his production of *The Sea Gull*. They were so brilliantly particular that instead of freeing the creative imagination of the poor young actress playing Nina, they paralyzed her, and she failed in the role. Chekhov was especially distressed by her performance, but no actress could have fulfilled what Stanislavski envisioned without having imagined and re-created for herself the reality he so exhaustively described.

Toward the end of his life, however, Stanislavski had come full circle. Ultimately, he took great care to preserve the personal creativity of the actor from the incursions of the director. He learned to appreciate the tremendous value of the actor's imagination and focused on means of reaching that imagination in such a way as to stimulate the actor to fulfill the director's concept of the play willingly, organically, and creatively.

Strasberg's own directorial experience in this regard is worth citing. He was known for the degree of freedom he gave his Group Theatre actors to find their characters without his interference, and notorious for avoiding the giving of stage directions, much less line readings, to his performers. Group actor J. Edward Bromberg reportedly once bet a fellow member of the company that Strasberg could not be induced to give the simple stage direction, "Cross left," in the course of an afternoon's rehearsal. For hours, the actor wandered aimlessly all over the stage, trying by every subterfuge to provoke the director into giving the desired order. But Strasberg was impervious to the scheme, and Bromberg won some money on the wager.

On the other hand, Strasberg was critical of an overpreoccupation with the work of the actor, to the detriment of the play itself. The emphasis in the Directors Unit was not only on the relationship of the director to the creative work of the actor, though that was a central concern, but on the totality of the director's creative obligation to his production. The "basic procedure" not only dealt with the director's approach to the actor, but with the overall, step-by-step handling of the aural, visual, and acting elements of the production. In the discussions of the work that directors brought into the Unit, in fact, little or nothing was said about the acting per se. The director was not particularly obligated to use Studio or even Method actors. While it was hoped he would learn enough about dealing with actors to be able to get from them what he wanted, his work in the Unit was judged solely on the basis of how close it came to his own conception of what he was after. (Again, Strasberg worked from the formula, "What did you expect? What did you get?") What Strasberg and the Unit were prepared to offer was help toward the realization of the director's intentions.

The intent of the director was a central concern of the Directors Unit, just as the intent of the playwright was a central concern of the Playwrights Unit. While the directors' group was being planned, Kazan had quipped, "We think that we'll have a little sideline course for directors in how to change the authors' main idea; and then in the Playwrights Unit, we'll have a little sideline course in how not to let the director change the writers' main course." [3] But the defining of an intention was serious business to Strasberg because he believed that if a director intended one thing, but wound up with something else, he was not a good director—no matter how striking the result of his efforts.

Strasberg encouraged the members of the Unit to study how such outstanding directors as Stanislavski, Meyerhold, Vakhtangov, Brecht, and Reinhardt had realized their directorial intentions in their famous productions. He decried the fact that theater artists were constantly starting from scratch, with no awareness of the wealth of experiment that had preceded them. He discussed with the Unit his own directorial awakening after his trip to Russia and his exposure to the great productions he saw there.[4]

Many of these issues were first touched on during the initial meeting of the Unit, which consisted of discussions between Strasberg and the members. After encouraging the directors to start bringing in projects so that the talk could become less general and more concrete, Strasberg witnessed the group's first project when his own codirector, Kazan, brought in some improvisations from Aeschylus's *Agamemnon* he had been working on with Avra Petrides and Andreas Voutsinas. This was only the beginning of Kazan's involvement with the Aeschylean *Oresteia*. The following year he presented some work from *The Libation Bearers* in which he tried to solve the problem of the chorus in "a more individually characterized approach." His interest in the Greek trilogy went so far as his having considered opening the Vivian Beaumont Theater at Lincoln Center with it. (Kazan says he yet might do it someday. "I'm still thinking about it.") The second season of the Directors Unit (1960–1961) began with some work on Douglas Moore's opera, *The Ballad of Baby Doe*, directed by Martin Fried. Later in the year, on December 8, Fried also presented what was perhaps the first American staging of Eugene O'Neill's *Hughie* with Joe Sullivan and Vincent Gardenia.*

After three and a half seasons of operation, from the spring of 1960 through the spring of 1963, Strasberg decided to suspend the

---

* Joe Sullivan says that Henry Hewes, the critic, brought the one-act to his attention. Hewes had seen it performed in Sweden and had returned with a copy of the play. He called Sullivan about it because he wanted to direct the actor in it at the Studio. But Fried eventually got to direct it, and Sullivan played it on three different occasions at the workshop. A Broadway production of the long one-acter, starring Ben Gazzara and directed by Fried, would open at the Golden Theatre some fifteen years later on February 11, 1975.

Unit. He had been disturbed by the level of work and the frequency of sessions in which discussion filled the void left by the failure of directors to schedule scenes. During the fall of 1963, he considered ways of restructuring the group both as to the makeup of its membership and as to the handling of directorial projects. On January 9, 1964, he resumed the activities of the Unit with the first of a series of talks on "The Art of Directing." The first six lectures constituted, in effect, a history of directing, focusing especially on the work of Stanislavski, Meyerhold, Vakhtangov, Brecht, and Reinhardt. The seventh lecture dealt with the first week of rehearsal, including a step-by-step analysis of the director's tasks in approaching a play and his actors during this crucial period. The eighth lecture dealt with problems of casting, and the ninth and last with the questions of putting the finishing touches to a production.

The work of the Directors Unit was to continue intermittently into the seventies. In the course of its existence, the names of many outstanding American directors graced its roster, among them: Joseph Anthony, William Ball, Michael Bennett, Melvin Bernhardt, Vinette Carroll, Shirley Clarke, Frank Corsaro, Vincent Donehue, Allen Fletcher, John Frankenheimer, Gerald Freedman, Martin Fried, Michael V. Gazzo, André Gregory, Ulu Grosbard, Wynn Handman, Michael Kahn, Milton Katselas, Jack Landau, Jacques Levy, Arthur Penn, Frank Perry, Ernest Pintoff, Nikos Psacharapoulos, José Quintero, Lloyd Richards, David Ross, Gene Saks, Alan Schneider, Edwin Sherin, John Stix, Arthur Storch, Gladys Vaughn, and Stuart Vaughn.

Some of these directors participated actively and continuously over many years; some sat in on only a handful of sessions. For many of them—participants and observers—the "directed stimulus" of the Unit was to be a telling influence. For those who were more or less casual or passive onlookers, the Unit provided, at the least, some insight into more fruitful ways of working with actors. For those who participated actively and intensively, the Unit was, in many cases, the basic source for an entire approach to directing.[5]

The early sixties also witnessed some important changes and developments in the Playwrights Unit. Molly Kazan, who had been heading the Unit for four years, submitted a letter of resignation on January 31, 1962. Arthur Penn had nominally been her associate in the running of the Unit, but because of his busy professional schedule, in effect, she had been solely in charge ever since William Inge's departure from the scene. (Frank Corsaro and John Stix helped her on occasion.) Weary of the responsibility, and recognizing that she could not effectively delegate the Unit's producing functions to other people, she offered to finish out the season in an attempt to "pull the operation back into shape" while the search for her successor could be carried out.

In the interim, she tried to interest Walter Kerr and others in the position, consulted with various playwright-members of the Unit about their thoughts on the future of the group, and prepared a thirty-eight-page report, "The Playwrights' Unit: The condition, the temperment [*sic*] and the needs of playwrights; a history of the Unit; suggestions for the future," which she hoped would provide a rationale and a framework for the transition from her leadership.

During the summer of 1962, a Playwrights' Committee consisting of William Archibald, Edward Albee, William Goyen, Paul Richards, and Mark Rydell consulted with Harold Clurman and Gaynor Bradish, a professor of English literature at New York University, about their possible participation in the Unit during the following season. The idea was that Clurman and Bradish share its leadership, each to handle thirty-six sessions during the season. The committee also called for the reevaluation of the membership status of each playwright in the group and suggested new operating procedures for the presentation of work. Finally, they outlined a program for inviting such eminent figures as Robert Lowell, W. H. Auden, Harold Pinter, Jo Mielziner, Leonard Bernstein, and others to help generate an "atmosphere of theatre" in the Unit.

As things worked out, Gaynor Bradish led the group during the 1962–1963 season. (Clurman, who wanted to be paid for moderating, had dropped out of the picture during the preceding summer.) The Unit was reconstituted to contain fewer members than previously—sixty-two, under Bradish's tenure. More radical changes were to come. By the end of the season Bradish was recommending that the group's membership be further reduced until a comparatively small circle of only the most important writers remained.

Edward Albee, Jack Gelber, Arthur Kopit, and Jack Richardson met with Strasberg to discuss the entire operation of the Unit and why they believed the group was too large to function effectively. They were given authority to cut the Unit's membership to twenty.

Aside from Albee, Gelber, Kopit, and Richardson, those asked to remain were Lawrence Alson, William Archibald, James Baldwin, Conrad Bromberg, William Goyen, James Leo Herlihy, Adrienne Kennedy, Norman Mailer, Terrence McNally, Eleanor Perry, Muriel Resnick, William Snyder, Sol Stein, Deric Washburne, Lawrence Weinberg, and Arnold Weinstein.

The manner in which these twenty writers were selected angered and upset a great number of people (mostly those not chosen), who felt the choice was carried out undemocratically and on the basis of favoritism. Those not included in the reorganized Unit characterized the committee's action as "a power grab," "arbitrary," "Hitlerian (and/or Stalinist)," and "underhanded." June Havoc resigned in disgust from all three of the Studio's units. The whole course of events created such feelings of ill will around the Studio that Albee, Kopit, and Richardson finally felt obliged to send out a report in which they defended the actions that had led to the reorganization.

When the 1963–1964 season began, the twenty-member Playwrights Unit was no longer headed by Gaynor Bradish. The group announced that it was reverting to a policy of inviting Studio members and observers to attend their sessions only when the playwright being presented wanted them there. At their first meeting they voted in eleven additional writers as "participating observers." [6]

Albee took the occasion of the Unit's reorganization to invite Tennessee Williams to participate in it. Williams, who had never been an official member despite his long association with the Studio, expressed an eagerness to be involved.

For some reason, bad breath or bad toilet habits or an itinerant way of life, I never was invited to participate in the Unit. With playwrights being discharged as well as not invited, it sounds like a rather formidable unit, but what isn't? I am not scared off. And I certainly do have things I would love to have tried out. My career has turned to a try-out it seems, anyway. I can't think of any better place to have a try-out. Most of my work now, and from now on, I suspect is in the short-long or long-short form, intensely personal, and highly eclectic, and maybe unfit for public exposure. But I know, from past experience with plays such as the short form of Camino Real and Night of Iguana [*sic*], both of which were explored by the Studio, that the atmosphere there is sympathetically creative and experimental, and it would be of the greatest help to me to have one or two of them tried out as class-room exercises, culminating in the sort of in-group presentation that the Studio provides to nerve-shattered playwrights. So if you will accept me as a probationary or novitiate sort of a contributor, I will *gladly* contribute.[7]

Despite this expression of his characteristic goodwill, there is no evidence that Williams, who lived much of the time in Key West, Florida, actually ever did get around to contributing to the Unit.

Albee himself contributed little to the Unit in the period after the reorganization. No play of his was produced there after *The Zoo Story* and *The Death of Bessie Smith* during the 1959–1960 season. The first of those plays had been assigned to John Stix to direct, with Shepperd Strudwick and Lou Antonio in the roles of Peter and Jerry. They had only a brief rehearsal, and carried scripts when they presented the work to the Unit. According to Stix, it was not a very good performance, but the play was received with acclaim by Albee's fellow playwrights, first and foremost by Norman Mailer, who said, "That's the best one-act play ever written in this country." Arthur Penn concurred. Evidently Albee was pleased with what Stix had achieved in a short time because he subsequently asked him to direct *Bessie Smith* in the Unit.[8]

By 1963 Albee's career was in full bloom. *Who's Afraid of Virginia Woolf?* had been an enormous success the previous season, and at the very moment the new Playwrights Unit was getting under way, he was busy with the previews for his second Broadway production, *The Ballad of the Sad Café.* By the following spring, he had left the Studio to found an independent playwrights' unit run and financed by Richard Barr, Clinton Wilder, and himself.

Albee's four-year experience at the Studio seemed to make little impression on him. He firmly resisted the idea of discovering a play in production that Strasberg and the Studio sought to encourage and was quite touchy on the matter of the actor's creative contribution to the finished text of his plays. He held to certain preconceived, idealized visualizations of how his texts should look and sound. When he worked with a director, his attitude was "I hear the line this way, I want to hear it that way on stage." Though this was his artistic prerogative, it was strangely at odds with his involvement with the Studio.

Albee's attitude reflected a basic aesthetic argument offered by a number of other writers and theatrical figures against the Studio, namely, that the workshop's preoccupation with the "theatrical" was at the expense of literary values, and that its focusing on the

elicitation of idiosyncratic behavior in the work of the actor, however provocative the results, was inevitably at the expense of dramatic
clarity and faithfulness to the author's intent.

The Studio's answer to this charge was that the theater is not a
branch of literature, and that while the actor and the director do their
utmost to make manifest the author's vision, the creativity of theater
does not end in the playwright's study. The really knowing playwright, as a true man of the theater, extends his vision to encompass
the creative role of the actor and sees the realization of his play as
a collaborative process in which the writing of the text is the first
step, and the embodying of it on stage a further, difficult, painful,
sometimes compromising, often enhancing, final step.

Strasberg himself has held that several of the playwrights involved
with the Unit during this period (Albee, Jack Gelber, Jack Richardson, Arthur Kopit, and Terrence McNally included) have not lived up
to expectations because they were not appreciative enough of and did
not take advantage of "what they could get from the Studio, which
was a sense of theater . . . of what the theatrical medium could do
for the word."

During the summer preceding the 1963–1964 season, the Playwrights' Committee, as part of the attempt to generate "the experience of theatre in action," had applied for a grant from the Ford
Foundation to enable the Unit to set up a "Monday Night Theatre"
program. The aim of this project was to put on full-scale productions
of Unit members' plays. Ford turned down their request, but three
months later the Rockefeller Foundation awarded the Studio $56,400
to enable the Playwrights Unit to go ahead with their plan.

Out of this grant, thirty-five thousand dollars was immediately set
aside for five experimental productions of Unit members' plays. The
first of these was *Dynamite Tonight*, a musical with a book by Arnold
Weinstein and a score by William Bolcom, which was to move on to a
commercial production under the auspices of The Actors Studio. The
second presentation, Arthur Kopit's two short plays, *The Day the
Whores Came Out to Play Tennis* and *Mhil'daiim*, received such a hostile reception that the playwright resigned from the Unit in protest at
the audience's "rudeness." The audience's booing and acrimonious remarks were evidently aimed not only at the plays' artistic shortcomings, but at the monies lavished on the settings and at the use—unfairly
and unnecessarily, it was felt—of many non-Studio actors. The re-

maining three plays, all of which had been worked on at earlier times in the Unit, were Laurence Alson's *Party*, Conrad Bromberg's *Defense of Taipei*, and Maxime Furlaud's two one-acts, *Fitz* and *Biscuit*. There were to be supplementary Rockefeller grants to the Unit in the seasons ahead and a number of further experimental productions as a result.

Yet another area in which the Studio expanded its activities during the early sixties was one it had often been accused of neglecting: physical training technique. As a result of Strasberg's visit to Montreal in the late summer of 1960 to see the Peking State Opera, the official theater of the People's Republic of China, an awareness of the American actor's deficiencies in the department of physical expressivity once again took hold at the workshop (as it had at the time of Decroux's tenure at the Studio). Strasberg was thrilled by the Chinese actors' technique, which was characterized by incredible flexibility and agility rather than fixed forms. At the opening meeting of the 1960–1961 season, he spoke to the Studio membership about what he had seen and projected an "ideal" training program that would combine the work of the Chinese with the Studio's Method. He explained his belief that a five-year course of study, starting with children of about thirteen and fourteen years of age, could lead to the development of the idealized master actor that Gordon Craig had called for in his vision of the theater of the future.

While such a program did not fall within the purview of The Actors Studio, Strasberg's enthusiasm on the subject of the Chinese theater eventually led to a gesture in that direction. Sophia Delza was invited to the workshop to give a demonstration of T'ai Chi Ch'uan, "the ancient Chinese 'Exercise Art,' " which, Strasberg believes, "trains without making rigid." The response from members was very strong, and Miss Delza was asked to work with the Studio actors throughout the 1962–1963 season.[9]

The greatest hope for the "expansion" of the Studio's activities during the late fifties had been the liaison with the future Lincoln Center. After several years of inconclusive negotiation, the appointment of Kazan in 1959 as "an associate in the development and direction of the Lincoln Center Repertory Theatre" had seemed the first really tangible foot in the door for the Studio. But matters were not what they might have appeared to the Studio membership. At the same opening meeting of the 1960–1961 season in which he described his encounter with the Chinese Opera in Montreal, Strasberg told the members that, although no final decision had been handed down, the Lincoln Center project was off as far as the Studio was concerned. During the previous year, and ever since his appointment, Kazan had been attempting to bring the Studio and Strasberg into a working relationship with Lincoln Center, but apparently with no success. For various reasons, the Studio's ambition to become the theatrical arm of the new cultural complex was to be stymied after almost five years of tantalizing expectation.

The negotiation with Lincoln Center had been problematic from the start. At first Kazan himself was uncertain of his involvement. After receiving from Kazan the project brief, in which the director proposed a theater setup that was, in effect, an extension of the Studio, John D. Rockefeller III inquired further as to Kazan's ideas about the size and technical facilities of the theater building and about the possible organizational structure for the theater administration. Kazan, after consulting with his colleagues, answered Rockefeller's questions, proposing that Strasberg, Miss Crawford, and he administrate the theater as a troika, with the three of them making all the basic organizational and artistic decisions. Although he received no specific response to his proposals, the Center's continuing interest evidently persuaded Kazan to commit himself to building a theater in the New York cultural complex.

Strasberg, however, soon grew leery of the discussions with the Center people, which he felt always ended with little more than polite statements like "Well, we'll see you soon again." One meeting, at which the Studio's artistic director was interviewed by Dr. George D. Stoddard, dean of New York University's School of Education, about how the Studio proposed to handle Shakespeare—how the Method might be applied to Shakespearean texts—especially rankled Strasberg. "He treated me as if I were an applicant for a doctorate," Strasberg recalls, "interrogating me with a smirk and a smile, which I still remember, and for which I could have killed him then and there."

Strasberg was also suspicious of the Center's "edifice complex," which for him bespoke a certain confusion of aesthetic priorities. He referred to this obliquely in summing up an article he wrote for *The New York Times* in July of 1958 on the prospects of the American theater:

But while my hopes are optimistic, my practical vision is pessimistic. The conditions for great theatre today exist. But there exists equally too much of a tendency to confuse a theatre with the building which houses it, a dream against a ledger, great theatre with good manners.[10]

A prime example of this putting the cart before the horse, according to Strasberg, was the appointing of Robert Whitehead as the organizing director of the Lincoln Center theater before the choice of an artistic leadership had been made. While expressing only admiration and respect for Whitehead, Strasberg nevertheless felt it was an indication that Lincoln Center was moving in a direction very much at odds with the vision of the theater Kazan had outlined in the original proposal to Rockefeller.

It was apparent that there were also differences in cultural ideology between what the Studio proposed and what Lincoln Center wanted. Rockefeller's cultural advisers seemed to be orienting the project toward a classical theater on the European model, as opposed to the uniquely American theater, celebrating the American classics, which the Studio advocated. When the Juilliard Foundation brought Michel St. Denis from France to advise the Center on the formation of a projected theater school, Strasberg saw it as "the first indication that . . . Lincoln Center was not at all . . . receptive to the idea of continuing to develop the basis of an indigenous American theater movement." Kazan and Crawford, who were sitting on the Center's theater advisory board, strongly disagreed with this move and threatened to resign. But it was decided that they would stick it out to see what could be salvaged from their original hopes.

Cheryl Crawford, however, did subsequently quit her position over another incident that reflected on the Studio's advocacy of the American classics. At one board meeting, Vivian Beaumont, after whom the Lincoln Center theater was to be named because of the extent of her financial contribution to it, declared that she hoped the theater she was supporting would not house such sordid American playwrights as Tennessee Williams, among others. Miss Crawford, who had produced Williams's *The Rose Tattoo* in 1950 and was in the process of preparing *Sweet Bird of Youth* in 1959, resigned in protest when none of the Lincoln Center officials present spoke up in defense of the American playwright. Ironically enough, the most successful production in the history of the Lincoln Center Repertory Theater, as of 1980, was the revival of Williams's *A Streetcar Named Desire* in 1973.

When Kazan was invited to join Whitehead in running the Lincoln Center theater, the expectation was that he could somehow effectuate the absorption of the Studio into the operation. This is where matters stood in the fall of 1959. But apparently there was resistance to the Studio and to Strasberg. Miss Crawford has suggested that the people at Lincoln Center were afraid of the Studio directors. According to her, Kazan, Strasberg, and she herself were too emphatic and knew too precisely what they wanted in dealing with the Lincoln Center organization, thereby scaring them and putting them off. Kazan says there was a feeling among the powers at the Center that the Studio was "a cliquish thing." He also felt "the main reason for deciding against the Studio was that they wanted it in the hands of Bob Whitehead. Bob brought me in. They didn't want me. If Whitehead was going to be the responsible person, he wanted to be the responsible person. The same would have been [true] if the Studio had been brought in. They wouldn't want Bob Whitehead there. I mean it's one or the other."

Nevertheless, Kazan made an effort to see what he could do. "He pitched quite hard for the Studio," Whitehead remembers. But to no avail. Despite his admiration for Studio actors, many of whom he had starred or featured in his prestigious commercial productions, Whitehead was clear on one thing about his new enterprise: "I didn't simply want it to be a theater born out of The Actors Studio. I felt we had new ground that we had to uncover, and that we should try to make the Repertory at Lincoln Center a theater that embraced its own character and its own style."

While recognizing Strasberg's special gifts as a teacher, Whitehead opposed what he considered the director's overemphasis on "the psycho-sexual interpretation of the subtext." "At Lincoln Center," he stated for the record, "we will be anti-psychoanalytic. We want to establish a new character for our performers, as well as the theatre." [11] Whitehead maintains it was entirely his decision to exclude the Studio from Lincoln Center.

As a gesture to Strasberg, however, he did later suggest to Kazan that the Studio be invited to do two productions each year in the small downstairs playing space (now the Mitzi Newhouse Theater) that was to be included as part of the Vivian Beaumont Theater building.

Kazan, for his part, persuaded Whitehead to offer Strasberg the co-leadership with Michel St. Denis of the projected theater-training program at the new Juilliard School, which was to be part of the Lincoln Center complex. Whitehead agreed to this despite his strong reservations about Strasberg dominating the training of actors who might eventually be involved with the repertory company. He was leery about this, he has said, because he hoped to break new ground with the American actor's handling of language in classical drama, and he felt that this was an ideal to which Strasberg, the son of non–English speaking immigrant parents, who himself spoke only Yiddish when he arrived in America, was insufficiently sensitive.

As it turned out, he need not have worried. Strasberg refused both offers. Without The Actors Studio as its official theater, he had no desire to become involved with any aspect of Lincoln Center.

The mood of the membership during the 1960–1961 season was dominated by the indecision over Lincoln Center; it was one of restlessness and discontent marked by a growing sense that the Studio was missing yet another boat in its long struggle to become more than a workshop. Carroll Baker vented some typical feelings of disappointment in an interview:

The Studio has lost its spirit. Lots of people who went to it are disillusioned because much of what they hoped would happen just didn't. The only one of the old group who still goes is Geraldine Page, but none of the others are there. The Studio was never the catalyst in theater we hoped it would be. . . . Things just never seemed to work out. We are all striving toward some sort of permanent theater and a lot of us gave up professional work to be in Studio projects which just petered out because of the lack of a strong driving force. Let's drink a toast to it. It was a wonderful place to learn and work. Long may it live.[12]

By the spring of 1961 it was clear that the situation was hopeless for the Studio. Kazan told Strasberg that he was going ahead with the Lincoln Center theater as an independent agent. Strasberg was severely disappointed, for he had thought of Lincoln Center as the coming "apex of our contribution." With the larger plans of the Studio so finally frustrated, he came to wonder about the workshop's role in the American theater. After anticipating a theatrical fulfillment for so long, was there any rationale for the Studio to continue as it had? "I began to question our reason for existence. Perhaps we had contributed as much as we had to contribute. Or maybe we hadn't been as valuable as we thought we had been. Was there something new we could go on to do? Or was there, possibly, no need for a Studio?" [13] At the somber final session of the season he stated quite bleakly, "The future of The Actors Studio is uncertain. At the moment we have reached a dead end." He left for Europe that summer wondering if he would be returning to the Studio in the fall.

Any doubts Strasberg may have had, however, were dispelled by his visit to various theaters abroad. He encountered inspiring work at the Berliner Ensemble and elsewhere, but he also came across a startling lack of creative ambition among the younger actors—an absence of dedication to greatness in acting, or of belief in its possibility. He was pleasantly surprised to find immense interest in the Studio and esteem for it as an idealistic standard of theater. It made him appreciate anew the inspiration the Studio had become for young American actors, and he returned to New York reassured of the importance of the workshop on the American theater scene. The only question remaining was how to channel the energies of the membership, how to reinvigorate the Studio's "responsibility" to the theater.

Despite rumors during the summer that the Studio would not reopen, the 1961–1962 season began in October as usual. As if in rededication, the membership had spent the summer months giving the Studio building its first ceiling-to-cellar renovation and repainting since it had been taken over by the workshop six years earlier.

At the opening meeting on October 24, the three Studio directors addressed the members. Miss Crawford talked of the financial situation, mentioning that in its fourteen-year history the Studio had raised over a quarter of a million dollars to keep operating, but as usual was still "just ahead of the sheriff." Kazan expressed confidence in the workshop, stated that his involvement with Lincoln Center would in no way affect his relationship with the Studio, and that in fact he hoped that some kind of working relationship might still develop between the two organizations. Strasberg spoke of his month-long visit with the Berliner Ensemble, which had so stirred and excited him, as did Franco Zeffirelli's production of *Romeo and Juliet*, which he saw in Venice. He also spoke of the Planchon Company's production of *Georges Dandin*, which he saw at the Berlin Festival. He strongly reaffirmed his belief that the Studio was a unique phenomenon in the theater world, and exhorted the entire Studio community, himself included, to use it more fully.

His report on what he had discovered during his European "work trip" was considered important enough for arrangements to be made for a midnight lecture at the Morosco Theatre on November 27 so that members of the New York theater could share in his impressions and conclusions. Strasberg discussed the Zeffirelli and Planchon productions as dramatic examples of how classic plays could be refreshed and brought to new life by means of a thorough following-through of the kind of approach to reality and honesty the Studio tried to inculcate.

The emphasis of his talk was on the Berliner Ensemble and the significance of their approach to theatrical reality. Strasberg was no stranger to Brecht. As early as 1936, he had worked briefly on one of the playwright's short didactic pieces with some of the Group's actors. Brecht, who was present during the work, and whose special demands on the actors Strasberg was apparently successful in communicating to the performers, sent Strasberg a note thanking him for demonstrating that it was possible to realize Brecht's kind of theater in the United States. The same year Strasberg used the Brechtian technique of "narrative emotion" in his Group Theatre production of Erwin Piscator's *The Case of Clyde Griffiths*, an adaptation of Theodore Dreiser's novel, *An American Tragedy*.[14]

In the summer of 1956 Strasberg had seen the Berliner Ensemble perform in London and had given a detailed appreciation of their work at the Studio the following October. But it was not until he spent almost six weeks watching rehearsals of the theater, talking to Helene Weigel (Brecht's widow and a leading actress in the company) and others involved with the Brecht productions, that he was able to state quite positively, "What I saw on the Brecht stage is the most outstanding theatrical achievement of the last twenty years. It is the greatest contribution to the theatre of the post-Stanislavski period." [15]

Two months later, Cheryl Crawford presented *Brecht on Brecht*, George Tabori's collage of Brecht materials, which had originally been produced as an ANTA matinee showcase at the Theatre De Lys. A "floating company" of mostly Studio actors worked on the production throughout its run. Besides Lotte Lenya and George Voskovec, who were not Studio members, the original cast included Anne Jackson, Viveca Lindfors, Michael Wager, and Dane Clark, replacing Eli Wallach, who appeared in the original showcase performance. Among the Studio actors who later took over roles in the play were Kevin McCarthy, Rosemary Murphy, Lou Antonio, Barbara Baxley, Lenka Peterson, Alfred Ryder, David Hurst, and Madeleine Thornton-Sherwood.

But all was far from well at the Studio. The usual financial crisis, which in previous seasons had been somehow averted, took on truly dangerous proportions. At the beginning of December the workshop announced there were only enough funds to continue operations through January. Then at a meeting with the membership on February 16, 1962, Cheryl Crawford revealed just how grave the financial situation was. Pleading her weariness of repeated attempts, not always successful, to raise money for the Studio after so many years, she announced that there were enough funds to keep the Studio open for two weeks, and no longer. Promised contributions had failed to come through, and it was now up to the members themselves to find the wherewithal to keep the workshop functioning. She then left the meeting. Suggestions were made about doing a television show to raise funds, also for the Studio involving itself in raising money for a national theater, but these seemed distant prospects at best. The atmosphere of the meeting was grim.

An emergency members' meeting was called for the following Tuesday, February 20, in place of the regular acting session. At that gathering ten thousand dollars was given by an anonymous donor, and another fifty-four hundred pledged to keep the Studio running till June 15. The assembled members, with the approval of the three directors, also voted to set up a Committee to Secure the Long Range Financial Stability of The Actors Studio. Composed of representatives of the three units and three members appointed by the directorate, the committee included Rip Torn, Paul Newman, Geraldine Page, Fred Stewart, Michael Wager, Rona Jaffe, Anne Bancroft, Nan Martin, Rosemary Murphy, and John Stix. (Alternates to the committee were Aza Bard, Salem Ludwig, William Smithers, Muriel Resnick, and Frank Corsaro.) Torn, who from the start was to give the group its dynamic impetus, was elected its chairman. Stewart was made secretary. The committee voted to ask the three directors for permission to examine the Studio's books and charter, and proceeded to call a special meeting on the sixth of March to hear suggestions and opinions from the membership at large on the problem of long-range financing for the Studio.

Thus began a period of heady excitement during which the members felt themselves taking control of the life of the Studio. At several meetings throughout the month of March—most of them held late at night at Michael Wager's apartment on Sixty-third Street—the committee investigated the legal standing of the members of the Studio, and began feeling its way toward an assertion of power. They talked of "moving into areas of greater authority," and commented on the three directors "being tired" and of the need for being "weaned" from dependence on them. They expressed an often reiterated desire for "training on a broader scale." Most centrally, they discussed the possibilities of production and the relationship of Studio work to the presentation of plays, specifically, the relationship in artistic, organizational, and financial terms of Studio classes to the running of a theater. And Strasberg's role in all of this was closely and carefully examined. The committee was keenly aware that Strasberg, despite his dream of a theater, could be expected to temporize out of caution and skepticism. "We kept reminding ourselves at every meeting," Geraldine Page recalls, " 'Now we must arrange to go ahead around Lee's objections and always keep in mind that he would try in every way to pull out of it.' So we were always careful to explore ways of being able to overcome that."

The committee presented their findings and recommendations to the three directors on April 2, the day before their report was to be discussed at a general membership meeting the committee had called. The thirteen-page document, titled "Towards Securing the Long Range Financial Stability of the Actors Studio," outlined a variety of suggestions, including setting up a "Board of Patrons," devloping a public-relations policy "to combat the erroneous image [of the Studio] that has been allowed to develop in the public mind," and, most important, creating a "Production Unit" for The Actors Studio. At the meeting on April 3 with the membership, the atmosphere was electric as Geraldine Page dramatically emphasized the common determination to create a theater. She proclaimed, "If our directors don't go along with us, we must drive our directors to the wall." Later that evening the committee met to evaluate the morning's events and voted to call themselves thenceforth "The Members Committee" of The Actors Studio.

Members had had experience in dealing with Strasberg in committee before. Seven years earlier there had also been a members' group, an "Actors Studio Co-ordinating Committee" set up by the three directors in the fall of 1955. When that committee had tried to define its responsibilities and authority, it had run headlong into Strasberg's resistance to any encroachment on what he felt were his prerogatives as the Studio's artistic director. He explained at that time that he approved of the "housekeeping" activities the committee had defined as within its province, but rejected any intrusion on its part into the area of "policy." He granted they had responsibility for the former, but absolutely denied them any authority in the latter. In the artistic field, he noted, matters cannot be run by committee.

One of the points Strasberg touched on at the April 3, 1962, meeting, during the general membership's discussion of the report of the Committee to Secure the Long Range Financial Stability of The Actors Studio, was that the idea of a theater governed by a committee needed serious and careful deliberation. (He still carried the scars of his experiences with the Group Theatre Actors' Committee, of course.) This is precisely what the Members Committee involved itself with when on April 4 the three directors gave the committee authority to implement its recommendations. Later, when the workshop went into production, Kazan would say, "The Actors Studio theatre is run by a committee. I wouldn't sit on a committee with Jesus Christ, never mind Stanislavski, and you can quote me. I'm me!"

The artistic questions of "a theater governed by a committee" aside, the Members Committee proceeded to investigate the "political" and legal aspects of the issue. They discovered that, by law, control of the Studio resided in five "corporate" members: Kazan, Strasberg, Crawford, and the lawyers, John Dudley and William Fitelson. These five *were*, in fact, The Actors Studio, Inc. The committee was astonished to find that the "membership," made up of the Studio's hundreds of actors, had no *legal* standing. The five corporate members elected the board of directors (in this case the same five people), who exercised legal authority in making policy for the Studio. The corporate members, they learned, are like stockholders; the board of directors is the governing body. The Studio bylaws call for the corporate members to elect directors and officers, and for the directors, in turn, to elect new corporate members. The three directors also held the titles of president, vice-president, and secretary of the corporation. The only way the Members Committee could have any legal authority over the Production Unit they wanted to create was to have members of their group elected to corporate membership or to the board of directors.

The committee debated among themselves how assertive they should be in their quest for authority. Some argued that all sixteen members of the Members Committee should be elected to the corporate membership. Concern was expressed over the actors' attitudes toward Kazan and Strasberg as "father figures." Molly Kazan made a deep impression on the members at the April 3 meeting when she exhorted them to realize that they were "no longer kids." Fred Stewart summed it up during the committee's period of soul-searching, when he observed that it was not a question of learning to live with the "fathers," but of realizing that "we are now the fathers and mothers."

The mood of the membership and the determination of the committee evidently made an impression on Strasberg. His nervousness about sharing power was to a certain extent offset by the irresistible force of the members' enthusiasm. Strasberg, after all, wanted a theater, and if Lincoln Center was out of the question, the most logical recourse was to support the Studio members' driving ambition to create one.

Therefore, when the issue of giving the membership some real power was presented to him, Strasberg proved amenable to having two of the committee's members join the board of directors in place of the lawyers, Fitelson and Dudley. It was not the large-scale capitulation some of the committee members had hoped for, but at least, as Strasberg explained, whenever there was a difference of opinion over some matter, the two actor-members of the board would only have to persuade one of the other three board members in order to have a majority. The committee responded by nominating Rip Torn and Geraldine Page to fill those positions. The first official announcement of the Studio's plans to start its own theater appeared two weeks later, on May 11, 1962.

Cheryl Crawford was happy to go along with the fast-unfolding developments. She too had been disappointed with the outcome of the Lincoln Center business, and was stirred by the possibility that the members' energies might produce an Actors Studio theater organization after all. Kazan, however, was another matter entirely.

Once it had become apparent that the Studio as an organization would not be absorbed into the Lincoln Center complex, Kazan had hoped that the members' dream of a theater would be sublimated into a renewed dedication to the traditional workshop role of the Studio. In September of 1961 he had written a letter to Strasberg in which he had outlined the situation as he saw it and emphasized his belief that there were "two separate and distinct needs" for a Studio and a theater. "The organization for a Studio is not the organization for a Theatre and the inner spirit of one is different than that of the other. In other words I do not agree with the inference . . . that if the Studio did not become a Theatre it would disintegrate. I don't think it should become a Theatre. And I don't think it will disintegrate. But I do think there should be adaptations and changes now. The course of your work has made these necessary." He suggested that Strasberg devote his time to creating "projects" at the Studio, and concluded by making the "official offer from Lincoln Centre to the Actors' Studio" to present two Studio productions a year in the smaller theater at the Center. He also told Strasberg, "When we were able to bring you into the Studio I thought the movement had found its perfect leader. I still think so. I said to Cheryl at the time that I wanted to 'give' the Studio to you. And I did. At the same time I have never been far away. And I have no intention of leaving it, now or later." [16]

When it became evident that the Studio would not be satisfied with remaining just a workshop, that it would in fact be creating a theater independently of Lincoln Center, Kazan was faced with a dilemma. Such a theater would, of course, be directly competitive with his own fledgling Lincoln Center Repertory Theater. But even more troubling was the very sticky conflict-of-interest problem that would eventually force Kazan to reconsider his intention not to leave the Studio "now or later."

With the Studio going into production, Kazan would wind up on the board of directors of two competing institutions. In an effort to forestall such an untenable situation, he wrote a letter to Strasberg and Miss Crawford proposing that the Production Unit being created by the Members Committee be set up outside the corporate structure of the Studio so that he, in effect, would not be legally associated with it. The committee's response to this was that such an arrangement would make it impossible for the Production Unit to enjoy the tax-exempt status of the Studio, and, equally as important, that the members of the Studio wanted the Unit to be known as The Actors Studio Theatre.

The committee was of no mind to accommodate Kazan, even though he was the Studio's founder. However else the situation might be viewed, they felt that the membership had been traduced in the matter of Lincoln Center, and it was suggested that Kazan was largely responsible. It was suggested, too, that if he had really wanted the Studio at the Center, it would have been there. And in the light of this sentiment, anything he might suggest on the subject of the Studio's turning to production might be construed as self-serving. Nor were they reluctant to voice their disenchantment publicly. At one of the late-night meetings to which Kazan was invited, for instance, Anne Bancroft put the question to him directly: "Would you be terribly upset if we didn't ask you to direct our first production?" The director uncharacteristically lost his poise as he was momentarily struck speechless.

Strasberg and Miss Crawford met with Kazan to try to persuade him to stay on the board of directors and to simply disassociate himself from the new Production Unit. They also recommended at that meeting that the two committee members be added to the board and that the Production Unit be created under official Actors Studio auspices. Kazan, deeply troubled by the turn of events, asked for forty-eight hours to think matters over.

On May 18 of 1962, after several "hellish" days of indecision, Kazan agreed to the two Studio members' joining the board of directors and acceded to his colleagues' intentions to set up a Production Unit within the legal structure of The Actors Studio. But he was still uncertain about remaining on the board. On May 27, following a week and a half of sober self-counsel, Kazan resigned as a director of The Actors Studio. Posted on the Studio bulletin board two days later was the following note:

To All: I resigned as a director—only. That was necessary. But I'm still with you. And very much for any and all efforts you make. I'm sure that whatever you do will bring credit to our years of work and to Lee's teaching.

The First Member [17]

The membership, caught up in the excitement of the Studio's movement toward a theater, was generally indifferent to Kazan's announcement. Later that summer, he asked that the Studio newsletter continue to be sent to him.

In his statement to the press explaining his departure as a conflict of interest, Kazan noted that The Actors Studio production program would overlap and even compete with some of the activity for which he would be responsible at the repertory theater of Lincoln Center. The newspapers immediately predicted a contest between Kazan and Strasberg for the loyalties of Studio members. (Among the headlines: "Talent Raid Foreseen as Kazan Shifts Jobs" and "Studio 'Divorce': Will Kazan Get the Kids?") There was good reason. Kazan made it clear that he had "quite a few" Studio actors in mind for his company. But the responses to his overtures were cool. According to certain members, while the workshop itself was being kept at bay, Kazan had quietly tried to get some of the more prominent Studio personages to join his theater. This had created enormous resentment and had actually spurred the movement for the Studio to create its own theater. As one prominent member put it, "All of these people turned him down because they thought it was an act of betrayal and double-timing, which indeed it partly was."

As it turned out, only seven of the initial twenty-six actors in the Lincoln Center Repertory were Studio members.* One of the main reasons for this, undoubtedly, was that Kazan demanded a two-year contract from his performers plus a total devotion to the work of his theater, whereas the Studio organized the bulk of its membership as a "floating company" of actors committed for a minimum of five months out of the year (a month's rehearsal and four months of performing), which left them seven months free for other activities.

Geraldine Page recalls how, one evening during the run of *Sweet Bird of Youth*, Kazan and Whitehead came back to her dressing room and began describing their theater in all its lavishness-to-be: "Oh we're going to have a theater! We're going to spend millions of dollars. It's going to be the most beautiful . . . it's going to have so

---

* Mildred Dunnock, Salome Jens, Clinton Kimbrough, Patricia Roe, David J. Stewart, Michael Strong, and David Wayne. A number of the other Lincoln Center company members joined the Studio at a later time: Stanley Beck, Mariclare Costello, Barbara Loden, Barry Primus, Diane Shalet, and Jack Waltzer.

much gilt . . . so much chandeliers and crystal and red plush carpets
. . . and you must come and work for us." She asked them what
they were going to pay the actors. They told her, "Minimum. And
nobody can work for anybody else. They're going to have to promise
to stay with the theater for five years [*sic*] and not work outside of
it." She said, "Five years for minimum and not work outside of it?
But are you going to work outside of it?" Kazan said, "Well, I have
to. You know, I have movies to direct." She notes with amusement
that Kazan was genuinely surprised that the Studio actors were reluctant to join his theater when faced with this offer. "From the
minute I heard about it, from the word *go*, I didn't want to work
there."

Strasberg, nevertheless, was obviously both surprised and moved
by the number of members who signed up to show their solidarity
with the Studio while passing up the opportunity of working at
Lincoln Center.

With Kazan's departure from the Studio some basic disagreements
between Strasberg and Kazan on the subject of actor training were
brought to light: there had always been differences of emphasis between the two men, with Kazan focusing chiefly on actions, Strasberg on emotion. But in an article in *The New York Times Magazine*,
written four months after his resignation from the Studio, Kazan
underscored what he felt were the Studio's shortcomings and what he
hoped to avoid at Lincoln Center:

The Actors Studio has made a historic contribution to the American
theater. It is now no longer a young group of insurgents. It is itself an
orthodoxy. It takes particular pride in its roster of stars and "names." It
deserves the acclaim it has received and so does its artistic director, Lee
Strasberg. My great disappointment with the work there has been that
it always stopped at the same point, a preoccupation with the purely
psychological side of acting. I am speaking of my own failure there as
well as that of others.

Regrettably, too much of the "Method" talk among actors today is a
defense against new artistic challenges, rationalizations for their own
ineptitudes. We have a swarm of actors who are ideologues and theorists.
There have been days when I felt I would swap them all for a gang of
wandering players, who could dance and sing, and who were, above all
else, entertainers.[18]

At the final session of the 1961–1962 season on June 12, Rip Torn read to the assembled members the statement that the Members Committee had released to the press the day before. It announced the election of himself and Miss Page to the Studio's board of directors; the establishment of The Actors Studio Theatre as a legal entity, with Strasberg as its artistic director, Miss Crawford as its executive producer, Roger L. Stevens as its general administrator, and Michael Wager as its executive administrator; the formation of a Production Board for the Theatre to include Edward Albee, Anne Bancroft, Frank Corsaro, Paul Newman, Arthur Penn, Fred Stewart, and Michael Wager; and the selection of the Theatre's initial productions for the premier season of 1962–1963: June Havoc's *Marathon '33* and Edward Albee's first three-act play, *Who's Afraid of Virginia Woolf?*

After brief reports from the various subcommittees of the new Members Committee, Roger L. Stevens spoke briefly, and Cheryl Crawford read some telegrams. Among them: "Please Read. Dear Lee and Cheryl. Wish I was there, but I'm with you. Maureen Stapleton." "Please read. *Shalom.* Luck and blessings. Clifford Odets." "Please read. Dear Lee. Our thoughts and feelings are with you and the Actors' Studio that you represent. We would like you to know that to be part of any activities that you and the Studio will guide will be more than we can hope. Love. Jane Fonda and Andreas Voutsinas." "Please read. Dear Lee and Cheryl. Here's to the future. Marilyn M." Before calling on Strasberg to address the meeting, Torn read a telegram from Fred Stewart: "At this moment in the life of the Actors Studio I send you a message from Victor Hugo, who once said 'There's nothing so powerful as an idea whose time has come.' "

Strasberg spoke at length about his disappointments over the long negotiations with Lincoln Center, about his ambition to serve the American playwright, and of his hopes and fears for the future. After being presented with a symbolic key to the new Theatre, he announced to the gathering that champagne was waiting for the members downstairs, and then read a note from those in Hollywood who could not be there in person: "We send this champagne to toast the future. We are all drinking a toast at the same time. . . . Signed: Joanne Woodward, Jennifer Jones, Paul Newman, Tony Franciosa,

Marilyn Monroe, Judy Franciosa, Jane Fonda, George Peppard, Andreas Voutsinas, Maureen Stapleton, Clifford Odets, Bill Durkee, Eva Marie Saint, Jeff Hayden, Carroll Baker, and Jack Garfein." The greeting was received by prolonged applause, after which the members repaired downstairs to return the toast. And so The Actors Studio Theatre was born.

CHAPTER **7**

Venture into Production: The Actors Studio Theatre

FROM ITS INCEPTION The Actors Studio Theatre was a study in paradox. Aspiring to the highest ideals of ensemble acting, service to the American playwright, and to the development of a producing organization of artistic distinction that would endure, it achieved decidedly mixed results and died, after a relatively brief one and a half seasons, virtually aborning. The sudden fulfillment of years of hopes and dreams, the Studio Theatre wound up an opportunity fumbled as it succumbed to lack of planning, plain bad luck, and, sad to say, a number of ill-conceived artistic decisions.

Unlike the Group Theatre, whose aesthetic philosophy and operational structure had been thrashed out long before it started functioning, the Studio Theatre was propelled into existence by the collective enthusiasm of its Studio members without a program and without a clear understanding of how authority, artistic or otherwise, would be exercised. While the membership, represented by the Production Board, created the Theatre and provided its primary impetus, its role in the organizing and running of the enterprise was essentially advisory. Despite their willingness to help and be active, the members actually did little to shape the Theatre's course. The leadership, on the other hand, with the exception of Michael Wager, who was paid a salary of fifteen thousand dollars to serve as executive administrator, did not devote their energies to it exclusively; they made decisions, but they gave the Theatre little definitive guidance or direction.

Cheryl Crawford was busy with productions of her own during the period, while Roger L. Stevens, after his initial services in raising money for the organization, participated progressively less as his attention turned to his theatrical interests in Washington, D.C. Lee Strasberg, who continued his teaching, searched for a pragmatic compromise between the prerogatives of a true artistic director, traditionally the final and absolute arbiter of artistic matters, and the exigencies of working with established and fiercely independent directors and actors. As a result, he seemed to have been swept along despite his better judgment while fitfully, and not always productively, asserting his authority.

In the process, the distinctive qualities that might have been expected from a theater born of The Actors Studio and claiming the heritage of the Group Theatre were never fully or satisfactorily realized. The Group's conception of a theater, not as a producer of individual plays but as an organic entity defining its aesthetic profile over a lifetime of work, was lost sight of. Instead, as it developed, The Actors Studio Theatre was marked by a series of compromises in the name of expediency that reflected no consistent creative vision and that left no discernible artistic signature. The plays that were selected for production, for one thing, were in most cases not among the Theatre's first choices. For another, the kind of intensive exploratory work advocated by Strasberg in Studio sessions was slighted in the rush of rehearsals, so that the actors' performances in most of the plays, while generally respectable, were not, with one or two exceptions, especially distinguished or exciting for an organization that prided itself on the quality of its players.

The pattern that the Studio Theatre fell into once it was established was, in a word, disappointing. It was not the pattern of an ensemble functioning in a long-lived "organic" national theater that had been a Studio ideal for almost a decade.

Lee Strasberg had advocated such a theater for years. "Listen, we've probably got as much talent between 59th and 42nd Street, between two subway stops, as they've got in England or France. But the American theatre has no base. . . . There isn't a permanent center, an *ensemble*. . . . The way the theatre is done here, you have a bunch of strangers coming together for the first day of rehearsals. The cast never has time to become friends. They've no opportunity to form a real company because everybody is too busy trying to knock Brooks Atkinson dead on opening night." [1]

Strasberg had a vision of an American Old Vic, where the talents of the younger and older members of the Studio, reinforced by a common way of working and a deep knowledge of one another's personalities and temperaments, might create "an ensemble that could be second to none in the world. . . . The Moscow Art Theater had only six top people. The Group didn't have that many. We have 20 or 25. We would be able to engage on a greater variety of levels than any theater there ever has been. . . . We could do work that Stanislavsky might never have dreamed of." [2]

The unique approach of The Actors Studio Theatre to the establishment of such an ensemble was the "floating company," an idea originated by Strasberg in the early sixties to facilitate the involvement of as many of the major Studio "names" in the Theatre's productions as possible. Under this arrangement, members committed themselves to the Theatre for a limit of five months, floating in and out of active service, as it were. By making participation so flexible, and therefore attractive to the Studio's leading players, Strasberg sought to avoid some of the pitfalls of the usual "permanent" year-round ensemble which has to tailor its repertory to the range of talents of a small number of actors who are willing and financially able to be tied down for long periods of time. Such long-term commitment, Strasberg observed, "usually eliminates the best people that you want." The "floating company" was his accommodation to this American reality, and he believed that the "shared kinship" of Studio members would overcome any problems such a loose-knit structure might create.

Inevitably, there were some who viewed this arrangement, which essentially designed the Theatre for the convenience of its most celebrated members, as symptomatic of Strasberg's star-consciousness and as an attempt by him to have his cake and eat it too: he wanted an ensemble theater, but he also wanted his stars and was willing to compromise a more demanding ideal of commitment to get them.

The difficulty was not that the lesser-known members were jealous of their star colleagues, though some undoubtedly were. Everyone acknowledged that a large part of the excitement of having a Studio Theatre was to bring those gifted and famous performers back to the stage. The question was one of priorities. For the bulk of the Studio membership, name value seemed to receive disproportionate consideration in the planning for the Theatre despite ample evidence that many a Broadway production had achieved outstanding artistic and commercial success with relatively unknown talent. "Who were the 'superstars' in *A Streetcar Named Desire* when it opened?," the question might have been asked. Members had always been taught that "the work comes first," yet there seemed to be implicit in Strasberg's attitude an overvaluing of fame for its own sake.

Strasberg's "star-consciousness" was viewed as a besetting sin by the Studio membership at large. It generally elicited knowing smiles among them while genuinely rankling and distressing them, especially in those instances when he could be both adamant and insensitive on the subject.

One incident years later is especially telling. Long after the period of The Actors Studio Theatre, during the late nineteen seventies when the Studio was presenting a variety of plays in workshop form, Joanna Miles once persuaded Strasberg to observe her there at work with the talented young Michael Moriarty in a drama by Israel Horovitz. Afterward, when Miss Miles suggested to him that the play be sponsored for a regular commercial production by the Studio, he seemed open to the idea. She was stunned to hear him explain, however, that such a production would of course be contingent on Paul Newman and Joanne Woodward's being available to play the roles Moriarty and she had just performed. Incensed and incredulous, she said, "What are you talking about, Lee? Michael and I both won Emmy awards for our work in *The Glass Menagerie* with Katharine Hepburn, and Michael won a Tony for his Broadway debut in *Find Your Way Home!*" Strasberg was unimpressed, she reported, and insisted that only stars of the Newmans' stature would make it possible to produce the play successfully.

Despite his feelings about the need to feature celebrated members of the Studio in order to make a major artistic statement and ensure The Actors Studio Theatre's success, however, Strasberg was not unmindful of the problems a star-centered Theatre could create. He addressed himself to that very question in some of his earliest official pronouncements on the Theatre in the making. He was eager to point out in these first statements that while The Actors Studio Theatre had in fact been born of the efforts of the Studio members themselves, it was not going to be an "Actors Theatre." "If that were so it would be doomed to failure. For a theatre in which the actors' needs are primary would quickly dissolve into a battle for individual prominence and egotistical gratification. Only when the actors serve the play do we possess the proper environment for a theatre." [3]

The responsibility to the playwright was to be much discussed during the formative months of The Actors Studio Theatre in 1962. It certainly was an important item when the Production Board met with W. McNeil Lowry of the Ford Foundation during the summer of that year to talk about funding the new Theatre. Lowry, who first became interested in the Studio Theatre idea when Gordon Rogoff discussed its possibilities with him three years earlier, offered a grant of $250,000 to cover the first two years of the Theatre's existence, contingent on Roger L. Stevens's raising a matching grant by January 1963. The total $500,000, together with box-office revenues, would allow The Actors Studio Theatre to do several large and small-scale productions. Stevens later fulfilled that obligation, personally guaranteeing the necessary funds in the process. Among the monies raised was a contribution of $10,000 from Elizabeth Taylor.

Lowry emphasized that he was especially interested in the development of a "Playwrights Theatre" and expressed the hope that the Studio's new enterprise would prove the logical place for it to be realized. Any future funding, he told the members of the Production Board, would be decided on the basis of the kind of plays chosen and the quality of their presentation, not on the basis of box-office receipts or critical reviews.

The Actors Studio Theatre as a nurturing home for the playwright, a place "where the highest demands will be made upon him, where he will be encouraged to seek the fullest embodiment of his vision," was the theme of Strasberg's first public statement about the aims of the Theatre. It was also the main point of a letter he wrote to Tennessee Williams in the fall of 1962, trying to allay the author's fears that The Actors Studio Theatre was indifferent to producing his plays.

Williams had been one of the first to offer a play to the Theatre when it officially came into existence in June 1962. This new work, *The Mutilated*, was never really taken up for consideration by the Theatre's Production Board, because they were much more interested in the possibility of a production of his *Battle of Angels*, an earlier version of *Orpheus Descending* which Strasberg and Miss Crawford especially admired. As late as the fall of 1964, there were discussions about Patricia Neal and George Peppard appearing in it. There was also talk of doing *Camino Real*—Alan Arkin expressed interest in working on it as a Studio project at one point. But the Production Board ultimately came to focus on other plays as first-choice possibilities. As it would turn out, The Actors Studio Theatre never did present a Williams play.

The intention to produce a variety of American and European playwrights was serious and ambitious, but, as in the case of Williams, consistently frustrated. Week after week, the Production Board met at their offices in the Squibb Building at 745 Fifth Avenue to discuss the impressive list of plays they were interested in—plays for many of which negotiations had been initiated. Strasberg was keen on producing Odets's *The Flowering Peach*, which he felt had not been "fully realized" when the playwright had himself directed it some years earlier on Broadway. He wanted to open the Theatre's first season with Thornton Wilder's *Alcestiad*, and there were discussions of possible productions of such other American plays as Lillian Hellman's *The Autumn Garden*, Norman Mailer's *The Deer Park*, and even Royall Tyler's 1787 comedy, *The Contrast*.

The Theatre spent a great deal of time and effort in trying to secure the rights to a number of outstanding European plays. Among these, there was special interest in Jean Genet's *The Screens*, Georges Bernanos's *The Dialogue of the Carmelites*, Ariano Suassuna's *The Rogues' Trial*, John Arden's *Sergeant Musgrave's Dance*, and, most important, Bertolt Brecht's *The Caucasian Chalk Circle*, which the Theatre took an option on and which Strasberg wanted to produce in the style of the Berliner Ensemble with Geraldine Page playing the lead. Other Brecht projects that were discussed in the context of The Actors Studio Theatre were *The Resistible Rise of Arturo Ui* with Marlon Brando and Anthony Quinn, *Galileo* with Rod Steiger, and a special production of *The Measures Taken* to be directed by Jerome Robbins.

Some of these plays eluded the Theatre's grasp through no fault of its own. Thornton Wilder, for instance, would not release his *Alcestiad* for production because he felt it needed to be drastically rewritten; he could not be persuaded otherwise. A number of the plays, however, might have been done in later seasons if there had been a tenacious enough determination to follow through in securing the rights to them. Many possibilities were apparently fumbled away with unnecessary delays and equivocation. Though every theatrical producer has his stories about plays he let slip out of his hands for one reason or another—Harold Clurman, for instance, recounts in *The Fervent Years* how he and the Group Theatre turned down Saroyan's *The Time of Your Life* and Anderson's *Winterset*—the Studio Theatre somehow managed to let *most* of their first choices go by the boards.

The case of *Who's Afraid of Virginia Woolf?* perhaps typifies The Actors Studio Theatre's characteristic bungling of an opportunity. Edward Albee's play was originally to have been produced on Broadway by Clinton Wilder, Richard Barr, and Albee himself. But as Albee was a member of the Studio Theatre's Production Board and had been favorably impressed by the positive handling of *The Zoo Story* in the Studio's Playwrights Unit, the three partners decided to offer a coproduction to the Studio.

Michael Wager received a copy of the play from Richard Barr and read it while he was appearing in *Brecht on Brecht* at the Theatre De Lys. He was so excited by it, he called Strasberg from backstage to tell him, "I have just read the best play, I think, since *Long Day's Journey into Night*. An absolutely sensational play. This is the play we should open the Theatre with." Strasberg said, "If you think that strongly about it, we'll do it." Wager said, "We've got to do it. It's perfect for Gerry Page." The Studio agreed to finance the production and provide Geraldine Page as its star and Alan Schneider as its director. *Virginia Woolf* was then announced as one of The Actors Studio Theatre's first two productions.

It soon became apparent, however, that there were forces opposed to the Studio Theatre's doing the play. Roger L. Stevens, for one, thought it "a dull, whiny play, without a laugh in it." He told Strasberg he thought it was "one big yawn." Moreover, he objected to the play's language: "I will never be a party to subsidizing the speaking of those dirty words on the stage." Cheryl Crawford, while willing to go along with it, was "scared of its bitterness and brutality." Most crucially, Geraldine Page hated *Virginia Woolf* and was reluctant to appear in the role of Martha so soon after having played another "loudmouthed drunken lady, who was very strong," the Princess in *Sweet Bird of Youth*. Strasberg, who was enthusiastic about the play—he had suggested Eli Wallach for the role of George —sat Miss Page down in his kitchen one afternoon to convince her to do the role for the good of the Theatre; he was quite adamant about it.

She reluctantly allowed herself to be persuaded, but unfortunately to no purpose, as the situation, in the meantime, had changed. Barr and Wilder, evidently sensing something of the Theatre leaders' mixed feelings toward the play, were having second thoughts about getting involved with the Studio. Despite some last minute efforts by Michael Wager and others to convince them otherwise, they withdrew the offer of coproduction "to protect Albee's interests." Miss Page was apparently relieved at not having to do the play after all. In a letter to Cheryl Crawford, she confided that she felt its negativity would have marked the Studio with an indelible taint of bitter animosity and childish immaturity that the Theatre was very fortunate in having avoided.

Who's Afraid of Virginia Woolf?, of course, went on to become one of the most celebrated and successful dramas of the sixties, and there are those who feel that The Actors Studio Theatre would still be alive today if it had produced it.

Albee, for his part, seemed to hold no grudge against the Theatre. In January of 1963, still a member of the Production Board, he told an interviewer, "I'd be grateful if a play of mine were done by Actors Studio. . . . I can think of no happier home for a playwright." [4] Strasberg and he in fact "shook hands" over the Theatre's doing his second play sight unseen. When Albee sent Strasberg the first act of *The Ballad of the Sad Café*, the artistic director reaffirmed his promise to do the play, but expressed reservations about the "talkiness" of the script and how he felt it would not "play that way" though he liked the material and was ready to go ahead with a production. He received no further communications about the play from Albee, and the Studio did not produce it. In April of 1964, with neither of his plays nor the various projects he championed in the councils of the Production Board being realized, Albee resigned from The Actors Studio. He cited the press of his own business and his disenchantment with the Studio Theatre's artistic course as the reasons for his decision.

As the discussions over possible repertory continued, it became increasingly difficult to pin Strasberg down to a particular play he would be willing to approve of as the Theatre's opening effort. Though he was not anxious to rush into production and seemed content to wait out developments on *Alcestiad* and *The Flowering Peach*, the Production Board was eager to get started.

It was Rip Torn who first suggested that they stage Eugene O'Neill's *Strange Interlude*. Everyone, including Strasberg, had agreed at the very beginning that an O'Neill play would be a properly prestigious project to start with. But Cheryl Crawford had gone to see Carlotta O'Neill, the playwright's widow, and discovered that the production rights to all the O'Neill plays had been given to Lincoln Center. Torn, however, found out that despite this arrangement, José Quintero was preparing an authorized production of *Desire Under the Elms* at the Circle in the Square. He went to Quintero, got himself cast as Eban in that presentation, and talked the director into approaching Mrs. O'Neill to give The Actors Studio Theatre permission to stage a production of *Strange Interlude*, which Quintero would direct.

Strange Interlude, which had originally won O'Neill his third Pulitzer Prize, had not been seen in New York since its memorable 1928 production starring Lynn Fontanne. In the interim it had gained a reputation as a landmark work in the playwright's *oeuvre*, with its massive nine-act construction and its innovative use of soliloquies and asides.

The Actors Studio Theatre production of the play, directed by José Quintero with Geraldine Page in the leading role of Nina Leeds, opened on March 11, 1963, at the Hudson Theatre and became one of the theatrical events of the season. Also in the cast were William Prince, Franchot Tone, Ben Gazzara, Pat Hingle, Betty Field, Richard Thomas, Jane Fonda, and Geoffrey Horne. Settings and lighting were by David Hays, costumes by Noel Taylor (Miss Page's costumes were by Theoni V. Aldredge). It received a generally warm critical reception from the daily press, though there were reservations over the "flaws," "absurdities," and "naiveties" of the play. Walter Kerr called it "this curious and uneven but illuminating and extremely interesting experience." [5] Howard Taubman saluted the opening as a major event: "With a brilliant revival of Eugene O'Neill's 'Strange Interlude' the Actors Studio has taken a step forward. It may turn out to be a giant step forward for the good of the theater in America." [6]

Other critics, however, were harsher, characterizing O'Neill's play as an overblown melodrama with shallow psychologizing and turgid language. They also attacked the production for what they considered its lack of distinction and its deficiency in true ensemble work. They said it was "star-infected and underrehearsed" [7] and that its cast, with the exception of Geraldine Page, had "a familiar kind of journeyman excellence which lacks the rarefied subtlety expected of the Actors Studio method." [8] Harold Clurman said Geraldine Page was playing herself, and generally expressed his disappointment in a production he felt did not truly represent the Studio.[9] Various members of the Studio felt the same: the production had become a vehicle for Geraldine Page, and the acting did not reflect the essential nature of Studio work. And from Strasberg himself, "The production, while it had our people and therefore had certain elements that were very good, was not the kind of thing that I would have wanted to be represented by."

There were also indications from the start that the lines of artistic control had not been clearly defined. José Quintero, since he brought the play to the Theatre, naturally wished to realize it his own way. As a non-Studio director, he did not want any interference from Strasberg or the Production Board. By agreeing to do the play under the implied condition that neither Strasberg nor the Production Board would interfere, the Studio in effect had compromised its own creative authority before the fact, thereby sowing the seeds of inevitable conflict. When rehearsals bogged down, Quintero and Rip Torn had furious arguments over what corrective action should be taken. Torn, by virtue of his position on the Production Board and as the initiator of the *Strange Interlude* project, functioned as a sort of unofficial executive producer, although Cheryl Crawford, as the Theatre's executive producer, was technically in charge of the production. Strasberg, who in his capacity as the artistic director of the Theatre theoretically had a say in all matters of production, was reduced to working with some of the cast behind the director's back.

For many Studio members, the decision to cast Betty Field and Franchot Tone, two non-Studio actors, was seen as a breach of faith in the Studio family, even though Tone, as a Group Theatre alumnus, had spiritual ties with the workshop. (Strasberg further justified bringing in Tone by pointing to the shortage of older character actors in the Studio.) There was also resentment that certain actors were cast more for their "name" value than for their suitability. Resented, too, was the exception granted in the case of Ben Gazzara and Jane Fonda, who were hired even though they could work for only four months despite the understanding that everyone would be required to devote five months to the Studio. These violations of the agreed-upon organizational and functional principles not only indicated a looseness in the Theatre protocol, but a dangerous tendency to be too readily accommodating when it seemed momentarily convenient.

Even so, *Strange Interlude* achieved a popular success. It did well at the box office and might have shown a financial profit except for problems resulting from the rental of the Hudson Theatre. When the Studio Theatre sought to renew its lease there, the Hudson's owners tried to negotiate an exorbitant rise in rent, so the production was transferred to the Martin Beck Theatre for what was hoped would be an extended run. Unfortunately, the move proved damagingly costly: eleven thousand dollars for transportation of the scenery; an added weekly expense of several musicians the production did not use, but who had to be paid under the union contract at the Martin Beck; and, most crucially, the disruption of the production's advance sale. After a month at the Martin Beck, the play closed.*

In 1964 the production was invited to London to participate in the Royal Shakespeare Theatre's international commemoration of Shakespeare's birthday. But initial plans to accept the invitation and to proceed with a European tour afterward had to be abandoned because of a lack of funds.

The switch of theaters during the run of *Strange Interlude* was an unfortunate reminder of the Studio Theatre's problem in not having a home of its own. In an effort to start the 1963–1964 season off with a more secure base of operation and to avoid putting itself at the mercy of a variety of theatrical landlords, the Studio Theatre announced a plan to take over the Riviera Terrace, an unused ballroom at Broadway and Fifty-third Street, and convert it into an all-purpose theater suitable for at least part of its production schedule. The idea was to operate under a cabaret rather than a theater license,

---

* On April 7, 1963, Columbia Records made an original-cast recording of the production, Columbia DOS-688 (5 records).

which would allow the serving of food and liquor in what would be called The Actors Studio Theatre Club. The design concept of the projected $100,000 renovation was to allow for conversion to a thrust stage, a modified proscenium arrangement, or complete theater-in-the-round seating, depending on the production—a flexibility that would accommodate a variety of plays from the season's repertory. Unfortunately, arrangements fell through when the cabaret license was refused at the last moment and Columbia University, the owner of the property, decided to sell the building for other purposes.

The loss of the Riviera Terrace was especially unfortunate in terms of the first production of the new season, June Havoc's *Marathon '33*. The ballroom structure would have served admirably to re-create the milieu of the dance-marathon craze of the thirties, the background for Miss Havoc's highly theatrical piece. It was an ingenious plan to enhance the excitement and period color of the production by establishing an environmental atmosphere of the time, with the audience mixing with the actors, seeing their dressing rooms, and observing the goings-on as if they were in an actual dance hall of the early thirties. When the play was moved to the ANTA Theatre, much of the effect of this idea was lost. Despite the construction of a thrust forestage, the planting of actors in the front row, and the use of the house for some entrances and exits, the production was severely restricted by the traditional proscenium arrangement.

Even more damaging to the production was the loss of income suffered through the failure to rent the Riviera Terrace. When *Marathon '33* was originally scheduled to open in the fall of 1963, The Actors Studio Theatre signed theater-party contracts for approximately $200,000. With additional individual orders, the production enjoyed an advance sale of more than a quarter of a million dollars, which would have assured it of at least a four-month run. In the three months it took to find and secure the ANTA Theatre, the advance sale evaporated.

Marathon '33 was based on June Havoc's biographical reminiscence, *Early Havoc*.[10] Julie Harris, who was appearing with Miss Havoc in *The Warm Peninsula* at the time of the book's publication, persuaded her to turn it into a play, promising to do the leading role if it were ever produced. At one point a Broadway production was planned by David Merrick with Gower Champion set to direct, but

Miss Havoc withdrew her play because of "artistic differences" with them. When *Marathon '33* was offered to The Actors Studio Theatre, Strasberg suggested that she develop it further in the Studio.

For over a year there was continuing experimentation on the material of the play, with exciting theatrical results. Assisted by Tim Everett, a Studio member with outstanding credits as both actor and choreographer, Miss Havoc encouraged a wide range of exploratory improvisations to "find the life" of the play and its characters. In one respect, this work was Miss Havoc's audition for the job of directing her own play, which she was determined to do after failing to see eye-to-eye with Frank Corsaro and Burgess Meredith, the first and second directors who were brought in to stage the production. Strasberg assumed overall supervision of the production when Miss Havoc took on the directorial chores. He also encouraged her to continue working on the script.

In the opinion of various Studio members who saw the original draft, the revisions were for the worse. Strasberg was concerned with the "literary deficiencies" of the script. Miss Havoc had, in fact, taken offense at his remarking that the Broadway critics would find the play strong in theatricality, but lacking literary content or philosophy. Certain members of the Production Board felt that Strasberg was overly concerned with strengthening the dramatic conflicts in the play, or, depending on the point of view, insufficiently assertive with Miss Havoc in getting his ideas across, because in the course of developing the property, the play became, in the opinion of many, "*very* sentimental" and "incredibly third rate" compared with the original script. Rip Torn, for one, wished it had never been tampered with. "June gave us a marvelous two-headed calf to exhibit," he said of it. "Everybody in the world would have paid two cents to come see this two-headed calf. Lee chopped off one of the heads, and all you had was a calf with a big sore on the side. Nobody wanted to see it."

Miss Havoc believes her admiration for Strasberg caused her to defer to him too willingly at the time. While she was delighted with his initial enthusiasm for the script, she now feels he did not really understand the vaudeville milieu of the play. She believes that a good deal of humor was lost because of his emphasis on the "inner work" with the actors in the production.

Strasberg and others have recollected matters somewhat differently.

Once the play had gone into production, according to them, Miss Havoc's attitude toward the creative contributions of others experienced a sea change. She insisted on details being executed precisely to her order. When Strasberg tried to encourage even greater theatricality through more choreography, for instance, his suggestions were ignored. On several occasions he gave notes to Tim Everett that Miss Havoc refused to carry out. In fairness to Strasberg, it must be stated that Miss Havoc's rewriting of her play was totally within her control. Though it may have been Strasberg's error in judgment not to have gone with the original rough-hewn version of the script, it is hard to believe he encouraged the growing sentimentality in the work. He tried to heighten the element of struggle between the characters in the face of the somewhat mawkish atmosphere Miss Havoc's staging had created. As the play was autobiographical, there is some reason to believe that Miss Havoc had tended to sentimentalize her own memory of herself. When Strasberg attempted to suggest ideas to dispel that sentimentality, she resisted.

Then, too, one must remember the prevailing mood of those dark days in the autumn of 1963. At one rehearsal, during the emotionally trying week following President Kennedy's assassination, the conflict between Miss Havoc's direction and Strasberg's reached an explosive climax. The company sat in the house as Miss Havoc gave them notes. Several of her remarks were addressed to Julie Harris, who was starring in the play as she had promised. What Miss Havoc said to her evidently contradicted what the actress had just been told to do by Strasberg, for Miss Harris suddenly exploded in a cold fury. "Who is the director here!" she demanded. "I cannot work this way! I cannot listen to one person say this and then another person say that, and work! I am an actor; I can do it this way or I can do it that way, *but I cannot do it both ways at the same time!*" Overwrought by months of physically and spiritually exhausting rehearsal, she continued her tirade of agonized frustration for several minutes, speaking in a "Medea-like" voice so passionate and so powerful it made her listeners' blood run cold.

Miss Harris's anger seems eminently justified under the circumstances. It dramatically crystallized one of the shortcomings of The Actors Studio Theatre—the absence of a definitive policy of artistic control over production—a deficiency that was to provide endless problems for the Theatre.

When *Marathon '33* opened on December 22, 1963, Strasberg's prediction was confirmed. While many of the critics found the play's evocative atmosphere entirely sufficient unto its purposes, others did not. Howard Taubman, who was complimentary about the production's "theatrical flair and gusto" and Miss Harris's performance, for example, nevertheless concluded that " 'Marathon' is thin in dramatic content; it can only be recommended as a tour de force of theatricality." [11]

The third presentation of The Actors Studio Theatre, and the only musical it produced, was the "comic opera for actors," *Dynamite Tonight*, with libretto by Arnold Weinstein and score by William Bolcom. This satire on war had originated in the Playwrights Unit as the first experimental project under the Rockefeller Foundation grant of 1963. It was codirected for the Unit by Paul Sills, the founder and director of the Second City, and Mr. Weinstein. When it was shown at the Studio, according to Strasberg, "it was a knockout," and several producers offered to continue it Off-Broadway. The Actors Studio Theatre, however, decided to sponsor the venture itself.

Unfortunately, in the process of transferring *Dynamite Tonight* to Off-Broadway, something went awry. Partially as a result of cast changes—Gene Wilder and Anthony Holland replaced William Redfield and Alvin Epstein in two of the central roles—the chemistry among the performers was disturbed; a certain sparkle and flavor was lost. What had seemed genuinely hilarious in the intimate confines of the Studio now came across as sophomoric and flat. Director Mike Nichols was called in to salvage the production, but to no avail. When the show opened on March 15, 1964, at the York Playhouse with George Gaynes, Lou Gilbert, John Harkins, Barbara Harris, David Hurst, and James Noble, in addition to Wilder and Holland, it received a number of enthusiastic reviews.[12] But the Theatre's leaders apparently agreed with Howard Taubman's observation that "in presenting it . . . the Actors Studio Theater [gave] its judgment of what is viable on the stage a thoroughly black eye." [13] It was closed immediately.

The Studio Theatre's fourth production, the only one that was to show a financial profit at the end of its run, was James Costigan's *Baby Want a Kiss*. The reason for this monetary success was the play's small cast—three characters and a sheepdog—and the fact that Paul Newman and Joanne Woodward, who starred in the production with their author and friend Costigan, worked for Actors' Equity minimum salary. At $117.50 per week apiece, each of the two Hollywood stars was earning a fourth of Costigan's wage and less than either the assistant stage manager or their own understudies. The decision to subsidize their production in this manner reflected the Newmans' enthusiasm for the whole Theatre enterprise and a characteristic generosity that was to come to the aid of the Studio itself on many occasions.*

Newman had expressed his support for the movement toward a theater as early as the summer of 1959, shortly after the Studio had announced its plans for an expanded program. He wrote to Strasberg declaring his willingness and desire to participate in a theater that on a regular basis would embody the kind of work done at the Studio. In the same letter he acknowledged the Studio's contribution to his own artistic growth and successful career.

At the time of that letter, while he was appearing with Geraldine Page in *Sweet Bird of Youth* on Broadway, Newman attended the Studio faithfully. An interesting side result of his observation of the work there was the decision to produce and direct his first film, Michael Strong's performance of Chekhov's comic monologue, *On the Harmfulness of Tobacco*. He had seen Strong present the piece at one of the acting sessions "and felt it deserved a wider audience." It was shot over a five-day schedule in the auditorium of the Orpheum Theater on Second Avenue in New York's East Village. During the 1961–1962 season, Newman returned to the Studio to work on the character of Petruchio in *The Taming of the Shrew*.

The decision to appear in *Baby Want a Kiss* was "a whim" of the Newmans, according to Frank Corsaro, who is a friend of theirs

---

* The Studio Theatre's schedule had a one-thousand-dollar top, which was paid to its most prominent players. This amount was substantially less than these leading players could earn in a commercial production. Similarly, all Studio members worked for less than they would normally be paid. Thus, it would be fair to say that all Studio Theatre actors subsidized the plays they were appearing in.

The Newmans' gesture is, nevertheless, an especially munificent one. They apparently felt their financial situation allowed them to forgo the top Studio Theatre salary to which they were entitled. If *Baby Want a Kiss* had been a commercial production, they would have commanded many thousands of dollars plus a large percentage of the weekly house gross.

and who directed the production. They wanted to do it because Costigan also was a friend and because the notion of playing a glamorous Hollywood couple amused them. The plot line was simple: two movie stars visit a writer pal of theirs, whom they have not seen in fifteen years. Through the course of an evening, they play a game of acting out their dreams and otherwise bare their souls and reveal the hollowness of their lives while indulging in a dense and bewildering exchange of wisecracks. Corsaro himself felt it was a "talented play," but an unfinished one that should have been done Off-Broadway. Strasberg was taken by "a fantasy element in the play, which, unfortunately, did not come across in the production." Corsaro says the author was obdurate and unwilling to change things in the play once they went into rehearsal. "The truth was he couldn't change it. . . . The last ten minutes, the play sank like the *Titanic*." When it opened on April 19, 1964, at The Little Theatre, the production received almost unanimously unfavorable notices. Nevertheless, because of the Newmans, it played to sold-out houses for four months.

Four days after the opening of the Costigan play, The Actors Studio premiered its fifth production, James Baldwin's *Blues for Mister Charlie*. A drama of potent social comment, it proved to be a *succès d'estime* that rekindled respect for the Studio Theatre after the "unsubstantial" efforts that had preceded it earlier in the season. The fact that Baldwin offered the play to the Theatre in the first place was something of a competitive victory over Kazan and Whitehead at Lincoln Center, who had fought to get it for themselves.

Kazan's interest in the property was understandable. It was he who had originally given Baldwin, his assistant on the productions of *J.B.* and *Sweet Bird of Youth*, the idea for a play based on the Emmett Till case. He corresponded with the young author for two years about the drama, suggested its climax, and even discussed the set with him. When it came time to produce the play, Baldwin told Kazan he was giving it to The Actors Studio Theatre because there were no blacks on the board of Lincoln Center. Actually, the reasons were profounder, and were finally revealed when Baldwin informed Kazan that he felt overly bound to him, like a son to a father, and that he needed to be free of this paternal influence to do the play on his own. Kazan was bitterly disappointed. "I should have produced it," he said, recollecting the episode. "I initiated it. He did something wrong in doing what he did. . . . I certainly would have been much tougher on him rewriting, he was right about that. . . . I believe in rewriting a lot. I didn't like [what the Studio did with it]. I didn't think it was well done. I thought Jimmy was a fool to do what he did."

Rip Torn once again, played a crucial role in getting the play for The Actors Studio Theatre. He discussed the script with Baldwin at every opportunity, occasionally offering him helpful suggestions about it. He challenged Baldwin to finish it by telling him that various people around town were saying he would never see it through to the end. The provocation was effective. Baldwin finally came up with a workable draft, though when it was ready, he was reluctant to offer it to the Studio Theatre. "They'll never do it the way I wrote it," he said. Torn assured him it would be done word for word the way he wrote it. When Cheryl Crawford later tried to blue-pencil some of Baldwin's raw language (she particularly objected to the word *motherfucker*), the volatile Torn flew into one of his famous rages and then explained his promise to the playwright that the work would be done as written. The other directors outvoted Miss Crawford, and the cuts were restored.

Frank Corsaro was originally supposed to direct *Blues for Mister Charlie* and Sidney Poitier early on was named as one of the stars, though he later withdrew. Corsaro, Strasberg, and Baldwin worked on revisions up to the point where the author refused to acquiesce further in making the play "less polemical and more humane." The playwright, who spent two months in Strasberg's summer home on Fire Island revising, had at first been amenable to softening the drama's strident condemnation of whites. But ultimately, according to Corsaro, Baldwin decided that for certain political reasons the play had to remain a polemic against the white race. He finally had a "crisis of confidence" with Corsaro and insisted that he be relieved of his job since the director's ideas were opposed to his own political vision of the play. Though Burgess Meredith, who was willing to direct the play on Baldwin's terms, was brought in to replace Corsaro, conflicts with the playwright did not end. There were several stormy sessions, including one especially dramatic afternoon when

Baldwin mounted a ladder to shower the members of the company and the Theatre's leaders with a lengthy stream of vilification over the Studio's incompetence.

The Studio Theatre's Production Board originally voted to give *Blues for Mister Charlie* a simple workshop production because the play's initial five-and-a-half-hour length seemed to preclude a commercial presentation. Strasberg had concurred with that vote, but after leaving the meeting at which it took place, on his way to catch a plane, he changed his mind. In the strikingly offhanded and impulsive manner in which such matters were sometimes decided, he phoned the board from Kennedy airport to announce that the play would be given a full-scale production. "This decision was final," Cheryl Crawford recollects in her autobiography, "and it is an example of the kind of administration that became our downfall. We never planned to give the artistic director the power to overrule the Board; it simply happened." [14]

Even as a full-scale production, *Blues* was initially intended to be presented simply and straightforwardly as a modest endeavor requiring a minimal monetary outlay. But it soon became apparent that there would be little saving and no prospect of financial profit on the project. When Meredith took over, he elaborated the concept, filled out the cast to twenty-seven actors, and augmented the rather barren, open-stage space of platforms and pieces of furniture with a very effective lighting scheme by designer Abe Feder. The constant revision and condensation of the inordinately long script made it impossible to schedule an opening date so that an advance sale could be built up. The cutting also entailed the further expense of re-lighting and recuing. Finally, it was decided that in order to draw a sympathetic and eager audience—particularly blacks and students—ticket prices should be set as low as $2.30 a seat with $4.80 as a top price.

When it opened on April 23, 1964, at the ANTA Theatre, the production received a generally enthusiastic critical reception. Reservations were expressed at the play's sprawling structure and its stereotypes of the southern red-neck, but there was high praise for the "fierce energy and passion" of the piece and for its relevance and authenticity as a shout of protest. There was also particular commendation for the outstanding performances of Pat Hingle, Al Freeman, Jr., Diana Sands, and Rip Torn. [15]

Because of the weekly production costs and the low prices of tickets, *Blues for Mister Charlie* consistently lost money. When the play, despite "strongly positive audience reaction," was threatened with closing the following month, Baldwin led a campaign to keep it open. His effort was supported by a ten-thousand-dollar contribution from two daughters of Nelson Rockefeller and by the personal exhortations of such individuals as Roy Wilkins, the executive secretary of the NAACP, who sent out a mailing on his organization's letterhead urging attendance at the play. An ad, taken out in support of the play by the Reverend Sidney Lanier and signed by such figures as Geraldine Page, Lorraine Hansberry, Marlon Brando, Lena Horne, Shelley Winters, Sammy Davis, Jr., Percy Sutton, Ossie Davis, Harry Belafonte, Studs Terkel, Tennessee Williams, Miles Davis, Leontyne Price, James Farmer, William Warfield, Lillian Hellman, James Foreman, A. Philip Randolph, Sidney Poitier, Diahann Carroll, Whitney Young, and Brock Peters, among others, appeared in *The New York Times* (p. 43) and the *New York Herald Tribune* (p. 15) on May 28, 1964. The campaign was successful enough to keep the play running through the summer. By then, it was estimated that the audiences consisted of approximately 80 percent blacks. Unfortunately the ANTA Theatre was booked by another production for the fall season and *Blues* was forced to close on Saturday, August 29, because of the lack of eight thousand dollars required to move the production to the Martin Beck Theatre.

The sixth and final production of The Actors Studio Theatre was dedicated to Marilyn Monroe. The tragic death of the famous movie star in August of 1962, less than two months after she had sent her telegram congratulating Strasberg and the Studio membership on the new Theatre, had come as an enormous shock to them. She had named Strasberg as a principal beneficiary in her will, bequeathing him 60 percent of her estate and all of her personal effects, and he was among the few invited to her funeral in Westwood, California, where he delivered the eulogy for her.[16] On June 1, 1963, the thirty-seventh anniversary of her birth, he announced that the Studio would establish a Marilyn Monroe Fund in her memory and that his first production for The Actors Studio Theatre, Chekhov's *The Three Sisters*, would be dedicated to her.

Strasberg had been contemplating a production of Chekhov's play for many years. His memories of the Moscow Art Theater's production of the classic were still quite vivid, and he spoke frequently of how moved he had been by the emotional power of the Russians' performances.

I remember when Stanislavski as Vershinin came to say good-by to Masha in *The Three Sisters*. They have tried not to show their love for each other, but the band was playing, and they looked at each other, and then they grabbed each other. I'll never forget that grabbing. I remember literally holding onto the seat. The simple reality of that good-by, of the two people holding on as if they wouldn't let go, of both literally clinging to each other, will stay with me always.[17]

Despite these impressions, he had his own ideas about *The Three Sisters* and how, in general, Chekhov should be realized. He thought the MAT's "rich and full" production was not quite what Chekhov was after—which was something less emotionally obvious, something more hinted at than baldly stated, something fulfilling in theatrical terms the aesthetic principle that less is more. Strasberg felt a strong affinity between his perception of Chekhov's "vision" and the nature of the training his own tastes had developed at The Actors Studio. In class sessions, he talked of how Chekhov should ideally be approached and of how the Chekhovian sensibility related to the work in the Studio:

Chekhov was insistently opposed to fake dramatic vision. He didn't like sentiment. He didn't like the actors to be too aware of acting. He didn't like points to be made too emphatically on the stage—or for that matter off the stage. . . . Only by the approach that we follow can we possibly attain the kind of evanescent reality which Chekhov sensed. Somebody once described Chekhov very well. "Chekhov," he said, "is like something you see reflected in water." . . .

It is possible that the technical work we do here, which strips the actor of obvious theatricalities, can lead to the fulfillment of Chekhov's intention.[18]

Strasberg's continuing preoccupation with *The Three Sisters* inspired hopes among his students that he would realize his long-avowed ambition to resume his directing career with a production of the play. Opportunities had come and gone. In 1959, for instance, when Gordon Rogoff unsuccessfully tried to arrange for the Studio to produce some plays for a European tour under the sponsorship of the State Department, one of the projected items was *The Three Sisters*, to be directed by Strasberg. Kim Stanley has reported that she and Geraldine Page had tried to get him to do the play for three years prior to the founding of the Studio Theatre. "We begged, pleaded, cajoled.... We didn't care which parts we played." With the advent of the Theatre, it became a foregone conclusion that Strasberg would finally turn his wish/dream into reality, especially with Misses Stanley and Page putting pressure on him to get started by turning down other roles to keep themselves available for the production.

When it came time to cast *The Three Sisters*, Strasberg had a very clear idea of whom he wanted in most of the roles. Geraldine Page originally expressed an interest in playing Natasha, having come to appreciate the possibilities in the role after seeing Ruth Gordon do the part. But Strasberg rejected the idea, insisting that she should play the eldest sister Olga. According to Miss Page, Strasberg's original choice for Natasha was Anne Bancroft, who declined to appear in the production because she wanted to play Masha "or nothing." From the start, Strasberg had decided on Kim Stanley for Masha. Barbara Harris was briefly considered a likely Natasha, but the part was ultimately given to Barbara Baxley. Susan Strasberg was announced to play Irina, the youngest of the sisters, but she withdrew early on, and Shirley Knight finally created the role.

As for the men, Strasberg would have loved Marlon Brando to play Vershinin. According to Martin Fried, *The Three Sisters* production stage manager, Brando was offered the role, said he would do it, and then at the last minute wrote a letter to Strasberg declining the offer with the explanation that he was just too nervous about returning to the stage at that time. Kim Stanley said of Brando, with whom she was once scheduled to tour *Hamlet* through Europe before he backed out, "I love Marlon's talent; hate his cowardice."

Negotiations were started with Ben Gazzara to play Vershinin, but were suspended because Miss Stanley reportedly felt he was too young for the role. She herself hoped Montgomery Clift would play the part. But the artistic director had already made his choice: Kevin McCarthy. When Miss Stanley expressed her chagrin at Strasberg's decision—she felt no affinity for McCarthy and feared this would damage her performance—he explained that the actor had the perfect combination of qualities for the role, which was not really that of a romantic hero, and that, besides, it did not matter how unimpressive he was to the audience because anyone she, Miss Stanley, would be in love with would seem worthy and interesting to them. This explanation infuriated her—she stormed out of the restaurant where they were discussing the matter—much to Strasberg's perplexity, and she never was reconciled to playing opposite McCarthy.

Strasberg invited certain actors to participate in the production, including Tamara Daykarhanova, who played Anfisa and served as a consultant on Russian customs and dress; Luther Adler, one of the leading lights of the Group Theatre, but not a Studio member, as Chebutykin; Robert Loggia, as Solyony; and Salem Ludwig as Ferapont. The other parts were open for audition by any Studio member who wanted to sign up. Having to audition, ironically, seemed offensive to some of the actors. While on the one hand it seemed a fair way of giving those who wanted to be considered a chance, it alienated many who had worked at the Studio for Strasberg for five or ten years "to have to go through that same rejection and humiliation from the place that was supposed to be home." Quite likely, however, the alternatives of auditioning every role or precasting every role would have proved equally unpopular. There was also at least one "accommodation" to a busy actor's schedule. Gerald Hiken, whom Strasberg wanted in the role of Andrei, was given the part despite the fact that he was unable to attend the first week of rehearsals and could only play eight weeks of the prescribed twelve-week run. The final cast included, in addition to those already mentioned, James Olson as Tuzenbach, Albert Paulsen as Kulygin, John Harkins as Fedotik, Brooks Morton as the Adjutant, David Paulsen as Rode, and Janice Mars as the Maid. (The last three were not Studio members.)

About Strasberg's artistic role in this production there are a variety of opinions, each subjectively colored by the individual encounters with the director during rehearsals. Some of the actors were very responsive to his direction and found his approach to the work nurturing and creative. He gave these players the reassurance that each was ideally suited to their role and that he and the performer simply had to work together to reveal what was already there. He fired their imaginations with penetrating observations of character motivations, social customs and mores relating to the era of the play, and by his own sensitivity to the poetic nuances of Chekhov's world.[19]

With some of the other actors, there were the characteristic Strasbergian confrontations. He was very severe with James Olson and

Barbara Baxley by all accounts. At one point the actress threatened to walk out of the theater and fly home to California if he did not apologize for yelling at her.

It has been suggested that some of his flare-ups with the featured performers were the result of his frustrations with his stars. He gave many people the distinct impression that he was largely intimidated by his leading actresses and had difficulty dealing with them easily or effectively. Kim Stanley once blew up at him for berating Shirley Knight. "Why don't you yell at me!" she challenged him. "I'm the one you want to yell at!"

The clash of temperamental egos is all too common in the professional theater and it is difficult, if not impossible, to ascertain who is more fundamentally at fault in the resulting artistic conflicts. But for Geraldine Page, her work with Strasberg was a series of shocks. She characterized his approach to the production as "an attempt of somebody trying to act like a Broadway director." Perhaps to assert his authority at the outset—and to head off some anticipated self-indulgence—he insisted that she play certain moments in a very specific way. (He even gave line readings à la George Abbott, she says.) She consequently felt that she was never really able to explore anything and that Strasberg directed her by imposition.

Kim Stanley also experienced and somewhat resented the pressure of certain ideas he attempted to "impose" on the performance. She especially remembers his staging of the final tableau, which she claims the actors never felt comfortable with. He brought in a recording of the Moscow Art Theater production and played over and over again the scene of departure between Vershinin and Masha that had moved him so deeply some four decades earlier. Miss Stanley felt he almost wanted the actors to catch and reproduce the very intonations of the Russian speech, and she found this intolerable.

But then Miss Stanley definitely had a mind of her own. At one rehearsal, Michael Wager, observing her entrance in the third act, her hair streaming down her back, turned to Strasberg in concern. "What is this?" he asked the director. "She looks like she's playing the mad scene from *Lucia di Lammermoor!*" According to Wager, Strasberg, who was livid with rage and exasperated beyond endurance at his total inability to influence her performance, said with strangled fury, "She's playing it that way because Kim Stanley thinks Masha goes crazy in the third act!"

Among the members of the Studio there were a variety of responses to the production. For some it was a memorable artistic experience. For others it was a hodgepodge of brilliant moments and unrealized effects, which like much of the rest of the work of the Studio Theatre did not fulfill what they felt the Studio was ideally capable of. Even among members of the company there were differences of opinion. Some thought the production was very successful at what it was trying to accomplish. Others felt that the work was variable and not consistently distinguished. From his point of view, Strasberg believed the major part of it worked out quite well. Some of the casting was less than ideal, but the sisters themselves he felt were "quite successful."

The production, designed by Will Steven Armstrong, with lighting by Feder and costumes by Theoni V. Aldredge and Ray Diffen, opened at the Morosco Theatre on June 22, 1964, and received a number of highly favorable reviews. Brooks Atkinson called it "a tender, spontaneous, truthful performance . . . [which captured] the grace of Chekhov's compassionate spirit." [20] Jerry Tallmer was particularly exuberant in his praise:

The Actors Studio talks a good deal about truth. Last night at the Morosco Theater it nailed for our lifetime the right to do so and Lee Strasberg proved to a world waiting 20 years that he could direct a play—if it's the right play—with all the creative truth and strength a human being can command.

The Actors Studio also talks a good deal about inner life. I do not think I have ever seen 16 or however many actors walking a stage with more valid and inter related inner lives than those Mr. Strasberg has elicited from his brilliant cast for Chekhov's "The Three Sisters" at the Morosco.[21]

There were also negative reviews, and reviews expressing strong reservations: Judith Crist talked of "a diffusion of character, a variety of acting styles and a diversity of mood that vitiates the cumulative impact of the play." [22] Others criticized what they considered the failure at ensemble playing and the tendency to solipsistic acting. Henry Hewes observed that "the performers seem less involved with each other than they do with their personal selfish needs and feelings." [23]

Something all the reviews agreed upon was the outstanding quality of one character portrayal: Kim Stanley's. "With her performance as Masha, the sister who is closest to the play's center, she confirms her position as our greatest actress. . . . Miss Stanley seizes this role and takes it to its limits. From the opening scene, where she lies on a couch without speaking, she dominates the stage in her silences as in her speeches. It is a performance of such intensity, depth, complexity, and imagination that it comes close to enkindling the production. At the very least, it touches it with splendor." So ended *Newsweek*'s negative review.[24]

A performer widely admired as an "actors' actor," Miss Stanley represented the very best the Studio could offer. Yet there were those who pointed out that the sheer brilliance of her portrayal tended to disturb the balance of the play and to make of the drama a one-woman show. Some of her fellow actors in *The Three Sisters* thought she was a little *too* dramatic and a little too strong, especially toward the beginning of the run. Reportedly, she agreed with this, saying at one point that "her Masha *would* have gone to Moscow." Harold Clurman, who considers Miss Stanley "a brilliant, a wonderful actress," nevertheless thought her Masha "a latter-day neurotic, ridden by spasms of torment caused not so much by her situation in the play as by an experience of life far more complex and sophisticated than that of Chekhov's character." [25]

Randall Jarrell, whose translation of Chekhov's play was used by the Studio Theatre, said that, although he admired her performance greatly, he thought the "laconic" quality of Masha was somewhat lost. "Nearly one-fourth of the lines she uttered, he estimated, were not in the script but were her own invention, introduced perhaps to help her through the role." [26] After one performance Miss Stanley reportedly went up to Jarrell and said, "I love your adaptation," to which he replied, "I love yours."

But it was chiefly the critical raves for Miss Stanley's performance that drew the audience to *The Three Sisters*. When she became ill later in the run, the production was desperately hurt. Miss Crawford and Strasberg wrote to Patricia Neal in England asking her to step into the part for a limited time in order to save the production. As it turned out, Geraldine Page took over the role of Masha, while Peggy Feury played Olga. The play continued through the summer, closing on October 3 after a run of 119 performances.

On October 19, 1964, The Actors Studio Theatre and the Ely Landau Company announced that they had entered into a special agreement by which *The Three Sisters* would be the first of twelve Studio Theatre productions to be recorded on tape and film in the process called Electronovision, previously used to film a performance of Richard Burton's *Hamlet*. The original cast—except for Barbara Baxley and Shirley Knight, who because of previous commitments were replaced by Shelley Winters and Sandy Dennis—was directed by Paul Bogart. The resulting film, a rather grim affair which does not do justice to the finer qualities of the original stage presentation, remains the only record, however flawed, of an Actors Studio Theatre production. It has rarely been seen.*

In the meantime, The Actors Studio Theatre had once again been invited to London, this time to take part in the second annual World Theatre Season under the sponsorship of the Royal Shakespeare Company and Peter Daubeny in conjunction with the London *Sunday Telegraph*. Daubeny, who as the festival's artistic director had brought such outstanding theater companies as the Berliner Ensemble and the Comédie Française to the first World Theatre Season, was especially eager to have the Studio Theatre participate as the representative of American theater, because of the tremendous interest in Strasberg's work and teaching in England and Europe.

For years the Studio had greeted theater companies from abroad, who, in recognition of the workshop's international standing, came to visit its headquarters while they were playing in New York. During the early sixties alone, such welcomes were extended to the Teatro Piccolo Milano, the Comédie Française, the Old Vic, the Swedish Royal Theater, the Habimah Theater, and the members of the Moscow Art Theater who gave the MAT seminars in 1965. These troupes, representing the theater of their respective countries as they did, paid the Studio a singular honor by expressing their interest in the work of the organization. The idea of finally achieving an equal standing with them by performing at the prestigious World Theatre Festival as America's representative theater was enormously appealing to the Studio's leaders.

They decided to send *The Three Sisters* and *Blues for Mister Charlie* to appear at London's Aldwych Theatre from May 3 through 22 as the climax to the festival. The effort to raise the money to send the two companies to England proved, unsurprisingly, something of

* Vincent Canby gave it a scathing review in *The New York Times* (June 30, 1977) when it was released for a brief theatrical run in the summer of 1977.

a struggle. Appeals to the State Department were rejected and an effort to enlist the support of individual corporations also proved fruitless. It was only at the eleventh hour that the fifty-five thousand dollars required was supplied to the Studio Theatre through the generosity of Columbia Pictures, Pan American World Airways, MGM, Paramount, Seven Arts, Twentieth Century-Fox, and Warner Brothers. Paul Newman was instrumental in raising about 60 percent of the total, including his own personal financial contribution.

Preparation for the trip to London progressed slowly. According to Geraldine Page, Rip Torn had urged some decisive action on the invitation to England as soon as the Theatre had received it; he pointed out that it would be difficult to get the original cast members were they not contracted with early on. But Strasberg and Miss Crawford began to make arrangements only at the last moment, when, indeed, many of their actors had other commitments. They therefore suffered some major losses. Because she was starring in *The Owl and the Pussycat*, *Blues for Mister Charlie* no longer had Diana Sands, whose performance had been one of the highlights of the production; Pat Hingle, another of the show's strengths, was involved with a film. They were replaced by Beverly Todd and Larry Blyden, neither of whom were Actors Studio members. A good number of the show's featured players were also unavailable. And by the time the company departed for London, Rip Torn was absent as well.

Torn had had a series of fights with Baldwin over the changes the playwright insisted on for the London production. Baldwin wanted Torn's character, Lyle Britten, to be played as an outright villain in accord with his own more militant view of the play. Torn objected that to do so would be to underestimate the intelligence of one's enemies and would weaken the persuasiveness of Baldwin's polemic. One day at rehearsal Baldwin proceeded to read a list of words he was eliminating from the script to allow the play to pass the censorship of the Lord Chamberlain. Torn looked on in disbelief. After the confrontations he had had with Miss Crawford over the play's language, he could not comprehend what he saw as the playwright's self-betrayal. He embarrassed Baldwin by confronting him before the company with his accusative questions, "Jimmy, *what* are you doing? *What* are you doing?"

Torn also had confrontations with Burgess Meredith over the way the director was proceeding with the rehearsals. Meredith's attitude, faced with a largely new company, was to approach the play anew, to explore it afresh. Torn said to him, "Burgess, you've got one week. You better get the stage-manager's notebook out and check the blocking and light cues." Torn's outbursts were finally too much for both playwright and the director and he was fired for his "corrosive attitude," and replaced by Ralph Waite.

The London opening of *Blues for Mister Charlie* was the beginning of a nightmare for The Actors Studio Theatre. There had been difficulty with the lighting so the production proceeded in a murky darkness. During the second act, two members of the British National Party began shouting "Filth, why don't you go back to Africa?" [27] The following day, the response of the London critics was lethal. While several reviews had some kind words for the play, the majority supported the view that it was a "straggling, overloaded propaganda tract." *The Times* of London said that Baldwin was "exchanging creative writing for demagogic oratory." As for the production, *The Times* critic added, ". . . one had hoped the performance would override these objections; and that if there was any company in the world equipped to dig through the rhetoric to a core of true human feeling it was the Actors Studio of New York. Nothing of the sort took place in last night's performance; and it was with astonishment that one realized that the company, far from deepening the play, were broadening and coarsening it even more." [28] The critic for the *Financial Times* noted that "throughout the whole of the first act the players gave a display of uniformly bad acting." The *Guardian* critic concurred, observing that "this first view of the celebrated method was a disappointment." [29]

The morning after the opening, Strasberg held a news conference at which he discussed the shortcomings of both the play and the production and answered questions about the Method. "There is confusion in the play between Mr. Baldwin's dynamic anger at the racial situation and the human involvement beneath it," he said. "It is partly his fault, partly ours, if the human emotions are not sufficiently conveyed in the production." He explained that most of the performers in *Blues for Mister Charlie*, though good actors, were not members of The Actors Studio and that in any case, both the Baldwin play and the Chekhov did not necessarily represent the work of the Studio. "They are only part of the effort of the first year. We are not a repertory company and have had a company for only a year. We have no regular actors under contract, and we are really only beginning to put on productions. We thought it might be interesting for you to see us from the beginning, and then follow our work and progress." [30]

The apologetic tone with which he spoke and the excuses which he offered for the state of the play and production angered and upset the Studio Theatre people. The black members of the cast who were not Studio members were particularly irate over what they took as a belittlement of their contribution. Those in the company who were Studio members were equally embarrassed and, vis-à-vis the other actors, placed in an awkward position by Strasberg's remarks. Burgess Meredith reacted to some of Strasberg's comments about the direction of the play with stunned surprise. Cheryl Crawford listened to part of the news conference but left abruptly. "I couldn't take it," she recalls. "He wasn't defensive. He was offensive." Baldwin, it goes without saying, was furious.*

The critical commotion over the Baldwin play was but a mild foretaste of the vituperative scorn which was to greet Strasberg's production of *The Three Sisters*. Admittedly, the Chekhov play was not presented under the best conditions. To begin with, only one of the sisters from the original New York production traveled with it to England. Geraldine Page, who became pregnant and was unable to journey to London to play Olga, was replaced by Nan Martin. Shirley Knight, because of other commitments, was replaced by Sandy Dennis. To complicate matters further, Kim Stanley refused to go to London if Kevin McCarthy played Vershinin. Her first choice was Montgomery Clift, with whom she had worked on the Vershinin/Masha scenes in her apartment. Clift was eager to do the part, but when Miss Stanley proposed his name to Strasberg, the artistic director, concerned about Clift's physical and mental condition, refused. McCarthy was, however, replaced by George C. Scott. In addition, Miss Stanley refused to fly to London, so the company had to begin rehearsal without her during her ocean voyage. There was little time in London to get acclimated to the raked stage of the Aldwych Theatre (the actors had to sit tilted awkwardly forward on rented

* Baldwin's portrait of Strasberg, thinly disguised as the character Saul San-Marquand, who runs "The Actors Means Workshop" in *Tell Me How Long the Train's Been Gone* (New York: The Dial Press, Inc., 1968), is not very flattering.

antique furniture that could not be adjusted to the incline), nor to work out the myriad technical problems of the production. The lighting was so poor, the actors had difficulty seeing one another. Two days before the opening Tamara Daykarhanova was knocked down in an accident, suffering a fractured arm.

But none of these problems can explain away the debacle of opening night, which was the result of "an unbelievably self-indulgent performance," in the opinion of many observers. "The calamity was Sandy Dennis," reported Strasberg. "With her nervous tics, you couldn't watch it." The artistic director had had enormous fights with her during rehearsals, but there was no ridding her of the stuttering mannerism that particularly irritated the critics. Kim Stanley, usually a tower of strength according to Strasberg, fell to pieces. She moved at a lethargic pace and indulged in interminable pauses. "She waddled on the stage. . . . I don't know what she did," Strasberg remembers sadly. The curtain went up late, and the show took almost four hours because of the delays between the acts and during the scenes. The expectant English audience was greatly dismayed by what they saw, and many left before the final curtain. When Miss Dennis came out in the third act and said, "Oh it's been a terrible evening," someone yelled out, "It sure has been!" and the remaining spectators burst into laughter. The curtain came down to a shower of boos and catcalls, which stunned the cast. Laurence Olivier came backstage to comfort the actors with his supportive presence and helped cushion the blow of the catastrophic opening by sweeping the company off to a party prepared for them at which they proceeded to drink "heartily."

The critical outcry over the next few days was unprecedented. The reviews were calamitous. The most savage was undoubtedly Penelope Gilliatt's in *The Observer*. "The admirable World Theatre Season's last dismal task has been to mount the suicide of the Actors' Studio," she began. "The whole endeavor [was] absurd and agonising, like playing the harpsichord in boxing gloves, like filling the Spanish Riding School with hippopotami." [31] For the English, all the familiar criticisms of Method acting—the mumbling, the lack of skill with the classics, the coarsening of emotion into hysteria, "the use of art as a way of flexing private neuroses"—seemed finally and unhappily to be confirmed. It was a devastating and humiliating blow to the reputation of The Actors Studio and to the hopes of The Actors Studio

Theatre.* [32] The morning after the opening, Strasberg called the company for a ten o'clock rehearsal. When he arrived he was livid. The cast, slightly hung over and still tense from the previous night, listened as he launched into an angry analysis of their performance. He commented on how he felt the English reviewers were right in their criticism of the opening. George C. Scott stood up and, barely controlling his own rage, said threateningly, "Mr. Strasberg, you called us together here to tell us the papers were right? That we're lousy actors? Do you mean to blame the actors for last night's fiasco!" Several of the actors feared for the artistic director's safety. Strasberg quickly turned around and walked out.

Kim Stanley was distraught from the whole experience, feeling betrayed and guilty. Betrayed, because she had been "sucked into the thing" and Strasberg had not "been there" to stand behind her, to work with her, to help her. Guilty, because she and Geraldine Page had talked him into directing *The Three Sisters* in the first place, feeling as they did that it was what he really wanted and that he had a big statement to make, only to discover they were wrong. "He should not have been put in that position; he had had a dream and it should have been left alone." Her unhappiness over the production left her with a lingering distaste for acting and contributed to an eventual nervous breakdown.

Back in New York the future plans of The Actors Studio Theatre were suddenly thrown in doubt. At the beginning of the 1964–1965 season, there had been talk of a full schedule of plays, including *The Flowering Peach*, to feature Rod Steiger, Shelley Winters, and Susan Strasberg; *Mourning Becomes Electra* to star Patricia Neal; and productions of *Macbeth*, *The Caucasian Chalk Circle*, and *Sergeant Musgrave's Dance*. But when the Ford Foundation was approached about renewing its grant to the Theatre, the answer from W. McNeil Lowry was no.

When attempts were made to raise money for the Theatre in the 1965–1966 season, after the disastrous trip to England, they were unsuccessful. Plans were put in abeyance for the year. In succeeding seasons there would be a number of efforts to get Theatre activity

* There were several sympathetic reviews, notably from critics who saw the production later in its brief run. See, for example, Francis Wyndham, "Actors Studio Ambushed," *New York Herald Tribune Magazine*, July 4, 1965, pp. 22, 24.

started again, but they would all fizzle out. For all practical purposes, the career of The Actors Studio Theatre ended with the final performance of *The Three Sisters* in London.

In truth, however, the lack of funding was not the essential cause of the death of the Theatre. The long-dreamed-of Actors Studio Theatre had died a victim of poor planning, poor organization, and mixed motives. The cherished ideal of ensemble-playing-through-unified-training in a theater serving the playwright had been undercut at almost every turn by lapses of taste in the choice of plays and in their handling, by the unspoken assumption that an impressive array of Studio celebrities would, in and of itself, guarantee both the artistic quality and the economic success of the Theatre, and by the repeated failure conscientiously to build productions on the basis of Studio work. The Studio Theatre undermined its integrity by striving to embrace incompatible goals: to be an ensemble company, yet to be infinitely flexible; to exist outside the Broadway-production syndrome, yet to be inside it fervently looking for a hit; to create a living theatrical tradition based on considered artistic principles, yet to produce a series of plays with no ruling sensibility or identifiable aesthetic, in the blind hope that something good would emerge.

In this last respect, the trip to London was not only a gross miscalculation, but a bizarre culmination of the Studio Theatre's general tendency to proceed without proper planning or purpose and of its willingness to compromise ideals of work, preparation, and ensemble in order simply to get something on.

Strasberg, accepting at least partial responsibility for the Theatre's shortcomings, blames himself for not having been more assertive as artistic director. Others point out that Strasberg's problem was not only that he did not exercise enough authority, but that he had no discernible profile as artistic director insofar as he failed to establish and administer a coherent, significant artistic program.

Subsequent seasons of work might have helped the Theatre resolve its problems, clarify its purpose, and find its true voice. England's National Theatre, for example, enjoyed a number of shakedown years of performing outside of London before it was expected to give an account of itself. The Studio Theatre's record, after all, was not totally undistinguished. The organization did mount six full productions on funding originally intended for three plays, and it had mustered many outstanding theater artists to its cause. But, as the

New York theater world has never been conducive to extended and expensive essays in self-discovery by major arts organizations, The Actors Studio Theatre never got the chance to develop into the artistic force it had hoped to become.

The failure of the Theatre took a lot of wind out of the Studio's sails. A number of members were permanently alienated from the organization as a result of the whole experience. For Strasberg, it signaled a period of disillusionment, dejection, and personal grief. (His wife, Paula, died in 1966.) He seriously contemplated going abroad, dropping The Actors Studio, and finding "something else."

CHAPTER 8

The Studio
Till Now:
1965–1980

THE YEARS AFTER the ill-fated expedition to London were
taken up with efforts to ensure the financial security of The Actors
Studio and to prepare the way for a possible return of the Studio
Theatre. Before the trip to the World Theatre Festival, in 1965, a
New Year's Eve party at the Studio raised approximately ten thousand dollars for the workshop with the assistance of such entertainers as Judy Garland, Liza Minnelli, and Carol Channing, who
performed gratis. But as enjoyable and successful as such events
proved, a conviction was growing among the Studio's leaders that
such small-scale projects were no solution to the workshop's long-
range need for funds.

Early in 1966, under the supervision of Carl Schaeffer, then serving as "national administrator and treasurer of The Actors Studio,"
the workshop announced the formation of a committee of businessmen to help raise a million dollars to revive the Studio Theatre and
to remodel and expand the Studio's building on West Forty-fourth
Street. The committee laid plans for a season of four plays, including
a Kazan-directed *Oresteia;* seventy thousand dollars was actually
pledged by various leaders in finance and industry. By the fall of the
1966–1967 season, however, it was evident that the necessary funding would not be forthcoming and that plans for the Theatre
would have to be postponed at least until the following year. As late

as December 1968, the Studio seriously discussed going back into production with promised support from the Walter Reade Organization. But like earlier efforts, this plan failed to get past the talking stage. Announcements of further postponement evolved over the years into expressions of hope for a Theatre "someday."

Attempts to involve businessmen in the operation of the Studio, however, continued throughout the seventies. Liska March, who organized most of the annual benefits that raised money for the Studio, worked to expand the workshop's board of directors for many years, arguing that a properly constituted board rather than benefits, annual or whatever, should be the primary source of the Studio's yearly funding.

In late 1968, Carl Schaeffer set up an "Advisory Board" with Paul Newman as its chairman and Jack Valenti as its cochairman. Unfortunately, it was disbanded within less than a year because most of its members felt that they were only being asked for money and never for advice. It was replaced with a group called "Friends of The Actors Studio," whose efforts were equally unsuccessful. During the seventies there were additional attempts to create a board similar to those that support the major arts organizations in New York, but each development in that direction was short-lived. It seemed that the leadership of the Studio, while eager for the financial security and "legitimacy" such a board would provide, was still leery of outside influence on the structure and functioning of the workshop, and such wariness was, in turn, reciprocated by potential financial supporters.

The Studio's essential unwillingness to embrace the changes that would have given it a solid financial base and propelled it forward from its "cottage-industry" footing into the status of a major arts organization is typified in the Studio's response to a report on the workshop's fiscal outlook commissioned from the Victor Weingarten company in 1967.

The Weingarten report pointed out that the Studio's loose administrative and organizational setup was outmoded and, for the purposes of achieving future growth and financial stability, would have to be restructured with a clarification of the now familiar question, "Who's minding the store?" It specifically addressed itself to necessary priorities: an annual operating budget, methods for proceeding with a three-part capital fund drive that would encompass everything from the rehabilitation and enlargement of the Studio plant to the creation of a theater, and an enlargement of the board of directors that would include representatives of industry, banking, real estate, foundations, construction, education, as well as members and "friends" of the Studio.

But the Studio's leaders made little effort to put the Weingarten recommendations into effect, and so the report had no impact on the workshop's course of affairs. Though a number of people were added to the board in 1968, its subsequent composition shifted radically from year to year and never achieved, for any significant time, the consistency of representation counseled by the study. There was no real movement toward a theater, the structure of the organization remained loose, and the primary source of income remained the annual benefit.

The Studio did make a move toward implementing the plan to enlarge the workshop's plant with a backyard extension to house additional rehearsal space when it commissioned an architect to evaluate the condition of the existing structure and to prepare a feasibility study of the projected construction. But the upshot of this gesture was not the enlargement of the Studio—only a certain amount of renovative shoring-up underneath the building to arrest the gradual deterioration of the century-old edifice.

The Studio, despite the aspirations and visionary projections of its leadership, remained a small-scale, "candy-store" operation—its heyday apparently past. Those innovations in Studio activity that did take place were of a modest nature, and were born, as in so many instances in the workshop's history, from the efforts of individual Studio members.

One such modest attempt to expand the scope of the organization was the "Special Evening." A creation of Fred Stewart, who first presented the idea to Strasberg during the summer of 1965, these events, to which friends and supporters of the Studio were invited, consisted of scenes, one-act plays, and full-length projects that had been worked on in one or another of the workshop's units, plus special lectures by Strasberg. The point of the Special Evenings, of which half a dozen or more were given each season, was to share some of the Studio's work with a larger public while raising funds to help continue that work.

As an introduction to the first season's Special Evenings in 1965–1966, the Studio presented Maxime Furlaud's two short plays, *Biscuit* and *Fitz*, directed by Frank Corsaro and featuring John Harkins, Sam Waterston, and Sally Kirkland.* The season itself included Special Evening performances of "Legend in a Garden" an experiment in "style" based upon Japanese music, painting, and drama in which a single actor, Robert Viharo, using only a bathrobe and an umbrella as costume and props, played three characters: a lady, her lover, and her husband; a Jules Feiffer sketch, "A Little Play"; Act I of Verdi's *La Traviata*, "An experiment in creating environment, relationships and events to match the music"; two films: *Marilyn*, produced by David Wolper, and *The Actors Studio*, a documentary on a day at the workshop, produced for French television by Philippe Berard; an evening of "informal entertainment" with Eli Wallach and Anne Jackson; and a full-scale production of Ariano Suassuna's *The Rogues' Trial*, "A satire on human frailties in the form of a Miracle Play—based on ballads and folk tales of Northeastern Brazil," directed by Fred Stewart.

In the fall of 1966, the second season of Special Evenings began with Strasberg lecturing on Duse, Bernhardt, Réjane, Mrs. Fiske, and John Barrymore, in tandem with showings of the Museum of Modern Art's films of their performances in various roles. This event, enthusiastically received, was to become a specialty of the artistic director, who has repeated it a number of times over the years at the Studio and elsewhere. Later in the series, he also discussed the "problem of Shakespearean soliloquies," illustrating his talk with recordings of famous actors. In subsequent seasons he lectured on "Hamlets I Have Known" and on the thirties.

Other noteworthy presentations during the six-year history of Special Evenings, (1966–1972) included Kenneth H. Brown's *The Happy Bar*, directed by Rip Torn and featuring several actors from the Living Theater; two scenes from a work-in-progress by Michael V. Gazzo and his full-length play, *And All That Jazz*; two early Tennessee Williams one-acts, *The Last of My Solid Gold Watches* and *The Yellow Bird*; Heathcote Williams's *The Local Stigmatic*, with Al Pacino (later produced Off-Broadway); a dramatization of Yasunari Kawabata's *Snow Country*; an adaptation of Romain Gary's *The Ski Bum*, conceived and directed by Tim Everett; a symposium on Grotowski with Strasberg, Sidney Kingsley, and John Simon; an

---

* On May 6, 1966, the plays opened Off-Broadway at the Circle in the Square with the same cast under Corsaro's direction.

"informal evening" with Charles Gordone, Studio member and author of the Pulitzer Prize–winning *No Place To Be Somebody*, sampling some of the dramatic pieces he worked on at the Studio; and Shelley Winters's *The Noisy Passenger*, featuring Robert De Niro, Diane Ladd, Joanna Miles, Sally Kirkland, Will Hare, and Peter Masterson.

This last project, a series of three one-act plays reportedly based on incidents from the actress's own life, demonstrated that Miss Winters had a good ear for dialogue and could skillfully limn a character (this despite the critical panning she received when the work was later produced Off-Broadway as *One Night Stands of a Noisy Passenger*). It was not her first playwrighting effort, either. More than a decade earlier she had written and directed a play titled *Hansel and Gretel in the Oven*, which she presented at one of the acting sessions. At first the audience's response on that occasion took Miss Winters aback. In writing her play, she had drawn from her relationship with one of her handsome Hollywood costars for what she felt was a serious and very personal drama. To lend authenticity to the piece, she even supplied her own clothes to her leading lady, Patricia Bosworth. But the Studio audience found the play terribly funny, which was upsetting to Miss Winters until Strasberg pointed out that she had written, and obviously had the talent for writing, a comedy.

Many of the plays presented at the Special Evenings evolved from the Playwrights Unit, where they were first presented. The dramatists' group was quite active between 1964 and 1967, with Harold Clurman joining the Studio to moderate many of the Unit's sessions during this period. The Rockefeller Foundation also continued to support the Playwrights Unit, ultimately providing it with a grand total of approximately $100,000.[1]

A year later, however, the situation had changed. With the Rockefeller funding coming to an end and the Studio strapped for money on all fronts, it became necessary in 1968 to suspend the Unit.[2] The Directors Unit met the same fate, but in 1969 both units were revived, and a ten-thousand-dollar grant from the New York State Council on the Arts and five thousand dollars from Lawrence Shubert Lawrence kept them running for the next few seasons.

Between 1969 and 1971 the Playwrights Unit was administered by John Stix and Liska March, who brought in a number of guest moderators to share the work of guiding the group. Among them were Walter Kerr, Leonard Harris, Martin Gottfried, Harold Clurman, and Paddy Chayevsky. The quality of criticism provided by these men created a new excitement at the sessions. The playwrights, nevertheless, had mixed feelings about the long-range effectiveness of the new arrangement. They missed the critical benefit of continuity that a single moderator's sensibility and intelligence could provide. When Stix and Miss March yielded to other commitments, the rotating-moderator approach was abandoned. In the spring of 1973, after two seasons of what the Studio directorate considered unsuitable leadership, the Unit was once again suspended. During the seventies, the Directors Unit was to experience the same sporadic existence it had throughout its history. It was disbanded and revived as funds ran out or became available and as interest waned or renewed itself. At the urging of the Studio membership, who called for the reconstituting of both groups, the directors and playwrights were brought together into a single unit in January of 1975, first under the joint artistic leadership of Lee Strasberg and Arthur Penn, and later, in the fall of 1978, under the direction of Harold Clurman, who has moderated it since.

A separately functioning playwrights group, The New York Playwrights Lab at The Actors Studio, was established under the leadership of Israel Horovitz in November of 1977. Working in closed, seminar-type sessions, Horovitz and his ten playwrights produced a number of new plays that were presented in a series of staged readings in May of the following year. This "First Annual New Plays Festival" has been followed by a second season of "The Lab" at the Studio and by a "Second Annual New Plays Festival" in May of 1979.

The revitilization of the Playwrights and Directors units was invariably welcome news at the Studio, but the principal activity there, at all times, was the twice-weekly sessions with Strasberg, whose work with the actors still provided the organization its *raison d'être*. During the late sixties, in the period after The Actors Studio Theatre, when the Studio's presence as an active force on the American theater scene went into eclipse and its influence seemed to wane, there was ample proof of the abiding vitality of Strasberg's teaching. International curiosity about the Studio hardly abated as foreign observers continued to visit and attend classes. Scores of actors still sought entry into the workshop.

Any doubts that Strasberg might have had about the continuing viability of the Studio and the relevance of his work there were dispelled by his experience during a trip to Paris, where he gave a seminar on the Method in 1967.

The artistic director went to France at the instigation of Alain Resnais, the French film director who had come to admire Strasberg's teaching when he attended the Studio and Strasberg's private classes on a number of occasions during a visit to America in 1964. He was introduced to the famous teacher by Delphine Seyrig, who had been a student of Strasberg's several years before she starred in Resnais's *Last Year at Marienbad*. "There is no other school like it in the world," Resnais said. "Only New York has an Actors Studio, and there are a million lessons to be learned from Lee Strasberg." [3] Resnais was eager to have Strasberg clarify what he felt were misunderstandings about the Method in France.

Between September 5 and 30, in sessions lasting a total of sixty hours, Strasberg held a class for some 350 people, including Jeanne Moreau, Jean-Louis Barrault, François Truffaut, and several members of the Comédie Française. The success of this seminar, as well as the interest in the Studio and the Method it represented, pleased and reassured Strasberg enormously.

The experience of Paris and the success of a similar seminar he offered the following spring at the University of California at Los Angeles convinced him that he should expand his teaching efforts and, in the process, systematize them as never before. To this end, he announced the establishment of the Lee Strasberg Theater Institute, his own school of acting with branches in New York and Los Angeles, which he set up and financed with the help of Carl Schaeffer.

At the opening session of the Studio's 1969–1970 season, he discussed the personal excitement and sense of triumph the two seminars had afforded him. "I became aware somehow in a more personal way of the enormous concern and interest and, in addition to that, the enormous need for the ideas that we here take for granted." He explained that his schools would not be competitive with the Studio, that they represented a logical extension of his work at the workshop, and that, in fact, they would make possible a greater devotion to the workshop on his part. "[They] will in no way affect my activity in The Actors Studio except for the better, in the sense that

I will be less concerned whether I am paid or not on those occasions (which are the majority of occasions) when I am not paid, and I will be able to give my time more freely and easily because I will be more active generally. Too much of my time in recent years has had to go into, simply, the problems of making a living. . . ." [4]

By sharing his work on a larger basis, Strasberg hoped to clarify his contributions as a teacher of acting and to dispel the mystery and misconception that had dogged the private work of The Actors Studio for so long. Earlier in the sixties, a very important step had been taken exactly in that direction with the publication of Robert H. Hethmon's book, *Strasberg at The Actors Studio.*

Hethmon had visited Strasberg in 1960 to discuss the possibility of depositing the archives of The Actors Studio and Strasberg's personal papers with the Wisconsin Center for Theatre Research at the University of Wisconsin. When he discovered that the sessions at the Studio had been recorded since 1956 and that all the tapes were on file at the workshop, he offered to edit and arrange the tapes for a book that would present Strasberg's ideas and teaching methods in a logical and comprehensive fashion.

Hethmon's offer was accepted by Strasberg: the first set of tapes was deposited at the Wisconsin Center for Theatre Research in 1962 and *Strasberg at The Actors Studio* was finally published in 1965.[5] At the time of publication, Strasberg and Hethmon announced that 10 percent of their royalties would go to The Actors Studio.

Strasberg at The Actors Studio received critical approbation for its documentation in relatively coherent form of Strasberg's "precepts and practices." There were some reservations, however, over the repetition of material and over the limitations imposed by the book's format in which the anonymity of the Studio actors was maintained through the use of code letters, while the actual exercises and scenes being discussed were not available to the reader. (For months after the book came out, several members had to suffer being addressed and introduced to others as Actress KK or Actor MM, and so on, by their straight-faced Studio cohorts.) For a few critics, the book confirmed all their worse opinions about Strasberg and the Studio, but for most it illuminated positively the unique contributions of both man and institution.[6]

The publication of Hethmon's book served as the occasion for inaugurating what was perhaps the major development in the Studio's history during the late sixties: The Actors Studio West, the workshop's West Coast branch in Hollywood. At a party given by Dennis Weaver and his wife on December 5, 1965, at their home in Encino, California, many "old members" who for years had been regretting the lack of a workshop stimulus in the movie capital gathered both to celebrate the appearance of *Strasberg at The Actors Studio* and to support a move to bring the Studio to Los Angeles. Strasberg flew out to join some seventy-two Studio actors at the Weavers' party, and, moved by the enthusiastic sentiments for the Studio to function where so many of its actors lived and worked, approved a committee to set up and guide a Hollywood branch and promised to visit California from time to time to look in on its activities.

It was only logical that the Studio should have a branch in the motion-picture capital of the United States. The Method, both in the Studio and pre-Studio periods, had had an enormous influence on acting in the American cinema. A number of the Moscow Art Theater veterans who had first taught the Stanislavski System in America, including Boleslavsky, Ouspenskaya, and Michael Chekhov, were working and teaching in Hollywood by the late twenties and early thirties. Many members of the Group Theatre had had successful film careers. After the demise of the Group in 1941, several of its actors established the highly influential Actors' Laboratory, Incorporated (the Lab) in Hollywood, marking the first large-scale introduction of the Method on the West Coast. During the late fifties various Method teachers, including Sanford Meisner, were working on the Coast as well.

The motion picture, by its very nature, demanded a realism in acting that was well served by the Method approach. The Method's emphasis on *experiencing* and on the actor's use of himself made it an eminently useful tool for such an intimate artistic medium.

More than one observer has noted that the Studio probably has had a greater and more lasting influence on film and television acting than on theatrical performance. Most of the Studio's more famous members have made their careers primarily in the motion pictures, and Strasberg himself ascribed the workshop's reputation to Kazan's use of Studio actors in his films. The support of the Studio over the years by many of the film industry's magnates, such as David O.

Selznick, Samuel Goldwyn, Spyros Skouras, Jack L. Warner, and Joseph Schenck, has reflected an awareness of the workshop's actual and potential contributions to the movies throughout the more than three decades of its existence. A not inaccurate gauge of the Studio's impact on American film acting is the record of its members' recognition by the motion-picture industry itself: in excess of a hundred and twenty-five Academy Award nominations and Oscars received in the various acting categories between 1948 and 1979. (Nine of the 1979 nominees were Studio members, and of these Jane Fonda and Christopher Walken won the Oscars in their respective categories.)

Jack Garfein was instrumental in the drive to get The Actors Studio West started. He was eager to encourage the Studio after the debacle in London, when it looked as if the workshop might founder, and consulted with similarly interested members about what could be done. He organized meetings at the Beverly Hills Hotel and at his own home to talk about setting up a branch of the Studio for those members who lived and worked in California and consequently had not been actively involved in the life of the workshop for many years. As a result, the party given by Dennis Weaver, the culmination of these preliminary efforts, was more than a social affair.

Shortly after that gathering, Garfein and Paul Newman explored Hollywood in the actor's MG for a suitable meeting place for The Actors Studio West. According to Garfein, Newman, always generous and enthusiastic on behalf of the Studio, was eager to work on *Hamlet* in the intimacy of the workshop. Upon investigating a dance studio at 1103 North El Centro Avenue, Newman's response was immediate and positive, "I like this place, Jack. It has the smell of Forty-fourth Street, the feel of a real New York rehearsal space." The landlady, wanting a cash down payment, looked somewhat askance at the casually dressed Newman. She accepted the actor's check only after Garfein, who was wearing a suit, cosigned and guaranteed it. Thus 1103 North El Centro became the Studio's first headquarters in the film capital.

Meeting once a week, first on Friday, later on Tuesday evenings, the approximately seventy-five actor/playwright/director members proceeded to work on acting exercises, problems, scenes, and projects under a group of moderators, including Jack Garfein, Mark Rydell,

Alfred Ryder, Bruce Dern, Lee Grant, and Michael Strong, who supervised the activities on a weekly rotation basis. Garfein was chosen to administer the workshop as its executive director along with a six-member committee consisting of Ryder, Rydell, Dern, Henry Scott, Lou Antonio, and Dennis Weaver. The group would later expand.

Since no scenes were planned for the first session, Dennis Weaver got up and spontaneously performed Lincoln delivering the Gettysburg address, and received the characteristic critical reaction of a class of Actors Studio members. His colleagues felt that he could have gone much further in capturing the reality of Lincoln's experience. They suggested that he create the cold of the day as well as deal with a number of other given circumstances that would have affected the president's behavior on that occasion. For example, someone pointed out that, just before he was to speak, Lincoln was informed that his young son had come down with pneumonia. Weaver, pleased with the group's observations, promised to work on what had been suggested and presented the speech again, considerably improved, the following week.

Preliminary auditions were held for the hundreds of California actors who expressed interest in The Actors Studio West, with Strasberg flying in to judge the final auditions (as well as attending several working sessions held over a weekend). Out of the first 120 applicants, however, only seven were passed for a final audition. It soon became evident that the small number of active West Coast members was not enough "to stimulate sufficient work" at the workshop, and that few participants would be added through the audition process. It was therefore decided that each member would be invited to sponsor an observer who would be expected to take part in the workshop's activities to a far greater extent than observers were allowed to in the New York Studio. Among the many who came to watch and to participate were such figures as Candice Bergen, Jack Albertson, Elizabeth Ashley, Red Buttons, Diahann Carroll, Patty Duke, Richard Dreyfuss, Mary Tyler Moore, Sally Field, Jack Nicholson, and Raquel Welch. In later years, the sheer number of participating observers would create conflict at the workshop and result in a retrenchment on the question of their involvement, but they would continue to play an important role throughout The Actors Studio West's history.

As observers became predominant, a few of the older, more famous members—some of the very ones it was hoped would become its most active participants—became disaffected with the Studio West. A sense of intimacy, of the true collegiality of peers, seemed lost to them. The problem, however, was not exclusively with observers. There was a certain tension between older, established members and newer ones. A case in point is Karl Malden, who was very active in the early days of the Studio West—he worked on Shylock and moderated some sessions—but dropped out after a while, citing his displeasure at the "arrogance" of some of the younger Studio members newly arrived from New York, who overstated their critical comments. "Just because they had passed a five-minute audition in New York, they felt they could say whatever they wanted. It didn't matter who you were or what you had achieved—they were experts," he complained to Jack Garfein.

On November 14, 1966, The Actors Studio West came into possession of its present home, the 8341 Delongpre Avenue estate of the deceased silent-screen cowboy star, William S. Hart. Surrounded by the tall apartment houses of West Hollywood, the Hart home, a modest, two-story frame structure set on an acre or so of steeply sloping land running from the Sunset Strip at its upper edge down to residential Delongpre Avenue, was leased to the workshop by the city of Los Angeles, virtually as a gift, at a rent of one dollar a year. The property, which for the previous two years had housed the American National Theater and Academy, had been donated to the city by Hart in the nineteen fifties, along with fifty thousand dollars for its development as a park. Through the efforts of Carl Schaeffer, who was on the ANTA board, and Cay Forrester, an actress who as Kate Archer later became a member of the workshop, it was turned over to the Studio West with the understanding that it would be put to use as "a cultural-theatrical center designed to further elevate the artistic reputation of the city." The date the workshop moved in officially, November 15, was proclaimed "Actors Studio West Day" by Los Angeles Mayor Samuel W. Yorty.

The Actors Studio West, for its part, was to refurbish the property, developing some of it into a park, and oversee drama programs in various city parks. The workshop did spend more than twenty thousand dollars renovating "the white colonial mini-mansion" to include a general office, library, prop and dressing rooms, and rehearsal space; the small adjacent garage was converted into a 120-seat theater designed by Ralph Alswang, which was dedicated in February 1967. Other plans—to construct a six-hundred-seat theater for public performances on the property and to convert the surrounding acreage into a Shakespeare Theatrical Park—however, were never realized.

On two subsequent occasions over the next decade there would be attempts by various theatrical groups interested in using the property for their own purposes to have the Studio's tenancy revoked. These organizations, including a couple of city-sponsored projects, accused the Studio of violating the terms of the Hart deed, which called for public use of the facility in a manner that contributed to the community at large. But in both instances the workshop was able to muster impressive support for its continuing presence on the Hart estate by demonstrating that it did contribute to the community.

During the workshop's premiere season in its new home, a new Playwrights Unit was established. It was originally headed by William Inge,[7] who granted The Actors Studio West permission to present his play, *Don't Go Gentle*, as one of the first projects in its 120-seat theater. Directed by Jack Garfein and featuring the author in one of the roles, it was subsequently presented at the University of California at Los Angeles as part of a "Plays in Progress" series sponsored by the school in cooperation with the workshop. The other plays in the series were the premieres of Calder Willingham's *How Tall Is Toscanini?* (on a double bill with Chekhov's *The Harmfulness of Tobacco*), Lonny Chapman's *Echoes*, and Harvey Perr's *The Adventures of Jack and Max*. (An attempt at a second series, featuring Irwin Shaw's *A Choice of Wars* and James Bridges's *Bachelor Furnished*, would not be as well received the following fall.)

It was Garfein's hope that plays emanating from The Actors Studio West would find their way to Broadway. Robert Alan Aurthur's *Carry Me Back to Morningside Heights* made the trip, but not successfully. A number of plays that were first read or worked on in the ASW Playwrights Unit did eventually get produced elsewhere in Los Angeles, in regional theaters, or Off-Broadway. It was the Studio West's Acting Unit, however, that gave birth to what was eventually turned into one of Broadway's most innovative musicals. This was George Furth's *Company*, which evolved out of scenes he wrote expressly for Collin Wilcox and Clinton Kimbrough, who were looking for material to work on in the acting sessions. Furth dedicated the work to Lee Strasberg.*

The California membership had long been eager to produce plays under the banner of The Actors Studio West, but this ambition had been frustrated by the lack of a suitable theater on the Hart estate and by the failure of the Plays in Progress series to evolve into a permanent program. Then the fortuitous generosity of Merle Oberon in the spring of 1972 gave further impetus to the workshop's theatrical aspirations. Miss Oberon owned a former post office building at 817 North Hilldale Avenue, which Albert McCleery and some partners leased from her and converted into a theater called the McLoren. When, a year and a half later, their organization defaulted, Alejandro Rey approached her on behalf of the Studio West and she offered it to the workshop for one dollar a year for five years. The Studio West renamed the building the Merle Oberon Theater and made immediate plans to produce their first play in it.

Lonny Chapman's *Hootsudie* opened there on April 28, 1972. The play, about a baseball player named Hoot and a stripper named Sudie, did not impress the critics. But the performances by Jim Antonio and Lane Bradbury were greeted as a promise of exciting theater to come. The following September the Studio West luxuriated in a full-scale production of Brecht's *The Threepenny Opera*, directed by Lee Grant and featuring Paul Winfield as Macheath, Burgess Meredith as Mr. Peachum, and Pat Carroll as Mrs. Peachum. After opening at the Merle Oberon Theater, the production was shifted to the larger Huntington Hartford Theater in the hope that it would have a healthy run. Its impression on both critics and public was slight, however, and its run was brief.

The aftermath of the Brecht production, predictably, was an enormous financial debt, which was eventually paid off through a benefit given in honor of Miss Oberon, and some supplementary aid by the New York Actors Studio. When the Studio West raised some additional money the following March 1973 at a benefit premiere of *Last Tango in Paris* "co-hosted" by Lee Strasberg and Barbra Streisand, plans were announced for a 1973–1974 season of six plays at the Merle Oberon Theater. But as it turned out, there were to be no further productions. The benefit money was ex-

* His play, *Twigs*, which was done on Broadway with Sada Thompson and on television with Carol Burnett, also originated at The Actors Studio West.

hausted in the everyday operations of the Studio West, and eventually, the burden of maintaining the unused Oberon Theater—among other things, the workshop was responsible for property taxes and insurance on the building—led the Studio West to relinquish its lease arrangement.

The Actors Studio West's production plans were put in abeyance, but the working sessions of its Acting Unit continued without interruption. (Its Playwrights Unit broke away, however, to follow an independent existence in 1974 after a series of artistic differences with the Studio West's administrators.) The workshop's leadership had changed over the years—a number of people succeeded Garfein in directing its operations (among them Lonny Chapman, Lou Antonio, Burgess Meredith, Martin Landau, Milton Sperling, Mark Rydell, and Lee Grant)—and its constituency had varied as new members were added and older members became more or less involved. Fresh flushes of enthusiasm kept the organization humming. Many members who frequently moved from coast to coast for their work became active at both branches of the Studio. By the seventies Strasberg was dividing his time equally between the two, spending six months in New York and the rest of the year in his first home on the West Coast, a seventeen-room mansion in the heart of Hollywood that once belonged to John Barrymore.*

The New York Studio, in its home on West Forty-fourth Street, by now had witnessed the evolution of several generations of actors. Having endured many vicissitudes—surviving more than twice as long as its spiritual ancestor, the Group Theatre—it continued to function. In the process it had accumulated a body of over four hundred members, some who remained deeply devoted over a period of many years, some whose tenure was brief, some whose participation was peripheral at most, and others who left only to return again. For most of the actors, the ties were strong and durable.

One formal expression of the permanence of such ties was the newsletter started back in October 1961 and sent out on a monthly basis throughout the sixties. When it ceased appearing for two and a half seasons (the fall of 1967 through the winter of 1969), its absence was felt. Aside from serving as a record of scenes and projects

---

* The Strasbergs moved out after several years when the house was donated to Los Angeles by its owners, the John Paul Getty Foundation, for use as the official residence of the city's mayor.

in all the units, it had been a useful tool for keeping members in touch with one another. It was instrumental in helping to raise funds at several crucial junctures, in setting up and continuing the pattern of Special Evenings, and in gathering California members together to form The Actors Studio West. The feeling among many of the members "that something valuable in their connection with the Studio was missing" prompted Fred Stewart to reactivate it in March 1970. It has continued to appear, though with great irregularity, up to the present.

It was logical that Fred Stewart oversee the newsletter's resurrection. His special province, his uniquely self-imposed responsibility, had always been to keep Studio people in touch with one another. A genial walrus of a man, he exemplified the noncelebrity Studio loyalists who, over the years, devoted themselves to the welfare of the organization. An initiator of countless projects, including the entire Special Evenings program, he stood in the forefront of efforts to support the work of the Studio, working on committees, supervising and sharing in household chores, and stimulating others to participate more fully. "The squire, the grand chatelain (with keys and all) of the Studio," Stewart, who lived in the nearby Whitby Apartments, was at the workshop nearly every day; it was, in every sense, his second home. His presence was infectious and made the place feel like home for others.

Tragedy struck on Saturday evening, December 5, 1970, when Stewart was overseeing a particularly popular Special Evening, Lee Strasberg discussing some rare films of the world's great actresses. Having introduced the artistic director, Stewart left the room in a jovial mood to man the reception desk downstairs. Stricken by a massive heart attack, he died there, just two days short of his sixty-fourth birthday.[8]

The memorial service held for him in place of the regular 11:00 A.M. acting session on Tuesday, December 8, was a very special moment in the history of The Actors Studio. It brought together there, for the first and only time, all the founders of both the Studio and the Group Theatre—Stewart had worked for the Group—who came to pay their respects. The atmosphere was familial, the occasion crystallizing palpable feelings of camaraderie, of shared history, and, above all, of shared values. Lee Strasberg, Cheryl Crawford, Elia Kazan, Robert Lewis, Harold Clurman, and other members, observers, and friends spoke with warm remembrance of their association with Stewart, while his brother-in-law, the Reverend Ewing Wayland, officiated. Kazan was especially touching in his remarks:

They called and told me the old Senator was dead. That's pretty hard to believe, I thought. If it's true, it's sickening—first David Stewart, then Frank Silvera, now Fred.*

Then they told me where it happened and I believed it. I hope they have the good sense to bury him in the backyard. He's certain to haunt the place. I've been away from here quite a few years now. But Fred Stewart kept me up on the news, what new projects were being worked on. "Some very interesting work's being done there, you ought to come look at it," he'd say. Or other times he'd say, "I'm doing some very interesting work on this project, the best work I've ever done." He looked at himself objectively, Fred did!

For quite a few years Fred was somewhere or other in everything I did. No small parts, only small actors; Fred made that stand up. And he fought back at the inevitable, the disintegration that most of us accept as inevitable. Fred, perhaps foolishly but always gallantly, believed in forward movement, in progress. He was really a unique person, middle-America into Stanislavski—and Strasberg. . . .[9]

Stewart's death deprived the Studio of one of its most conscientious stalwarts. The responsibility for many activities that he had handled devolved on several others (most notably Liska March) who were willing to fill the vacuum he had left. Some projects came to an end. A series of lectures on the "Practical Traditions of Professional Courtesy in the Theatre, Television and Films," which he had created especially for young actors and had inaugurated less than a week before his death, was never concluded. More important, the program of Special Evenings was, in effect, terminated at the close of the 1970–1971 season.

One of Stewart's projects that did survive was the annual presentation of *The Masque of St. George and the Dragon*, an "old English Christmas Mummers Play," which Stewart had put together from several traditional sources and which he staged in broad and boisterously colorful strokes. First presented in 1955 as a means of sharing the Studio's first Christmas in its new home with the children of the

---

* Both Studio members, David J. Stewart died December 24, 1966, and Frank Silvera died June 11, 1970.

neighborhood, *The Masque of St. George* was subsequently forgotten as the workshop became busy with other things. Stewart decided to revive it in 1968 as a means of involving the Studio with the community on a regular basis. After his death, Walter Lott directed the presentation for a couple of seasons. By 1974, the production had become an annual affair. Under the supervision of Anna Strasberg, it would tour to children's hospitals and homes for the aged during the Christmas season as well as play a dozen performances at the Studio for children bused in from all over the city.

The continuing production of *The Masque of St. George* was, perhaps, the most tangible evidence of the Studio's efforts to dissipate its reputation for hermetic privatism that forever seemed to plague the organization in its efforts to find financial support. There is no doubt that members of the Studio made contributions on many levels to the community-at-large. Many worked in regional theaters, taught in schools, and were involved with minority groups. There was a good argument to be made for the Studio's influence in all this. But it all seemed indirect. "What do you contribute to the community?" the workshop was constantly being asked. As an institution, the Studio was looked upon as an isolated, inward-looking entity by the various foundations to which it turned for aid.

Since the Weingarten report of 1967 there had been an awareness that some accommodation had to be found between the Studio's need for privacy and its obligation to come out into the world. "The actor's career develops in public, but his art develops in private"— Goethe's observation often quoted by Strasberg—was a point of view no longer sufficient to preserve the workship as a *viable* organization. In terms of both its administrative structure and its relationship with the public, it had to become more accessible. Thus, the efforts to renovate the "close corporation" setup by enlarging and diversifying the board of directors, the introduction of the Special Evenings, and the constant outlook for a possible reentry into production.

During the seventies there would be a heightening of pressure to show a more public-service orientation as the Studio's financial situation deteriorated. Peter Masterson arranged for the workshop to participate in the Great Lakes College Association apprenticeship program, whereby students of the member colleges could observe at the Studio and participate in any of the classes that were offered and on any production work that was going on. The Studio received some useful remuneration under this plan. There were some behind-the-scenes explorations of possible linkups between the Studio and Hunter College, the City University, and the Brooklyn Academy of Music, but as of 1980 nothing had come of these possibilities.

Because of its critical financial problem, the Studio broke with a long-standing tradition in 1971 and instituted a new policy whereby "each participating member and observer" was to contribute ten dollars a month to the workshop. But this was only a partial solution at best and, as it turned out, a short-lived one. The Studio still eyed the prospect of foundation funding as a prime source of aid. To interest the various foundations that contributed to arts organizations, however, the Studio had to demonstrate that it was prepared to show its work to the public. This commitment would mean production in some form or other.

The members of the Studio, always eager to move in that direction, had for some time advocated turning the workshop into a quasi-Off-Off-Broadway experimental theater by adding a Production Unit to whose presentations the general public would be invited. The Members Committee eventually investigated the legal possibilities of converting the Studio building into just such a theater. Strasberg, who was never very sympathetic to the idea of a small-scale operation representing the Studio, at first was "loath to engage" the workshop in public activities. His dream was of a full-fledged theater, and the Studio, he hoped, would give birth to it. Even then, however, the Studio would continue to function as a workshop. "I have always felt that the special character of the studio required that it be a private place," he told *The New York Times* in a 1972 interview.[10] But the enthusiasm of the membership—"the natural pull of the younger generation"—and the growing realization that it might, after all, be a fruitful move finally persuaded him to acquiesce. A Production Unit at The Actors Studio, he reasoned, would not interfere with his larger ambition: a national theater evolving from the workshop.

During the 1971–1972 season a Production Unit was established with Arthur Penn as its executive producer. A Theater Board was selected, and with a five-thousand-dollar grant from the Billy Rose Foundation specifically earmarked for that purpose, three plays were presented in the spring: *Felix* by Claude McNeal, which opened on February 20, 1972, and received several favorable reviews; the previously unproduced and unpublished Clifford Odets play, *The Silent Partner;* and Dennis J. Reardon's *Siamese Connections.*

The Studio's decision to present plays for the public in its home, and the encouraging reception of the first three productions, evidently had the desired effect. Several institutions offered grants-in-aid for the following 1972–1973 season's activities. The Edward J. Noble Foundation gave the Studio ten thousand dollars to be used for projects and for moderators for the Playwrights and Directors units. The New York State Council on the Arts awarded seventy-five hundred dollars for similar purposes, while additional awards from the CBS and the Shubert foundations were made available for the workshop's basic expenses.

Over the next eight seasons play production became an integral part of the functioning of The Actors Studio with the workshop mounting some twenty additional projects for the public. These ranged from a decidedly burlesque version of Aristophanes's *The Birds* to relatively conventional stagings of *Othello* and *Richard III,* the latter featuring Ron Leibman in a bravura performance as Shakespeare's villain, and included the annual presentation of *The Masque of St. George and the Dragon* with the statuesque Julie Newmar gracing the old English mummer's play on several occasions as a pulchritudinous "Princess Sabra." A number of the projects bore the cautionary labels "rehearsal version," "staged reading," "work in progress," or "open rehearsal of a work in progress"; but for the most part they were fully staged, polished workshop productions.

Among the varied endeavors were plays written by members of the Studio—as, for instance, June Havoc's *Oh Glorious Tintinnabulation!,* a musical whimsy directed by the author and featuring Estelle Parsons as one of the bizarre denizens of a fantastical bordello; productions of O'Neill's *Long Day's Journey into Night* and Pinter's *Old Times* directed, in a tradition harking back to the earliest days of the Studio, by the cast members themselves; a "revisionist" account of the life of Jesus, *From the Memoirs of Pontius Pilate,* by the eminent theater critic and scholar, Eric Bentley; an ambitious trilogy of Israel Horovitz dramas called *The Wakefield Plays,* which featured Michael Moriarty's sensitive and evocative performance in the leading role; and, most recently, Elizabeth Stearns's *Hillbilly Women*, a piece of lyrical theater based on the lives of actual Appalachian women as recorded in Kathy Kahn's book of the same name.

One production that gained special public attention by virtue of its attempts to use the full experimental potential of the Studio was Paul Zindel's *Ladies at the Alamo*, a project that turned out to be something of a traumatic experience for everyone involved. Zindel, the Pulitzer Prize–winning author of *The Effect of Gamma Rays on Man-in-the-Moon Marigolds*, expanded his one-act play, "The Ladies Should Be in Bed," into the full-length *Ladies at the Alamo* by utilizing an unusual procedure involving five Actors Studio actresses: Madeleine Thornton-Sherwood, Jacqueline Brookes, Elaine Aiken, Doris Roberts, and Susan Peretz. The playwright began developing his ideas "on the situation of women in power" by taking the singular step of interviewing each of his actresses about their personal lives, privately and at length. He transcribed the tapes of these intimate and "confessional" talks, edited them down, and created monologues from the performer's own words, including some harsh and embarrassing things they had to say about one another. These were grafted to the substance of the original one-act play, which was thereby substantially fleshed out into a full-length drama about five women involved with a resident theater company in Texas. The actresses received copies of the new script several months later when they gathered to read it at Zindel's home in the country. Their experience that afternoon was "brutal and horrendous," in the words of one of the participants. The actresses were shocked and hurt at how their own words had been wedded to the characters they were assigned to play and at what they were made to say about each other. There were tears and silence afterward and fretful and apologetic phone calls back and forth later that evening. Despite the fact that Zindel had given each of the actresses a percentage of the play for their contributions to the writing of it, two of them, Miss Thornton-Sherwood and Miss Brookes, who spoke of feeling "used" and of having their words distorted, quit the project the following day when the cast met at the Studio. They were replaced by Arlene Golonka and Lily Lodge, and the play was put into rehearsal. The script was further developed by the author and his performers over the following weeks and finally presented for twelve sold-out performances as a full-scale workshop production. Many well-known theater people attended these performances, and the play was subsequently produced on Broadway, though with only Susan Peretz of the original cast re-creating her role. The show's producers felt that the others had to be replaced by more prominent names to make the play commercially viable. Unfortunately, the New York critics had harsh things to say about the play's venomous tone and shrill characters, and it closed quickly.[11]

Perhaps the most dramatically successful of these projects was *The Best Little Whorehouse in Texas*, which began as an article in *Playboy* and wound up a long-running Broadway musical hit. The original magazine piece by Larry L. King, an account of the forced closing of a century-old Texas bordello called "The Chicken Ranch," was "discovered" by Studio member Peter Masterson as a likely starting point for a country-and-western musical comedy. Masterson and King worked on the dramatization and presented scenes from the developing script in the Studio's acting sessions, while Carol Hall wrote the show's music and lyrics. During its twelve-performance run at the Studio, Universal Pictures became interested in the property. The film company bought the stage rights and a screen option and backed a move first to Off-Broadway and, ultimately, to the Forty-sixth Street Theatre, where the musical has enjoyed a great popular success (and in the process provided a small financial return for the Studio).

Of all the projects in the 1970s, *The Best Little Whorehouse in Texas* is the only one whose success seems to have fed on itself. But as pleasantly diverting (and as commercially successful) an entertainment as it turned out to be, it hardly represented the kind of distinguished theatrical creation that Strasberg had envisioned emanating from and representing the Studio in its role as the precursor of a national theater.

Despite the values Studio members found in having a production program and the positive impact the program had on the membership, it was no secret that Strasberg was barely tolerant of the whole operation. He could never be particularly happy with what he perceived as a "penny-ante" approach to theater.

The dream of a national theater was increasingly on his mind during the seventies. As he became more preoccupied with the Strasberg Institute, where his training methods were utilized much more rigorously and systematically than at the Studio, he began "souring" on the workshop. By the late seventies he had limited his participation there to a single two-hour Friday session a week. Much of the stimulation he once derived from the Studio he now found in his schools. Now more than ever for Strasberg, it was the natural purpose of the Studio to serve as the foundation for a theater. "The major area of our progress is to show the world the unified concept of our work, which they see only on an individual level and therefore must draw erroneous deductions from," he explained.

Looking back on the experience of The Actors Studio Theatre, Strasberg frankly acknowledged "some serious mistakes," both organizationally and artistically. Nevertheless, he insisted that the fact the Studio Theatre was able to produce six plays for $500,000 proved, from a purely financial point of view at least, that a Studio Theatre could be successful. By the grace of a "forward looking hindsight," as one of the Studio Theatre prospectuses put it, the errors of The Actors Studio Theatre could be avoided in any future effort to set up a producing organization. And the efforts to do so were renewed.

In January of 1975, Strasberg, Liska March, and Arthur Penn applied to the National Endowment for the Arts for a two-year matching grant, in excess of $600,000, to establish in connection with the American bicentennial what they hoped would become a national theater. They were turned down. It was evidently inappropriate that such a large request be made from an organization with such a small operating budget. Then there was the rumor that Strasberg was disliked by certain people in the government's arts program. As a practical matter, it may well be that his opinions on the futility and artistic wastefulness of the government's funding policies, expressed by letter to the National Endowment on an earlier occasion and in the press on subsequent occasions, contributed to the Studio's failure to obtain grants from the federal government. More recently, under the professional guidance of a "Director of Development and Public Affairs" at the Studio, and with a new administration at the Endowment, the workshop has begun to receive some funds to support its work, though by any standard these are modest amounts and are not intended to finance a major theatrical undertaking.

One last attempt to establish a theater during the seventies was made in the summer of 1976 when the Studio announced that it had entered into a multimillion-dollar deal with Twentieth Century-Fox TV and a production company called Four Star International to mount at least three productions a year. With $750,000 "in the bank" for the first season's presentations, Strasberg discussed how he hoped to bring some of the major Studio figures back to the Broadway stage in a wide repertory of plays that would be staged for limited ten-week runs and later recorded and sold to television.

But it was not meant to be. There was by now a familiar lack of follow-through—a characteristic inability to implement the visionary scheme in the face of the cold, hard realities. The choice of plays could not be agreed on, the burning impetus to precipitate it cooled, and the dream of a theater remained only a dream. Though the Studio has remained a workshop, Strasberg has continued to speak of the future, and of a theater—someday.

The failure to create a theater did not affect the life of the workshop. Under Strasberg's stewardship it continued to function quite actively, with actors still applying for membership in large numbers and many talented individuals continuing to find value there. Throughout the late sixties and the seventies, the Studio nurtured many prominent new players.

Christopher Walken, who won the best supporting actor Oscar in 1979 for his performance in *The Deer Hunter*, was an observer at the Studio for years before becoming a member. In contrast to the contemporary roles he has played on stage and screen, he passed his final audition with a scene from Camus's *Caligula* and has worked on both Hamlet and Iago at the workshop. Harvey Keitel, who auditioned many times before he was admitted with a scene from *Carnal Knowledge*, once worked on a J. D. Salinger short story for Strasberg, interpreting his part in a subtly convincing homosexual manner. The artistic director said to him, "If I didn't see this with my own eyes, I wouldn't have believed how brilliantly you created the character's homosexuality. What did you work on?" "The character's hands I got from you," Keitel told him, causing everyone in the room to roar with laughter, Strasberg included. Ellen Burstyn, who became a member on the West Coast in 1968, has been especially active in recent years, moderating sessions, joining the workshop's Corporate Board, and frequently testifying to the enormous influence Strasberg and the Studio have had on her career and her life. In August of 1979 she made her directing debut at the Studio when she staged Norman Krasna's comedy, *Bunny*, with Catlin Adams in the title role. Robert De Niro, Jill Clayburgh, and Michael Moriarty all became Studio members during the seventies. Dustin Hoffman's membership dates from 1966, when he passed his preliminary and final auditions with two different scenes, one from *The Journey of the Fifth Horse* and the other from *The Subject Was Roses*.

Another member who joined the Studio in 1966, when he passed his final audition with a scene from *Counsellor at Law*, is perhaps the single most visible personage of this latest generation of Studio actors: Al Pacino. His very first appearance at the Studio, which he said "terrified and frightened him," established Pacino as an especially ambitious and adventurous talent: he performed one of Hickey's monologues from *The Iceman Cometh* and then segued into Hamlet's "O what a rogue and peasant slave am I" soliloquy! Strasberg told him right then and there to repeat what he had just done, but to play Hickey as Hamlet and Hamlet as Hickey. Evidently the people watching were impressed with what they saw because they applauded the young actor's work. Strasberg turned to the members and commented, "See, we take all kinds here."

Since that debut in January of 1967, the quality of his talent has, of course, become widely appreciated. Although he has not worked on a scene there in a very long time, Pacino continues to identify himself with the Studio. He observes sessions from time to time; he plays on the Studio's softball team in the Broadway Show League competitions; and he has accepted positions on the workshop's Corporate Board and board of directors.

The Studio was home and family to Pacino, as it has been to many, at a crucial period of his life—when he was hungry and struggling for recognition. He once borrowed fifty dollars from the James Dean Fund to pay his rent. His feelings about the Studio are perhaps most tellingly revealed in the very generous gesture he made to revive or pass on that tradition of family help. In May of 1978, to honor the memory of a friend and fellow Studio member who, tragically young, had died of cancer, Pacino anonymously established the Norman Ornellas Fund with a grant of twenty-five thousand dollars.

On the face of it, the Studio, as it enters the eighties, would seem to be enjoying a new vitality; there is a great deal of activity and the sessions are crowded at the old church building on West Forty-fourth Street. Strasberg has been present every Friday during the six months he is not moderating similar sessions at The Actors Studio

West. A host of moderators have taken over the Tuesday sessions (on both coasts) and fill in for him whenever he misses a Friday because of his other commitments. Shelley Winters has supervised several months of meetings in Los Angeles, while Ellen Burstyn, Vivian Nathan, Frank Corsaro, Estelle Parsons, Arthur Penn, and others have taken turns at the job in New York. Eli Wallach points out that, when he moderates, he will not sit in Strasberg's seat, the canvas-and-wood director's chair with "Lee" printed on it. His feeling in the matter is very understandable—the Studio is still very much Lee Strasberg; there is no taking his place, and there has not been for well over a quarter century.

The Studio celebrated its twenty-fifth anniversary on December 6, 1973—a year late. When Strasberg was asked to comment on the fact that it was actually the Studio's twenty-sixth anniversary, he observed wryly, "That's how poorly organized we are." It was a fitting remark. Even so, a "gala Silver Ball" was planned for both coasts, with Elia Kazan as the guest of honor. Ever since the memorial service for Fred Stewart, Kazan had taken a renewed interest in the Studio mostly because Carl Schaeffer persuaded him to drop by the sessions occasionally. Whenever he did so, he created the same kind of excitement he had in previous years. He also rejoined the Studio's Corporate Board and is a member of the workshop's board of directors.

Kazan attended the Silver Ball in New York while Strasberg hosted the festivities in California. A film montage of Kazan's work was prepared especially for the occasion. In the course of his remarks at the celebration, Kazan spoke, inevitably, of Strasberg:

If I had to select one image to represent the Studio, one symbol, it would be the back of Lee Strasberg's head. I've watched it year after year, as he paid equal attention, formidable attention, to scenes that were good and scenes that were awful. Lee, who's been coming down to Forty-fourth Street in rain and snow and as the sun shone, his devotion unwavering, his patience that of a stone saint, answering the same questions, making the same explanations. Lee finally brought us here tonight.[12]

Changes have been detected in Strasberg over the last decade. Sidney Kingsley once said of him, "Lee can be as close to actors as a psychoanalyst and as distant as a god." In both capacities, he has apparently made certain adjustments. In the late sixties, the emphasis of his work with actors seemed to shift. There was less psychological probing as he began, generally, to deal more with the actor's problems than with the individual's problems. In recent years, Strasberg's friends, associates, and Studio members have noted a mellowing of the man. He seems warmer, happier, and somewhat more approachable in his eighth decade. "Lee has improved with age," Kazan has observed. "Success hurts some people; it's helped him."

In spite of whatever mellowing may or may not have occurred, still perceptible is the feisty dogmatism that attracts or repels people according to their perception of the man as a whole. His sense of rectitude and self-importance, tainted by elements of megalomania, occasionally creates ill will, and when indelicately expressed, can wound. He once went backstage to congratulate Christopher Plummer after a performance to say, "That was very good. You should work with us; you'll benefit by it." Cordial and misunderstood.

And yet there is something admirable in the hard-nosed consistency with which he has pressed his views over the years. His zealous trumpeting of his ideas on acting still evokes belief in the power of the theater in others, and continues to inspire them as Gordon Craig had originally inspired him. Strasberg is recognized by the world theater community as an authentic and original voice, and as he approaches his ninth decade the testimonials to that fact have increased. He accepted his first honorary doctorate, conferred by Florida State University during a three-day "Salute to the Actors Studio," in January of 1977 while New York City recently gave him its highest cultural award, the Handel Medallion. It is part and parcel of what Kazan calls Strasberg's "success."

As a benediction, the last ten years have been especially kind to Strasberg: his new family (Strasberg has two young sons, Adam and David, by Anna Mizrahi Strasberg); the success of his schools, and the attendant financial security they represent; the continuing acknowledgment of his importance in the history of the American theater; and, most unexpectedly, his remarkable debut as a motion-picture actor in *Godfather II*, which resulted, some fifty years after his first professional appearance as a performer, in an Academy Award nomination and in the resurrection of his long dormant career.

His friends, colleagues, and students came together to salute the man and his accomplishments on the occasion of his seventy-fifth birthday. The November 1976 Actors Studio benefit party at the Pierre Hotel was crowded with well-wishers, including many Studio celebrities. Those who could not be there in person sent filmed or taped greetings. Paul Newman and Rod Steiger, photographed together on a beach in California, offered, "Lee, after seventeen beers we've decided you have to take the credit or blame for what we've become." Many speakers praised the artistic director and thanked him for his contributions to their lives and careers and, by extension, to those of five generations of American actors.

How is such a career to be measured? There is no denying Strasberg's monumental influence on American acting, just as there is no calculating the precise nature and extent of it. That influence is not necessarily a question of the deliberate and systematic use of all the techniques he advocates. Surprisingly few Studio members use every aspect of the Method in the manner or with the consistency he considers essential. Moreover, the majority of Studio actors have done most of their training under other teachers. Strasberg's influence is more properly measured in terms of the members' perception of themselves as serious creative artists.

In that respect, Strasberg's influence, refracted through the fame of The Actors Studio and the emulation that that fame has engendered, has been fundamental. It could almost be said that through the Studio, Strasberg has affected every medium of performance—theater, television, and film. Through him, The Actors Studio, however falteringly and controversially, has achieved a historic place as one of the fountainheads of "American" acting.

The Studio continues to attract the gifted performer. Both the ideals of acting it represents and the promise of exciting and possibly profitable associations it holds (there is a perennial element of "hoping to be discovered" in the air there) sustain the Studio's reputation as more than an organization to which one strives to belong. It is a way of life. For Lee Strasberg it seems a way of life ungovernable by the strictures of time. "I feel that the work I'm doing, in advancing the basic idea of the actor's craft, is of historical importance," he told *The New York Times* in 1975. "I don't expect to give it up." [13]

Carl Schaeffer, who has been a major force in keeping the workshop afloat both financially and spiritually for the last fifteen years—he has contributed great amounts of time and effort on numerous Studio projects to nurture and develop the institution he esteems as a "national asset"—recently approached Strasberg about grooming a successor to fill the artistic director's shoes. Strasberg laughed off the suggestion and said, "When I die, someone will arise. That's the way it is in art."

Who will take over after Strasberg, and how the new leadership will affect the future course of the workshop is simply idle speculation at this time. Strasberg is robust and still very much in charge, and there is no denying that The Actors Studio as it exists today is still, fundamentally, Lee Strasberg. After his departure, there may be dramatic changes that will set the Studio on new paths, but his imprint—that spirit of dedicated seriousness that has made the Studio what it is—will undoubtedly remain.

Three decades is a remarkable term of endurance for as frail a vessel as an artistic workshop. The Actors Studio, which has survived that time of trial with accomplishment, influence, and prestige, has more than earned a right to its historical eminence as the fostering source of so much that has been rare and precious in the actors' art in in America.

Life Members of The Actors Studio as of January 1980

CATLIN ADAMS, Elaine Aiken, Sally Alex, Jean Alexander, Jared Allen, Lee Allen, Penny Allen, Sage Allen, Tamzen Allen, Clinton Allmon, Mathew Anden, Mary Angela, Mary Anisi, Susan Anspach, Joseph Anthony, Jim Antonio, Lou Antonio, Kate Archer, Robert G. Armstrong, Sidney Armus, Beatrice Arthur, Beverly Hope Atkinson, Tom Avera, Eleanor Valente Ayer.

Joel Bailey, Barbara Bain, Carroll Baker, Joe Don Baker, Sybil Baker, Pat Baldauff, Judith Baldwin, Martin Balsam, Anne Bancroft, Aza Bard, Katherine Bard, Geraldine Baron, Martine Bartlett, Susan Batson, Barbara Baxley, Betty Beaird, Stanley Beck, Vincent Beck, Nancy Praeger Berg, Herbert Berghof, Mel Bernstein, Sabin Bernstein, Jack Betts, Richard Beymer, Edward Binns, Don Blakely, Richard Blofson, Rudy Bond, Richard Boone, Patricia Bosworth, Sully Boyar, Ray Boyle, Lane Bradbury, Richard Bradford, Jocelyn Brando, Marlon Brando, John Branon, Beth Brickell, Stanley Brock, Jacqueline Brookes, Hildy Brooks, Vanessa Brown, Roscoe Lee Browne, Jan Burrell, Susan Burns, William Burns, Ellen Burstyn, Chad Burton, Tony Burton, William Green Bush.

Zoe Caldwell, Hope Cameron, Carolee Campbell, Anthony Cannon, Anna Capri, Pat Carroll, Judith Chapman, Lonny Chapman, Dane Clark, Jill Clayburgh, Odessa Cleveland, Julie Cobb, Al Cohen, Harry Cohn, Miriam Colon, Carlton Colyer, Dimo Condos, Michael Conrad, Marilou Conway, Anita Miller Cooper, Charles Cooper, Joan Copeland, Pat Corley, Bonnie Leaders Corsaro, Frank Corsaro, Katherine Cortez, Anthony Costello, Mariclare Costello, John Costopoulos, Barbara Covington, Eric R. Cowley, John R. Crawford, Neil Brooks Cunningham.

Rebecca Darke, Brad David, Clifford David, Altovise Davis, Harry Davis, Tamara Daykarhanova, Libby Dean, Olive Deering, Domenic De Fazio, Gabriel Dell, Jerome Dempsey, Robert De Niro, Sandy Dennis, Bruce Dern, Richard Derr, Francesca De Sapio, Bradford Dillman, Dolores Dorn-Heft, Kay Doubleday, Keir Dullea, Mildred Dunnock, Richard Durham, Robert Duvall.

Joan Ellis, Robert Emmett, Hal England, Tom Ewell.

Margaret Fairchild, Norman Fell, Don Fellows, Joe Feury, Peggy Feury, Sally Field, Robert Fields, Gail Fisher, Jane Fonda, Richard Forbes, Milton Earl Forrest, John Forsythe, Anthony Franciosa, Nancy Franklin, James Frawley, Al Freeman, Jr., Marilyn Fried, Martin Fried, George Furth.

Martha G. Galphin, Rita Gam, Jennifer Gan, Vincent Gardenia, Jack Garfein, David Garfield, Sean Garrison, Lorraine Gary, George Gaynes, Ben Gazzara, Michael V. Gazzo, Stefan Gierasch, Patricia Gilbert, Linda Gillin, Wendy Girard, Paul Gleason, Scott Glenn, Carlin Glynn, Sharon Goldman, Arlene Golonka, Allen Goorwitz, Charles Gordone, Lee Grant, William Greaves, Karlee Green, Gayle Greene, Mary Grey, Wayne Grice, Charles Grodin, David Groh, Mary Grover.

Michael Hadge, Don Hanmer, Will Hare, John Harkins, Barbara Harris, Fox Harris, Julie Harris, Ted Harris, Laurence Hauben, Marcia Haufrecht, June Havoc, Terese Hayden, Barbara Hayes, Linda Haynes, David Hedison, Frances Heflin, Anne Hegira, John Heldabrand, Robert Heller, Alva Hellstrom, Ann Hennessey, Jan Henry, Hanna Hertelandy, Shelby Hiatt, Gerald Hiken, Marianna Hill, Steven Hill, Pat Hingle, Zen Hirano, Dustin Hoffman, Jane Hoffman, Ellen Holly, Celeste Holm, Claire Hooton, Geoffrey Horne, Israel Horovitz, Joan Hotchkis, Jennifer Howard, Michael Howard, Robin Howard, Gloria Hoye, Marcie Hubert, Michael Patrick Hughes, Dianne Hull, Kim Hunter, David Hurst, Lisabeth Hush, Earle Hyman.

Diana Ivarson.

Anne Jackson, Jacqueline Jacobus, Nicole Jaffe, Clifton James, Conrad Janis, Mark Jenkins, Salome Jens, Charlene Jones, Joanne Moore Jordan, William Jordan, Bill Joyce, Vern Joyce.

James Karen, Bernard Kates, Gloria Kaufman, Elia Kazan, Lainie Kazan, Don Keefer, Harvey Keitel, Sally Kellerman, Elizabeth Kemp, Maya Kenin, Philip Kenneally, Clinton Kimbrough, Sally Kirkland, Terry Kiser, Virginia Kiser, Adelaide Klein, Jacqueline Knapp, Shirley Knight, Suzannah Knight, Karen Kondazian, Edward Kovens.

Diane Ladd, Margaret Ladd, Martin Landau, Elizabeth Lane, Robin

Lane, Nicholas La Padula, Wesley Lau, Cloris Leachman, Bryarly Lee, John Lehne, Ron Leibman, June Levant, Viveca Lindfors, Joanne Linville, Robert Lipton, Barbara Loden, Lily Lodge, Robert Loggia, Tanya Lopert, Jack Lord, Walter Lott, Tina Louise, Phyllis Love, Salem Ludwig, Robert Lupone, Richard Lynch, Eleanor Lynn, Robert F. Lyons.

Cynthia McAdams, Sandra McCabe, Kevin McCarthy, Peggy McCay, Rue McClanahan, Darren McGavin, Johnny Rae McGee, Bill McKinney, Allyn Ann McLerie, Steve McQueen, Jay MacIntosh, Janet MacIntyre, Janet MacLachlan, Henry Madden, Kathleen Maguire, Karl Malden, Liska March, Nancy Marchand, Steven Marlo, Scott Marlowe, Marc Marno, Linda Marsh, E. G. Marshall, Ernest Martin, Nan Martin, Peter Masterson, Walter Matthau, Peggy Maurer, Nona Medici, Julio Medina, Mary Mercier, Burgess Meredith, Jo Anne Meredith, Margaret Middleton, Joanna Miles, Sylvia Miles, Kenn Mileston, Tom Milian, Allan Miller, Sally Moffat, Reginald Montgomery, Yvonne Mooney, Bill Moor, Terry Moore, Michael Moriarty, Benjamin Murphy, Matthew C. Murphy, Rosemary Murphy.

Joanna Nail, Vivian Nathan, Patricia Neal, Mitchell Nestor, Lois Nettleton, Corinne Neuchateau, Paul Newman, Julie Newmar-Smith, Jack Nicholson, Alex Nicol, Leslie Nielsen, Eulalie Noble, James Noble, Kathleen Nolan.

Carroll O'Connor, Eavan O'Connor, Gerald O'Loughlin, James Olson, Alba Oms, Patrick O'Neal.

Al Pacino, Geraldine Page, Harrison Page, Betsy Palmer, Estelle Parsons, Lucille Patton, Albert Paulsen, Jacqueline Pearce, Arthur Penn, Leo Penn, Christopher Pennock, George Peppard, Susan Peretz, Lazaro Perez, Anthony Perkins, Eleanor Perry, Felton Perry, Frank Perry, Nehemiah Persoff, Phil Peters, Lenka Peterson, Avra Petrides, Margaret Phillips, Wendell K. Phillips, Ben Piazza, Sidney Poitier, Sydney Pollack, Anthony Ponzini, Robert Porter, Joan Potter, David Pressman, Gilbert Price, Barry Primus, William Prince, Andrew Prine.

James Quinn, Pat Quinn.

Joseph Ragno, Steven Railsback, Logan Ramsey, Pat Randall, Robert G. Reece, Robert Reed, Elliot Reid, Alejandro Rey, Lisa Richards, Paul E. Richards, Peter Mark Richman, Ronald Rifkin, Eli Rill, Martin Ritt, Jerome Robbins, Doris Roberts, Cliff Robertson, Randy Rocca, Percy Rodriguez, Patricia Roe, Bea Roth, Joyce Roth, Mickey Rourke, John Ryan, Mitchell Ryan, Mark Rydell, Alfred Ryder.

Fred Sadoff, Eva Marie Saint, Raymond St. Jacques, Christopher St. John, Gene Saks, Patricia Sales, Albert Salmi, Jaime Sanchez, Irma Sandrey, Sam Schacht, Carl Schaeffer, Thelma Schnee, Alan Schneider, Charles Schull, Henry Scott, Sandra Seacat, Ed Setrakian, Martin Shakar,

Diane Shalet, Adriana Shaw, Paula Shaw, Kathy Shawn, Pearl Shear, Joshua Shelley, Henry Silva, Ron Silver, Robert Simon, Delos V. Smith, Jr., Lane Smith, Lois Smith, Patricia Smith, Savannah Smith, William Smithers, Barry Snider, Harvey Solin, Brett Somers, Hedy Sontag, Katherine Squire, Kim Stanley, Anna Stanovich, Maureen Stapleton, Elizabeth Stearns, Rod Steiger, Anna Sten, Nancy Stephens, Jan Sterling, Sandy Stevens, Warren Stevens, Jean-Pierre Stewart, Marvin Dean Stewart, John Stix, Arthur Storch, Anna Mizrahi Strasberg, John Strasberg, Sabra Jones Strasberg, Susan Strasberg, Michael Strong, Shepperd Strudwick, Nuba-Harold Stuart, Maxine Stuart, Joseph Sullivan, Gary Swanson, Inga Swenson, Ken Sylk, John Sylvester.

Dennis Tate, Vic Tayback, Audrey Taylor, Madeleine Thornton-Sherwood, Joseph Tobin, Rip Torn, William Traylor, Lynn Tufeld, Manu Tupou, Mimi Turque.

Joan Van Ark, Trish Van Devere, Jo Van Fleet, Clyde Ventura, Robert Viharo, Lynn Von Kersting, Elissa Von Zobor, Andreas Voutsinas.

Michael Wager, Ralph Waite, Robert Walden, Christopher Walken, Ellie Wood Walker, Adrienne Wallace, Eli Wallach, Alexandria Walsh, Ray Walston, Jack Waltzer, Janet Ward, Lesley Ann Warren, David Wayne, Gary Waynesmith, Dennis Weaver, Ann Wedgeworth, Jessie Welles, Tom Wheatly, Lois Wheeler, Christine White, James Whitmore, Mike Whitney, Collin Wilcox, Shannon Wilcox, Gene Wilder, Ann Williams, Cindy Williams, Frank Wilson, Paul Winfield, Shelley Winters, Iggie Wolfington, Kate Woodville, Joanne Woodward, Patricia Wylie.

Melanie York.

Eleanor Zee.

DECEASED MEMBERS OF THE ACTORS STUDIO

Tod Andrews, Geraldine Brooks, Joan Chandler, Montgomery Clift, Curt Conway, Norma Crane, Rupert Crosse, James Dean, Annette Erlanger (Carell), Tim Everett, Betty Field, Lou Gilbert, Steve Gravers, William Hansen, Alexandra Holland, Joyce Lear, Michael Lewin, Gene Lyons, Joan McCracken, Patrick McVey, Norman Ornellas, William Redfield, Diana Sands, Frank Silvera, David J. Stewart, Fred Stewart, Paula Strasberg, Franchot Tone, Nadyne Turney, Frances (Sivy) Waller, Richard Ward, Mary Welch.

Notes

INTRODUCTION

1. Quoted in a Studio brochure for "A Season of Special Evenings," n.d. [ca. Winter 1968], Actors Studio files.
2. Tony Richardson, "An Account of The Actors' Studio: The Method and Why," *Sight and Sound* 26, no. 3 (Winter 1956/57): 134.
3. Robert Brustein, "Are Britain's Actors Better Than Ours?" *The New York Times*, April 15, 1973, sec. 2, pp. 1, 30.
4. Norman Mailer, *Marilyn, a Biography* (New York: Grosset & Dunlap, 1973), p. 151.

CHAPTER 1: THE GROUP THEATRE HERITAGE

1. David S. Lifson, *The Yiddish Theatre in America* (New York: Thomas Yoseloff, 1965), p. 153.
2. Ibid., pp. 194–96.
3. Besides *On the Art of the Theatre*, he read Craig's *Towards a New Theatre* (London: J. M. Dent & Sons, Ltd., 1913) and *The Theatre—Advancing* (Boston: Little, Brown and Company, 1919). Among the many volumes that made a lasting impression on him were the following: Hiram Kelly Moderwell, *The Theatre of Today* (New York: John Lane, 1914); Sheldon Cheney, *The Art Theatre* (New York: Alfred A. Knopf, 1917), and *The New Movement in the Theatre* (New York: Mitchell Kennerley, 1914); Kenneth Macgowan and Robert Edmond Jones, *Continental Stagecraft* (New York: Harcourt, Brace & Co., 1922), and Kenneth Macgowan, *The Theatre of Tomorrow* (New York: Boni & Liveright, 1921); Huntly Carter, *The New Spirit in Drama and Art* (New York: Mitchell Kennerley, 1913), and *The New Spirit in European Theatre* (New York: George H. Doran, 1925); Oliver Sayler, *The Russian Theatre* (New York: Little, Brown and Company, 1920), and *Inside the Moscow Art Theatre* (New York: Brentano, 1925).
4. Lee Strasberg, "Renaissance?" *The New York Times*, July 20, 1958, sec. 2, p. 1.
5. Edward Gordon Craig, *On the Art of the Theatre* (Chicago: Browne's Bookstore, 1911), pp. 1–2.
6. David Magarshack, *Stanislavsky, a Life* (New York: The Chanticleer Press, 1951), p. 336.
7. Strasberg, "Renaissance?" p. 1.
8. Craig, *On the Art of the Theatre*, pp. 132–136.
9. Sayler, *Inside the Moscow Art Theatre*, gives a full account of the MAT tour in America, including the number of performances of each play.
10. Lee Strasberg, "History of the Method" (unpublished transcription of a series of five lectures, January–February 1958). I, p. 61.
11. Ronald Arthur Willis, "The American Laboratory Theatre, 1923–1930," Ph.D. dissertation, University of Iowa, 1968, pp. 12–13.
12. Konstantin Stanislavsky, *My Life in Art*, trans. G. Ivanov-Mumjiev (Moscow: Foreign Languages Publishing House, n.d.), p. 408. "The preparatory work was in the hands of Richard Boleslavsky, with Sulerzhitsky in charge of production [p. 407]."
13. Willis, "The American Laboratory Theatre," pp. 31–32, explains that an unpublished set of Boleslavsky's lecture notes entitled "Creative Theatre"—translated by Michel Barroy and on file in the Theater Collection of the New York Public

Library at Lincoln Center—are, in fact, the Princess Theater lecture notes.
A selection from these notes, under the title "Living the Part," has been published in Toby Cole and Helen Krich Chinoy, eds., *Actors on Acting*, rev. ed. (New York: Crown Publishers, 1970), pp. 510–17.

14. Christine Edwards, *The Stanislavsky Heritage* (New York: New York University Press, 1965), p. 203.
15. Richard Boleslavsky, *Acting: The First Six Lessons* (New York: Theatre Arts Books, 1933).
16. Richard Boleslawsky, "Stanislavsky—The Man and His Methods," *Theatre*, 37, no. 4 (April 1923): 74.
17. Cole and Chinoy, *Actors on Acting*, p. 512.
18. Marcel Proust, *Swann's Way*, trans. C. K. Scott Moncrieff (New York: Random House, 1928), pp. 62–66.
19. Ronald Arthur Willis, "The American Lab Theatre," *Tulane Drama Review* 9, no. 1 (T-25, Fall 1964): 116.
20. Strasberg, quoted in Victor Seymour, "Stage Directors' Workshop: A Descriptive Study of The Actors Studio Directors Unit, 1960–1964," Ph.D. dissertation, University of Wisconsin, 1965, p. 335; see also Victor Seymour, "Directors' Workshop: Six Years' Activity of the Actors Studio Directors Unit," *Educational Theatre Journal* 18, no. 1 (March 1966): 25–26.
21. Harold Clurman, *The Fervent Years* (New York: Alfred A. Knopf, 1945), pp. 10–11.
22. Ibid., p. 41.
23. Helen Krich Chinoy, ed., "Reunion, A Self-Portrait of the Group Theatre," *Educational Theatre Journal* 28, no. 4 (December 1976): 498. (Entire issue devoted to the Group Theatre.)
24. Clurman, *Fervent Years*, pp. 44–45.
25. Stark Young, *Immortal Shadows* (New York: Charles Scribner's Sons, 1948), pp. 127–28.
26. Lee Strasberg, "Acting and the Training of the Actor," in John Gassner, *Producing the Play*, rev. ed. (New York: Holt, Rinehart and Winston, Inc., 1953), p. 154; also recollected in Robert H. Hethmon, ed., *Strasberg at The Actors Studio* (New York: The Viking Press, 1965), p. 106.
27. This project was filmed by the Group's photographer, Ralph Steiner, as *Café Universal*. Thirteen stills from this motion picture are on file in the Theatre Collection at the New York Public Library at Lincoln Center.
28. E[ugene] Vakhtangov, "Preparing for the Role," in *Acting, A Handbook of the Stanislavski Method*, comp. Toby Cole, rev. ed. (New York: Crown Publishers, 1955), pp. 116, 120.
29. Schmidt's translations for Strasberg and the Group included (1) Boris Alpers, *The Theatre of the Social Mask* (copyrighted and published by the Group Theatre in 1934 in mimeograph), about the work of Meyerhold; (2) Pavel A. Markov, *The First Studio* [of the MAT], *Sullerzhitsky–Vackhtangov–Tchekhov* [*sic*] (copyrighted and published by the Group Theatre in 1934 in mimeograph); (3) "The Theatrical October," a collection of essays on the Soviet theater; (4) Nikolai Volkov, "The New Manner," a section of his biography, *Meyerhold*, covering the years 1910–1917; (5) "Gogol and Meyerhold," a collection of essays on Meyerhold's production of *The Inspector General;* (6) S. Radlov, " 'The General Inspector' in Meyerhold's Staging"; (7) "At Rehearsals of 'Inspector-General' (Stenographic record of V. Meyerhold's work with the actors)" (published in Toby Cole and Helen Krich Chinoy, eds., *Directors on Directing: A Source Book of the Modern Theater*, rev. ed. [Indianapolis/New York: The Bobbs-Merrill Company, Inc., 1963], pp. 311–25); (8) I. Y. Sudakov, "Talks on the Primary Elements of the Actor's Creative Work" (published, in part, as

"The Actor's Creative Work" in *Theatre Workshop* 1, no. 2 [January–March, 1937]: 7–42; and as "The Creative Process," in *Acting, A Handbook of the Stanislavski Method*, pp. 69–104; (9) Michael Chekhov, "Stanislavsky's Method [from Chekhov's notes]" (as adapted by Molly Day Thatcher), *New Theatre* 1, no. 11 [December 1934]: 12–13, 29, and 2, no. 2 [February 1935]: 6–7; (10) "From E. B. Vakhtangov's Diaries and Entries" (published, in part, as "Fantastic Realism" in *Directors on Directing*, pp. 185–91); (11) B. E. Zakhava, "Yevgeniy Vakhtangov" (published, in part, as "Preparing for the Role" in *Acting, A Handbook of the Stanislavski Method*, pp. 116–24); (12) V. [B. E.; B. M.] Zakhava, "Can We Use Stanislavsky's Method?" (as edited and condensed by Molly Day Thatcher), *New Theatre* 2, no. 8 [August 1935]: 16–18; (13) Sergei Mokulsky, "The Masks of Comedy as a Historical Problem"; (14) "Vsevolod Meyerhold Works on *La Dame aux Camelias*"; (15) Michael Chekhov, "The Road of the Actor: Memoirs." The original manuscripts and typescripts of all these items are in the possession of Lee Strasberg.

30. Chinoy, "Reunion," p. 517.
31. An account of his trip to Russia, including selections from his notes on his stay there, appears as Lee Strasberg, "Russian Notebook (1934)," *The Drama Review* 17, no. 1 (T-57, March 1973): 106–23.
32. Quoted in Harold Clurman, *On Directing* (New York: The Macmillan Company, 1972), p. 152.
33. Published in Robert Lewis, *Method—or Madness?* (New York: Samuel French, Inc., 1958), between pp. 34 and 35.
34. Chinoy, "Reunion," pp. 508–9.
35. "Three Meetings [with Stanislavski]," in Boris Filippov, *Actors Without Make-up* (Moscow: Progress Publishers, 1977), p. 59.
36. Cole and Chinoy, *Actors on Acting*, p. 605.
37. Clurman, *Fervent Years*, p. 194.
38. Michel Ciment, *Kazan on Kazan*, Cinema One series (New York: The Viking Press, 1974), pp. 20–22; also quoted in Chinoy, "Reunion," pp. 535–36.
39. Clurman, *Fervent Years*, p. 195.
40. Ibid., pp. 191, 204.
41. Ciment, *Kazan on Kazan*, p. 19.
42. Ibid., pp. 18–19.
43. Brooks Atkinson, review of *Five Alarm Waltz*, *The New York Times*, March 14, 1941, p. 16.
44. Clurman, *Fervent Years*, p. 42.
45. Chinoy, "Reunion," pp. 504, 508, 516.
46. Ibid., 497.

CHAPTER 2: BIRTH OF THE ACTORS STUDIO: 1947–1950

1. Ciment, *Kazan on Kazan*, p. 15.
2. Ibid., pp. 33–34.
3. Elia Kazan, "Actors Studio Twenty-Fifth" (speech given on the occasion of Kazan's being honored at the "twenty-fifth" [actually the twenty-sixth] anniversary celebration of The Actors Studio, December 6, 1973), p. 2, Studio Archives [The aggregate of Studio records and files will hereinafter be referred to as "Archives"]; also printed (in mimeograph) in *The Actors Studio Newsletter*, September 1973–July 1975, p. 4.
4. Elia Kazan, "Candid Conversation," *Show Business Illustrated*, February 1962, p. 26; also Kazan, "Actors Studio Twenty-Fifth," p. 3, and *The Actors Studio Newsletter*, September 1973–July 1975.
5. The founding of the Moscow Art Theater during a historical eighteen-hour

meeting between Stanislavski and Nemirovitch-Dantchenko at the Slavyansky ("Slavic") Bazaar is discussed in their respective autobiographies: Stanislavsky, *My Life in Art*, pp. 217–22 and Vladimir Nemirovitch-Dantchenko, *My Life in the Russian Theatre* (New York: Theatre Arts Books, 1968), pp. 79–83.

6. Mel Gussow, "Actors Studio Thrives at 25 . . . er 26," *The New York Times*, December 6, 1973, p. 60.

7. Cheryl Crawford and Harold Clurman at a colloquium on the Group Theatre at Hunter College, New York, December 10, 1973.

8. One of the Group Theatre publications first presented the history of the First Studio, including the work and influence of Vakhtangov, in English. See P. A. Markov, *The First Studio, Sullerzhitsky–Vackhtangov–Tchekhov* [sic], trans. Mark Schmidt (New York: Group Theatre, Inc., 1934).

9. Incorporation papers of The Actors Studio, Archives.

10. Lou Gilbert's notebooks. Other classes held by Lewis at the Union Methodist Church included a special lecture on G. B. Shaw (December 5, 1947) and the following representative scenes: Michael Strong and Joan Chandler in *Beyond the Horizon*, John Straub and John Becher in *Thunder Rock*, Will Hare and Maureen Stapleton in *Homecoming*, Karl Malden and Anne Jackson in *The Angel That Troubled the Waters*, Jerome Robbins and Jay Barney in *Waiting for Lefty*, William Redfield in *Winterset*, Peter Cookson and Peggy Meredith in *Clash by Night*, Jay Barney and Fred Stewart in *Laburnam Grove*, Tom Ewell and David Wayne in *Of Mice and Men*, Tom Ewell and Thelma Schnee in *Ghosts*, Mary Welch in *Saint Joan*, William Redfield and Thelma Schnee in *Golden Boy*, Herbert Berghof, Jane Hoffman, and Thelma Schnee in *The Lady of Larkspur Lotion*, Ty Perry and Thelma Schnee in *Merton of the Movies*, Anne Jackson and Jay Barney in *The Petrified Forest*, and Patricia Neal and Peter Cookson in *Elizabeth Barrett Browning*.

11. Lester Bernstein, "How the Actors Prepare at the Studio," *The New York Times*, November 9, 1947, sec. 2, p. 3.

12. Ibid.

13. See Elia Kazan, "Look, There's the American Theatre," *Tulane Drama Review* 9, no. 2 (T-26, Winter 1964): 73–74; and Ciment, *Kazan on Kazan*, pp. 40–41.

14. Examples from Lou Gilbert's notebooks.

15. Robert Rice, "Actors Studio [Article I]," *New York Post Magazine*, May 13, 1957, p. M8.

16. Robert Lewis, "Foreword," in Edwards, *The Stanislavsky Heritage*, p. xii.

17. Bessie Bruer, *Sundown Beach* (Brooklyn, N.Y.: Grindstone Press, 1973).

18. L. A. Sloper, "Sundown Beach," *The Christian Monitor*, July 27, 1948 [Two-Star edition, Boston], p. 4. This review does not appear in the microfilmed editions of the *Monitor*.

19. In the cast were Nehemiah Persoff, Martin Balsam, Treva Frazee, Jennifer Howard, Ellen Mahar, Vivian Firko [Nathan], Elmer Lehr, Ralph Cullinan, Steven Hill, Don Hanmer, Joe Sullivan, Michael Lewin, Joan Copeland, Anne Hegira, Edward Binns, Warren Stevens, Tom Avera, Lenka Peterson, Kathleen Maguire, Phyllis Thaxter, Joseph Fallon, Julie Harris, Cloris Leachman, John Sylvester, Ira Cirker, Robert Simon, Alex Nicol, George Joseph, and Lou Gilbert.

20. Brooks Atkinson, review of *Sundown Beach*, *The New York Times*, September 8, 1948, p. 37.

21. Ibid.

22. Brooks Atkinson, "Sundown Beach Also Closes—Mr. Kazan's Direction of the Actors Studio," *The New York Times*, September 12, 1948, sec. 2, p. 1.

23. See Clurman's *On Directing*, pp. 115–17, for an account of how he handled Brando in that production.

24. "NOTES: Production Meeting August 12, 1948, 8:30 P.M., TV Program, Actors Studio, Inc.," Cheryl Crawford Files, NYPL-LC. This is the earliest document associating Lee Strasberg's name with The Actors Studio.
25. Only a few of those Meisner brought to the Studio during his tenure there remained life members. These include, in addition to the above, Margaret Feury, James Karen, Lucille Patton, David Stewart, and Melanie York.
26. Compiled from various lists in the Studio Archives. To complete the total: Curt Conway, Robert Emmett, William Greaves, Adelaide Klein, Phyllis Love, Eleanor Lynn, Gene Lyons, Alex Nicol, Leslie Nielsen, James Noble, Fred Sadoff, Henry Scott, Henry Silva, Frances Waller, and Janet Ward.

CHAPTER 3: STRASBERG TAKES OVER: 1951–1955

1. Brooks Atkinson's (and Lewis Nichols's) review of these plays appeared in *The New York Times* as follows: *Many Mansions* by Jules Eckert Goodman and Eckert Goodman, October 28, 1937, p. 28; *Roosty* by Martin Berkeley, February 15, 1938, p. 21; *All the Living* by Hardie Albright, March 25, 1938, p. 14; *Dance Night* by Kenyon Nicholson, October 15, 1938, p. 20; *Flight into China* by Pearl S. Buck, September 12, 1939, p. 28; *Summer Night* by Vicki Baum and Benjamin F. Glazer, November 3, 1939, p. 17; *The Fifth Column* by Ernest Hemingway (adapted by Benjamin F. Glazer), March 7, 1940, p. 18; *Clash by Night* by Clifford Odets, December 29, 1941, p. 20; *A Kiss for Cinderella* by Sir James M. Barrie, March 11, 1942, p. 22; *R.U.R.* by Karel Capek, December 4, 1942, p. 30 (reviewed by Nichols); *Apology* by Charles Schnee, March 23, 1943, p. 14 (reviewed by Nichols); *South Pacific* by Howard Rigsby and Dorothy Heyward, December 30, 1943, p. 11 (reviewed by Nichols); *Skipper Next to God* by Jan de Hartog, January 5, 1948, p. 14; *The Big Knife* by Clifford Odets, February 25, 1949, p. 27; *The Closing Door* by Alexander Knox, December 2, 1949, p. 36; *Peer Gynt* by Henrik Isben, January 29, 1951, p. 15.
2. *The New York Times*, March 25, 1938, p. 14.
3. *The New York Times*, December 29, 1941, p. 20.
4. *The New York Times*, March 27, 1940, p. 18.
5. Lee Strasberg, "An Answer to the Riddle of the Theatre," *The New York Times*, August 31, 1947, sec. 2, pp. 1–2.
6. Strasberg, "Acting and the Training of the Actor," in John Gassner, *Producing the Play*, pp. 128–62.
7. Lee Strasberg, "Introduction," in *Acting, a Handbook of the Stanislavski Method*, pp. 10–17.
8. Paul Gray, "Stanislavski and America: A Critical Chronology," *Tulane Drama Review* 9, no. 2 (T-26, Winter 1964): 41.
9. Ciment, *Kazan on Kazan*, p. 37.
10. See, for instance, Elia Kazan, "Actors Studio Alumni Working 'East of Eden,'" *New York Herald Tribune*, February 27, 1955, sec. 4, p. 3; and Kazan, "Actors Studio Twenty-Fifth."
11. Gray, "Stanislavski and America: A Critical Chronology," p. 43.
12. Ciment, *Kazan on Kazan*, p. 37.
13. "Eli Wallach," in *Working with Kazan* (Middletown, Conn.: Wesleyan University, 1973), unpaginated.
14. Tennessee Williams, *Camino Real* (Norfolk, Conn.: New Directions, 1953).
15. C. P. Trussell, "Elia Kazan Admits He Was Red in '30's," *The New York Times*, April 12, 1952, p. 8; Elia Kazan, "A Statement by Elia Kazan," *The New York Times*, April 12, 1952, p. 7.
16. Ciment, *Kazan on Kazan*, p. 12.

17. Ibid., p. 83.
18. Michel Ciment, *Kazan par Kazan, Entretiens avec Michel Ciment* (Paris: Stock, 1973), p. 40. Kazan's discussion of his longtime friend, Odets, is one of the items in this original French edition of Ciment's book that does not appear in the English and American editions.
19. Letter from Elia Kazan to Cheryl Crawford, n.d. (ca. 1952), Cheryl Crawford Files, NYPL-LC.
20. Crawford, *One Naked Individual* (Indianapolis/New York: The Bobbs-Merrill Company, Inc., 1977), p. 220.
21. From an informal talk given by Earle Hyman on January 15, 1977, at the Williams Building, Florida State University at Tallahassee, as part of "A Salute to The Actors Studio" sponsored by the Charles MacArthur Center for American Theatre in association with The Florida State University School of Theatre.
22. Lee Allen, Richard Blofson (stage manager), Gabriel Dell, Sandy Dennis, Al Freeman, Jr., Conrad Janis, Percy Rodriguez, Diana Sands, and Iggie Wolfington.
23. Ronald Martinetti, *The James Dean Story* (New York: Pinnacle Books, 1975), p. 84.
24. Frederic Morton, "Actors' Studio," *Esquire*, December 1955, p. 216.
25. Howard Thompson, "Another Dean Hits the Big League," *The New York Times*, March 13, 1955, sec. 2, p. 5.
26. Hethmon, *Strasberg at The Actors Studio*, p. 27. Lee Strasberg at The Actors Studio, October 5, 1956: Tape no. 10, side 1, of The Actors Studio Tape Recordings at the Wisconsin Center for Theatre Research, series 339A (hereinafter called "Wisconsin Tapes").
27. The plays were *Maya* by Simon Gantillon, *The Scarecrow* by Percy MacKaye, *The School for Scandal* by Richard Brinsley Sheridan, and *The Little Clay Cart*, a Hindu play by King Shudraka translated from the Sanskrit by Arthur William Ryder.
28. Stuart W. Little, *Off-Broadway: The Prophetic Theater* (New York: Coward, McCann & Geoghegan, Inc., 1972), p. 78.
29. Letter from Stark Young to Jack Garfein, December 10, 1953, Archives.
30. Morton, "Actors' Studio," p. 211.
31. See, for example, Michael V. Gazzo, "A Playwright's Point of View," *Theatre Arts*, December 1958, pp. 20–22, 80, and his letter to the editor, *Columbia Forum* 3, no. 2 (Spring 1960): 3.
32. Brooks Atkinson, "Everybody's Busy, Several Interesting Productions, And 'A Hatful of Rain' in Particular," *The New York Times*, December 4, 1955, sec. 2, p. 1.
33. Lee Strasberg, "Introduction," *Famous American Plays of the 1950s*, selected by Lee Strasberg (New York: Dell Publishing Co., Inc., 1962), p. 20. *A Hatful of Rain* is included in this collection.
34. Morton, "Actors' Studio," p. 212.

CHAPTER 4: THE STUDIO IN THE SPOTLIGHT: 1955–1959

1. Among the earliest were Frederic Morton's "Actors' Studio"; Seymour Peck's "The Temple of 'The Method,'" *The New York Times Magazine*, May 6, 1956; Maurice Zolotow's "A Study of The Actors Studio," *Theatre Arts*, August 1956 and September 1956; Maurice Zolotow's "The Stars Rise Here," *Saturday Evening Post*, May 18, 1957; and Robert Rice's "Actors Studio," *New York Post Magazine* (in six installments), May 13–17, 19, 1957.
2. Shull made a number of interesting suggestions to Strasberg, including holding seminars with professional and academic theatrical people to discuss the work

and findings of the Studio, tape-recording Studio sessions, and publishing pamphlets and texts.

3. The USIA requested information for an article to be published in *America Illustrated* for distribution in the USSR.

4. A detailed account of the filming, including Strasberg's involvement with the project, is given in Fred Lawrence Guiles, *Norma Jean, The Life of Marilyn Monroe* (New York: McGraw-Hill, 1969), pp. 230–38.

5. Harold Clurman, "The Famous 'Method,'" in *Lies Like Truth* (New York: The Macmillan Company, 1958), p. 251.

6. Guiles makes several minor errors in his book here. He has Miss Monroe attending Strasberg's classes at the Paramount Building (p. 189) and states that the Studio had been at the Malin Studios from its inception (p. 186). According to Delos V. Smith, Jr., Miss Monroe first attended the private classes when they were being held at the Malin Studios and subsequently when they were moved to the *Capitol* Theater Building. The Studio, of course, was only at the Malin Studios for a single season.

7. Lee Strasberg, "Remarks at the Funeral," *Marilyn Monroe, A Composite View*, ed. Edward Wagenknecht (Philadelphia: Chilton Book Company, 1969), p. 113.

8. Kazan, "Actors Studio Alumni Working 'East of Eden.'"

9. He was also asked to write entries on John Garfield, William Gillette, Laurette Taylor, and the development of the Method in the United States. Only the ones on Belasco, Chekhov, and Mrs. Fiske were completed.

10. Lee Strasberg, "Introduction," in William Archer, *The Paradox of Acting by Denis Diderot and Masks or Faces?* (New York: Hill and Wang, Inc., 1957), pp. ix–xiv; Lee Strasberg, "Acting," *Encyclopaedia Britannica*, 14th ed. I (1957), 104–7. [Strasberg later wrote a new article on acting for the *Britannica*'s 15th ed., I, 58–64]. Stanislavski's article, "Directing and Acting," is reprinted in Cole, *Acting, A Handbook of the Stanislavski Method*, pp. 22–32. A different translation of this material was made by Elizabeth Reynolds Hapgood for publication in Constantin Stanislavski, *Stanislavski's Legacy*, ed. and trans. Elizabeth Reynolds Hapgood, rev. ed. (New York: Theatre Arts Books, 1968), pp. 182–94.

11. A number of Stanislavski's works, available in the integral Russian edition, are still unavailable in English. In addition, there has been a continuing controversy about the completeness and accuracy of Miss Hapgood's translations.

12. Quoted in Sister M. Doris Ann Bowles, O.P., "The Influence of Stanislavski Upon American Acting as Practiced by the New York Actors Studio," M.A. thesis, Catholic University of America, 1960, p. 48.

14. Stark Young, "Letter to Julia Young Robertson [his sister]," June 2, 1954, *Stark Young, A Life in the Arts, Letters, 1900–1962, Volume II*, ed. John Pilkington (Baton Rouge: Louisiana State University Press, 1975), pp. 1289–90.

15. Hethmon, *Strasberg at The Actors Studio*, p. 67.

16. Molly Kazan, "THE PLAYWRIGHTS' UNIT: The condition, the temperment [sic] and the needs of playwrights; a history of the Unit; suggestions for the future," a mimeographed, thirty-eight-page paper addressed to Cheryl Crawford, Lee Strasberg, The Members Committee, and all members of the Playwrights Unit, n.d. [ca. 1962], Archives, pp. 5–6.

16. Kazan, "Actors Studio Alumni Working 'East of Eden.'"

17. This is what John Gassner calls him in *Directions in Modern Theatre and Drama* (an expanded edition of *Form and Idea in Modern Theatre*) (New York: Holt, Rinehart and Winston, Inc., 1967), p. 57.

18. Geraldine Page, "The Bottomless Cup," *Tulane Drama Review* 9, no. 2 (T26, Winter 1964): 129.

19. Truman Capote, "Profile, Duke in His Domain [Marlon Brando]," *The New Yorker*, November 9, 1957, p. 56.

20. William Bast, *James Dean* (New York: Ballantine Books, 1956), p. 66.
21. Lewis Funke and John E. Booth, eds., *Actors Talk About Acting* (New York: Random House, 1961), p. 322.
22. Robert Rice, "Actors Studio (Article II)," *New York Post Magazine*, May 14, 1957, p. [M8].
23. Seymour Peck, "The Temple of 'The Method,'" p. 27.
24. Lillian Ross and Helen Ross, *The Player, a Profile of an Art* (New York: Simon and Schuster, 1962), pp. 166–67.
25. Page, "The Bottomless Cup," p. 121.
26. Lee Strasberg, "View From The Studio," *The New York Times*, September 2, 1956, sec. 2, p. 3.
27. Ross and Ross, *The Player, a Profile of an Art*, pp. 14–15.
28. See, for instance, José Ferrer's complaints about "Method People" in Funke and Booth, *Actors Talk About Acting*, pp. 124–27.
29. Joe Hyams, "This is Hollywood, Film Stars Call Studio Grads 'Unfair,'" *New York Herald Tribune*, August 3, 1956, p. 6.
30. Jean Domarchi and André S. Labarthe, "Entretien Avec Elia Kazan," *Cahiers du Cinéme* 22, no. 130 (April 1962): 2. (Retranslated from the French.)
31. Clurman, *Lies Like Truth*, p. 256.
32. Zolotow, "The Stars Rise Here," p. 84.
33. Tyrone Guthrie, "Is There Madness in 'The Method'?" *The New York Times Magazine*, September 15, 1957, pp. 82–83.
34. Joe Hyams, "Marlon Brando Thinks 'The Method' a Fiction," *New York Herald Tribune*, September 9, 1957, sec. I, p. 13.
35. Quoted in Martinetti, *The James Dean Story*, p. 120.
36. Walter Kerr, *Pieces at Eight* (New York: Simon and Schuster, 1957), pp. 236–37.
37. Elia Kazan, "An Interview [with] Elia Kazan," *Equity Magazine* (December 1957), p. 12.
38. Gordon Rogoff, "The Hidden Theatre," *Encore* 10, no. 1 (January–February 1963): 35.
39. Gordon Rogoff, "Lee Strasberg: Burning Ice," *Tulane Drama Review* 9, no. 2 (T-26, Winter 1964): 131–154.

CHAPTER 5: STANISLAVSKI AND THE STUDIO: THE METHOD CONTROVERSY

1. *Webster's New Collegiate Dictionary* (Springfield, Mass.: G. & C. Merriam Company, 1974), p. 723.
2. Stanislavsky, *My Life in Art*, pp. 345–56.
3. Constantin Stanislavski, *An Actor Prepares*, trans. by Elizabeth Reynolds Hapgood (New York: Theatre Arts Books, 1936), p. 14.
4. Stanislavski, *Stanislavski's Legacy*, p. 203.
5. M. O. Knebel, "Superior Simplicity," in *Stanislavski Today, Commentaries on K. S. Stanislavski*, comp., ed., and trans. Sonia Moore (New York: American Center for Stanislavski Theatre Art, Inc., 1973), p. 44.
6. Quoted in Ruben Simonov, *Stanislavsky's Protégé: Eugene Vakhtangov*, trans. and adapt. Miriam Goldina (New York: DBS Publications, Inc., 1969), pp. 11–13.
7. Quoted in Sonia Moore, *The Stanislavski System*, rev. ed. (New York: Compass Books, The Viking Press, 1974), p. 102.
8. Hethmon, *Strasberg at the Actors Studio*, p. 41. Strasberg has stressed these points on many occasions at the Studio and in lectures.
9. Henry Hewes, "'The Method's' Mouth," *Saturday Review*, January 24, 1959, p. 25.

10. Edwards, *The Stanislavsky Heritage*, p. 261. Also, see Hethmon, *Strasberg at The Actors Studio*, pp. 40–41.
11. The earliest discussion of his teaching procedures appears in Strasberg, "Acting and the Training of the Actor" in Gassner, *Producing the Play*, pp. [128]–162.
12. See his article, "Acting," p. 59, in the *Encyclopaedia Britannica*, on this point. He also discusses this distinction in Lee Strasberg, "On Acting," *Texas Quarterly* 3, no. 2 (Summer 1960): 83–87.
13. Quoted in Constantin Stanislavski, *Building a Character*, trans. Elizabeth Reynolds Hapgood (New York: Theatre Arts Books, 1949), p. 167.
14. Sonia Moore's characterization in *Training an Actor* (New York: The Viking Press, 1968), pp. 40 41. See also Paul Gray's tendentious and distorted presentation of the exercise in "Stanislavski and America: A Critical Chronology," p. 49–51.
15. See Lee Strasberg, "Working with Live Material," *Tulane Drama Review* 9, no. 1 (T25; Fall 1964): 126.
16. See Stanislavski, *Stanislavski's Legacy*, pp. 187–88.
17. See Michael Schulman, "Backstage Behaviorism," *Psychology Today*, June 1973, pp. 51–54, 88, for an analysis of Strasberg's Method procedures in terms of behaviorist psychology.
18. See Constantin Stanislavski, *An Actor Prepares*, pp. 136–42 (on physical actions) and pp. 154–81 (on emotion memory); and *Stanislavski Produces Othello*, trans. Helen Nowak (New York: Theatre Arts Books, 1948), pp. 150–54 (on physical actions).
19. Strasberg, "Acting," p. 106.
20. They were Victor Manyukov, a director and teacher; Vladimir Prokofiev, an historian and theoretician; Angelina Stepanova, an actress; and Vasily Toporkov, an actor and teacher.
21. See, for instance, P. V. Simonov, "The Method of K. S. Stanislavski and the Physiology of Emotions," in *Stanislavski Today, Commentaries on K. S. Stanislavski*, comp., ed., and trans. Sonia Moore, pp. 34–43.
22. See above, Chapter Four, p. 161, and n. 39.
23. Theodore Hoffman, "Stanislavski Triumphant," *Tulane Drama Review* 9, no. 1 (T-25; Fall 1964): 16–17.
24. Robert Brustein, "The Keynes of Times Square," *The New Republic*, December 1, 1962, p. 29.
25. Michael Redgrave, *Mask or Face* (London: Heinemann, 1958), p. 31.
26. The eight lectures were given at the Playhouse Theatre in New York in April, May, and June. They were later published as Robert Lewis, *Method—or Madness?*
27. Strasberg, "Working with Live Material," p. 122.
28. Strasberg, "View from the Studio," p. 1.
29. "Drama Mailbag," *The New York Times*, September 16, 1956, sec. 2, p. 3.
30. Michael Chekhov, *To The Actor, On The Technique of Acting* (New York: Harper & Row, 1953), p. 178.
31. Suzanne O'Malley, "Can The Method Survive The Madness?" is just the latest round in their ongoing feud. See *The New York Times Magazine*, October 7, 1979, p. 32.
32. Nikolai M. Gorchakov, *Stanislavsky Directs*, trans. Miriam Goldina (New York: Funk & Wagnalls Company, 1954), p. 52.

CHAPTER 6: KAZAN DEPARTS: 1960–1962

1. "Topics," *The New York Times*, May 14, 1960, p. 22.
2. Seymour, "Stage Directors' Workshop," pp. 12–13.

3. "Elia Kazan's Talk, Actors' Studio Benefit Party, October 8, 1959," p. 4, Archives.

4. Strasberg wrote about Meyerhold in the fall after his trip to Russia. See Lee Strasberg, "The Magic of Meyerhold," *New Theatre*, September 1934, pp. 14, 15, 30; and Strasberg, "Russian Notebook (1934)," pp. 106–23.

5. Aside from Mr. Seymour's dissertation, which I have freely drawn upon, there is his article which briefly summarizes the work of the Unit (see p. 282 n. 20, above).

6. Harold Brodkey, Lonny Chapman, Lewis John Carlino, Alice Childress, Lorraine Hansberry, Janine Manatis, Lawrence Osgood, Lou Peterson, Arnold Sundgaard, Douglas Taylor, and Richard Townsend.

7. Letter from Tennessee Williams to Edward Albee, October 21, 1963, Archives.

8. According to Stix, Mailer asked him to direct *The Deer Park* for the Unit, but he demurred because he could not see a way to do it. "When Mailer talked in the Unit," Stix also noted, "people listened."

9. See Sophia Delza, "T'ai Chi Ch'uan: The Integrated Exercise," *The Drama Review* 16, no. 1 (T-53, March 1972): 28–33. "T'ai Chi Ch'uan is a system for activating the body for the simultaneous development of physical, emotional and mental well-being. It is useful for the actor because it promotes a heightened perceptivity, sensitive awareness and stamina. Since the exercise has no stylistic mannerisms, it enhances the ability to manipulate the body expressively for any desired effect" (p. 28).

10. Strasberg, "Renaissance?"

11. Quoted in Gray, "Stanislavski and America: A Critical Chronology," pp. 53–54.

12. Joe Hyams, "Carroll Baker and School Spirit," *New York Herald Tribune*, May 11, 1961, p. 17.

13. John Keating, "Actors Studio at Crossroads," *The New York Times*, January 21, 1962, sec. 2, p. 1.

14. See "Lee Strasberg Directs *The Case of Clyde Griffiths*," *Educational Theatre Journal* 28, no. 4 (December 1976): 457.

15. Lee Strasberg at the Morosco Theatre, November 27, 1961. See Hethmon, *Strasberg at The Actors Studio*, pp. 389–395, for excerpts from this talk.

16. Letter to Lee Strasberg from Elia Kazan, September 18, 1961, Archives.

17. Dated: Tuesday, May 29, 1962, Archives. Kazan did not resign from the corporate board till April 23, 1965. Thus, when Torn and Miss Page joined the board of directors, only Miss Page was at the same time a corporate member of The Actors Studio, Inc.

18. Elia Kazan, "Theater: New Stages, New Plays, New Actors," *The New York Times Magazine*, September 23, 1962, p. 28. His comments on emotional memory in Kazan, "Look, There's the American Theatre," pp. 72–73, are quite antithetical to Strasberg's views on the subject.

CHAPTER 7: VENTURE INTO PRODUCTION: THE ACTORS STUDIO THEATRE

1. Morton, "Actors' Studio," p. 212.

2. Robert Rice, "Actors Studio (article VI)," May 19, 1957, p. M5.

3. Lee Strasberg, "The Actors Studio Theatre," *Playbill* for *Strange Interlude*, July 1, 1963, inserted after pp. 6, 26.

4. "Group Sets Broadway Debut," *The Christian Science Monitor*, January 28, 1963, p. 4.

5. Walter Kerr, "Strange Interlude," *New York Theatre Critics' Review*, *1963* 24 (May 27, 1963): 317. Kerr's review was not published in the *New York Herald Tribune* because of a newspaper strike.

6. Howard Taubman, "Strange Interlude," *The New York Times*, March 13, 1963, p. 5.
7. Robert Brustein, "Revivals: Good, Bad, and Insufferable," *The New Republic*, March 30, 1963, pp. 28–29.
8. *Newsweek*, March 25, 1963, p. 97.
9. Harold Clurman, "Theatre," *The Nation*, March 30, 1963, pp. 274–75.
10. June Havoc, *Early Havoc* (New York: Simon and Schuster, 1959).
11. *The New York Times*, December 23, 1963, p. 20. Also in the company were Lee Allen, Sally Alex, Tom Avera, Joe Don Baker, Lane Bradbury, Dick Bradford, Lonny Chapman, Libby Dean, Olive Deering, Gabriel Dell, Marcella Dodge, Philip Dorian, Tim Everett, Don Fellows, Will Hare, Robert Heller, Robin Howard, Maya Kenin, Philip Kenneally, Adelaide Klein, Janet Luoma, Janice Mars, Peter Masterson, Brooks Morton, Margret O'Neill, Lucille Patton, Gordon Phillips, Patricia Quinn, James Rado, Logan Ramsey, Pat Randall, Doris Roberts, John Strasberg, Ralph Waite, Iggie Wolfington, and Conrad Janis and his Tail Gate 5 Band. The setting was by Peter Larkin, the lighting by Tharon Musser, and the costumes by Noel Taylor.
12. John McClain, *New York Journal-American*, March 16, 1964, p. 19: "'Dynamite Tonight' is really quite a fresh conception—mad music brilliant bedlam carefully congealed—and I believe it should take its place with the best of Off-Broadway." Martin Gottfried, *Women's Wear Daily*, March 16, 1964, p. 21: ". . . a marvelously exciting and bitterly entertaining music-play." The production was designed by Willa Kim, the lighting by Peter Hunt. Charles Turner was the musical director.
13. *The New York Times*, March 16, 1964, p. 36.
14. Crawford, *One Naked Individual*, p. 236.
15. In the cast were Frankie (Downbeat) Brown, Rip Torn, Al Freeman, Jr., Percy Rodriguez, Wayne Grice, Clyde Williams, Otis Young, Hilda Haynes, Diana Sands, Lincoln Kilpatrick, David Baldwin, Pat Hingle, Ann Wedgeworth, John McCurry, Pat Randall, Patricia Quinn, Ralph Waite, Joe Don Baker, Ann Hennessey, Bill Moor, Pat Corley, Dick Bradford, Billie Allen, Grachan Moncur III, and Pearl Reynolds.
16. See Strasberg, "Remarks at the Funeral," in *Marilyn Monroe, A Composite View*, pp. 112–13.
17. Hethmon, *Lee Strasberg at The Actors Studio*, p. 74.
18. Ibid., pp. 72–73.
19. For a detailed account of Strasberg's work on the play see Seymour, "Stage Directors' Workshop," pp. 125–56.
20. Brooks Atkinson, "Critic at Large," *The New York Times*, July 28, 1964, p. 26.
21. Jerry Tallmer, "Across the Footlights," *New York Post*, June 23, 1964, p. 16.
22. Judith Crist, "Chekhov on Broadway Illumined by Kim Stanley," *New York Herald Tribune*, June 23, 1964, p. 10.
23. Henry Hewes, "Broadway Postscript," *Saturday Review*, July 18, 1964, p. 25.
24. *Newsweek*, July 6, 1964, p. 45.
25. Harold Clurman, "The Three Sisters," *The Nation*, July 27, 1964, p. 39.
26. Seymour, pp. 151–52.
27. Peter Daubeny, *My World of Theatre* (London: Jonathan Cape, 1971), p. 324.
28. Quoted in James Feron, "'Charlie' Scored by London Critics," *The New York Times*, May 5, 1965, p. 52.
29. Ibid.
30. R. B. Marriott, "Strasberg Explains," *Stage* [London], May 13, 1965, p. 8.
31. Penelope Gilliatt, "Theatre," *The Observer Weekend Review*, May 16, 1965, p. 24.

32. See Penelope Gilliatt, "The Actors Studio in London, or the Broadway Boiler-house Abroad," *Harper's*, September 1965, pp. 32, 34, 36.

CHAPTER 8: THE STUDIO TILL NOW: 1965–1980

1. Some of the Unit productions funded by the Rockefeller grant during the mid-sixties were Joyce Carol Oates's *The Sweet Enemy*, directed by Frank Corsaro (later presented Off-Broadway as an "Actors Studio Workshop Production," February 15, 1965); Mark Van Doren's *The Last· Days of Lincoln*, directed by Fred Stewart (later presented as an "Actors Studio Workshop Production" at The Library of Congress, April 12–14, 1965); Herbert Schapiro's *Teddy;* Douglas Taylor's *The Sudden and Accidental Re-education of Horse Johnson* (later produced on Broadway, December 18, 1968); Robert Unger's *Bohikee Creek* (later produced Off-Broadway, April 28, 1966); Michael V. Gazzo's *Death of the Kitchen Table in Our Fair City;* Kenneth H. Brown's *The Happy Bar*, directed by Rip Torn; Douglas Taylor's *Oh, Pioneers;* and Aldo Giunta's *The Implausibility of Imperial Noon.*
2. The Rockefeller Foundation turned down a new request for aid in 1970, but a year later it gave Ronald Tavel a "Playwright in Residence" grant to work at the Studio, with a thousand dollars going to the workshop as part of the arrangement.
3. John Gruen, "Actors Studio, Mon Amour," *New York Herald Tribune Magazine*, October 11, 1964, p. 30.
4. *Actors Studio Newsletter*, March 1970, p. [5], Archives.
5. Directors Units tapes covering the period February 1960 through June 1961 were delivered August 6, 1962 (they are numbered D1–D38); the first set of Actors Unit Tapes, covering the period March 1956 through June 1962, was delivered August 30, 1963 (they are numbered 1–191); the second set of Actors Unit tapes, covering the period November 1963 through January 1969, was delivered July, 1969 (they are numbered A1–A163).

    A duplicate set of this last group of tapes (A1–A163) is on file at The Actors Studio; all the rest, being the originals and unduplicated, are available only at the Wisconsin Center for Theatre Research.

    Tapes made at the Studio subsequent to January 1969 have not been deposited at the Wisconsin Center and are on file only at The Actors Studio.
6. For a representative unfavorable review see Richard Gilman, *Bookweek*, October 24, 1965, pp. 4, 36, 37. For a representative favorable review see Howard Taubman, *The New York Times Book Review*, December 26, 1965, p. 10.
7. Robert Alan Aurthur took it over after the first year.
8. His obituary appeared in *The New York Times*, December 7, 1970, p. 48.
9. "Comments by Elia Kazan at the Memorial Service for Fred Stewart at The Actors Studio, December 8th 1970," Archives.
10. McCandlish Phillips, "Actors Studio Opening Its Doors to General Audience," *The New York Times*, March 7, 1972, p. 44.
11. See Patricia Bosworth's article, "The Effect of Five Actresses on a Play-in-Progress" in *The New York Times*, April 3, 1977, Sec. 2, p. 1, 8, 9.
12. Kazan, "Actors Studio Twenty-Fifth."
13. Joan Barthel, "The Master of the Method Plays a Role Himself," *The New York Times*, February 2, 1975, sec. 2, p. 13.

A Selected Bibliography

BOOKS

Adler, Stella. "The Actor in the Group Theatre." In *Actors on Acting,* edited by Toby Cole and Helen Krich Chinoy. Rev. ed. New York: Crown Publishers, 1970.

Baldwin, James. *Blues for Mister Charlie.* New York: The Dial Press, Inc., 1964.

Boleslavsky, Richard. *Acting: the First Six Lessons.* New York: Theatre Arts Books, 1933.

————. "Living the Part." In *Actors on Acting,* edited by Toby Cole and Helen Krich Chinoy. Rev. ed. New York: Crown Publishers, 1970.

Breuer, Bessie. *Sundown Beach.* Brooklyn, N.Y.: Grindstone Press, 1973.

Ciment, Michel. *Kazan on Kazan.* Cinema One series. New York: The Viking Press, 1973. Published in French as *Kazan par Kazan, Entretiens avec Michel Ciment.* Paris: Stock, 1973.

Clurman, Harold. *The Fervent Years.* New York: Alfred A. Knopf, 1945.

————. *Lies Like Truth.* New York: The Macmillan Company, 1958.

————. *On Directing.* New York: The Macmillan Company, 1972.

Cole, Toby, comp. *Acting, A Handbook of the Stanislavski Method.* Rev. ed. New York: Crown Publishers, 1955.

————, and Chinoy, Helen Krich, eds. *Actors on Acting.* Rev. ed. New York: Crown Publishers, 1970.

————, and Chinoy, Helen Krich, eds. *Directing the Play.* Rev. ed. New York: The Bobbs-Merrill Company, Inc., 1953.

Corsaro, Frank. *Maverick; A Director's Personal Experience in Opera & Theatre.* New York: Vanguard Press, Inc., 1978.

Costigan, James. *Baby Want a Kiss.* New York: Samuel French, Inc., 1966.

Craig, Edward Gordon. *On the Art of the Theatre.* Chicago: Browne's Bookstore, 1911.

Crawford, Cheryl. *One Naked Individual.* Indianapolis/New York: The Bobbs-Merrill Company, Inc., 1977.

Easty, Edward Dwight. *On Method Acting.* New York: HC Publishers, Inc., 1966.

Edwards, Christine. *The Stanislavski Heritage.* New York: New York University Press, 1965.

Funke, Lewis, and Booth, John E., eds. *Actors Talk About Acting.* New York: Random House, 1961.

Gazzo, Michael V. *A Hatful of Rain.* In *Famous American Plays of the 1950s,* selected and introduced by Lee Strasberg. New York: Dell Publishing Co., Inc., 1962.

Gorchakov, Nikolai M. *Stanislavsky Directs.* Translated by Miriam Goldina. New York: Funk & Wagnalls Company, 1954.

Guiles, Fred Lawrence. *Norma Jean, The Life of Marilyn Monroe*. New York: McGraw-Hill, 1969.

Havoc, June. *Marathon '33*. New York: Dramatists Play Service Inc., 1969.

Hethmon, Robert H., ed. *Strasberg at The Actors Studio*. New York: The Viking Press, 1965.

Lewis, Robert. Foreword to *The Stanislavsky Heritage*, by Christine Edwards. New York: New York University Press, 1965.

————. *Method—or Madness?* New York: Samuel French, Inc., 1958.

Magarshack, David. *Stanislavsky, A Life*. New York: The Chanticleer Press, 1951.

Mailer, Norman. *Marilyn, a Biography*. New York: Grosset & Dunlap, 1973.

Markov, Pavel Aleksandrovich. *The First Studio, Sullerzhitsky—Vackhtangov —Tchekhov* [sic]. Translated by Mark Schmidt. New York: Group Theatre, Inc., 1934.

Martinetti, Ronald. *The James Dean Story*. New York: Pinnacle Books, Inc., 1975.

Moore, Sonia. *The Stanislavski System*. New rev. ed. New York: Compass Books, The Viking Press, 1974.

————, comp., ed., and trans. *Stanislavski Today, Commentaries on K. S. Stanislavski*. New York: American Center for Stanislavski Theatre Art, Inc., 1973.

Redgrave, Michael. "To Be Me or Not To Be Me, Notes on 'The Method.'" In *Mask or Face*. London: Heinemann, 1958.

Ribot, Théodule. "The Memory of Feelings." In *The Psychology of the Emotions*. London: Walter Scott, Ltd., 1897. Originally published as *La Psychologie des Sentiments*. Paris, 1896.

Ross, Lillian, and Ross, Helen. *The Player, a Profile of an Art*. New York: Simon and Schuster, 1962.

Simonov, Ruben. *Stanislavsky's Protégé: Eugene Vakhtangov*. Translated and adapted by Miriam Goldina. New York: DBS Publications, Inc., 1969.

Stanislavski, Constantin. *An Actor Prepares*. Translated by Elizabeth Reynolds Hapgood. New York: Theatre Arts Books, 1936.

————. *An Actor's Handbook*. Edited and translated by Elizabeth Reynolds Hapgood. New York: Theatre Arts Books, 1963.

————. *Building a Character*. Translated by Elizabeth Reynolds Hapgood. Introduced by Joshua Logan. New York: Theatre Arts Books, 1949.

————. *Creating a Role*. Translated by Elizabeth Reynolds Hapgood. Foreword by Robert Lewis. New York: Theatre Arts Books, 1961.

————. *My Life in Art*. Translated by G. Ivanov-Mumjiev. Moscow: Foreign Languages Publishing House, n.d.

————. *The Sea Gull Produced by Stanislavski*. Edited with an introduction by Prof. S. D. Balukhaty. Translated by David Magarshack. New York: Theatre Arts Books, 1952.

————. *Stanislavski's Legacy*. Edited and translated by Elizabeth Reynolds Hapgood. Rev. ed. New York: Theatre Arts Books, 1968.

————. *Stanislavski Produces Othello*. Translated by Dr. Helen Nowak. New York: Theatre Arts Books, 1948.

————. *Stanislavsky on the Art of the Stage*. Translated, with an Introductory

Essay on Stanislavsky's "System" by David Magarshack. New York: Hill and Wang, 1961.

Strasberg, Lee. "Acting." In *Encyclopaedia Britannica.* 14th ed. Vol. I, 1957.

———. "Acting." In *Encyclopaedia Brittanica.* 15th ed. Vol. I, 1958.

———. "Acting and the Training of the Actor." In *Producing the Play,* by John Gassner. Rev. ed. New York: Holt, Rinehart and Winston, Inc., 1953.

———. Introduction to *Acting, a Handbook of the Stanislavski Method,* compiled by Toby Cole. Rev. ed. New York: Crown Publishers, 1955.

———. Introduction to *Famous American Plays of the 1950s,* selected by Lee Strasberg. New York: Dell Publishing Co., Inc., 1962.

———. Introduction to *The Paradox of Acting,* by Denis Diderot and *Masks or Faces?,* by William Archer. New York: Hill and Wang, 1957.

———. "Remarks at the Funeral." In *Marilyn Monroe, a Composite View,* ed. by Edward Wagenknecht. Philadelphia: Chilton Book Company, 1969.

———. *Strasberg at The Actors Studio.* Edited by Robert H. Hethmon. New York: The Viking Press, 1965.

Vakhtangov, Eugene. "Fantastic Realism." In *Directors on Directing,* ed. by Toby Cole and Helen Krich Chinoy. Rev. ed. New York: The Bobbs-Merrill Company, Inc., 1963.

———. "Preparing for the Role ['notes from the diary of Vakhtangov originally arranged by B. E. Zakhava']." In *Acting, A Handbook of the Stanislavski Method,* compiled by Toby Cole. Rev. ed. New York: Crown Publishers, 1955.

Williams, Tennessee. *Camino Real.* Norfolk, Conn.: New Directions, 1953.

———. *Working With Kazan.* Middletown, Conn.: Wesleyan University, 1973.

Young, Stark. *A Life in the Arts, Letters, 1900–1962.* Vol. II. Ed. by John Pilkington. Baton Rouge: Louisiana State University Press, 1975. Letter about Young's visit to The Actors Studio, pp. 1289–90.

PERIODICALS

Adler, Stella. "The Reality of Doing." *Tulane Drama Review* 9, no. 1 (T-25, Fall 1964): 143.

Alpert, Hollis. "Autocrat of the Sweat Shirt School." *Esquire,* October 1961, pp. 88–89, 179–85.

Bentley, Eric. "Who Was Ribot? or: Did Stanislavsky Know any Psychology?" *Tulane Drama Review* 7, no. 2 (T-18, Winter 1962): 127–29.

Boleslavsky, Richard. "The Laboratory Theatre." *Theatre Arts* 7 (July 1923): 244–50.

———. Stanislavsky—The Man and His Methods." *Theatre* 37, no. 4 (April 1923): 27, 74, 80.

Brustein, Robert. "The Keynes of Time Square [Lee Strasberg]." *The New Republic,* December 1, 1962, pp. 28–30.

Capote, Truman. "Profiles, The Duke in His Domain [Marlon Brando]." *The New Yorker,* November 9, 1957, p. 53.

Chinoy, Helen Krich, ed. "Reunion, A Self-Portrait of the Group Theatre." *Educational Theatre Journal* 28, no. 4 (December 1976).

Coger, Leslie Irene. "Stanislavski Changes His Mind." *Tulane Drama Review* 9, no. 1 (T-25, Fall 1964): 63–68.

Crohem, Daniel. "Du côté de l'Actors Studio: l'art dramatique de base est une névrose." *Paris-Théâtre* 11, no. 117 (1957).

De Sanctis, Filippo M. "Origine e influenze dell 'Actors' Studio." *Bianco e Nero*, nos. 3–4 (1960).

Flanner, Janet. "Profiles: A Woman in the House [Cheryl Crawford]." *The New Yorker*, May 8, 1948, pp. 34–58.

Gazzo, Michael V. Letter to the editor. *Columbia University Forum* 3, no. 2 (Spring 1960): 3.

———. "A Playwright's Point of View." *Theatre Arts*, December 1958, pp. 20–22, 80.

Gilliatt, Penelope. "The Actors Studio in London, or, the Broadway Boiler-house Abroad." *Harper's*, September 1965, pp. 32, 34, 36.

Gottlieb, Morton. "Morton Gottlieb Talks About Actors Studio." *Harper's Bazaar*, May 1966, pp. 98, 102, 104.

Gray, Paul. Reply to Lee Strasberg's Letter to the editor (same issue). *Tulane Drama Review* 11, no. 1 (T-33, Fall 1966): 241–42.

———. "Stanislavski and America: A Critical Chronology." *Tulane Drama Review* 9, no. 2 (T-26, Winter 1964): 21–60.

Hewes, Henry. " 'The Method's' Mouth." *Saturday Review*, January 24, 1959, p. 25.

Hoffman, Theodore. "At the Grave of Stanislavski, or How to Dig the Method." *Columbia University Forum* 3, no. 1 (Winter 1960): 31–37.

———. "Stanislavski Triumphant." *Tulane Drama Review* 9, no. 1 (T-25; Fall 1964): 9–17.

Journal of the Actors Studio 1, no. 1 (January-February 1968).

Kazan, Elia. "Candid Conversation." *Show Business Illustrated*, February 1962, pp. 26–27.

———. "An Interview [with] Elia Kazan." *Equity Magazine*, December 1957, pp. 10, 12–14.

———. "Look, There's the American Theatre." *Tulane Drama Review* 9, no. 2 (T-26, Winter 1964): 61–83.

Lewis, Robert. "Emotional Memory." *Tulane Drama Review* 6, no. 4 (T-16, June 1962): 54–60.

———. "Would You *Please* Talk to Those People?" *Tulane Drama Review* 9, no. 2 (T-26, Winter 1964): 97–113.

Meisner, Sanford. "The Reality of Doing." *Tulane Drama Review* 9, no. 1 (T-25, Fall 1964): 144.

Morton, Frederic. "Actors' Studio." *Esquire*, December 1955, p. 107.

Page, Geraldine. "The Bottomless Cup." *Tulane Drama Review* 9, no. 2 (T-26, Winter 1964): 114–30.

Richardson, Tony. "An Account of the Actors' Studio: The Method and Why." *Sight and Sound* 26, no. 3 (Winter 1956/57): [132]–136.

Roberts, Peter. "Method or Madness?" *Plays and Players* 5, no. 11 (August 1958): 4–5.

Rogoff, Gordon. "The Hidden Theatre." *Encore* 10, no. 1 (January-February 1963): 33–43.

————. "Lee Strasberg: Burning Ice." *Tulane Drama Review* 9, no. 2 (T-26, Winter 1964): 131–54.

————. Reply to Lee Strasberg's Letter to the editor (same issue). *Tulane Drama Review* 11, no. 1 (T-33, Fall 1966): 239–241.

Schulman, Michael. "Backstage Behaviorism." *Psychology Today*, June 1973, pp. 51–54, 88.

Seymour, Victor. "Directors' Workshop: Six Years' Activity of the Actors Studio Directors Unit." *Educational Theater Journal* 18, no. 1 (March 1966): 12–26.

Strasberg, Lee. "Actors Studio Is Not a School." *Plays and Players* 4, no. 5 (February 1957): 9.

————. "The Actors Studio Theatre." *Playbill* for *Strange Interlude*, July 1, 1963, inserted after pp. 6, 26.

————. "How to 'Be' an Actor." *Saturday Review*, July 9, 1955, p. 18.

————. "In the Words of Lee Strasberg." *Cue*, January 10, 1970, pp. 16–17.

————. "Introductory Note [on acting]." *Theatre Workshop* 1, no. 1 (October 1936): 3–4.

————. Letter to the editor. *Tulane Drama Review* 11, no. 1 (T-33, Fall 1966): 234–39.

————. "The Magic of Meyerhold." *New Theatre*, September 1934, pp. 14, 15, 30.

————. "On Acting." *Texas Quarterly* 3, no. 2 (Summer 1960): 83–87.

————. "Past Performances." *Theatre Arts*, May 1950, pp. 39–42.

————. "Russian Notebook (1934)." *The Drama Review* 17, no. 1 (T-57, March 1973): 106–23.

————. "Talking It Over [Review of Robert Lewis' *Method—or Madness?*]." *Playbill*, March 9, 1959, p. 3.

————. "Working with Live Material." *Tulane Drama Review* 9, no. 1 (T-25, Fall 1964): 117–35.

Theatre Workshop 1, no. 2 (January–March 1937): 94.

Vinaver, Michel. "La fin et les moyens d'acteur." *Théâtre Populaire*, no. 32 (1958), pp. 1–28.

Wasserman, Debbi. "Developing An American Acting Style." *New York Theatre Review*, February 1978, pp. 5–9. ["Lee Strasberg, John Houseman, Sonia Moore, Robert Lewis and Stella Adler Talk Abous Stanislavsky/The Method/Contemporary Acting Styles."]

Weaver, Neal. "A Place to Come In Out of the Rain: The Actors Studio." *After Dark*, May 1968, pp. 31–[37].

Willis, Ronald A. "The American Lab Theatre." *Tulane Drama Review*, 9, no. 1 (T-25, Fall 1964): 112–16.

Yale/Theatre 8, nos. 2 and 3 (Spring 1977). Interviews with Lee Strasberg, Stella Adler, and Sanford Meisner, among others.

Zakhava, V. [B. M.] "Can We Use Stanislavsky's Method?" *New Theatre* 2, no. 8 (August 1935): 16–18.

Zolotow, Maurice. "The Stars Rise Here." *Saturday Evening Post*, May 18, 1957, p. 44.

————. "A Study of The Actors Studio." *Theatre Arts*, August 1956, pp 70, 71, 91; September 1956, pp. 95–96.

NEWSPAPERS

Barthel, Joan. "The Master of the Method Plays a Role Himself." *The New York Times*, February 2, 1975, sec. 2, pp. 1, 13.

Bernstein, Lester. "How the Actors Prepare at the Studio." *The New York Times*, November 9, 1947, sec. 2, pp. 1, 3.

Bosworth, Patricia. "The Effects of Five Actresses on a Play-in-Progress." *The New York Times*, April 3, 1977, pp. 1, 8, 9.

Bracker, Milton. 'Slow Route to Big Time." *The New York Times*, January 10, 1954, sec. 2, p. 3.

Brustein, Robert. "Are Britain's Actors Better Than Ours?" *The New York Times*, April 15, 1973, sec. 2, pp. 1, 30.

Fife, Stephen. "Lee Strasberg: A Double Life in the Theatre." *The Village Voice*, June 26, 1978, pp. 40–41.

————. "No Place to Be Somebody; Acting Schools: Only the Strong Survive." *The Village Voice*, March 13, 1978, pp. 39–43.

Gelb, Arthur. "Behind the Scenes at the Actors Studio." *The New York Times*, April 29, 1951, sec. 2, pp. 1, 3.

Gruen, John. "Actors Studio, Mon Amour." *New York Herald Tribune Magazine*, October 11, 1964, p. 30.

Gussow, Mel. "Actors Studio Thrives at 25 . . . er 26." *The New York Times*, December 6, 1973, p. 60.

Guthrie, Tyrone. "Is There Madness in 'The Method'?" *The New York Times Magazine*, September 15, 1957, pp. 23, 82, 83.

Kaufman, Wolfe. "Actors Studio Makes its Bow on Broadway." *The New York Times*, September 5, 1948, sec. 2, pp. 1–2.

Kazan, Elia. "Actors Studio Alumni Working 'East of Eden.' " *New York Herald Tribune*, February 27, 1955, sec. 4, p. 3.

————. Letter to the editor in the "Drama Mailbag." *The New York Times*, July 15, 1948, sec. 2, p. 1.

————. "A Statement by Elia Kazan." *The New York Times*, April 12, 1952, p. 7.

————. "Theater: New Stages, New Plays, New Actors." *The New York Times Magazine*, September 23, 1962, p. 18.

Marriott, R. B. "Strasberg Explains." *Stage* [London], May 13, 1965, p. 8.

O'Malley, Suzanne. "Can The Method Survive The Madness?" *The New York Times Magazine*, October 7, 1979, p. 32.

Peck, Seymour. "The Temple of 'The Method'." *The New York Times Magazine*, May 6, 1956, p. 26.

Phillips, McCandlish. "Actors Studio Opening Its Doors to General Audience." *The New York Times*, March 7, 1972, p. 44.

Rice, Robert. "Actors Studio [in six installments]." *New York Post Magazine*, parts I–VI, May 13–19, 1957, sec. 2.

Schumach, Murray. "Strasberg Fears 'Hams' in Theater." *The New York Times*, December 25, 1970, p. 34.

Shepard, Richard F. " 'Problems' of Success Happily Beset Actors Studio." *The New York Times*, May 26, 1963, sec. 2, pp. 1, 3.

Strasberg, Lee. "An Answer to the Riddle of the Theatre." *The New York*

Times, August 31, 1947, sec. 2, pp. 1–2. Replies to this article: "Drama Mailbag." *The New York Times*, September 14, 1947, sec. 2, p. 2.

———. "Renaissance?" *The New York Times*, July 20, 1958, sec. 2, p. 1.

———. "View from the Studio." *The New York Times*, September 2, 1956, sec. 2, pp. 1, 3.

The New York Times. "Topics [editorial]," May 14, 1960, p. 22.

RECORDING

Strange Interlude. Original [Actors Studio Theatre] cast recording. Columbia DOS-688 (5 records).

OTHER MATERIALS

Actors Studio Newsletter. 1961–1979. Mimeographed and Photo Offset.

Actors Studio Tape Recordings, 1956–1969 (series 339A). Wisconsin Center for Theatre Research. The University of Wisconsin. This collection includes Actors and Directors Unit Tapes (commentaries on scenes and exercises by Lee Strasberg); taped discussions by Lee Strasberg; taped lectures by Etienne Decroux and Cheryl Crawford; and welcomes to such groups as the Comédie Française and the Moscow Art Theater.

Actors Studio Tape Recordings, 1963–1979. The Actors Studio, New York. The collection of tapes at The Actors Studio includes duplicates of tapes presented to the Wisconsin Center for Theatre Research covering September 1963 through June 1969; Actors and Directors Unit tapes from 1969 to the present; and miscellaneous taped discussions and lectures by Lee Strasberg and others.

Bowles, Sister M. Doris Ann, O.P. "The Influence of Stanislavski Upon American Acting as Practiced by the New York Actors Studio." M.A. thesis, Catholic University of America, 1960.

Roberts, Jerry Wayne. "The Theatre Theory and Practice of Richard Boleslavsky." Ph.D. dissertation, Kent State University, 1977.

Scharfenberg, Jean. "Lee Strasberg: Teacher." Ph.D. dissertation, University of Wisconsin, 1963.

Seymour, Victor. "Stage Directors' Workshop: A Descriptive Study of The Actors Studio Directors Unit, 1960–1964." Ph.D. dissertation, University of Wisconsin, 1965.

Strasberg, Lee. "History of the Method." Typewritten. Unpublished transcription of a series of five lectures (I, 68 pp.; II, 65 pp.; III, 4 pp.; IV, 77 pp.; V, 69 pp.). January-February 1958.

Willingham, Calder. "End as a Man." Mimeographed. Unpublished play, New York Public Library Theater Collection at Lincoln Center.

Willis, Ronald Arthur. "The American Laboratory Theatre, 1923–1930." Ph.D. dissertation, University of Iowa, 1968.

Acknowledgments

MANY PEOPLE HAVE HELPED ME with my research. First and foremost, I am indebted to Lee Strasberg for the many hours he patiently discussed historical and theoretical questions with me. His cooperation was of crucial importance to this book, and he gave it generously.

I am also grateful to those connected with the Studio who were of assistance, especially to Liska March, who arranged for me to examine the Studio Archives and who aided me in numerous other ways, and to the Studio coordinators: Betsy Crawford, Robert Charles, Ellen Chenoweth, and Janet Doeden in New York and Mary Mercier in Los Angeles, who allowed me access to their files during working hours.

I want to thank the many members and others with whom I discussed the Studio: Elaine Aiken, Mathew Anden, Lou Antonio, Tom Avera, Jay Barney, Barbara Baxley, Herbert Berghof, Larry Blyden, Rudy Bond, Patricia Bosworth, Joan Chandler, Lonny Chapman, Harold Clurman, Joan Copeland, Frank Corsaro, John Costopoulos, Cheryl Crawford, Dorothy Davis, Tim Everett, Robert Fields, Marilyn Fried, Martin Fried, George Furth, Jack Garfein, William Gibson, Lou Gilbert, Steven Greenberg, Will Hare, Julie Harris, June Havoc, Terese Hayden, Anne Hegira, Jane Hoffman, Earle Hyman, Celeste Holm, Geoffrey Horne, Anne Jackson, Elia Kazan, Harvey Keitel, Robert Lewis, Viveca Lindfors, Kevin McCarthy, Joanna Miles, Vivian Nathan, Geraldine Page, Arthur Penn, Harvey Perr, Lenka Peterson, Lou Peterson, David Pressman, Gordon Rogoff, Carl Schaeffer, Alan Schneider, Delos V. Smith, Jr., Anna Sokolow, Kim Stanley, Maureen Stapleton, John Stix, John Strasberg, Joe Sullivan, Michael Wager, Eli Wallach, Arthur Waxman, Dennis Weaver, Leslie Weiner, Christine White, Robert Whitehead, Shelley Winters, and Paul Zindel.

I should also like to express my gratitude to Paul Myers, Roderick Bladel, Maxwell Silverman, Monty Arnold, Dorothy Swerdlove, and David Bartholomew of the New York Public Library Theater Collection at Lincoln Center as well as the staffs of the New York Public Library at Forty-second Street, the Newspaper Collection at West Forty-third Street, the Wisconsin Center for Theater Research, and the New York University Library.

For help and advice with my manuscript, I should like to thank Theodore Hoffman, Richard Hayes, Edwin Kennebeck, and Cara DeSilva. And finally, my heartfelt appreciation to Steven Dansky, Kitty Benedict, and Charles Corn, for their confidence, support, and assistance in this project.

Index